Salvation in the Slums

Salvation in the Slums

Evangelical Social Work, 1865–1920

Norris Magnuson

BAKER BOOK HOUSE
Grand Rapids, Michigan 49516

Clothbound edition published 1977 by
The Scarecrow Press
and The American Theological Library Association

Paperback edition published 1990 by
Baker Book House Company

Library of Congress Cataloging-in-Publication Data

Magnuson, Norris A., 1932–
    Salvation in the slums : evangelical social work, 1865–1920 / Norris
Magnuson.
        p.   cm.
    Reprint. Originally published: Metuchen, N.J. : Scarecrow Press, 1977.
Originally published in series: ATLA monograph series ; no. 10.
    Includes bibliographical references (p.   ).
    ISBN 0-8010-6261-6
    1. Church work with the poor—United States—History. 2. Evangelistic
work—United States—History. 3. Urban poor—United States—History.
4. City missions—United States—History. 5. Evangelicalism—United
States—History. 6. United States—Economic conditions—1865–1918.
I. Title.
[BV639.P6M34 1990]
261.8'32'0973—dc20
                                                                89-28714
                                                                CIP

Printed in the United States of America

CONTENTS

FOREWORD

I am delighted to see this dissertation made more accessible in its revision for publication in the American Theological Library Association Monograph Series. Since I first became aware of its existence a few years ago, this study by Norris Magnuson has been a major source of my understanding of the development of popular evangelicalism in the late 19th and early 20th centuries. My copy of an earlier draft has as well circulated around the country to aid the research of others. With the appearance of this revised version my copy can now retire to its shelf for a well-deserved rest.

Norris Magnuson has carefully surveyed the activities and convictions of such revivalist movements as the Salvation Army, the Volunteers of America, the Christian and Missionary Alliance, the "rescue mission" movement, the circles around the Christian Herald, and the Florence Crittenton homes for "fallen women" during the period from 1865 to 1920. He details how the commitment of these "slum workers" to "saving souls" did not preclude their involvement in a wide range of social concerns (food, shelter, recreation, health, unemployment, and so forth) among such dwellers of the inner-cities as the poverty-stricken, recent immigrants, racial minorities--as well as among the more socially deviant derelicts, prisoners and prostitutes. This part of his work has not so much altered our understanding of these movements as it has fleshed out (in both detail and breadth) the story of such "evangelical social welfare work." Of the groups here surveyed only the Salvation Army has hitherto received extended critical analysis.

But Magnuson has gone further to uncover a great deal of caricature-shattering material. He has shown how these movements were permeated with a "gospel egalitarianism" that affirmed the ministry of women (and often manifested itself in support of suffrage and other tenets of feminism) and transcended its cultural context remarkably in overcoming race and class prejudice--not only in theory but also in practice. Perhaps even more interesting is the demonstration that these "gospel slum workers" at least on occasion broke through to a more "structural" and "causal" critique of American society. Obedience to biblical injunctions to "preach the gospel to the poor" required a changing physical location and close identification with the objects of their concern. In such work they came to understand the structural and environmental causes of poverty and social oppression. And viewing society from the bottom up made them more sympathetic with some of the radical social critics and reformers.

This study also emphasizes the intense piety of these revivalists, especially their profound commitment to the pursuit of "personal holiness." In so doing it confirms the earlier work of Timothy Smith, who argued in his Revivalism and Social Reform (New York: Abingdon, 1957) for the social significance of the Wesleyan doctrine of "Christian Perfection." Magnuson notes that these "holiness slum workers" characteristically "centered their faith in an ethical principle, love, rather than a doctrinal creed" and thereby broke through to a level of acceptance and affirmation that proved to be a powerful force for social rehabilitation--a quality perhaps too lacking in some contemporary (and modern) forms of social work.

One measure of the creativity of a thesis is the extent to which it opens up new questions and other areas needing study. Is it not possible to discern among the persons who are the subjects of this study a certain narrowing of focus on conversion (by comparison with antebellum revivalistic reform) that will later undercut the commitment to reform--especially as the themes of the new "pre-millennial" eschatology become more dominant and upward social mobility begins to remove some of these revivalists and their converts from physical proximity to those occupying the lower rungs of society? Is there any way that we could measure the actual broader social impact of these groups as they participated in the "discovery of poverty" and were driven to support the progressive legislation and social reforms of the period? Is it possible to further specify the exact relationship of these conservative revivalist movements to the more liberal "social Christianity" of the time, to the emerging "fundamentalist" movement, and to the development of later American "evangelicalism." The post-World War I outworkings of these currents especially summon researchers to complete the story.

Finally, Magnuson's study illustrates the extent to which some received historical wisdom will have to be rethought in the process of further penetration into popular religious literature. Such literature (and related movements) reveal often unexpected religious and social innovation--cut loose as they are to some extent from the sometimes more culturally conservative dominant theological and ecclesiastical traditions. Unfortunately the sources for such study are often more inaccessible since they have not been as carefully preserved by the usual libraries and repositories to which researchers turn. Norris Magnuson has obviously had to maximize his skills as both historian and librarian in pursuing this study. But he has done well, and we can only be thankful for his careful and painstaking work.

Donald W. Dayton
Director, Mellander Library, and
Assistant Professor of Theology
North Park Theological Seminary
Chicago, Illinois

ACKNOWLEDGMENTS

I am indebted to the American Theological Library Association for the grant that funded the initial research for this volume, and to the Institute for Advanced Christian Studies for a fellowship that enabled additional study and writing during a post-doctoral sabbatical research year. I am also grateful for the assistance of staff members--too numerous to name--of the headquarters and school libraries of the groups under consideration here, as well as to the staffs of various other libraries that happily had retained the materials upon which this study is based.

To two of my colleagues--Professor Garth Rosell of Bethel Seminary and Professor James Johnson of Bethel College--I am indebted for a helpful critical reading of the text. Professor Timothy L. Smith of Johns Hopkins University, who guided this study in its dissertation stages, has continued to be of assistance far beyond what an advisee and former student could ordinarily expect. While their suggestions have greatly improved this work, I bear full responsibility for any errors of fact or of interpretation that remain.

                                    Norris Magnuson
                                    Bethel Theological Seminary
                                    St. Paul, Minnesota

INTRODUCTION

When Ernest Fremont Tittle, the noted liberal preacher, wrote more than three decades ago that "Evangelical religion" could never hope to produce a humane social order, he gave voice to what has been the opinion of many throughout the present century. Tittle thought that evangelicals had since the Reformation era habitually sanctioned the social order and refused "to cry out against social injustice," thus clearly demonstrating the social impotence of a gospel of individual salvation.[1*] Such a blanket judgment, generally perplexing to many students of evangelical religion, seems especially inapplicable to the revivalistic welfare enterprise of the Progressive Era, with its social programs, warm acceptance of the dispossessed, and support for basic reform. Indeed, why did evangelical social Christianity fall into such bad repute?

That kind of question originally motivated this study of the historical relationship of inward faith and humanitarian concern. Years of participation in evangelical congregations, together with the critical impact of studies in history and religion, combined to awaken my interest, while the identification of liberal religion with the rise of the "Social Gospel" led me back into the formative decades of modern urban-industrial America. Against the background of discussions of social Christianity by historians like Charles Hopkins, Aaron Abell, and Henry F. May, as well as more general accounts, I sought, then, to determine what contributions evangelistic religionists had made.

Beginning with the Salvation Army the story gradually unfolded of a large body of earnest evangelicals who entered the slums because of their concern for the souls of men and women, but who soon developed wide-ranging social service programs. The Volunteers of America, urban rescue mis-

---

*Notes to Introduction and chapters I-XV begin on page 179.

sions, chains of rescue mission homes for women, the Christian and Missionary Alliance, and the Christian Herald magazine became the other focal points for the story, although they do not by any means exhaust the account of the social contributions of evangelicals during the Progressive Era. [2] Moreover, the degree to which the personnel of "gospel welfare" groups interacted with each other and with other evangelicals, including such prominent urban pastors as F. B. Meyer, J. H. Jowett, and A. J. Gordon, and such popular evangelists as J. Wilbur Chapman, Henry Varley, Gipsy Smith, Sam Jones, and D. L. Moody, indicates a "movement" of fairly large proportions. And the support they received from proponents of social Christianity like Lyman Abbott, Josiah Strong, Charles Sheldon, and W. T. Stead, reinforces the other evidence of their size and influence. My mounting surprise at the unfolding record of concern and of welfare activities gradually came to include surprise at the relative absence of historical attention to the social contributions of gospel welfare organizations. On the contrary, historians generally have associated these revivalists with irrelevant and reactionary conservatism that ignored or fought the cause of the common man during those decades. Why has that kind of an interpretation persisted?

One important reason for the neglect of gospel welfare groups has been the unavailability of their publications to scholars. Very few academic libraries bothered to save, if indeed they ever received, the literature of the Salvation Army, the Volunteers, and the Alliance, or of rescue missions and homes for derelict men and women. Even the Christian Herald, one of the most widely circulated religious magazines of that day, and a mine of information on evangelical humanitarian and religious activities, has rarely been preserved. Aside from the Library of Congress, which has fairly complete runs of the Herald, the War Cry, and the Volunteers' Gazette, I know of no library with considerable holdings of more than one of these magazines. Annual reports of individual institutions are even more scattered and inaccessible. This situation militated against research by the writers who established the first prevailing interpretation of the era. When such writers may have happened upon rescue literature, moreover, its preoccupation with evangelism and intense personal religion, and its casting in language geared to an unsophisticated constituency, did not give much promise for the fruitful use of limited research time.

Even had these materials been widely available, the

spirit of the age has not been conducive to an appreciation of revivalistic sects. The triumph of liberal religion after decades of heated controversy, for one thing, did not make for a balanced evaluation of persons of a contrasting persuasion. The bitterness of that controversy, together with the conscious withdrawal of twentieth-century religious conservatives from an emphasis on social welfare, have greatly obscured the larger evangelical contribution to human welfare. The Fundamentalist withdrawal was itself, however, an accidental by-product of the fact that the era witnessed not only the severe social problems of an emerging urban-industrial society, but also widespread defections from historic Christian orthodoxy. For Fundamentalism the defense of the faith received first priority, and the intensity with which that defense was marshalled left little energy for a social gospel often identified with modernism and secular humanism. At the same time, an age emancipating itself from its former religious moorings and reacting against the excesses of Prohibitionism and the controversy over evolution found it easy to read back into the past the apparent irrelevance of conservative and evangelistic Christianity.

Probably the pivotal contribution toward a reevaluation of the role of earnestly evangelistic faith in American social life was Timothy L. Smith's study of the humanitarian crusades of the mid-nineteenth century. His Revivalism and Social Reform demonstrated that revivalism's concern for souls and for personal holiness produced a profound social consciousness.[3] Appearing not long after Carl F. H. Henry and others had begun to arouse the slumbering social conscience of contemporary evangelicals,[4] Smith's book helped restore historical awareness that earlier generations of revivalists had concerned themselves effectively with human need. Indeed, the considerable optimism which permeated social Christianity during the Progressive Era gained inspiration from that fact, as writers like Charles Loring Brace and F. H. Stead stressed the important contribution Christian men and women had made to social welfare across the centuries.[5] Significantly, one of the brightest chapters of that long story was the impact which the evangelical revivals of the eighteenth and nineteenth centuries had upon the elimination of the slave trade and the abolition of slavery, as well as upon the dilemmas created by the developing Western industrial society.[6]

The present work extends that larger chronicle of earnest, experiential religion, and particularly the story of nineteenth century American revivalism related by Professor

Smith. Focusing upon the period from the Civil War to about 1920, this study attempts to portray the sizeable body of Christians whose extensive welfare activities and concern sprang similarly from their passion for evangelism and personal holiness. To the latter date, at least, there had apparently occurred no "great reversal" of what one recent writer has termed evangelicalism's earlier "major role in both social reconstruction and social welfare."[7]

If the triumph of liberal religion after decades of controversy was not conducive to a balanced evaluation of the proponents of a more evangelical faith, neither was the triumph of the welfare state conducive to an appreciation of contrasting social and economic views. Only after mid-century, in fact, did secular historians gain a clearer perspective on the later nineteenth century, modifying the sharply contrasting hues with which they had earlier sketched its outlines.[8] The story of social Christianity, although not drawn in as exaggerated tones as Vernon Parrington and other historians employed for the larger American account, demonstrates a similar need for more balanced portrayal. Here, too, historians have found heroes and villains, with a tendency to neglect both the limitations of the former and the strengths of the latter. The heroes in the generally accepted picture of the Social Gospel Era have been the small group of Christian Socialists on the left and the more moderate but much larger number of social gospelers. The villains, in contrast, have been the main body of conservative churchmen on the right, at best irrelevant for the cause of social Christianity and at worst reactionary. It is with the latter that gospel welfare evangelicals have generally been placed.[9]

Although interpretations of modern social Christianity have thus sharply contrasted the social gospelers and revivalistic churchmen, they have also indicated limitations in the former group that are quite serious by the criteria of welfare state liberalism. James Dombrowski, writing in 1936, saw the social gospelers as "theorists" who stood apart from the workingman's struggles, counseled "patience and moral suasion," and in the end remained "individualists." Charles Hopkins, while stressing an increasing openness to socialism, concluded that most of those who embraced that ideology "left the fold," and that the social gospelers were markedly children of their age in their rejection of labor violence. And Henry F. May, besides remarking about frequent "extreme lack of understanding of labor's ... problems," stressed the sharp contrast between moderate social Christianity and the radical Christian social protest of that day.[10]

Washington Gladden, eminent pioneer among social gospel clergymen, illustrated one facet of this contrast when in 1899 he addressed the National Conference of Charities and Correction in terms more characteristic of the old than of the new approach to poverty. Chiding the "strenuous socialist" who saw the greed and heartlessness of capitalists and corporations but overlooked the selfishness of the poorer classes, he asserted that many of the unemployed did not want work, and urged cities to develop and persistently apply work tests. Agreeing with one authority that insincere work-seekers should be treated with prison-like constraint, Gladden declared that "the one thing that must be stopped, if we are to save the state from ruin, is the business of breeding paupers." This was for him a familiar and central emphasis. "I have said all this so many times," he declared, but argued that on a topic of such importance "no man has a right to be silent."[11]

Many of Gladden's hearers shared his viewpoint. Addressing the same conference two years earlier, Jane Addams, noted settlement house leader and social reformer, had rebuked its members for their fear that the people they aided might not really deserve assistance. Well past the turn of the century charity organization literature amply reflected that fear.[12] Part of the antipathy of some charity workers to the Salvation Army stemmed, in fact, from what they considered to be the Army's careless welfare practices. Salvationists, for their part, on more than one occasion emphasized what they judged to be the harshness of charity organizations toward the poor.[13] To some contemporaries, then, as well as to later observers, the attitude of many social workers differed markedly from the kind of acceptance that the social causes of the developing modern urban-industrial poverty warranted.

Robert Bremner, in his book From the Depths; The Discovery of Poverty in the United States, clearly shows both the developing awareness of that "new" poverty and the inappropriateness of the response of many reformers. For Bremner apparently found very few Americans who accepted the poor as worthy persons in the way in which the better of the young settlement house workers did.[14] At that very point the evangelistic welfare movement had one of its major strengths. No matter how troublesome the persons they helped--former prisoners, prostitutes, unwed mothers, vagrants, or the unemployed--revivalists accepted them with openness and warmth. Placing the blame largely on environmental pressures, rescue workers argued that given a proper

chance even the most difficult persons would perform credit-
ably. Frederick Booth-Tucker, commander of the Salvation
Army in the United States from 1896 to 1903, estimated that
90 per cent or more of the unemployed would gladly work if
they had the opportunity. That kind of optimistic acceptance
generally characterized these organizations. [15]

From the point of view of radical reformers an important reason for faulty attitudes toward the poor was the
failure to perceive the basic causes of poverty. Implicit in
the distance from socialism of social gospelers and social
workers, [16] this failure occasioned some direct criticism.
In an address before the nation's social workers in 1906,
Edward T. Devine charged the charity movement with "not
having at all appreciated the importance of the environmental
causes of distress." He might well have added that those
leaders who had begun to note environmental causes moved
only gradually after the turn of the century from such secondary elements as disease and poor housing into the emphasis
on wages, hours, industrial safety, social insurance, and
other factors that soon came to dominate the discussion of
social reform. [17]

Although the structural reform of society was not the
major thrust of the gospel welfare movement, its strengths in
that area, in combination with the limitations noted in the
position of social gospelers and social workers, makes it
evident that the groups do not stand in the sharp contrast
some have assumed. Certainly the openness of the revivalists toward the underprivileged, their criticism of the social
order, and their support for labor and for various progressive reforms, ought to weigh heavily against their being identified with an irrelevant or reactionary position. Indeed, as
this volume attempts to show, in a number of statements and
interests the revivalists moved close to the radical critics of
the established order. [18]

Among the elements in the story of the gospel welfare
movement that help explain their openness toward and identification with the poor was their knowledge of slum conditions,
a knowledge that came from continuing close personal contacts. Such knowledge, as the literature of that era makes
clear, often correlated positively with support of progressive
reforms. One example, of course, was Walter Rauschenbusch, perhaps the best-known representative of the social
gospel movement, whose pastorate in the "Hell's Kitchen" area
of New York City from 1886 to 1897 helped shape his passion

for reform as well as the larger development of his social
Christianity.   Another was the settlement house workers, who
became "neighbors of the poor" in the most literal sense,
and who attributed in large part to that experience their own
early understanding of the worth of the poor and the need for
reform. [19]

Such concrete knowledge was widely shared among
evangelistic welfare groups.   Many of their members and
some of their leaders, including the pioneer rescue missionaries Jerry McAuley and S. H. Hadley, were converted residents of the slums who remained there to help others.   Many
others became neighbors of the poor in the manner of the
settlement house workers.   The members of the Salvation
Army's slum brigade took apartments in the tenement areas,
for example, and spent their time helping their neighbors in
any way they could.   Still others, while not residents, had
long and intimate familiarity with conditions in the slums. [20]
Continuing contact on that scale helps to explain statements
in the secular press that the Salvation Army had better knowledge of the real conditions of life for the very poor than did
any other welfare organization, private or public.   Extensive
first-hand acquaintance also helps explain both the Salvationists' high estimate of the worth of the poor and the support
they and other gospel welfare workers gave to reform. [21]

As Robert Bremner's account makes clear, however,
familiarity with slum conditions did not always produce that
kind of response.   Even when knowledge did result in a recognition of oppressive social conditions, it often failed to bring
a changed attitude toward the poor.   Despite the fact that the
grounds for blaming the lower classes are removed to the extent that the causes of poverty are social, few contemporaries
seemed to share the responses of generous aid and acceptance of the poor as worthy persons that characterized many
of the settlement house workers as well as their counterparts
in the gospel welfare movement. [22]   Moreover, because the
reshaping of prejudiced attitudes is probably as important to
social reform as is the reshaping of unjust social and economic structures, this failure is a significant one.   And it
was at this essential point of attitude that gospel welfare
workers were most notable, not only in accepting the dispossessed with compassion and optimism, but in energetically
proclaiming their worth to all who would hear.   Why did they
so respond?

In the case of evangelistic welfare workers, acceptance

and aid occurred, it seems to me, because of the nature of their religious experience and teaching, which centered on "love"--practical, sacrificial sensitivity and helpfulness to others. That kind of sensitivity, at the heart of their faith, strongly predisposed them to respond wherever they encountered need. Their continuing presence in the slums, familiarizing them as it did not only with the urgent needs of the poor, but also with oppressive urban conditions, resulted naturally, therefore, in large-scale welfare programs and sympathetic acceptance. It resulted also in the placing of major blame upon the larger society and its prosperous members and in support for a wide range of progressive reforms. [23]

Because the response of these workers was rooted so deeply in that kind of sensitivity to human need it operated with unusual breadth and consistency. Rather than becoming narrowly preoccupied with the industrial problem, it embraced disadvantaged persons of all types, including blacks, Orientals, and "new" immigrants--classes the social gospelers and leaders of the larger progressive movement appear to have neglected. Opposing restrictive immigration laws, they received the "new" immigrant much as they had the "old." In a day when the plight of blacks was worsening, the Salvation Army and kindred organizations defended them and welcomed them into rescue institutions for assistance and as fellow-workers. Finally, these groups opened their highest offices to women, using them to preach and administer in numbers and with a freedom far in advance of most of their clerical and secular contemporaries. For them there did seem to be little distinction of persons, whether male or female, slave or free, rich or poor. [24]

URBAN REVIVALISM, 1865-1920

During the decades following the Civil War the United
States rapidly shifted from a rural and agricultural social
and economic order to urban-industrial status. Other factors,
like the increasing tide of city-bound immigration from southern and eastern Europe, intensified the poverty and attendant
miseries spawned by this transition. Social workers and then
the nation gradually awakened to the new poverty and its
causes. A small but increasing number of American Protestants responded to the plight of the urban poor with what
came to be known as the "social gospel," and Roman Catholicism, generally closer to immigrant and laboring classes,
similarly adjusted its emphasis. [1]

Other social evils that marked that era were partially
obscured for contemporaries as well as for most historians
until mid-century by the over-arching emphasis upon urban-
industrial reform. Recent studies, stimulated in part by the
shifting emphases of the past quarter century, have helped to
clarify the larger picture of the social evils of that day.
Black persons, Indians, women, and the foreign-born, as
well as alcoholics, prostitutes, and other outcast residents
of the slums, received neither the attention nor the help that
their need and the social causes of their problems warranted. [2]

A major crisis of faith added to the restlessness of
an era characterized, as Sydney Ahlstrom has said, at once
by a "strange formlessness" and by "severe duress" for
traditional Christianity. The progressive breakdown of the
intertwined orthodoxies that had dominated the nineteenth cen-
tury--socio-economic individualism and evangelical Protes-
tantism--heightened the disruptive impact of the new urban-
industrial order. In combination those developments helped
produce not only the army of chemically dependent and otherwise deviant persons in the slums, but also the multiplied

scores of thousands who consciously or unconsciously sought integration and wholeness outside of traditional Christian orthodoxy. Secularism, religious modernism, shrilly defensive Protestantism, and sectarian movements like Jehovah's Witnesses and Christian Science, all vied with the old orthodoxy with increasing success. [3]

During that troubled era an increasing number of revivalistic slum workers united to penetrate the blighted areas of American cities with their gospel of "salvation." Their hallmark was thorough supernaturalism and intense religious commitment. Beginning as a small body of earnest Christians from various Protestant denominations, these evangelists attracted hundreds of thousands of recruits and converts within a few decades. Their continuing experience in the slums soon led them into varied and extensive social welfare programs. Thus combining evangelism and welfare they formed one of the largest and most influential contingents of field workers in American cities during those decades. The following pages relate their important story.

The Booth Family, the Salvation Army, and the Volunteers of America

Late one night in 1865 William Booth, an itinerant evangelist then preaching in the slums of East London, returned to his home and announced to his wife, "Kate, I have found my destiny! These are the people for whose salvation I have been longing all these years." East London, made famous two decades later by the investigations of Charles Booth, was as blighted an urban area as the Western world then knew. The condition of its masses so moved the young evangelist that, as he told his wife, "there and then in my soul I offered myself and you and the children up to this great work." "That night," he later said, "the Salvation Army was born."[4]

Such concern for human welfare was not a new thing to William Booth. Born in Nottingham in 1829 and converted in his early teens, he immediately became "an apostle to the lads of Nottingham slums," and founded there, as he once described it, a "miniature Salvation Army." His preaching and personal contacts soon enabled him to marshal a shabbily-clothed company into his church, to the dismay of fellow members. For the next eight years in Nottingham and London, preaching, often in slum streets, and extensive personal "wit-

nessing, " occupied much of Booth's free time. In April,
1852, he determined to devote himself fully to the ministry,
and for nearly a decade thereafter he labored as a Methodist
preacher, primarily as an itinerant evangelist. The Booths'
letters and other records from that period describe increasing crowds and thousands of converts. During his campaign
in Cornwall in 1861 and 1862, for example, he claimed more
than 1000 converts in four months. Evangelism was his love,
and when his denomination insisted on confining him instead
to a regular parish, he resigned and entered with his wife
the independent ministry that was to occupy the rest of their
lives. Catherine Mumford, whom William Booth had married
in 1855, shared both his fervor and his effectiveness in
preaching. She is said to have urged the break with Methodism, and fully supported her husband's decision to enter
the East London slums, a decision that promised both difficulty and poverty for their growing family. 5

William Booth's revivalism did not spread beyond
England's capital city for several years, and thirteen years
passed before his "East London Christian Mission" became
the "Salvation Army." Yet an early "balance sheet" covering
the nineteen months through September, 1868, listed thirteen
"preaching stations" in London with a capacity of 8000 persons.
There and in the streets Booth's workers had held nearly 150
services each week; and since the Mission's beginning over
4000 "anxious inquirers" had responded to their preaching. 6
During the 1870s the Mission's expansion accelerated. Its
Conference of Workers in April, 1874, announced that during
the preceding twelve-month period its people had established
eleven new stations and had conducted nearly 11,000 services
resulting in the conversion of 3220 persons. 7

In 1878 the Christian Mission found its new name.
Early one morning as George Railton read aloud a report on
which he, Bramwell Booth, and the "General" were working,
the latter leaned over Railton's shoulder, crossed out "volunteer" in the phrase "volunteer army, " and replaced it with
the word "Salvation. " The phrase only accelerated a trend
toward military discipline in organization and methods which
was already underway, but it did that, and its electric effect
on Railton and Bramwell Booth was symbolic of the impact
the trend was soon to have. 8

William Booth's evangelistic fervor now caught on
among a rapidly increasing number of English adherents and
soon spread overseas as well. In February, 1880, George

Railton and seven young Army lassies sailed for the United
States, the first contingent of the missionary bands that during succeeding months and years planted the Salvation Army
standard around the world.[9] Railton's group was unofficially
preceded by other Salvationists. Nearly a decade earlier,
James Jermy, one of the Christian Mission's "most active
and successful" workers, had emigrated to Canada and then
to Cleveland, Ohio. Finding slums similar to those in East
London, Jermy "hoisted the Mission flag" and then wrote
Booth requesting recognition and advice. Within a year he
and several co-workers were operating at least two missions
patterned in spirit and approach on Booth's London enterprise. But the Christian Mission had neither the organization nor the personnel for international expansion at that
time, and when Jermy returned to England the experiment
died.[10] A few years later another worker, Amos Shirley,
sailed with his family for Philadelphia, where they soon began meetings in an abandoned factory and established the
first permanent branch of the Salvation Army. Booth's newspaper, the War Cry,[11] published its first account of their
meetings late in January, 1880; two weeks later Railton and
his party sailed for New York.[12]

Despite criticism from American churchmen, the new
endeavor made steady progress. Railton was perhaps the
Army's best known leader outside of the Booth family, and
his successors, Majors Thomas Moore and Frank Smith,
were competent and energetic men. By the time Railton returned to England in 1881, corps were operating in Philadelphia, New York, Newark, and St. Louis. In 1887 Major
Smith turned over to his successor, Ballington Booth, an
organization of more than 300 local corps, and double that
number of officers. For nearly half a century thereafter,
William Booth's children--Ballington and his wife Maud,
Emma and her husband, Frederick Booth-Tucker, and the
famous Evangeline--commanded the Salvation Army in the
United States. They guided the movement into large-scale
social work, and they helped win for it increasing public acceptance and steady growth.[13]

A serious breach in the Army ranks occurred in the
United States early in 1896 when Ballington Booth and his
wife resigned their command to begin a new and more "democratic" organization, the Volunteers of America.[14] Though
never rivaling the Salvation Army in size or world-wide expansion, the Volunteers quickly gained a wide following.

Benefitting from officers who followed them from the Army, and from the national goodwill built up during their decade of experience in America, Maud and Ballington Booth reported organizations in more than sixty cities and towns within twelve weeks, and 20,000 paid subscriptions to their Gazette. By year's end they had 140 posts in twenty states.[15]

Though the Volunteers often stressed differences, they resembled the Army closely in the combination of evangelistic fervor and social outreach as well as in military garb and organization. Ballington Booth's annual reports frequently mentioned converts in the thousands; he reported a total of 15,000 the first three years, over 6000 in 1903, and more than 8000 in 1908.[16] Meanwhile facilities for social service steadily expanded. Within weeks of the schism Maud Booth embarked upon the prison work which for several decades remained the Volunteers' most notable welfare effort. Gradually the group developed a diversified program of social service, including dinners and fresh air outings for children, orphanages, homes for women, and shelters and "hotels" of several varieties. Ballington and Maud Booth, along with several of the original company of officers, maintained a continuity of command and purpose right down to the outbreak of the Second World War.[17]

During these same years the Salvation Army in the United States, which had quickly recouped its losses, also steadily expanded both its social and evangelistic work. William Booth's fourth child and second daughter, Emma, known widely as the "Consul," and her husband, Frederick Booth-Tucker, were the leaders until 1904 when Evangeline Booth assumed a command that ended only when she became international General of the Salvation Army in 1934. The two daughters inherited a large measure of their parents' executive ability, and Booth-Tucker was their equal. An officer in the Indian Civil Service, and a product of D. L. Moody's revivalism, Booth-Tucker joined the Salvation Army in 1881 and led its first contingent back to India a year later. During his nine-year administration there, more than 3600 converts entered service as soldiers in some 250 stations.[18] Similar progress marked Booth-Tucker's term in the United States. From a low point of twenty-five corps after an initial schism late in 1884, the Army grew to more than 600 corps by the time Booth-Tucker arrived nearly twelve years later. When he departed in 1904 the American Army numbered over 900 corps and auxiliary institutions.[19]

On the world front a similar rapid growth took place. William Booth commanded fewer than 100 British Isles stations in 1878, but two decades later his world-wide organization numbered about 3500 posts, and by 1904 there were more than 7000.[20] Though the founder died in 1912, rapid growth continued; 4600 new corps came into being during the thirteen years immediately following his death.[21] This long-term expansion drew repeated praise from such leaders of American social Christianity as Josiah Strong and Charles Stelzle. The former, writing in the early 1890s, declared that the Army's "amazing success," which would have been "phenomenal in any class of society," was in fact more amazing because it had occurred among those whom the churches had "conspicuously failed to reach."[22]

Throughout the era before World War I, neither William Booth nor his Army lost the fervor for evangelism that had driven the founder into the slums of East London. If anything, it increased across the years. "Souls! Souls! Souls!" was the headline in one issue of the War Cry,[23] and those words and spirit were everywhere in evidence. George Railton, in an article written during his brief foray in America, declared that "this willingness to sever ourselves, if needs be, from the whole world, in order to save somebody," to "plunge down to the very depths of human contempt," was "the essence of the life of Jesus Christ." Shortly after his arrival as "commander" of the American forces, Railton slept in his chair in the dark basement rooms of his headquarters so that a drunken castaway could have his cot.[24] A few years later Ballington Booth exhorted his officers in council to make the Salvation Army "a greater soul-saving agency" than ever before.[25] His successor, Frederick Booth-Tucker, whose nine-year command was marked by a great extension of the social work, struck a similar note. Launching a farewell tour in 1904 under the dark shadow of the death of his wife, Booth-Tucker called for "seasons of spiritual baptism and power" in which souls would be saved. War Cry reports of that tour indicate that he had his wish; his command thus ended with the kind of spiritual emphasis that had permeated his years here.[26]

This same concern seemed to William Booth's officers the dominant trait in his character.[27] William T. Stead once termed William Booth a "miracle of energy," and the Anglican F. W. Farrar commented that the General had committed "every energy of his life" to his task.[28] That task, as Booth described it at the bedside of his dying wife, was "living and dying only for the salvation of men. "[29] Early in his ministry he had vowed that God would have "all of William Booth there was," and in the dark hour of the death of his wife he reaffirmed his intention to serve his God to "the last drop of my blood."[30] Booth led his Army with unabated energy for more than twenty additional years, intensifying, if anything, its evangelistic and holiness zeal and developing a wide-ranging social program. Yet near the end of his life he wrote with some dissatisfaction that if he could begin again he would work a "thousand times harder." His family and chief officers shared that kind of zeal; no matter what level of religious dedication they and their soldiers reached, they always called for more.[31]

Such enthusiasm helps to explain the mounting totals of the Army's conversions. By the turn of the century Salvationists claimed converts ranging as high as one-third of a million annually on their world-wide front, and up to 50,000 or more in the United States.[32] In addition to their on-going evangelism, annual special campaigns such as the "Siege" under Evangeline Booth produced about 10,000 converts each year in the space of a few weeks.[33] The impact of individual leaders in special services was equally impressive. Crowds repeatedly packed the largest churches and auditoriums in the land to hear the Booths; and the number who came forward to the mourner's bench seeking conversion or sanctification consistently ranged from a score or more to several hundred.[34] Other preachers such as Railton and Samuel Brengle, as well as a host of officers at lower levels, were intensely and successfully committed to the same evangelistic mission.[35] "Probably during no hundred years in the history of the world," Josiah Strong wrote, "have there been saved so many thieves, gamblers, drunkards, and prostitutes as during the past quarter of a century through the ... Salvation Army."[36] F. W. Farrar, a well-known Biblical scholar and church historian, declared that to find parallels to "the growth and force of this movement" one had to go back to St. Francis and St. Dominic, or to George Fox, the Wesleys, and the early church itself.[37]

Neither William Booth nor his officers were surprised at such estimates, nor at the results occasioning them; they felt that God's power was working through them, and that that power was the world's only hope. As they stated in one of the Army's well-known mottoes, "Go for souls, and go for the worst," Booth wanted to see in his people the conviction that they had a remedy capable of lifting the most depraved.[38]

The "salvation" they sought extended beyond individual reformation to all human problems. William Booth thus emphasized across his long life that salvation was the only cure
for the world's ills, and that any purported remedy omitting
it was a mockery. [39] American leaders repeatedly echoed
the same belief. A heart change, and not education or reform movements, was man's deep need, Ballington Booth declared; an educated devil was only a devil made more re-
sourceful. [40] And his wife Maud affirmed in 1894 at a symposium on the improvement of the city that the only way was
to change men's hearts, to bring them to Jesus Christ. [41]

The leaders of both the Salvation Army and the Volunteers of America emphasized the absolute importance of
keeping the "spiritual" primary in all of their welfare work.
Not long after the Army had begun to systematize and enlarge its social services, a serious shortage of funds caused
William Booth forcefully to reveal his own priorities. If
additional money was not forthcoming, he announced, the
social program would be curtailed, for the spiritual work
must continue. [42] His daughter Emma, in mild rebuke of the
many friends who preferred the Army's social to its spiritual
operations, declared that zeal for the latter carried them to
the depths to help the needy. [43] Ballington Booth struck that
same note before he left the Army, as did many others who
remained in it after his departure. [44] Later his various reports and official letters to the Volunteers of America invariably reached their climax in an emphasis on the spiritual.
Zeal, evangelism, was their supreme aim, the building as
against the mere scaffolding of methods. Though their philanthropic efforts had shown immense growth, he said, spiritual depth was ultimately their only source of power,
their strongest bulwark, the factor which made "all the difference."
Above all else they must experience God's presence. Without
this they would be nothing. To trust in any other power
would be "calamitous." [45] Edward Fielding, next to the
Booths as a leader of the Volunteers, whose Chicago area
appeared to sustain more welfare activity than any other in
the organization, repeatedly emphasized this same theme.
In 1903 he urged an assembly of officers that spiritual matters must keep first place. In his judgment only religious
persons, possessed of an "earnest, genuine desire to benefit
the people," could do effective philanthropic work. [46]

Jerry McAuley, S. H. Hadley,
and American Rescue Missions

"Do you love Jesus?"

"No, indade, do I love Jesus; and who is he?"

That brief conversation on the stairway of a Cherry
Hill tenement house in New York City in 1868 disturbed the
slumbers of a drunken "river thief" who lay on the floor of
his room a few feet away. The question came from a
Christian worker from the Howard Mission, the answer from
a large and rather belligerent woman who barred his way.
The drunk--a "frightful-looking object," he later admitted--
stumbled out of his room to locate the questioner. The ensuing conversation began a process which, over a period of
months, resulted in the permanent conversion of one Jerry
McAuley. [47] By the time of his death a decade and a half
later, McAuley's associates in rescue work claimed that the
New York City missions he founded had exerted a world-wide
influence, directly inspiring scores of similar institutions in
American and British cities. Certainly he was one of the
most important founders of the modern rescue mission movement. [48]

Jeremiah McAuley, a young Irish-born immigrant,
first professed conversion midway through a fifteen-year
term at Sing Sing prison. Soon after his release in 1864,
however, he lapsed into his earlier habits of crime and
drunkenness. His reconversion occurred in 1868, when the
celebrated "John Allen excitement" in Water Street brought
numerous missionaries into the Cherry Hill area in search
of lost men. [49] Several years passed before McAuley himself entered rescue work, though, as in prison, he enthusiastically told others about his "salvation"; he lost one job,
in fact, because he "preached Jesus too much." Meanwhile
his missionary friend Henry Little greatly influenced him
through frequent visits and such kindnesses as pawning his
own coat so McAuley could eat. During this period Jerry
also formed a lifelong friendship with a Wall Street banker,
A. S. Hatch, who helped him obtain employment. When,
therefore, he approached Hatch in 1872 with the story of a
remarkable "vision" of "working for the Lord down in the
Fourth Ward," his friend volunteered the use of a once notorious dance hall property at 316 Water Street, which became the permanent location of the Water Street Mission. [50]

McAuley opened what he at first called the "Helping

Hand for Men" in October, 1872. On Thanksgiving Day the next month friends provided food sufficient for 150 needy persons; in a religious service at the end of the day, "the Holy Spirit was poured upon" the group, as McAuley put it, and a great revival began. Three years later he wrote that a "gospel service" had taken place every evening from that time, with "hundreds of souls" converted and "as many as twenty-five or thirty" crowding the front and aisle at one time. "Had full records been kept," one friend affirmed later, the accounts of the numbers of converts could have been "multiplied a hundredfold."[51] In 1876, as a result of this continuing success, McAuley erected a new three-story building on the same spot, and renamed his enterprise the "McAuley Water Street Mission." Here he had fuller reign for the zeal that had marked the days of his conversion in prison as well as the period since his reawakening.[52]

After a decade in Water Street, McAuley founded the Cremorne Mission on West 32nd Street, the "worst" area, he said, that he had ever seen. There he worked with similar emphasis and results until his death in September, 1884. The huge crowd that thronged the Broadway Tabernacle and nearby streets for his funeral reflected the impact he had had across various classes of society during his twelve years in rescue mission work.[53] His widow Maria, also converted at the time of the John Allen revival and Jerry's co-worker from the beginning, assumed leadership at the Cremorne Mission, continuing until 1892, when ill health forced her to resign. During her superintendency, as in the farewell meeting in March, 1892, the primary emphasis continued to be upon evangelism.[54]

During Jerry McAuley's lifetime and for at least two decades thereafter, the Water Street Mission remained the most important American center in the rescue mission movement, though when the founder moved to the Cremorne project, attention shifted there for a time. In June, 1883, McAuley began publishing regularly a "newspaper" which became an informal organ of New York City missions, carrying accounts of the work of many others besides the Water Street and Cremorne efforts. A later superintendent at Water Street, John Wyburn, wrote that between 1872 and 1892 more than one hundred missions had opened in the United States and other lands as a result of the influence of McAuley's work.[55]

The continuing importance of the original mission owed

much to the reformation in 1882 of another drunken outcast,
Samuel Hopkins Hadley. Though he became the most influential leader in the rescue mission movement until his death in
1906, Hadley's name is almost unknown today. Raised in an
Ohio log cabin in a devout family, he claimed descent on his
mother's side from Jonathan Edwards. He had arrived in
New York in 1879, and though he prospered for a time, his
drinking increased until by early 1882 he was a spiritual and
physical wreck. [56] Depressed nearly to the point of suicide,
Hadley attended McAuley's Cremorne Mission. There he
heard Jerry tell his oft-repeated story, how he had been a
"thief, an outcast," and "one of the worst drunkards in the
Fourth Ward," when by faith in Christ he found redemption.
The testimonies of "probably twenty-five redeemed drunkards"
followed, "everyone of whom," Hadley said later, "told my
story." Wondering if he, too, could be changed, Hadley soon
was kneeling at the altar with other outcast men. There Mc-
Auley prayed with words the convert said he would "never
forget":

> Dear Saviour, won't You look down in pity upon
> these poor souls? They need Your help, Lord;
> they cannot get along without it. Blessed Jesus!
> These poor sinners have got themselves into a bad
> hole. Won't You help them out? Speak to them,
> Lord; do, for Jesus' sake. Amen.

McAuley then had each of his penitents pray, and after that
difficult experience, Hadley recalled, he "felt the glorious
brightness of the noon-day sunshine" in his heart, and believed himself "a free man." While praying that night, he
thought that his room "lightened up with a halo of glory."
"I cried, I shouted, I wept for joy," he said, "and I went to
sleep with tears raining from my eyes."[57]

Hadley, like his mentor McAuley, immediately began
trying to bring other men to what he felt was the amazing
change he had experienced. [58] That first evening he went to
his brother with his story; the next day he told it "to all who
would listen." That story, as Hadley repeated it across the
years, was "the boundless, deathless love of Jesus for the
sinner."[59] A. T. Pierson, editor of The Missionary Review
of the World, later judged Hadley the most successful "soul-
winner" of his generation, and estimated that he had led
75,000 persons to faith in Jesus. Similarly, A. B. Simpson,
founder of the fervently evangelistic Christian and Missionary
Alliance, affirmed that Hadley "had the genius of soul saving

as no other living man possessed it. " The Water Street
Mission reported converts almost daily and the annual totals
mounted to between 3000 and 5000 persons even after Hadley's passing. [60]

S. H. Hadley became leader of the Water Street
Mission in 1886, but his influence on rescue work extended
far beyond that institution. Earlier he had served as the
first editor of McAuley's rescue mission sheet. For most
of the period from 1886 until his death in 1906 he was the
most prominent leader and the chief guiding force within the
rescue mission world. Many of his converts entered mission work. His own brother, H. H. Hadley, converted at
Water Street in 1886, founded more than sixty rescue missions, brought the Anglican "Church Army" to the United
States, and inaugurated a widespread temperance effort. [61]
Mel Trotter, a convert at Chicago's Pacific Garden Mission
in 1897, and thereafter head of the Grand Rapids, Mich.,
City Mission, and founder of several score missions elsewhere, attributed the effectiveness of his own efforts to
Hadley's influence. Trotter, like many others, judged Hadley the most important person in advancing American rescue
work. [62]

Hadley initiated a cooperation among the heads of
American city missions which resulted in the organization
of a national federation. Each summer between 1900 and
1906, he, Trotter, and Harry Monroe, a converted criminal
who became director of the Pacific Garden Mission in 1892,
met with a few other leaders of rescue missions at the
Winona Lake, Ind., Bible Conference grounds to confer about
their work. [63] Earlier, such men had seen one another often
at the annual gatherings of the Convention of Christian
Workers, an organization significant both for beginning missions, and for informing and unifying mission personnel.
The presence of men like Jerry McAuley, Charles Crittenton, R. A. Torrey, George R. Clarke, A. T. Pierson, and
A. J. Gordon, as well as Hadley, indicates the tone of the
group. [64] Meanwhile, Hadley's increasing nation-wide speaking engagements, and his continuing activity in the important
rescue missions in New York City, greatly enlarged his national influence. [65] At his death, his fellow workers organized the National Federation of Gospel Missions, in order
to maintain the cooperation he had inspired. [66] While this
was neither the first nor the only national organization of
rescue missions, it did carry the thread of influence which

eventually issued in the most long-lived and significant of
such groups.

Another important organization was the National Gospel Mission Union, "designed to assist in planting ... missions ... in every city in the land." On the Union's Board
of Directors were such men as Charles N. Crittenton, evangelist and head of a chain of rescue homes for women, Louis
Klopsch, publisher of the Christian Herald, and Stephen Merritt, Klopsch's father-in-law and long time New York City
rescue worker. The Central Union Mission of Washington,
D.C., which opened in 1884 and occupied a new six-story
building by 1892, served as inspiration and model for a number of other "Union" or "Gospel Union" missions. In 1891
"Major" George Hilton, a man important in the Central Union
Mission's early history, opened the Pacific Gospel Union Mission in Los Angeles, patterned after the former institution.
Hilton influenced others, who in their turn began similar missions. John C. Appel, for example, an outcast converted by
Hilton in Los Angeles, attended Moody Bible Institute in Chicago before beginning the Gospel Union Mission of Portland,
Ore., in July, 1893. [67]

During 1913 the National Federation of Gospel Missions
gave way to the organization which has united rescue missions
since that time, the International Union of Gospel Missions.
The change was largely in name, for the officers of the new
body remained the same; its president was Sidney Whittemore,
whose wife, a vice-president, was head of the Door of Hope
rescue homes for women. Sarah Wray, director of New
York's Eighth Avenue Mission, which had been supported in
its early years by the Christian and Missionary Alliance, and
George H. Sandison, an editor of the Christian Herald, were
also vice-presidents. [68] As with its predecessor, the International Union of Gospel Missions promoted cooperation on the
district level. Leaders of the New York District met in
October, 1913, and elected John Hallimond, superintendent of
the Christian Herald's Bowery Mission, president, and Sarah
Wray, vice-president; John Wyburn, a veteran of the Bowery
Mission who had been associated with the Water Street Mission since 1900, was made chairman of the executive committee. The revivalistic emphasis of the movement is evident
from the fact that following the organizational meeting a
"Gospel" service lasting several hours ended with about
twenty people at the mourner's bench. [69]

A. B. Simpson and the Christian and Missionary Alliance

Less than two years after George Railton and his seven young Salvation Army women "invaded" New York in 1880, the Rev. Albert B. Simpson, who a few days before had resigned the pastorate of the 13th Street Presbyterian Church, met with six other persons in a nearby dance hall and laid plans to evangelize New York's poor. Three months later, in February, 1882, thirty-five persons joined Simpson in organizing a church "for the especial purpose of Gospel work, particularly among the neglected classes, both at home and abroad."[70] Within a year the church's membership reached 217, with Sunday evening congregations of about 700. In 1889, after having worshiped at twelve different places, Simpson and his people moved into a spacious new complex of buildings at Eighth Avenue and West 44th Street, with an auditorium seating 1000 persons.[71] By that date, the "Gospel Tabernacle," as the congregation called itself, was the mother church of a movement reaching into many cities in America and into mission fields around the world.

A. B. Simpson was graduated from Knox College, Toronto, in 1865, when twenty-one years old, and immediately thereafter became pastor of one of the largest churches of his denomination in Canada, the Knox Presbyterian Church at Hamilton, Ont. Successful as a preacher from the beginning, Simpson saw the Knox membership more than double by the time he left for a new charge in Louisville, Ky., nine years later.[72] A man of intense inward religion, at age seventeen he had dedicated himself to live for God alone in a "Solemn Covenant" in which he acknowledged at length his sinfulness and that of the world. He renewed that pledge more than once; in Louisville in 1878 he wrote, "My one desire now is ... souls, Christ's indwelling, and my church's salvation."[73] By that date Simpson had directed his congregation into a continuing evangelistic program. His missionary ambition, however, was reaching yet wider, and late in 1879 he accepted the pastorate of the 13th Street Presbyterian Church in New York City. There he began what Christian and Missionary Alliance writers have called the "first illustrated missionary magazine" on the American continent, The Gospel in All Lands.[74] And he launched an extensive effort to reach the poor and unchurched in the surrounding neighborhood. The congregation, however, was not happy with their new leader's aggressive evangelism. They refused to accept into membership a group of more than one hundred Italians converted through Simpson's visitation and street preaching in a nearby immigrant neighborhood. [75]

Not long after arriving in New York, Simpson experienced what his friend George Pardington called "the great spiritual and ministerial crisis of his life" at Old Orchard, Me., camp meeting grounds. Simpson later related his memory of the nights he had spent pacing its sandy beach in the summer of 1881, asking God "to raise up a great missionary movement" that would evangelize the unchurched of America and other lands. On his return to New York, he determined to resign his pastorate and begin a new "Gospel work" among the masses of that city. [76]

Apart from important intangibles of spirit, perhaps the key factor in the rapid expansion of Simpson's movement was the well-publicized conventions which he conducted beginning in 1884. The first, held in the temporary meeting place known as the "23rd Street Tabernacle," included in its objects "a special Baptism of the Holy Spirit for life and service" and the promotion of "the work of evangelization at home and missions abroad. "[77] At the following year's convention William S. Rainsford and Henry Wilson of St. George's Episcopal Church, New York, and Miss Carrie F. Judd, a well-known faith-healer, preached. As a result of those meetings, Simpson received invitations to hold similar gatherings that autumn in Buffalo, Philadelphia, Pittsburgh, Chicago, and other cities. Held in large halls or in leading churches of various denominations, these conventions attracted a widening circle. [78]

Simpson's conventions gradually resulted in the larger missionary organization for which he called as early as 1885, "A Christian Alliance of all those in all the world who hold in unison the faith of God and the Gospel of full salvation." The conference that precipitated this union took place at the Old Orchard camp grounds in 1886, the first of an annual series there. At it W. E. Blackstone, well-known preacher of the second advent of Jesus Christ, delivered an address on Tibet which prompted the first effort to begin foreign missionary work in areas other church groups had not entered. [79] At the Old Orchard convention the following summer, this movement took formal shape in twin organizations, the "Christian Alliance" for evangelism in North America, and the "Evangelical Missionary Alliance" for overseas lands. The membership consisted of like-minded groups of Christians

in cities and towns across the nation who were attracted to
Simpson by his increasing contacts through conventions and
journals and other writings. Some groups were already in
existence and others came together through his influence,
until by early 1889 the Alliance Weekly reported that groups
of this kind existed in almost every important American
city.[80] Despite Simpson's continuing insistence that his
movement was a supplement to the spiritual and missionary
work of the established churches rather than a new sect, the
distinctive Alliance emphasis and spirit increasingly drew its
local affiliates together and away from their original church
connections.[81]

During 1889 and 1890 Simpson's two organizations incorporated, with the Evangelical Missionary Alliance changing
its name to the International Missionary Alliance. In response to a growing consensus the groups merged as the
Christian and Missionary Alliance in 1897. The united body
continued the earlier objectives, emphasizing both "the deeper
Christian life" and the evangelization of "neglected classes"
here and abroad.[82] In its first annual report Simpson reaffirmed that the "pre-eminent work of the Alliance has been
the evangelization of the world." Despite fifty-five missionary
deaths, the Alliance by then had more than 300 missionaries
overseas, compared to twenty in 1890. From 1892 on the
organization had sent out from 70 to more than 100 new missionaries each year. Giving rose proportionately, from
$10,000 in 1889 and $91,000 in 1893 to $273,000 in the
eighteen months prior to his writing, cumulating to a total
of more than $1 million by 1897.[83]

Missionary volunteers came forward in such large
numbers during those years that the Alliance had difficulty
maintaining a home base sufficiently strong to support them.
Simpson wrote in 1897 that several hundred volunteers
awaited sending. Nearly a decade later the annual "Council"
of the Alliance declared the "crying need of more workers
in the home field." And in mid-1906, Simpson reported about
200 superintendents and evangelists in 150 formally organized
and 250 other branches on this continent.[84] By the time of
his death in 1920, those branches had channeled more than
$4 million into foreign missions. Writing in that year,
Robert H. Glover reported nearly 12,000 national members
in "full communion" in 125 organized churches on sixteen
overseas "fields." From their ranks 700 persons had entered full-time church or rescue work.[85] On both home and
foreign fronts the Alliance continued to grow; at its fiftieth

anniversary in 1937, its leaders reported the organization's previous two decades were the most impressive for expansion. [86]

An aggressive program of social work paralleled this evangelistic and spiritual activity of the Gospel Tabernacle and the Alliance during their early decades. The network of departments and agencies included a rescue home for women (1882), a home for "rest and healing" (1883), a Training College for missionaries, evangelists, and rescue workers (1883), an orphanage (1886), work with immigrants from Germany (1887), and several rescue missions. Such activities, supplemented by "open air meetings, services in jails, hospitals, on shipboard ... and in many other places," prompted Thompson's assertion that the Gospel Tabernacle was the "most aggressive center of evangelism in New York City."[87]

Tabernacle and Alliance ties with rescue work expanded steadily after 1890. S. E. Furry of the "New York Rescue Band" reported to the Old Orchard Convention in 1894 that the work in "hospitals, almshouses and charitable institutions" in New York was so extensive that Simpson himself did not know "how much the Alliance was doing for all [such] agencies of Christian work in that city." One of Simpson's associates wrote thirteen years later that scores of charitable institutions "within the limits of New York City, and, indeed, for many miles around" had felt the Tabernacle's impact, and that many of the leaders were members of the Alliance. [88] One of the channels for that influence was the annual "Rescue Day" held in connection with the important New York Convention. Rescue Day, which developed out of the Gospel Tabernacle's monthly "all-night prayer meeting ... for the city mission workers of New York," became an important gathering for other groups as well as for the Alliance, as it brought together many of the leading welfare workers of the area. [89]

Simpson supported the welfare activities of his people. Commenting on "An Ideal Church" in 1899, he noted that the first converts of the Alliance were among the poor, and asserted that "the great majority of our people are actively engaged either in rescue work at home or evangelistic work abroad." A few months later his own congregation's annual business meeting revealed "much useful work ... in nearly all the missions and charitable institutions of the city."[90]

More than once the pastor asserted that the "best evangelistic work" of his day was being done in rescue institutions in the city slums; and he instructed his followers elsewhere that if they wished to have a "strong Alliance branch" they should engage themselves in "practical Christian work," including, if possible, a city mission. [91]   That the branches shared his feeling is apparent from their reports to the Alliance Weekly. The first annual report of the combined national organizations mentioned the "hundreds of rescue missions" in which Alliance people were engaged.   Across the years their journal supplied details on many of these missions.   And local groups in Denver, Fort Worth, and elsewhere carried on a varied social program including orphanages, institutions for women, and "industrial" work, as well as rescue missions. [92]

Yet this considerable welfare activity was essentially a by-product of the deeper spiritual life Simpson and his co-workers sought to cultivate.   Thus while F. W. Farr pointed out with satisfaction the impact of the Gospel Tabernacle on "humanitarian enterprise" in the greater New York area, he emphasized that it did this "incidentally and mediately."   Unlike the "institutional" churches with their network of direct social programs, the Gospel Tabernacle was, Farr said, an "inspirational" church; its social impact came through the changed lives of its members. [93]   For him and for the Alliance this demonstrated the truth that evangelistic social work must spring from the concern and brotherhood that the Holy Spirit brought into the Christian's life.   Simpson more than once pressed home the point that the "liberal" churches, "with few exceptions," were not reaching the lowest classes. They had neither the message nor the spiritual drive, he said, to win such men. [94]

Among the reasons for the continuing growth of the Alliance was the caliber of the men whose cooperation Simpson attracted.   A list of speakers at the New York and Old Orchard annual conventions constitutes something of a "Who's Who" of the evangelicalism of that day: Andrew Murray and F. B. Meyer from abroad, and A. J. Gordon, A. T. Pierson, R. A. Torrey, D. L. Moody, J. Wilbur Chapman, S. H. Hadley, Frances Willard and Robert E. Speer from the United States. [95]   Others officially united with the Alliance in its missionary endeavors.   One such person was Henry Wilson, one of A. B. Simpson's closest associates and probably next to him in importance during the first two decades of Alliance history. [96]

Wilson, an Episcopalian clergyman in Kingston, Ont.,

for eighteen years, joined the staff of the now well-known institutional church, St. George's Episcopal Church in New York City, in 1884. The Salvation Army had arrived in Kingston months earlier, with Wilson attending its meetings. As a result, he related, he went with the fallen to its altar, seeing himself "as never before, a poor lost soul, just as much as they." He later judged this to have been the central spiritual experience for his life. And it was central for his ministerial career as well, for his support of the Salvation Army cost him his position in Kingston within a few months. Joining W. S. Rainsford's staff in New York, Wilson soon gravitated into A. B. Simpson's circle; there he found "sanctification," which, with his conversion, left him, he said, "on fire with love to God and a lost world."[97] His duties at St. George's Church included opening and supervising a gospel mission to the poor, as well as extensive pastoral visitation and occasional preaching in Rainsford's place. Amidst these tasks, he found time for increasing participation in the affairs of the Gospel Tabernacle and the Alliance.[98]

In 1891, Wilson severed his official connections with St. George's Church to become associate pastor at the Gospel Tabernacle. Ten years later he became field superintendent for Alliance operations in the United States, a post he occupied until his death in 1908. From near the beginning of his connection with the Gospel Tabernacle, Wilson was also president of the Seaman's Christian Association and chaplain of the Magdalene Home for girls.[99] His wide activity in welfare work is indicated by Simpson's assertion that "few men" in New York were "in closer touch" and a more helpful friend to the city missionaries. And Wilson was the key person behind the annual "Rescue Day" at which the Alliance featured those missionaries.[100] But the Alliance probably remembers him best for his work with children, in which for several years he marshalled 5000 children in the United States in support of about 1000 orphans in the care of Alliance missionaries overseas.[101]

Simpson and his associates pressed their mission among the poor from a base of supernaturalism and evangelism. The doctrines of the Christian and Missionary Alliance comprised a "four-fold Gospel," as Simpson called it, of conversion, entire sanctification, divine healing, and the second coming of Jesus.[102] Sin was a "terrible reality" for them, from which only the "power of the blood" could save; "most emphatically," George Pardington wrote, they had "no kinship or sympathy

with modern methods of salvation by character or culture."
Every Alliance branch, he exhorted, "should be first and
foremost a life-saving station for the salvation of souls."
That salvation, as Simpson emphasized, was to a "deeper
Christian life," to the experience of entire sanctification by
which the Holy Spirit took full control of the believer's
life.[103]

The Alliance gospel also stressed divine healing and
the imminent second coming of Jesus. Wary of the per-
versions to which these doctrines could lead, Simpson related them closely to his central message of regeneration
and sanctification, declaring that salvation was for the body
as well as the "soul," that the world's ultimate deliverance
from evil would come by cataclysmic change at the return
of Jesus, and that this second coming would not take place
until Christians evangelized the unchurched masses of the
world.[104] Thus Henry Wilson, a man characterized by "unfailing" friendship for the poor and needy and active participation in social welfare, would often close a sermon or a
prayer with the words, "Oh, come, and take away the sin,
the shame, the pain, And make this blighted world of ours,
Thine own fair world again."[105]

The Florence Crittenton and Door of Hope
Rescue Homes for "Fallen" Women[106]

While the reformed drunkards Jerry McAuley and S.
H. Hadley directed the Water Street Mission in the reclamation of outcast men, three rather wealthy New Yorkers
turned their attention during the 1880s to the salvation of
similarly needy women. Beginning in personal evangelism
in the slums, Sidney and Emma Whittemore and Charles N.
Crittenton soon encountered conditions that drove them to
provide "homes" where they could also supply material aid.
During the following several decades these workers not only
began scores of rescue homes for women, but became important leaders in larger circles of evangelistic social work.

The Whittemore chapter in evangelical slum work began in New York City in the late winter of 1875 when the
young couple attended separately a meeting conducted by a
prominent English evangelist, Henry Varley. Neither knew
the other was at that service, but both were stirred by
Varley's preaching and went forward to the mourner's bench,

where they made "firm resolutions to live a different life."[107]
The next Sunday the Whittemores reluctantly agreed to accom-
pany a friend to see Jerry McAuley in action at his first
mission in the Water Street dance hall. As was often the
case, the building was crowded, but the Whittemores located
seats near the front. Coming with a friendly but patronizing
spirit, they soon found themselves responding to the "testimonies" of McAuley and numerous mission converts, and
during the invitation raised their hands requesting prayer.
McAuley would not settle for that gesture, however, and
called them forward to the mourners' bench. Mrs. Whittemore later described the "motley group" with which they
knelt: "a drunkard, a gambler, a thief and a tramp on my
husband's side, and on my side one or two poor women" and
another drunkard.[108]

From that day the young couple moved steadily into
work for the kind of outcasts they had met at McAuley's
altar. Despite Mrs. Whittemore's poor health, they attended almost nightly, and became personal friends of the
McAuleys. In December, 1876, Sidney Whittemore became
one of the five incorporators of the "McAuley Water Street
Mission." He continued in official connection with the Mc-
Auley missions as long as Jerry or Maria McAuley were
active in rescue work.[109] Meanwhile the Whittemores assisted in personal contacts with the outcasts who came to the
mission, and in direct slum visitation and evangelism.[110]

This kind of contact, particularly after a marked improvement in Emma Whittemore's health in 1884, led her to
the conviction that she must do something for the "fallen"
girls she encountered. Accordingly, she opened the first
"Door of Hope" on October 25, 1890, at 102 E. 61st Street
in New York.[111] There she housed needy women, providing
food, clothing, and medical care in an atmosphere of acceptance and intense religious concern. Other similar refu-
ges soon followed, and during the next several decades Mrs.
Whittemore probably started or inspired more homes for
women than any other person. By 1903 she reported sixty-
one Doors of Hope to Christian Herald readers; before her
death in 1931 nearly 100 had joined the group.[112] The homes
early banded together in what became known as the Door of
Hope Union, an association aiming at encouragement and information, as well as at stimulating new homes and enabling
fresh starts in different locales for some of the girls.[113]

Both Sidney and Emma Whittemore gained increasing

prominence in the evangelistic welfare movement. Besides
working officially with the McAuley missions, they assisted
numerous other city missions by providing direct supervision,
enlisting staff, serving as trustees, and maintaining close
friendships with mission workers.[114] With this expanding
influence, the formal leadership of the rescue mission movement after the death of S. H. Hadley in 1906 came to reside
in considerable part with the Whittemores. Sidney Whittemore capped years of officership in the National Federation
of Gospel Missions with his election to the presidency of the
newly formed International Union of Gospel Missions in 1913.
After his death the following February his wife succeeded him
in that office, continuing as president until 1918.[115] Already
a high auxiliary officer of the Salvation Army, Emma Whittemore continued to speak frequently at its meetings as well
as at other gatherings, like the well-known summer Bible and
evangelism conferences at Winona Lake, Ind. Evangelist J.
Wilbur Chapman, who heard her often, reported that she
"moved the great audiences" as he had "rarely seen them
moved."[116]

Within her Doors of Hope, Mrs. Whittemore placed
primary emphasis upon evangelism. As she early reported
to the Alliance, of the 325 girls the Door of Hope had assisted to early 1894, "a large proportion" had been won "to
Christ," which for her was "the one important" goal. "Without Him," she asserted, "nothing can be accomplished."
Welfare agencies might bring the girls "out of the dens of
vice, but only Jesus can get the vice out of the girls." Of
the latter she was confident: "How surely do I know," she
wrote, "that the blood of Jesus cleanses, saves and keeps!"[117]
With that perspective Mrs. Whittemore sought to make the
girls she helped active in "soulwinning." Her most publicized
convert, Delia Loughlin, besides preaching widely, in her
turn converted more than 100 former friends. At Delia's
death in 1892, Mrs. Whittemore organized the "Delia Memorial," a missionary society which supported missionaries
overseas for the next several decades.[118]

Mrs. Whittemore heartily embraced the idea of devine
intervention in human lives. An invalid as a result of a
broken vertebra in her back, she claimed God "miraculously"
healed her in May, 1884, making possible her subsequent activity in evangelism and social welfare.[119] A timid person,
she traced her effective public speaking to a time when,
forced by circumstances to preach, it seemed as if someone

stood by her side, pouring into her ear what she should say.
"The moment this mysterious operation of the Spirit ceased,"
she wrote later, "I ceased talking and sat down ... with ...
amazement and gratitude."[120] And she professed complete
reliance upon God for the financial support of her homes,
withholding information about their needs even from her husband and others she knew would help. This principle was
central from the beginning of her work: God showed her
"very clearly," she asserted, that any home she opened
"must be strictly a Faith work." She early turned down a
substantial gift offered contingent on following normal fund-
raising channels. When, later, a steady flow of unsought
contributions ended after the arrival of one for which she had
hinted, she returned to her original principles and contributions began coming in again.[121] In later years she claimed
large donations had come unsolicited to meet such emergen-
cies as mortgage payments, guidance in organizing the growing chain of homes, and help in a multitude of minor needs.
Hot water bags, mismatched shoes, a barrel of apples, a
piano--the arrival of such gifts at the moment they were
needed seemed to her convincing evidence that divine intervention was the central factor in the success of her homes.[122]
The most important "miracle," however, was always the conversion of the girls her homes had sheltered.

Charles Crittenton's career as a pioneer in social
work reflected an equally fervent supernaturalism. Following
a conversion in 1882, precipitated by what seemed to him the
voice of his dead child, Crittenton moved progressively
through the Fulton Street Prayer Meetings, McAuley's Cremorne Mission, a camp meeting, and Methodist Phoebe Palmer's meetings for the promotion of holiness, into the intense
inner faith and evangelistic ministry that marked the last
twenty-five years of his life. During those weeks a radical
realignment of his life occurred, and from that point his
business received almost none, religion almost all of his
energies. Among the most active of American evangelists
after 1890, his Florence Mission resulted directly from one
of his first evangelistic excursions into the slums, and his
large chain of homes later developed similarly out of his efforts to convert the lost.[123]

In November, 1893, this evangelist-welfare worker
preached in St. Luke's Episcopal Cathedral in Atlanta, an
event of pivotal significance for the Crittenton homes. Characteristically concluding with an "invitation," he later related

that the rector's wife, Mrs. Kate Waller Barrett, experienced
"a real definite surrender" at that meeting, "changing her ...
into a Godly consecrated worker ... and a soulwinner."124
Mrs. Barrett herself wrote that she could "never forget" that
experience; "all of the bitterness" and pessimism left her,
she said, and "for the first time in my life I drew a breath
of real freedom...." Though her responsibilities in the Crittenton and other organizations increased greatly in ensuing
years, she affirmed that the same inner repose and strength
remained with her.125 Actively interested in work for women
even before this time, she gave able leadership to the Crittenton homes for nearly three decades. Joining the organization
officially after her husband's death in 1896, she was vice-
president and general superintendent from 1897 until Crittenton's death in 1909. Mrs. Barrett then assumed the presidency of the Association, a post she continued to hold for
sixteen years until her own death in 1925.126

During these years Mrs. Barrett also served at different times as president of the National Council of Women,
national chairman of the Congress of Mothers and Parent-
Teacher Associations, national president of the American
Legion Auxiliary, delegate to the Zurich Peace Conference in
1919, and special representative of the United States government on two occasions.127 And she continued to share the
fervent, evangelistic faith to which Crittenton had won her.
Playing a prominent part in the Crittenton Association's first
general convention in 1897, she affirmed that their homes
were "for the salvation of souls," and that they should make
"souls" their controlling aim. Similarly, the "Practical Suggestions" Mrs. Barrett wrote for the matrons of Crittenton
homes stressed conversion as the controlling objective in
work with girls.128

This emphasis, common to Crittenton and Mrs. Barrett, found frequent expression in the organization's publications and meetings. In the first issue of The Florence
Crittenton Magazine, the association attributed its advance to
its allegiance to Jesus Christ: "We are not in any sense a
reformatory organization; ... we believe that the only lasting
power is transformation through the power of the Cross."129
This spirit also predominated in their conventions. Crittenton
opened the gathering in 1897 of this "earnest band of soul-
winners" with a "devotional meeting"; at a second meeting
later that day he and two associates led in spontaneous sing-
ing while kneeling at the close of an "earnest" prayer.130
Reports from the homes constantly echoed this spirit, the

workers apparently fully sharing Crittenton's religious enthusiasm and evangelistic orientation.[131]

Louis Klopsch and the Christian Herald

While almost all of these evangelical welfare organizations published their own periodicals, one journal, the Christian Herald, more than any other brought their combined work
to the attention of the larger American public. Begun in the
United States in 1878 as an extension of the British periodical
of the same name, the Herald passed to the control of a New
York businessman, Louis Klopsch, in 1890. Klopsch's skill-
ful use of subscription premiums, his choice of writers, and
his alliance with social welfare activities combined to raise
the circulation of the Christian Herald from 30,000 at the
time of purchase to about a quarter of a million by his death
two decades later, making it one of the largest religious
magazines in the world.[132]

Besides regularly publishing accounts of evangelism
and welfare work here and abroad, the Herald was an important rescue institution in its own right. It raised and distributed nearly $3,500,000 to relief work during these de-
cades, including large-scale famine relief and aid to orphanages overseas, as well as support for its own Bowery Mission and Montlawn summer home for tenement children.[133]
At Klopsch's death in 1910, President Taft, the Viceroy of
India, and the president of the Red Cross in Japan were
among the hundreds who sent messages of sympathy.[134]

Interest in evangelism and welfare was in full harmony
with the Christian Herald's past. Indeed, as the issues of its
early years repeated regularly, its "aim" was to "make known
the way of salvation."[135] It featured the preaching of London's
Charles Haddon Spurgeon and New York's Thomas DeWitt Talmage, two of the most famous divines of that age, and both
staunchly evangelical. Talmage became the journal's editor
in 1890, and at his death twelve years later his successors
declared that the story of the cross and Christ's love had been
"the whole of his theology," controlling his life and permeating
"every sermon he ever preached."[136]

The Herald, moreover, shared with the Christian and
Missionary Alliance an emphasis on the imminent return of
Jesus. "To keep alive the expectation of his personal return
to the earth" was its single aim, the preface to its first

American volume stated in 1878-79. This aim found expression also in innumerable articles related to the "second coming" and the general subject of prophecy. W. E. Blackstone, whose little volume, Jesus Is Coming (1898), became a classic among evangelicals, George Müller of the well-known "faith" orphanages of Bristol, England, and Stephen Tyng of St. George's Episcopal Church of New York, were among the journal's other prominent contributors who stressed the second coming.[137]

During the first decade of its existence the Christian Herald also gave considerable attention to a wide range of philanthropists and gospel welfare work. It featured Jerry McAuley and his missions on more than one occasion.[138] Talmage wrote vigorously on the moral problems of urban America, and supported various relief projects. The journal's other featured contributor, Charles H. Spurgeon, an aggressive Liberal politically, and, as one writer has judged, an "extremely outspoken" critic of war and imperialism, sponsored and supported a wide range of philanthropic institutions and causes through his large inner city congregation in London as well as through his own personal income of more than £100,000 annually.[139] Thus the elements of the Herald's later evangelism and charity were quite clearly present during its first decade of American life.

Louis Klopsch, born in Germany to ardent republican parents in 1852 and married in 1886 to the daughter of the New York philanthropist-clergyman Stephen Merritt, served his publishing and business apprenticeship in originating a number of periodicals and services during the 1870s and 1880s. Among his ventures prior to purchasing the Christian Herald were the broadly inspirational Good Morning, the Daily Hotel Reporter, a print shop, the "Pictorial Associated Press," which supplied cuts of prominent persons to publishers, and the syndication of the sermons of his friend and pastor, T. DeWitt Talmage.[140]

Several factors contributed to Klopsch's success as publisher of the Herald. He secured as editor that same Talmage, whose printed sermons, world tours, and leadership of the mammoth 5000-seat Brooklyn Tabernacle, made him one of the most influential and popular clergymen of his day. Talmage brought to his editorial task evangelical fervor, a keen interest in the contemporary scene, sympathy for the needy, and readiness to cooperate in matters of reform and charity. His fame aided the Christian Herald and

his interests helped thrust it in the direction of welfare.[141]
Another of Klopsch's fruitful early ventures was to offer
Bibles as subscription premiums. Within five years the
Herald distributed well over 100,000 Bibles and New Testa-
ments in this way, greatly increasing its own circulation in
the process. At the time it stressed, with apparent sincerity,
the resulting "Bible revival" rather than its own gain, noting
Klopsch's determination to place Bibles in as many homes as
possible. And it estimated that in this and other ways "for
many years he issued not less than 60,000 Bibles and Testa-
ments annually."[142]

Of greatest significance, however, in making the
Christian Herald an influential paper was the decision of
Louis Klopsch to align it with the rising tide of interest in
social welfare, and specifically with evangelical rescue efforts. He came to the helm of the Christian Herald at a
time when the "social question" was perhaps the dominant
one of the age, when "social Christianity" was coming rapidly
to the fore in the churches, and when revivalistic elements
in the American religious scene were increasingly turning
their attention to the temporal needs of urban slum-dwellers.[143]
1890 was a pivotal year for other evangelical welfare groups
as well as for the Christian Herald: the Salvation Army's
blossoming social outreach received William Booth's enthusiastic sanction and direction in his In Darkest England and the
Way Out (1890); Charles N. Crittenton landed in San Francisco that spring upon completion of his world tour and immediately launched the twin ministries of welfare and evangelism that established that era's strongest group of homes
for "fallen women"; Mrs. Emma Whittemore opened the first
of her many Doors of Hope for the same class in October;
A. B. Simpson's recently organized Alliances for home and
foreign mission work entered their most significant decade of
expansion; and the rescue mission movement emerged from
its initial formative years into an important period of growth
and unification under the leadership of such men as S. H.
Hadley and Sidney Whittemore.

Louis Klopsch stepped enthusiastically into this developing situation early in the decade, making the Christian
Herald a direct participant, as well as greatly strengthening
its support of other evangelical welfare efforts. In 1892
Klopsch and Talmage inaugurated their journal's overseas
philanthropy in response to severe famine in Russia. It continued this kind of aid across the years, channeling its funds
and supplies largely into non-western lands, using Western

missionaries. It aided Simpson's Alliance missionaries during the successive Indian famines at the turn of the century, and included hundreds of children in Alliance institutions among the thousands it supported in India alone as a result of those famines. City missionaries took prominent part in the journal's "Food Fund" during the winter of 1894, and in staffing the summer home for tenement children begun that June. The Herald entered the rescue mission field a year later, assuming control of New York City's hard-pressed Bowery Mission, whose origin in 1880 made it one of the nation's oldest. Besides assisting or serving officially with such other missions as the Central Union Mission of Washington, D.C., Klopsch and the Christian Herald played a part in the unification and expansion of rescue missions. Klopsch and his father-in-law, Stephen Merritt, both served on the "Board" of the National Gospel Mission Union, and it was in the former's offices that the National Federation of Gospel Missions originated in 1906. But, besides this active participation, a stream of editorials and articles called for attention and support for the endeavors of other gospel welfare organizations.[144]

The Christian Herald supplemented its welfare and missionary orientation with a large emphasis and participation in direct evangelism. Although the deaths of Spurgeon (1892) and Talmage (1902) deprived the Herald of the sermons that had long been one of its staple ingredients, it continued to feature preaching from the leading evangelical pulpiteers of the land, including J. H. Jowett, A. J. Gordon, and A. B. Simpson, as well as its former editor's son, Frank Talmage.[145] The sermons of professional evangelists also appeared on its pages, including, after 1910, a lengthy series of unpublished messages by D. L. Moody, on topics such as "Have You Been Born Again?," "Looking to the Cross," and "Seeking the Lost."[146] It publicized R. A. Torrey's evangelistic campaigns with converts in the hundred thousand range, and the routine efforts as well as the great successes of other American evangelists. These included revivals in Kansas, the Billy Sunday meetings in Philadelphia and New York City, and the Stelzle-Biederwolf campaigns.[147]

The Christian Herald also provided direct financial support for varied evangelistic activities. Louis Klopsch lent his personal vehicle to a "gospel team" from George Dowkontt's medical and missionary college at least one summer.[148] His journal received and forwarded contributions to such agencies as the Society for Soul Winners, operating in

Southern mountain areas.[149] It extended considerable aid to
D. L. Moody and his schools in Northfield, Mass., and
Chicago. In fact, in spite of its increasing welfare program,
the journal once stated that its direct appeal from Moody was
of "infinitely greater importance than any other that could be
made."[150] But besides these undertakings, the missionaries
it supported in other lands, and the "evangelists" staffing its
own institutions,[151] the Herald underwrote direct evangelism
in the United States. George Sharp was its missionary
through wide areas of America for many years, and his
labors, while including welfare and educational work, focused
on gaining converts. Similarly, during the summer months
the journal often supported an evangelist who used the large
Christian Herald revival tent.[152]

Christian Herald evangelism shared the fervor that
characterized the Salvation Army and kindred rescue groups.
One of the emotion-laden passages on its pages was a request for prayer, repeated more than once, that its efforts
might be powerfully used to reach "souls."[153] And a re-
vealing incident as to its spirit and priorities was the instal-
lation in 1896 of John Wyburn as superintendent of the journal's newly acquired charge, the Bowery Mission in New
York.[154] In addition to talks by Emma Whittemore of the
Door of Hope homes and S. H. Hadley of the Water Street
Mission, Louis Klopsch spoke fervently about the importance
of evangelism in the Bowery Mission. Commenting on leading
men to the "blessed Saviour," and then on Wyburn's decision
to accept the position because of the potential for a "large
harvest of souls," Klopsch added, "as he told me this, I
said in my heart, 'this is the kind of man we want in the
Bowery Mission.'" He concluded with his hope that through
Wyburn's "genial, kind, sympathetic and loving ministrations,
multitudes [might] be brought to Christ."[155] "Multitudes,"
the journal affirmed, had already been redeemed through the
Bowery Mission, and it continued to enthusiastically report
converts through this and its other operations.[156] Feeling,
moreover, that its readers shared its fervor, the Herald
often expressed gratitude at their response to its projects.
That response was such, in fact, that the magazine called
them "perhaps the greatest body of earnest readers of any
religious journal in the world."[157] Together, journal and
readers did much to support the rising tide of evangelical
welfare after 1890.

II

HOLINESS SLUM WORK

"Many thousands of the starving poor have been relieved," William Booth's first official report from the Christian Mission revealed in the autumn of 1868. That report,
which covered nearly two years of operations, presented an
already wide-ranging social effort, including temperance
meetings, evening classes for "reading, writing, and arith-
metic," "Sunday, Day, and Ragged Schools," reading rooms,
and "Relief of the Destitute and Sick Poor" by the distribution of food and money as well as by "Soup Kitchens." The
Mission was also active in rescuing "fallen girls," obtaining
"situations" for unemployed persons, assisting the poor to
emigrate, and persuading "hundreds of drunkards" to sign
the total abstinence pledge.[1] The "appalling" destitution
which thus drew the Booths into welfare operations produced
similar results even more dramatically for Charles Crittenton.
Launching into gospel personal work among the derelicts of
New York City very soon after his conversion, one of Crittenton's first attempts at evangelizing brought home to him the
needs of the "fallen" with disturbing clarity. As a result,
he immediately began the dialogue that led to provision of
food, shelter, and other aid through the first Florence Mission.[2] Similarly, the "vision" that caused Jerry McAuley to
open the Water Street Mission in 1872 awakened him to the
physical needs of the destitute. During the first year alone,
McAuley reported dispensing more than 26,000 meals, 5000
lodgings, and a "great deal of clothing" to needy men.[3]

Knowledge of Slum Conditions

This kind of reaction resulted in part from the conditions gospel workers found in the burgeoning urban slums.
They were not alone in this, for an increasing number of observers from all walks of life were awakening to the physical

and inward destitution of the lower classes. This was the
age of Charles Booth, Washington Gladden, Jacob Riis, Robert Hunter, Walter Rauschenbusch, and many others. [4] Revivalistic slum workers joined them in focusing public attention on the wretchedness and necessity for change. In fact,
Ballington Booth wrote that the disclosures of the reformers
did "not begin to describe the want and destitution" that actually existed. His wife, in a lengthy article for Scribner's
Magazine, "fully endorsed" all she had seen written on tenement housing, but she was "sure the worst has not been
told." Their staff officers, the Booths said, constantly reported "most incredible conditions," the "sad and bitter existence" of the poor in American cities. [5] War Cry cover
illustrations and articles graphically portrayed their distress,
picturing barren and dirty rooms, shabbily clothed children
playing in treeless streets beside the tenements, and evicted
families standing helpless on the sidewalk. [6] William Booth's
famous prescription for England's social woes, In Darkest
England (1890), highlighted the plight of the "submerged
tenth." They lived in a "sea of misery," and against that
misery the Salvation Army would do battle. [7]

The Army's reaction--a reaction shared by other
rescue workers--arose largely out of close personal encounter.
"Our house-to-house visitation," Salvationists wrote less than
a decade after the Booths entered East London, "has brought
to light an amount of vice and misery that we could not have
conceived of." [8] Some revivalists, like T. DeWitt Talmage of
the Christian Herald, knew tenement conditions largely from
well-publicized investigative forays. Others, like Crittenton
and the Whittemores, knew from the same extended contact
the Booths had. Still others, Jerry McAuley, S. H. Hadley,
and many other rescue mission leaders among them, knew the
depths from long and bitter personal captivity there. [9] For
the Army's commanding officers in the United States, periodic
encounters renewed their awareness. Ballington and Maud
Booth professed themselves "heartsick" after their visit to
New York's "Inferno" in 1891, and their appearances that summer reflected that sort of impact. At San Francisco in July,
Ballington Booth stressed the terrible conditions in the city
slums, and his wife declared New York slumdom was "as terrible as that of London," which was for her a telling comparison. [10]

What ultimately gave gospel welfare organizations their
strongest insight and motivation for service, however, was
the continuing close contact of their field workers with the

poor. Those workers, the Booths and others felt, had an
almost unequalled knowledge of the conditions and needs of
the lower classes. Of Emma Bown, who by 1895 had headed
up the Army's American slum work for several years, a
sketch in the British War Cry remarked that she "probably
knows more of American slum life than any other woman in
the world." Ballington Booth's report of Army activities in
1892 began with an extended emphasis upon his officers'
identification with the masses in terms of origin and aim as
well as continuing residence. He concluded that perhaps no
organization had a greater awareness or "truer or larger
sympathy with the social condition of the masses of our
time...."[11]

Many outsiders familiar with the work of the Salvation
Army shared Booth's estimate. The prominent liberal clergyman, Lyman Abbott, urged his people of Plymouth Church in
Brooklyn to join him in the Army's Auxiliary League, commenting that Salvationists were accomplishing "a great work
in the slums, which no other organization can reach as effectively."[12] The Christian Herald's enthusiastic response
to In Darkest England pointed out that the Army's two decades
of experience gave them unequalled knowledge of the lower
classes.[13] The Chicago Mail, which chose the Army as its
outlet for the free distribution of thousands of loaves of bread
during the autumn of 1893, praised the group's work with the
observation that no people had more contact with the "real
poor." Somewhat later, Cleveland Plain Dealer reporters,
stymied in their attempts to reach the very poor, turned to
the Salvation Army and were promptly guided to scenes of
great misery. As a result that paper asserted the "generally accepted" truth that "no organization of public or private
charity" equalled the Army's ability to reach this class.[14]

Provision of Aid

This kind of knowledge of slum conditions quickly
shocked the Booths, Crittenton, and many others into providing concrete assistance for the destitute people they encountered. And while the aid varied in complexity and extent, its most characteristic form was also the simplest,
namely informal individual help for persons in need whenever that need appeared. Assistance usually began when,
in the course of personal visitation aimed at "soulwinning,"
rescue workers discovered material privation. Thus one of
Charles Crittenton's initial evangelizing forays led directly,

as we have seen, to the establishment of the first Florence
Mission.

Crittenton's kind of response continued to mark both
individuals and groups working in the slums. One of the
members of A. B. Simpson's congregation, kept from foreign
missions because of her poor health, turned her home near
the Gospel Tabernacle into a "shelter for the homeless and
unfortunate," often denying herself a bed and food in order
to help others. Similarly, a sergeant for the Volunteers of
America in San Jose, Calif., made the care of the sick and
suffering "a special object of her life."[15] The Booth children
early learned this response, possessing their parents' fierce
reaction against any oppression, and their sympathetic willingness to share with the needy. Bramwell, the second
general of the Salvation Army, showed this in an incident
Booth-Tucker related of choosing to give his "few ha'pence"
to a "poor boy" rather than spend it on himself.[16] Corps
and branches worked similarly for the poor. The Alliance
branches, despite their heavier "spiritual" orientation, often
emphasized relief. In New Castle, Pa., a group reported
that they frequently supplied the poor "with money, food, and
clothing." The Gospel Mission of Astoria, Long Island,
formed a "Society of Willian Gleaners," whose committees
included one for "Clothing" as well as for "Calling." And
New York's Wayne County Alliance resolved in 1896 that their
work should "become more and more practical," focusing
upon temporal needs.[17]

This charitable impulse stemmed partly from requests
for aid. Letters from the destitute so deluged the offices of
the Christian Herald that it instituted a "Relief Box" in 1893,
forwarding the name of one needy person each year to every
participating subscriber.[18] Simpson's Alliance frequently
answered similar appeals. A letter of thanks from a Kansas
family in March, 1896, acknowledged gifts of money and of
eight barrels of clothing, enough to carry them over com-
fortably to the next harvest, and to enable them to aid many
of their hard-pressed neighbors.[19]

As the Herald's "Relief Box" illustrates, experience
helped these workers anticipate and structure their response
to material need. Emma Whittemore's slum visitation was
one typical approach. Dressing as much as possible like the
people of the slums, she and her helpers would usually carry
such articles as a pail of gruel, soup, or tea, and a package
of old clothes. "Often" they helped "simply by sweeping out

a room, heating a cup of tea, or smoothing over [the slum person's] rumpled and untidy bed."[20] Fanny Tunison, a paralytic from birth, was one of Mrs. Whittemore's beneficiaries. In her turn and despite her handicap, she taught reading, cooking, and sewing to a class of small girls.[21] The Christian Herald assisted another long-term invalid, Bella Cooke, who had labored in slum areas in New York since mid-century, and elsewhere before that. Despite her own poverty, she carried on a program of regular visitation, distributing clothes, money, and other items with which charitable folk supplied her. Among larger projects, for Thanksgiving in 1889 Bella Cooke supplied more than 200 poor families with food and a gift. The following summer she provided day trips and country outings for nearly a thousand women and children.[22]

The Salvation Army more than any other gospel welfare agency formalized this kind of general assistance to the poor. By the 1880s its long experience in the slums gradually resulted in such specialized forms of aid as shelters, prison work, and rescue homes for women. Then in 1890 General William Booth published his well-known description and remedy for England's social woes, In Darkest England and the Way Out. Capitalizing on the current popularity of Stanley's "Darkest Africa," and using the literary talents of the reform journalist William T. Stead, Booth's volume graphically portrayed the "darkness" of England's masses. "Deliverance," he believed, required both urban and agricultural colonies, in which social workers would render aid across a wide spectrum of human need.

In Darkest England was a pivotal event for the Army's social efforts, bringing wide public attention as well as systematizing and giving official endorsement to the scattered beginnings of social work. And one of the forms of aid Booth described and proposed to extend was the "Slum Work." Serving in pairs, his "Slum Sisters" lived in the most depressed areas, their clothes and lodgings differing from those of their neighbors only in cleanliness and neatness. "Here they live all the year round," Booth wrote, "visiting the sick, looking after the children, showing the women how to keep themselves and their homes decent, often discharging the sick mother's duties themselves." They cultivated peace, advocated temperance, gave counsel on a variety of matters, all the while "ceaselessly preaching the religion of Jesus Christ to the outcasts of society."[23]

By the time Booth wrote, the formal slum work had expanded to fairly sizeable proportions. The English correspondent of the American War Cry wrote in early 1889 that although only two years old, the British program already included sixty officers. It gave sure promise, that writer felt, of being "at last" the avenue through which to reach "our struggling population."[24] The formal American slum work got underway about that same time. In February the editor of the War Cry announced the commencement of "The Garret, Dive, and Tenement Brigade": "In the midst of the squalor, misery, and sin of one of the worst neighborhoods of the great city of New York," he wrote, "two officers are commencing the Saviour-like work of visiting, helping, and reclaiming the lost." Adding that the officers would live in that neighborhood, he called upon "all lovers of precious souls to pray [for] this new departure...."[25]

Frequent calls for volunteers, a steady stream of reports and articles, and the support of the three Booth women resulted in the gradual expansion of the slum "brigade." The Army opened a second New York post in 1890, and by 1892 had inaugurated slum work in such other centers as Boston, Philadelphia, Cleveland, and Chicago.[26] Maud Booth--who had assisted in supervising the British program in its beginnings--worked closely with Emma Bown and the slum sisters during most of her time with the American Army, and Emma Booth-Tucker associated similarly with the work.[27] Evangeline Booth's first announced project as national commander was the institution of a slum settlement. Both of the latter made well-publicized appearances in tenement garb; one such for Mrs. Booth-Tucker was before an estimated crowd of 4000 in Buffalo, N.Y., with another 3000 persons turned away.[28] Slum officers quite often appeared with the Booth women, sometimes at Salvationist meetings, but also before other groups.[29] The name by which these women were often called--"Slum Angels"--indicates something of the feeling for them within the Army. So also does the observation of a ranking officer that "God had one son, and He was a slummer." And an article in the War Cry gave what was for the Army the unusual praise that "their labor is even more Christ-like" than that of other Salvationists.[30]

The slum sisters developed a varied program of aid which covered much of the range of the needs of their tenement neighbors. In keeping with the strong inclination of Salvationists and other gospel welfare groups toward verse and music, these workers had their own "slum song" depicting their spirit and tasks. They sang of tending the sick and ailing, scrubbing floors, washing clothes, and minding babies, all "gladly" done because of "Jesus' love."[31] Emma Bown's reports described the sort of help they were giving, one of the first including "visiting..., making gruel for the sick, washing dirty babies...," outfitting with clean clothes, and much other aid.[32]

Regular visitation undergirded the slum program. Ballington Booth began a pattern of three hours of visitation each day for corps officers, and Emma Bown early reported an average of nearly thirty visits a day for her slum sisters. Reports for the early years noted thousands of visits annually.[33] Maud Booth clarified the aim of those hours, calling on her officers to make their people "feel your love and concern for their welfare." As she later explained to outsiders, a visit "very often" meant "several hours spent in ... hard and difficult work." One of her first letters to the Volunteers declared that they were to find invalids and children who lacked food or clothes or coal, or perhaps a "weary mother" who would appreciate their help. If the people her officers visited were not needy like that, Mrs. Booth warned, they could "rest assured" that they were "switching off the right track."[34]

When one tenement resident declared that she forgot all of her misery when the "slum sisters" were with her, she vividly illustrated the identification with the people that Maud Booth sought.[35] So also did numerous requests for special aid, as when an anxious father came for help for his seriously ill child, one of the Army's nursery children; an all-night vigil ensued.[36] In 1900 two officers lost their lives attempting to rescue children during a fire in the Army's nursery in Cincinnati. One newspaper reported a third officer in a "complete collapse" as if she had lost her own child.[37] But it did not take death to touch their sympathies. Emma Bown early described a need pervasive and desperate enough to cause sleepless nights for her. In several articles she emphasized unnerving conditions, "wretchedness and misery" such that "I cannot put on paper or into words what my heart feels.... [I]s there any woman's heart that can remain untouched."[38]

Slum officers often provided used clothing for the poor. They requested friends to send any garments they could spare, complaining that it was hard to see the people in such rags. Readers responded, and the workers were enthusiastically grateful: "Glory to God! Hallelujah!" One wrote, describing a little girl she had in mind for one gift. [39] This need for clothing appeared in the communications of all gospel rescue groups, with rescue missions, homes for women, and orphanages joining the Army in requesting clothing to replace the inadequate and often vermin-ridden rags the poor owned. [40]

Another marked need the slum officers discovered was that of caring for infants and children whose mothers often faced the alternatives of leaving them alone all day, or starving. The first Army slum workers encountered both situations. As a result they began a "creche" or nursery within months of entering their slum quarters. That service became a characteristic feature, apparently much used by tenement mothers and much publicized within the Army and elsewhere. [41]

While Army workers were among the first "neighbors of the poor," actual settlement houses in the pattern of London's Toynbee Hall and Chicago's Hull House awaited larger resources and came rather late in the slum work. The first project Evangeline Booth announced after her arrival as Commander in 1904 was a "settlement house" to be established in the Cherry Hill area of New York City. This institution incorporated such features as a nursery to accommodate a hundred children, a laundry room, a sewing room, and a kindergarten. Within a few years Chicago, Cincinnati, and other American cities also had Army "settlements." [42]

That Salvation Army work in the slums continued along its early lines is indicated by the familiar account written by Hugh Redwood, the night editor of a London daily newspaper. Though penned several decades after the initial descriptions written by William Booth, Maud Booth, and Emma Bown, it embodied the same basic elements of wide-ranging aid infused with friendly and intense concern. Redwood's contact with Salvationist "slummers" made him a believer and then a participant in their work. With direct access to the records as well as to most of the persons of whom he wrote, he described officers cleaning quarters infested with vermin and rodents, caring for their almost equally infested tenants, and willingly risking their own lives in attempts to prevent violence. [43] And across these decades, it should be remembered, the Army's slum work was only a portion, and perhaps not the major portion, of what dedicated individuals from many evangelical welfare groups were doing on a general and relatively unstructured basis for the very poor. [44]

Holiness and Temporal Aid

Entering the slums, then, to help the poor spiritually, these evangelists found conditions that drove them to extend their help across a much wider range of needs. Staying to help, that very extension of aid progressively enlarged their knowledge, resulting in continuing improvements in both the range and effectiveness of their assistance. But the question rises-why did they stay to help? They might well have left in disgust or discouragement, or staying, might have been content only to exhort or rebuke. The answer in considerable measure seems to be that they helped because of a general large-heartedness tied closely to the central emphasis they placed on the Wesleyan doctrine of "holiness" or "perfect love."

"I literally worshipped Methodism," William Booth recalled of his early ministry. "To me there was one God and John Wesley was His prophet." Although Booth severed his official connections with Methodism, Wesley's perfectionism as well as his revivalism found important place in the Salvation Army.[45] Catherine Booth, speaking upon her favorite subject, early told her people that "the most important question" they could consider was "holiness," "how much like God we can be."[46] George Railton later judged that the central factor in the development of the mission in East London was the increasingly popular prayer and holiness meetings which the Booths conducted.[47] Thereafter, holiness meetings under varying names characterized the Army wherever it went.[48] Maud and Ballington Booth made their first joint appearance as American commanders in such a gathering.[49] William Booth's last directive to his son and successor was devoted to this subject; the doctrine and experience of holiness, he told Bramwell, was the key to any vigorous life for Salvationists.[50] A holiness preacher, Samuel Brengle, was perhaps the most important American-born leader during the Army's early decades. For him, as for the General, the gift of perfect love was the secret of the Army's power.[51]

Like the Salvation Army, other gospel welfare organizations all stressed holiness either explicitly or implicitly. Preoccupation with the idea of full consecration, of the "higher Christian life," marked McAuley and Hadley, Simpson and Henry Wilson, Crittenton and the Whittemores, and scores of less well-known workers. God demanded a radical change in human affections, they declared; His will required absolute consecration and service.[52]

The intensified devotion of these slum workers consistently sought the well-being of other persons. In part this reflected a practical and concrete bent, but it also reflected basic theory, namely that concern and sacrifice for others lay at the heart of the meaning of both conversion and sanctification. [53] "The law of Christ," A. B. Simpson wrote, "is the bearing of others' burdens, the sharing of others' griefs, sacrificing yourself for another." This, he continued, was "the law of Christianity ... [and] of the saint. It is the only way to be saved. From the beginning it has always been so."[54] His people learned at an Ohio convention in 1899 that "A good way to test your love to God is by the way you treat your brother.... God is more concerned by my conduct toward my brother than by my prayers to him."[55]

This orientation to others was central to "love," one of the most prominent words and concepts in rescue literature. William Booth wrote to his earliest lieutenants in America that the essence of Christianity was not in form or creed, or devotion to the Bible, but in the gift of love. The War Cry carried in bold print his summary word on the subject: "Every quality of our glorious religion can be resolved into one principle, and that is love."[56] Love, Simpson declared, was "the supreme law of the universe," and its essence was concern for others, "especially ... the most needy and helpless ones." Emma Booth-Tucker during her American command called on Salvationists to be a "people of a large and tender heart." William Booth saw as a prominent characteristic of his beloved wife, the Army "mother," her great capacity for sympathy for any person in need, no matter how lowly. In like manner, the man probably closest to him characterized the Founder as being first a person of great sympathies, his heart a "bottomless well of compassion."[57] And this quality such leaders called for in their followers: We "must have ... more sympathy--more affection--We want more heart."[58]

Evangelists in the slums displayed a marked ability and willingness to express affection. A. B. Simpson repeatedly referred to his co-workers and others as "dear brothers" or "beloved brothers." His Negro associates were his "beloved colored brethren." He and his fellows used similar expressions whether speaking of orphans, the Chinese among whom they worked, or any others. [59] Henry Wilson, himself widely loved throughout the Alliance, was notable not only for his ministry to adults, but also for his effectiveness with children, and particularly for the spontaneous affection

his messages and letters to them reveal. [60] And William
Booth, whose letters to and from his wife decades earlier
contained this same quality, wrote to his daughter Evangeline not long before his death in words that reveal him, as
well as the kind of compassion he sought. Salvationists'
love, the aged general wrote, must be "ambitious, boundless and eternal, O Lord, help me!..." And of his daughter
he said,

> My dear, dear Eva:
>   I had your letter. Bless you a thousand
> times! You are a lovely correspondent. You
> don't write your letters with your pen, or with
> your tongue, you write them with your heart.

He concluded, "Goodby, my darling child."[61]

This sort of affection revealed itself in situations
where one would normally react in disgust or anger. Mrs.
Whittemore's own initial loathing toward the physical and
moral filth she encountered in the slums ended in a "deep
hush of shame" during a crisis experience which transformed
her attitude. She subsequently related a number of instances
of the success of persistent and tender concern. One particularly difficult girl broke down when Mrs. Whittemore
found herself crying with "sad and deep concern" in her
presence. [62] S. H. Hadley of the Water Street Mission told
of the many down-and-outs who came repeatedly "to beat us
out of anything" they could. In response, he offered "no
word of reproof," he said, "not even a suggestion," affirming instead that "the tough heart ... is broken by the glorious
principle of love."[63]

Rescue workers did feel their "love" was effective.
One might even say that "love" was interchangeable with
"divine power" in their frequent assertion that nothing else
could transform men or their troubled world. For they felt
that love was the essence both of God and of the life he
wanted in men, and that it was impossible to attain apart
from a radical conversion in which God "filled" one's life.
Repeatedly these workers asserted that this love alone, and
almost without fail, would reach the hardened but empty
life. [64]

With this pervasive insistence upon Christian love went
an equally pervasive practicality. Maud Booth reflected a

general consensus when she asserted that religion must be "supremely practical." William Booth penned a lengthy series of letters on "Every Day Religion" for his people, Bramwell Booth's writings reflected the title of his frequently republished article, "Be as Good as You Seem," and the War Cry contained numerous pieces on such topics as slander, hasty tempers, grudgebearing, and various positive personal qualities. 65 Thus, while they centered their faith in an ethical principle, "love," rather than a doctrinal creed, their constant practical emphasis helped them keep that principle from evaporating into sentimentality: "The right kind of religion is love with its coat off, doing its best to help somebody"; "Acts of kindness rather than sentiments of emotional affection"--this they sought and seem generally to have achieved, though the emotion was present in generous portion also. 66

Frequently this kind of love sprang indignantly into action on behalf of the poor and oppressed. Hugh Redwood related the story of a woman who often came to a slum post badly beaten by her husband. Finally the officer in charge angrily told the woman to "hit him back.... Hit him with the rolling-pin. And if you can't hit him hard enough, bring him to me."67 William Booth, characterized by occasional irascibility as well as by sympathy, could act with similar anger whenever he encountered the oppressed or neglected. 68 And even so apparently mild-mannered a person as Charles Crittenton occasionally became aroused enough to bodily expel a man he felt to be callously exploiting women. 69

Self-sacrifice was another characteristic that conditioned and helped clarify the slum evangelists' idea of the nature of Christian love. The influential Anglican churchman, F. W. Farrar, thus judged the "chief secret" of the Salvation Army to be the "self-sacrifice not short of heroism which it has evoked in hundreds."70 A. B. Simpson of the Alliance declared sacrifice "the richest quality of love," holding that the willingness to make any sacrifice, even for the most unlovely person, was at the heart of the divine love which they must have. And a Salvationist writer claimed that the most striking feature of the Army's holiness was its insistence upon "absolute self-sacrifice for others."71 This quality rescue workers valued most highly in their fellows. After forty years of close association, Bramwell Booth called George Railton "the most completely unselfish man I ever knew." Maud Booth, who professed to have been drawn to the Army by the "love for others and disregard of self" which characterized its members,

said she had "never seen ... a selfish action" in Emma
Bown, her co-worker and director of the American slum
operations.[72]   Such persons knew well the Apostle's observation that a man might give all his possessions, and even
his own life, without having concern for others;   Booth-
Tucker was one who made the point that while sacrifice can
exist without love, there can be no genuine love without self-
giving: "Sacrifice," he declared, " is the language of
love."[73]

    This spirit expressed itself in various concrete ways.
Mrs. Kate Waller Barrett's little book of suggestions for
matrons of the Crittenton homes called on them to take a
small bedroom for themselves, leaving the larger and more
comfortable ones to the girls; to keep the preferred tables in
the dining room for the cooks and the girls who worked
there; to put the finest furniture in the girls' rooms rather
than in the parlor; and in general to give them the best possible attention, the kind their own daughter or a special guest
might receive.   For all of this, they should feel no self-
satisfaction, Mrs. Barrett emphasized, but only gratitude to
God that he had permitted them to add a little pleasure and
comfort to needy lives, in imitation of Christ and for his
sake.[74]   Crittenton displayed a similar attitude.   His co-
workers observed that while he would struggle before spend-
ing even a small amount on himself, he used his wealth un-
stintingly to meet the needs of others.   Among the few things
that angered him, they said, was an attempt to shield him,
at any hours, from the lowest supplicant.[75]   Fitting with this
was his willingness, and that of refined and sensitive persons
like Mrs. Whittemore and Mrs. Barrett, to give a large part
of their lives to working for and among the nation's seemingly
most degraded women.

    Others sacrificed their lives in even more dangerous
service.   Volunteers for overseas missions knew by reading
the death rolls what they were risking.   William Cassidy,
medically trained, and the first Alliance missionary, chose
the hardships of steerage passage in order to live with the
poorest travelers on ship, and died before reaching his desti-
nation of the disease he contracted en route.[76]   Among other
Alliance fatalities during those early decades were several
missionaries abroad whose illnesses began while they were
nursing seriously stricken persons during famines and epi-
demics.[77]   A similar carelessness for their own welfare often
appeared among missionaries at home.   Two women officers

of the Salvation Army died attempting to save their nursery children during a fire which destroyed their Cincinnati quarters in 1900.[78]

That kind of self-denial is perhaps more remarkable in that those who displayed it were themselves often recruited from the poorest classes. Indeed, such persons provided much of the financial support for gospel welfare groups. In September, 1899, the Alliance branch in New Castle, Pa., reported that it had raised $400 in cash and $250 in pledges for missions during the year, a feat which had seemed impossible, "as we are all poor working-men and women, and a few washer-women."[79] The annual convention in New York City in October, 1898, reported gifts and pledges of more than $110,000. As on other such occasions, Simpson noted the astonishment of newspapermen that "working girls ... cooks, laundresses and saleswomen in the stores" thought "nothing of giving as much as two hundred dollars a year for missions." Such participation, he asserted, stemmed from the love "which makes any sacrifice a joy."[80] Charles Crittenton, writing in The Florence Crittenton Magazine, noted similar sacrifice; outcast women in his chain of homes had contributed several hundred dollars to the work out of their difficult and poorly paid labor.[81] And for the Salvation Army, Emma Booth-Tucker wrote in 1901 that "many of our Rescue Homes are now practically supported by the work and contributions of the women who have gone through them."[82]

What seemed to them strong biblical support[83] for the perfectionist principle of practical love and sacrifice helps explain the fact of the continuing expansion of social welfare activities by slum evangelists. For despite a unanimous conviction that spiritual ministry must remain their primary concern, welfare projects came to have great importance, even to the point of preempting all other options. Charles Crittenton and Emma Whittemore were evangelists, yet they continued to exert themselves in behalf of their homes to the time of their deaths. Maud and Ballington Booth protested against social inroads on the spiritual work of the Army, and strongly maintained the primacy of the latter, yet the Volunteers of America moved in the direction of welfare from the beginning, and Maud Booth became the American leader perhaps most closely identified with the welfare of prisoners during these decades. William Booth, revivalist and holiness preacher to the end, continued to stress and expand the Army's social program in the most emphatic manner. His son and successor, Bramwell Booth, who had disputed Ballington's protests in 1896, two decades later denied that social work had diminished the Army's spiritual ministry. Instead, he argued, it gave the latter both strength and opportunity, and at the same time fulfilled the command of both Jesus and Paul.[84]

Leaders in evangelistic welfare agencies repeatedly invoked the Bible in defense of their social programs. Cover illustrations as well as articles in their journals frequently pictured Christ alleviating some physical need, or in other ways identified their particular forms of service with his life.[85] To Christ feeding the multitudes the War Cry gave the caption "Salvation Army Methods in Olden Times."[86] Among other scriptural passages its editors marshalled in support of social efforts were the well-known "Last Judgment" portrayed in Matthew 25, the account of Christ and the fallen woman, the story of the feeding of the multitudes, the Divine condemnation of him "who stops his ear to the poor," and the call for "mercy and not sacrifice."[87] When S. H. Hadley became superintendent of the Water Street Mission in 1886, the biblical passage that he said determined his decision was the fifty-eighth chapter of Isaiah, which emphasized justice and mercy in contrast to religious observance.[88] The important passages on love and mercy, the "great commandment" of Jesus, and the apostle Paul's discourse on love in First Corinthians 13, formed a constant backdrop for slum evangelism. Evangeline Booth's book, Love Is All (New York, 1908), for example, rested heavily upon the latter passage.

A. B. Simpson and his Alliance missionaries saw in the parable of the great feast in Luke 14 a sanction for evangelizing and aiding the poor in urban slums as well as in other lands. Simpson discussed this parable on numerous occasions, declaring that God's "mightiest working" in the last days had moved "from the church to the slums and the mission fields." Moreover, the feast which the parable described suggested "the special provision" Christians should make to alleviate "the physical needs and the material miseries of these lost multitudes." The faith men were accepting most widely, he declared, was "the Gospel of practical religion," of "real help for human suffering as well as human sin."[89] Here was divine endorsement along different but to them equally compelling lines, at once prophecy and command, that in the last days the lowest classes would be reached with a gospel of salvation for body as well as soul.

III

FOOD AND SHELTER

Early in 1879 the fledgling Christian Herald expressed its support for a "resolution" New York clergymen had adopted agreeing to preach sermons deploring the condition of tenement houses in the city. In that and succeeding issues, editorials and articles publicized conditions in the tenements and urged reform. T. DeWitt Talmage, the Herald's featured American contributor, had earlier explored the slums himself, and preached a series of sermons which were at once generous to the poor and harsh toward their landlords and housing. [1] Other evangelical rescue organizations, building on years of intimate knowledge of the slums, vigorously joined these protests. Jerry McAuley, recently graduated from both crime and tenement housing, took legal action to close up the filthy cellar apartments that he believed fostered crime near his mission. [2] Catherine Booth spoke harshly of the "Christian landlords who keep their tenants in buildings unfit for dogs." And she rebuked those who, when aroused about such housing, attempted to improve it "on the same principles as if ... [the poor] were cattle, mainly by means of buildings which pay a liberal interest."[3]

As Roy Lubove and Arthur Mann among others have shown, the housing of the poor was one of the most basic and publicized problems in the complex social question of that day. To that generation of liberals, Mann observes, the slum became "the microcosm of the evils" besetting Western civilization. [4] To this area of need Americans increasingly awoke, and here, perhaps more than in other areas, the awakening brought sympathy and desire for reform. [5] Evangelical rescue workers thus shared a growing awareness. Their knowledge may have been more adequate than that of most reformers simply because of daily contact with the tenements and their residents, and in such cases as Salvationist slum officers, from residing there themselves.

Fortunately, in the light of the painful slowness with which improvement came, [6] rescue workers not only publicized and protested those conditions, but sought to ameliorate the slum dweller's plight. They scrubbed and cleaned dirty, vermin-infested rooms, nursed ailing residents, provided fuel and food, furniture and rent money, and occasionally located quarters for an evicted or particularly ill-housed family. They also increasingly provided housing for the poor, ranging from the simplest shelter for the homeless to cheap lodgings for the working class.

The intensity and persistence of the reaction of rescue workers emerges in virtually every account of the origin of such projects. General Booth's eldest son and successor, Bramwell, noting that the "earliest and most typical institutions" the Army established for social work were its shelters, said they dated from the morning in 1888 when William Booth, greatly disturbed by what he had seen while crossing London the night before, exploded:

> 'Bramwell, did you know that men slept out all night on the bridges?'
>
> 'Well, yes,' I replied, 'a lot of poor fellows, I suppose, do that.'
>
> 'Then you ought to be ashamed of yourself to have known it and to have done nothing for them,' he went on vehemently.
>
> I began to speak of the difficulties, burdened as we were already.... My father stopped me with a preemptory wave of the brushes.
>
> 'Go and do something!' he said. 'We <u>must</u> do something.'
>
> 'What can we do?'
>
> 'Get them a shelter.'
>
> 'That will cost money.'
>
> 'Well, that is your affair. Something must be done. Get hold of a warehouse and warm it, and find something to cover them. But mind, Bramwell, no coddling!' [7]

William Booth's intense reaction was duplicated during that same decade when Charles Crittenton's sudden awareness of the mockery of preaching to women who had no "home" resulted in the Florence Mission, and then in a chain of homes for girls. And when, a few years later, Maud Booth began establishing "Hope Halls" for ex-prisoners, she declared that she would no longer preach to prisoners if she could not also offer them tangible help. [8]

"Shelter" thus became an essential element in much of the social work of evangelical welfare groups. Children's homes, prison missions, and efforts to rescue women, for example, were built upon it. [9] The general shelter efforts for the poor and homeless, meanwhile, ranged from emergency winter programs and dormitory beds in rescue missions to inexpensive "hotels" for working men and women. At all levels, rescue workers sought to provide adequate quarters as well as an atmosphere of kindness and acceptance.

Homes for Children

Homes for orphans and neglected children had constituted one of the earliest forms of evangelical welfare work. George Müller of Bristol, England, was one of the best-known Christian philanthropists of the nineteenth century. His large complex of orphanages received prominent attention in the Christian Herald from the beginning of its publication in America. [10] That journal's concern for orphanage work stemmed in part also from its interest in Charles Spurgeon's philanthropic efforts during the 1880s. [11] Later, after Louis Klopsch purchased the Herald in 1890, it raised money to support thousands of children orphaned by severe famines in India, China, and Japan as well as to provide summer vacations for 2000 tenement children annually at its Montlawn estate on the Hudson. [12]

The Christian and Missionary Alliance, the Salvation Army, the Volunteers of America, and to a limited extent the rescue homes for women, also sheltered children. One of the earliest, as well as most direct and official connections of the Alliance with welfare work was its Berachah Orphanage in New York City and nearby Nyack, begun in 1886. [13] Besides other direct and indirect support of orphanages in the United States, [14] the Alliance housed hundreds of famine orphans in India and elsewhere for more than a decade. [15] Moreover, though such institutions were not the focal point of the social program for the children's work of the Army or Volunteers, both groups operated homes for children in the United States from near the turn of the century. Ballington

Booth reported that the Volunteers had received and cared for nearly 500 children during 1903.[16]

The Rescue Missions

Stemming more directly from the peculiar problems of the new urban-industrial society were the other housing efforts of gospel welfare organizations. Jerry McAuley founded the Water Street Mission in New York City to feed and clothe as well as to evangelize homeless and destitute men. He reported furnishing more than 26,000 meals and 5000 lodgings during the mission's first year. S. H. Hadley, McAuley's successor from 1886 to 1906, wrote that he fed "thousands of men every year," and provided shelter for many of them in his building or in nearby lodging houses. He professed to help gladly anyone who came: "They are always received kindly," he wrote, "no questions are asked, and such food as we have is given them." During his super-intendency fifteen or twenty men could sleep in the upper floor of the mission. The new building constructed a few years after his death included larger quarters, thus more completely fulfilling McAuley's vision.[17]

One of S. H. Hadley's early responsibilities was to supervise the first Bowery lodging house opened by the Christian philanthropist, P. L. Tibbals. The Christian Herald called Tibbals, who also aided its own Bowery Mission and the Crittenton and Door of Hope homes, "the originator of the modern improved cheap lodging houses in the Bowery." His initial impulse was similar to that of William Booth, namely, dismay at seeing men without shelter one winter night. His directions for the first house were to "help the men, give them Christian counsel, and treat them with kind-ness." By 1895 six lodging houses were in operation, all of whose employees had themselves arrived out of work and penniless.[18]

Within his own Water Street Mission, Hadley's most striking quality was his sentimental but determined concern for the outcast men his mission sought to reach. "[We] pity them," he declared, "yes, we love them. We love them just because they are lost and poor and wretched and deceit-ful and utterly friendless...." On occasions where he became irritated with his clients, Hadley was unable to rest until he made amends.[19] Nor, as he claims, did he judge them, or attempt to pressure them into religious commitment:

He is asked no question. No promises are exacted.
He has no rules to observe except the one rule of
order. He is not lectured on his past. He is not
exhorted.... Neither Bible nor tract is forced
upon him.

He is left to himself without restraint of any
kind. He is neither watched nor suspected.... He
is treated as a brother, as if he were the best man
in the world. He meets with unvarying kindness on
every hand. [20]

Such men often came, Hadley wrote, simply because
they were desperate for food and shelter; they were "utterly
wrecked," "outcast humanity," "bankrupt mentally, physically
and morally." "Ninety-nine men out of a hundred," he affirmed, "come here because they are absolutely dying. They
have not a cent or a friend on earth ... and their clothing is
scarcely fit for a ragman."[21] Because of their severe need,
some men, finding a "snap," would work the mission "for all
it is worth," leaving "with a chuckle." Yet Hadley claimed
to accept the deception time after time: "... sooner or later
he is driven back again, by hunger," he wrote, "to the only
place where he can get shelter and food. On his return he
is met with the same welcome, the same kindness. There
is no word of reproof..., not even a suggestion ... that he
had not acted honourably."[22] Hadley was confident that
eventually the hardest case would break down before that kind
of treatment and experience the same conversion and change
that he had himself known. His writings described such
cases.

Prompted by this kind of concern, city missionaries
increasingly provided for the material needs of destitute men.
Despite S. H. Hadley's cheerfulness in the old Water Street
Mission building, its later workers sharply contrasted those
inadequate facilities with their own.[23] The manager of the
Beacon Light Mission in New York expressed the feeling of
many others when he emphasized his "crying need" for a
"building where the men could be lodged and cared for temporarily."[24] And, like the Water Street Mission, many missions were able to provide food and shelter.[25] The prominent Central Union Mission of Washington, D.C., incorporated
lodging in the new building it entered in 1892. Dean Peck of
the Alliance included similar accommodations in his complex
of welfare institutions in Denver at about that same time.
And the Christian Herald's Bowery Mission, besides housing

men at its "labor settlement" and its farm, gave lodging at
its central building. During the late 1890s it supplemented
beds for 150 men there with food facilities which dispensed
as many as 7000 cheap meals each day. [26]

Seasonal and Disaster Relief

As Agnes Palmer indicated in her review of Evangeline Booth's initial decades in the United States, hardly a
month passed that gospel welfare organizations did not render
service in the wake of storm, flood, or other disasters. [27]
Indeed, some of the earliest food and shelter projects
emerged out of special winter needs. In New York City,
Stephen Merritt, father-in-law of the Christian Herald's
Louis Klopsch and active in rescue and charity for many
years, began his "Travellers Club" for the unemployed and
destitute late in 1892. Located at the Eighth Avenue Mission, which he had also founded, the Club supplied coffee
and food to about 1800 persons each day that winter. [28] The
Christian Herald aided Merritt through the "Food Fund" it
started during a difficult cold spell a year later. By that
time he reported feeding 2000 men daily at breakfasts which
began at 4:30 a. m. in order to bring the homeless in out of
the cold. His guidelines remained unconditional and immediate response to need, as he professed to turn no one away
despite the "unheard of" numbers to which the program had
grown. [29] The Food Fund, meanwhile, was feeding 12,000
people each day by mid-February, 1894, and the total number
of meals served by the end of March, when it closed its activities, reached 800,000. [30] The Herald, which had emphasized that "sympathy for the destitute" was the best test of
one's faith, later attributed the generous response of its
readers to their Christian "love" and "zeal." [31]

The Christian Herald later continued this kind of
charity through the well-publicized "Bread Line" its Bowery
Mission operated during the first two decades of the new
century. Apparently originated in 1904, the winter Bread
Line featured breakfasts beginning at 1 a. m., for men in
"dire need." The notice in March, 1905, of the suspension
of the Bread Line from April 1 until the following Thanksgiving, reported 129,000 breakfasts that winter. [32] By 1913
that figure had mounted to 200,000, a daily average of well
over 1500 during the winter season. [33] The Mission's
"Brotherhood," which numbered 19,550 men that year, recruited its members largely from men who first came because

of the breakfasts. These men, "practically abandoned by society and by themselves, " were now clean, well-clothed, and satisfactorily employed, the journal recorded. 34

Heavy snowfalls prompted another form of temporary winter shelter. On January 24, 1905--described in the Christian Herald as "Blizzard Day"--a severe storm struck, and men without adequate clothing or shelter flocked to any potential cover. One typical individual wore a ragged coat and trousers, battered shoes, and no shirt, socks, or undershirt. Faced with that kind of "pathetic suffering, " Louis Klopsch, the Herald's publisher, directed that the Bowery Mission "be kept open all night, " and that the men be "well taken care of. " The Mission, filled to capacity, served food during the night and sent the more helpless cases to nearby lodging houses. The Salvation Army, meanwhile, provided food and temporary shelter in all of its halls in New York City. Similar news came from other rescue institutions, prompting the Herald's comment that while the Municipal Lodging House and police stations did what they could, "it was at the missions that ... [the needy] found their chief relief. "35

"Blizzard Day" was neither the first nor the last such response to severe winter weather. On occasion the Army offered its halls to municipal officials in areas struck by blizzards, supplementing shelter with food, and assisting anyone in need. 36 Programs of that kind gave impetus to the developing housing work. During the autumn of 1897, for example, in an article which reported Army shelters filled all that summer, the War Cry announced the securing of two large buildings in Chicago and Boston for additional housing during the winter months. A decade later the Army adopted the former Gault Hotel in Chicago as a major emergency shelter. 37

Floods, hurricanes, and other natural disasters similarly prompted temporary food and shelter programs. Although gospel welfare organizations had responded to earlier needs of this kind, 38 one of the first for which they effectively rallied their forces nationally was the hurricane-driven flood that struck Galveston, Texas, in September of 1900. The "Greatest Calamity of Modern Times, " the War Cry reported in calling for immediate aid from Salvationists and their friends. For weeks that magazine featured both the suffering at Galveston and the efforts of the Army's relief party, which

assisted 5000 refugees at its large tent in nearby Texas City.
As a "permanent memorial" to that aid, the Army erected a
shelter for workingmen. [39] The Christian Herald, which by
1900 had nearly a decade of experience in funding overseas
disaster relief, assisted the Army in its work.   Editor T.
DeWitt Talmage cabled a donation from Europe as part of
the immediate attention his journal gave to Galveston, and
Louis Klopsch, its publisher, was one of those who contributed at the large rally the Army held at Carnegie Hall in New
York. [40]

Severe floods continued to prompt relief from rescue
agencies.   "We have practically been working night and day
for the past week...," an officer in Kansas City notified the
War Cry during flooding of the Missouri and Mississippi
rivers in the early summer of 1903.   Besides serving several
hundred flood victims at its Fresh Air Camp near Kansas
City, the Army fed and sheltered others in a large building
provided by the leading bakery in the city.   In East Saint
Louis, Salvationists canceled all regular meetings in order
to make their hall available for the homeless.   To salvage
clothes, furniture, and other goods, eight wagons were busy
"night and day."[41]   The Gazette reported similar efforts as
the Volunteers fed and clothed hundreds of people and distributed ten wagon loads of clothes and furniture to the poor
during one week. [42]   The Christian Herald sent $2000 for
flood relief in response to what it termed the worst floods
in that region in three decades. [43]

One of the most famous and spectacular disasters in
American history was the San Francisco earthquake and fire
of April 18, 1906. This "almost unparalleled public calamity" prompted A. B. Simpson to forward immediate aid and
to invite continuing donations from readers of his Alliance
Weekly to be used especially for needy members of the
Alliance in the Bay area.   A week later his Gospel Tabernacle in New York City raised about $700 for this cause in
a single meeting. [44]   Other rescue groups also suffered
heavily from the earthquake; the Volunteers reported all
their property destroyed, and the Army claimed a loss of
approximately $150,000. [45]   These two organizations directed
their relief efforts to outsiders as well as to their own members.   The Gazette reported that by mid-June the Volunteers
had housed 46 persons and had dispensed about 2500 articles
of clothing, besides food and other assistance for the needy. [46]

The Salvation Army once again mounted the largest

single relief effort among evangelistic rescue groups. When the earthquake occurred, the Army's Commissioner for the Western United States was en route to California, a day's train ride from San Francisco. Informed by telegram, he immediately developed an emergency organization of about 700 persons, one-fifth of whom were officers from corps in the area. Besides using the Oakland Citadel as a shelter, the Army established a camp for refugees at nearby Beulah Park, to which government ferry boats and trucks transported the homeless.[47] Meanwhile, the national organization raised funds in support of the relief party. Commander Evangeline Booth's large rally in New York, chaired by Joseph Choate, the former ambassador to England, and generously supported by metropolitan newspapers, raised $2100. Salvationists in other lands soon forwarded a similar amount. And the editor of the War Cry promised that officers across the United States would work strenuously on behalf of the fund for San Francisco.[48] For at least three months the War Cry featured weekly news of relief work in the stricken Bay area. The issue for June 2 reported more than 2000 meals each day; two weeks later the total mounted to include food for 29,000 refugees and lodging for nearly 10,000. In addition, by early June officers had distributed nearly 20,000 garments and much other relief.[49]

The severe weather that necessitated the provision of emergency shelter and food also prompted rescue groups to supply food, coal, and, in summer, ice, to inadequately housed families.[50] The Christian Herald Food Fund, as well as various Army programs, aimed at this class in particular. An equally important facet of winter relief for families was the distribution of free or very low-priced coal. This most slum workers did as they encountered families without adequate heat. But the Salvation Army and the Volunteers carried on the most extensive program of coal distribution. William Peart, in a paper he prepared for the Army's International Social Council in London in 1921, spoke of dispensing small portions from carload purchases of coal, as well as issuing tickets redeemable at various coal yards. By that date the Army had been distributing coal in somewhat systematic fashion for well over two decades.[51]

During the "Great Blizzard" of early 1899 Salvationists opened depots where the poor could purchase twenty pounds of coal for a penny. Four winters later a coal strike brought an early beginning for this kind of charity. The War Cry of

November 8, 1902, featured needy persons coming to "cheap coal depots" that were already distributing twenty tons each day. [52] Totals rose gradually as the crisis and attendant suffering received strong emphasis throughout that winter. [53] In Sioux City, Iowa, the Journal channeled thirty tons of fuel to the poor through the Army. Eighteen distribution stations in Chicago supplied 8000 persons with coal during their first eight days of operation. And in New York City the Army dispensed more than 110 tons of coal during the week ending January 21. Of that total, matched during ensuing weeks as well, more than half was supplied by the New York American out of a stock of 1000 tons it distributed through the Army. [54] One of the city's largest dealers meanwhile assured Booth-Tucker of access to the Army's own supply for the poor. [55]

The Volunteers of America operated at least seven stations in Chicago alone during that same winter. At one post, a hundred families received coal in a single day, paying a total of 40 cents in exchange. Officers found "many" families without any fuel, the Gazette reported, although outdoor temperatures were well below zero. [56]

Summer's counterpart to cheap coal was "penny ice," which became a much publicized feature of the Army's summer philanthropy to slum families. By the turn of the century "Penny ice wagons" passed regularly through the poorer districts of Kansas City distributing "large" blocks of ice in a program which had begun two or three years earlier. [57] Before long other areas had similar undertakings; stations in Chicago gave away five tons one hot day in 1901. [58] While it is difficult to determine national totals, New York City's distribution of more than 175,000 pounds by mid-August in 1911 indicates an extensive program. [59]

Salvationists insisted that ice, like coal, was no luxury. The greater susceptibility of the poor to disease, stemming from their weakened constitutions brought about by crowded and impoverished housing conditions, made relief from extreme heat more of a necessity for them than for any other class. No one could know the "absolute misery" of the slums in summer except by personal experience, the editor of the War Cry asserted. [60] Accordingly, one cover illustration about "free ice" showed a lassie pushing back "death." Other covers stressed the suffering caused by the heat, including especially its effect on infants. And an article in the Kansas City Post in 1913 stated that the Army's ice program had "saved" 300 babies. [61]

The policy of making small charges for ice and coal reflected a determination to build inner strength by having the poor assist in their own support as much as possible. [62] Urban missionaries did distribute their supplies at a very low price, however, and often without any charge. They professed "no skimping" if the need warranted. They might give twenty-five pounds of ice instead of ten, for example, to a family with a sick baby. [63] Articles and excerpts from newspapers, besides commending the avoidance of pauperizing, showed the importance of the penny ice program in repeated descriptions of tenement residents thronging the distributors. [64]

Shelters and "Hotels"

At the same time as these emergency and seasonal programs were developing, the Salvation Army and the Volunteers of America began an extensive system of lodgings ranging from "shelters" for the destitute to cheap "hotels" for impoverished workingmen and women. The Army established its first food and shelter "depot" in London in February, 1888. By early 1890, British depots could feed 15,000 persons a day, and sleep 820 each night. [65] The following year, when Commander Ballington Booth returned from a study in England of the Army's developing "social scheme," he found that his wife had begun a "surprise" fund with which American Salvationists could inaugurate food and shelter work. Six months later they opened a depot in New York, which the editor of the War Cry hoped would begin an important program of housing. Visiting the "Lighthouse" in disguise in early February, 1892, he reported that the building, equipped to sleep about fifty persons, was usually full and always scrupulously clean, and the transient guests well satisfied. The editor claimed that the prices of five cents charged for meat pie, four cents for beef stew, and two cents for soup, could not be duplicated anywhere in the country for food of such excellent quality. [66]

Other shelters followed. The "Lifeboat" opened in San Francisco on Christmas Day, 1892. Within two months its officers fed 350 men daily, as well as arranging employment and providing some work within the shelter for the men. [67] On May 1, 1893, the Army began the "Ark" in Buffalo, N.Y., where a corps had been operating at the edge of the slum district for more than three years. An average of 117 men slept there each night to mid-July. In addition, its workers dispensed 8000 meals, found employment for 475 men, and gave other assistance. [68]

Rapid expansion characterized the shelter program after Booth-Tucker arrived early in 1896. In mid-August a Chicago paper reported his wish to open cheap lodgings for men, and also for women and children. By the turn of the century, Booth-Tucker's Social Relief Work announced, the Army had established six depots with capacity for 736 homeless men in New York City alone, and the total number in the United States had risen to forty-five with accommodations for 5000 persons. Early in 1903 the Army reported a monthly average of 137,000 lodgings and 365,000 meals at its eighty American institutions. [69]

The Volunteers of America launched shelter work during the first months of its existence, with corps in Council Bluffs, Iowa, and Syracuse, N.Y., announcing depots during 1896. Early in 1898 troops at Akron, Ohio, reported more than 1000 men "fed and lodged" in four months. In Chicago the Volunteers' program, which originated two years earlier, claimed 45,400 men lodged during the first three months of 1900. [70]

Officers of both the Army and the Volunteers took pride in the quality of the care which they claimed their shelters provided. Booth-Tucker wrote that the Army's shelters contrasted sharply with cheap private lodging houses, which were generally "of the meanest character." He had tried such an establishment himself; on a "bitterly cold night" there was no bedding or fire, while a chorus of "hacking coughs" and an army of bed-bugs made sleep "well nigh impossible." In contrast, he said, the Army shelters featured mattresses, pillows, sheets, and blankets on iron spring beds for 10 cents, with a private room costing an extra nickel. Equally important, the Army provided stoves, hot and cold baths, a reading room, freedom from bed-bugs, and an "officer in command [who] takes a kindly interest in the men." [71]

In addition to their shelters, after 1896 both the Army and the Volunteers maintained several "hotels" which featured more commodious lodgings for a slightly higher fee. The Army's "Dry Dock Hotel" which opened in New York late in 1896, charged 15 cents a night for each of 107 beds contained in its four stories. [72] Two of Booth-Tucker's published surveys of Army work reported similar lodging places for "clerks, storesmen, and others of the artisan classes." Although the preferred arrangement was a separate building, at times the better quarters were simply another floor or rooms in an ordinary shelter. The Army called for financial assistance from its friends so that it could enlarge this phase of its social program. [73]

Homes and hotels for working girls, like the hotels for men, were parental in purpose, "moral safeguards" which attempted to provide adequate lodging and a generally wholesome atmosphere for persons living on entirely inadequate wages. [74] Occasionally specified for "respectable" working girls, [75] they served the poor or unemployed, rather than reclaimed prostitutes or unwed mothers. Urban missionaries believed that such persons were in grave danger of being forced or lured into some form of prostitution. As Booth-Tucker asserted, it was "well-nigh impossible" to eat, rent a room, and dress on the wages they received. The alternatives were to "starve or sell their virtue. "[76]

In mid-1895 the editor of the War Cry expressed his satisfaction about the Army's new lodgings for women opening in the Bowery district of New York. A social work summary the following year reported that San Francisco also had such housing, and Booth-Tucker's Social Relief Work, published in 1900, included Boston, Chicago, and Los Angeles as well. By that date the Army had moved its facilities in New York's Bowery district to a larger building with accommodations for a hundred girls. [77] A few months later, a Boston paper reported that the Army's five-story Hotel Benedict was the finest establishment in that city for girls with inadequate wages. [78] A variation was the rest home for working girls at Tappan near New York City. Its officers were confident of the therapeutic effect of Tappan's country location upon slum-dwellers, twenty of whom were in residence in mid-1906. [79] Another departure was the "Martha Washington Club for Self-Supporting Girls" in Cleveland, an endeavor to provide fine surroundings and activities for girls of limited means. [80]

Again officers in charge stressed the quality of these institutions as well as the nominal fees. The listed price of 10 cents at one of the Army's first shelters for women, for example, included evening refreshments and bed as well as breakfast. [81] Officers at such institutions often assisted residents to secure suitable employment, in some cases by training them in domestic or other skills. Whenever possible they also provided reading rooms and other facilities to make their buildings cheerful and comfortable. [82] In the effort to

create "homes," friendship and kindness was all-important.
Thus a committee of clergymen commended the head of the
Volunteers' Girls Industrial Home in Toledo as a "sane and
sensible settlement worker, in the broadest and truest Christian sense, and a woman of warmest sympathy and truest
friendship for the girls...."[83]

Such quarters were often filled, reports claimed,
"and numbers have to be turned away." One officer related
"how they plead with us just to let them sleep on the floor,
or in the passages."[84] But if being filled to capacity forced
them to turn some women away, inability to pay did not.
The Volunteers made it plain that penniless applicants would
be "just as welcome." Furthermore, the homes invited
"graduates" to return whenever their finances made that
necessary.[85]

Rescue workers expressed their religious concern in
special evangelistic efforts as well as in the general spirit
of the homes. The Army's Working Women's Hotel in New
York City, for example, sponsored a brief meeting each
evening which reportedly resulted in frequent conversions.[86]
Yet officers conditioned neither entrance nor continuing residence on religion. And as Hadley pointed out for his work
with outcast men, they professed to avoid forcing their faith
upon those they helped.[87]

IV

HOLIDAY AND FRESH-AIR PROGRAMS

When William Peart remarked that the ambitious holiday "banquets" of the Salvation Army's early decades reflected their desire to bring "joy and gladness ... into ...
joyless homes and lives,"[1] he touched on a major element
in evangelical welfare. Almost none of their efforts dwelt
exclusively on physical relief, as important as that was.
But the holiday festivities and a variety of "fresh-air" projects aimed simply and directly at brightening lives.

Holiday Meals and Gifts

Though the first widely publicized banquets awaited the
early 1890s, modest precursors accompanied gospel welfare
operations from the beginning. Only a few weeks after Jerry
McAuley opened his Water Street Mission in 1872, for example, friends enabled him to provide Thanksgiving dinner for
150 neighboring slum dwellers. Similarly, not long after the
Salvation Army opened its campaign in American cities, individual corps provided special holiday meals; the War Cry
incidentally mentioned a Thanksgiving banquet as early as
1883. By the mid-1890s the Army's special dinners began
receiving prominent notice in its periodicals and increasing
attention in the secular press. For Thanksgiving of 1893
the War Cry presented extracts from newspapers in several
cities calling attention to "substantial" dinners for the very
poor. The Des Moines corps had served free meals for
most of Thanksgiving Day afternoon; in Jackson, Mich., the
Army hosted 200 and took food to others; and at Youngstown,
Ohio, the daily Vindicator reported 415 children fed, with a
crowd so large that police were necessary for a time to ensure order.[2]

For Christmas that same year a War Cry front page
pictured both a "slum angel" and "Cold" and "Hunger" hover-
ing over a banquet scene for the poor in a Salvation Army
hall.   Articles in that issue told of Christmas meals in such
centers as New York, Baltimore, Chicago, and Norristown,
Pa.   Though the Chicago troops had fed 2000 persons, San
Francisco claimed the largest event.   A reprint from the
San Francisco Examiner--which the War Cry noted was always a "friend" to the Salvation Army--described the large
Christmas Relief Fund that newspaper had decided to distribute through the Army.   The Christmas issue of the
Examiner devoted an entire page to the celebration, which
feted 4000 guests.   With the Fund's surplus of $4000, the
Army sent a large quantity of food, books, games, and other
gifts to the inmates of the "pest house."   The "delighted"
lassies also prepared boxes for the poor, filling each with
five pounds of fresh meat and many other items. 3

Thereafter the Army hosted the poor in rapidly
mounting numbers until for more than a decade after 1905
the War Cry featured a total of 300,000 or more dinners
every Christmas.   During 1895, while numerous corps reported meals for groups of from 100 to more than 1000,
Chicago supplied food for about 5000 persons.   Four years
later the Army claimed 150,000 such meals, a total which
in turn doubled by 1905. 4

The Volunteers stressed holiday meals from their
first year of existence.   Issues of the Gazette in December,
1896, reported a dinner for 800 newsboys, baskets of food
sent to needy families, and other meals for as many as 1000
guests. 5   The following Thanksgiving local corps fed approximately 20,000 children.   During these years the same Edward Fielding under whom Chicago had earlier become a
prominent Salvation Army center, made that city perhaps the
major area for Volunteer social work.   In 1897 his posts
served meals to 10,000 men and sent out food for 5000 other
persons, rivaling the Army's largest centers in the Volunteers' second year. 6

The Salvation Army report that it had had a number
of "trees" and distributed 500 garments in the slums of New
York and Brooklyn for Christmas, 1894, highlights another
facet of the holiday programs of evangelistic welfare organizations.   Thereafter, the Army's publications annually
stressed gifts for the poor during the Christmas season.   In

1896, for example, the War Cry featured New York's "Great
Christmas Tree" and the weeks of soliciting necessary to
gather presents that included 630 pairs of shoes. That account, in which Emma Booth-Tucker told "why she liked
little children," described the excitement of the guests, the
"dirtiest, hungriest, and noisiest" children they could find.
Those elements of sentiment and enjoyment appeared in many
other reports. A year earlier Mrs. Brigadier Perry had
stressed the children's delight with the Army's Santa, and
the officers' intention to have the celebration "as full as possible" of pleasure. And when William Peart later summed
up the Army celebrations for these early decades he noted
"usually a huge Christmas tree and entertainment ... with
the inevitable Santa Claus." After entertainment, he wrote,
came presents "for all the children," geared to age and individual need, and ranging from dolls for the youngest to
"wagons, sleds, and skates for the older boys." The most
needy received "warm clothing, selected to fit them by the
officers in touch with the situation." By the time Peart
wrote, the Salvation Army was hosting 125,000 children every
Christmas. [7]

Prominent officers lent their support to Christmas
festivities for the poor. Commander Evangeline Booth, successor to the Booth-Tuckers, played the part of the Army
Santa on one occasion, besides her more significant role in
maintaining this part of the social work. And Maud Booth,
under whose guidance American Salvationists had first entered
holiday efforts in force, not only generally supervised the
distribution of gifts by the Volunteers, one officer wrote for
Christmas in 1899, but "selected almost every article of
clothing, as well as toys" herself. Her well-publicized role
helped the Volunteers gain both attention and support from
outside sources. In 1904, for example, the organization received a "splendid" box of gifts from the "Little Mother Society" of the prominent Bethany Presbyterian Church of
Philadelphia, a church with which the Booths had frequent
and friendly contacts. [8]

Fresh-Air Programs

Summer's counterpart to holiday meals and gifts was
the picnic outing which both the Salvation Army and the
Volunteers utilized on a large scale. Probably the first of
these to get prominent notice in the War Cry was that undertaken by the Army in Kansas City, July 29, 1895. "Why not

give the poor children a day at one of the parks?" Brigadier
Sully thought as he reflected on the "want and misery" of the
slums of Kansas City.   Being, the War Cry added, a man of
action, Sully translated his idea into reality.   He soon found
that the Kansas City Star had a "Fresh Air Fund" which was
willing to underwrite the outing.   The result was a day of
games and food for 500 slum children, including free transportation which was itself an interesting diversion for the
poor.[9]

     The newly organized Volunteers of America also found
the fresh-air outing a simple and effective undertaking.   In
Chicago the organization stepped immediately into a city tradition of picnics for poor children which dated back to the
mid-eighties.   Their first summer--1896--saw them in charge
of a picnic for some 12,000 children in Chicago's Washington
Park.   The Gazette, which quoted the Chicago press at length,
continued to feature mayoral proclamations, press comments,
and illustrations regarding this annual affair for many years.
In 1899, for example, the editor printed a note in which
Mayor Carter H. Harrison commended the Volunteers for
their "good work ... especially in regard to the waifs and
homeless children."   The Chicago picnic remained the largest
event of this sort sponsored by any of these rescue groups,
consistently including children in numbers ranging from 10,000
to as high as 25,000.[10]

     Many other Army and Volunteer centers held picnic
outings, often adding boat or automobile transportation as a
special feature for tenement children.   In 1902 the Army's
annual picnic in Pittsburgh included steamship travel to the
park; a Chicago excursion in 1909 provided a free boat ride
on Lake Michigan for 2000 mothers and children; and that
same year the Volunteers took a group of 500 by steamer up
the Hudson from New York to a Tarrytown estate.[11]   Salvationists, following the example of William Booth's extensive
use of the recently developed automobile,[12] borrowed cars for
outings in Chicago and other cities after 1908.   The Army had
gotten the "auto habit," the editor of the War Cry wrote, but
was using it, "of course," for the poor and needy.[13]

     Overlapping in point of time with the quickly developing
program of picnic outings, was a system of summer homes
and camps to which rescue organizations took the poor for extended stays.   In mid-June, 1894, the Christian Herald opened
"Montlawn," its summer home for tenement children, on the

Hudson River at Nyack, a few miles above New York City.
Nurtured in general on a slum-ridden urban society's increasing idealization of the out-of-doors, Montlawn's immediate source was the Herald's first large domestic charity,
the Food Fund it operated during the winter of 1894. No
part of that work, the editor later affirmed, had "more
gratifying results" than the central effort to feed and clothe
tenement children, and to enlist them in the Sunday Schools
which were often their only education. Accordingly, in early
June, 1894, the Herald announced it would use surplus Food
Fund donations for a summer "Fresh Air Mission" for children, to open in Nyack on June 15, 1894.[14]

Montlawn, a two-acre estate overlooking the Hudson,
was donated for the journal's use by a ministerial friend of
Louis Klopsch. The home planned ten-day outings for 1500
guests that first summer. All of them were examined by a
physician to exclude any cases of contagious diseases.[15]
The children were then taken by steamer to Nyack in relays
of fifteen each day, up to the home's capacity of 120 children. The Herald promised adequate personal care from
Montlawn's large staff of Food Fund veterans, as well as a
homelike atmosphere in its many small rooms.[16]

Subsequent issues of the Herald related the story of
Montlawn in sentimental and extravagant terms. The first
Sunday dinner of roast beef, potatoes, sweet corn, pie, and
milk contributed to the assertion that Montlawn was "a veri-
table children's paradise." Those words--"children's paradise"--became a second name and a typical concept for the
home.[17] "Waifs Plead for Outings," one caption read, and
the characteristic picture the Herald drew of Montlawn was
one of happy and cooperative children delighting in good food,
woodland, stream, grassy lawn, and the assortment of equipment in the home's "outdoor gymnasium." One visitor described the estate as a "fairyland" such that it was no wonder
the children were "round-eyed and amazed." The editor of
the Herald contrasted the "heat and filth and disease and
vice" of the tenements with Montlawn's "glorious" environment.[18]

Montlawn annually celebrated the Fourth of July with
a patriotically oriented program at which Klopsch and other
distinguished guests talked to the children. In 1905, when
the home dedicated its "Children's Temple," the well-known
reformer Jacob Riis was the featured speaker. Five years
later, Independence Day guests included Judge Tomkins of

the Supreme Court of New York, Rear Admiral Charles Sigs-
bee, and China's ambassador to the United States, Chang Yin
Tang.[19]

The Montlawn program, which professed to be "absolutely non-sectarian," was avowedly evangelical Christian.
Prayers at meals and at bedtime and a daily religious service
expressed the home's orientation. More significant was the
general tenor of its spirit and writing. Workers attributed
their interest in the children to Jesus Christ, and in the example of his care for the child they found the pattern and
sanction for their own.[20] Miss Helen Collins, like many of
the home's early workers, had been active in city mission
work for several years before joining Montlawn's staff in
1894. Appointed matron two years later, she served in that
capacity for more than a decade. A graduate of A. B. Simpson's training school in New York, and active in the Alliance
for many years, she was also the first principal of its
"seminary" or prep school at Nyack. One of her early
helpers at Montlawn was a two-year veteran of New York
city missions, preparing for services as a medical missionary overseas. Another was from D. L. Moody's school in
Northfield.[21] Because they were, as the Christian Herald
affirmed, a "consecrated band" of young women, they frequently gave enthusiastic reports of "spiritual" results.
Letters from the journal's readers were similar in tone.
Gifts came, for example, "to help the cause of our blessed
Master," "as a token of God's favor," and to "do some poor
boy some good and be the means of leading him to Jesus."
One of the highlights of Montlawn's existence was the dedication in 1905 of its "Children's Temple," reported to be the
only church in the world expressly for children.[22]

The Herald made special provision for physically
handicapped children to visit Montlawn. At the close of the
season in 1895 and 1896, for example, the home hosted a
large number of convalescents. Years later the Herald reported its plan to send several children to Montlawn every
week from a Brooklyn school for the crippled.[23]

Early in September, 1894, the Christian Herald announced the arrival of Montlawn's 1000th child. A total of
approximately 1200 came that first season, well under the
projected 1500 to 2000. During the following year the home
increased its capacity to 250, and from that time averaged
about 2000 young guests each summer.[24] By 1913, Montlawn
had hosted 40,000 children[25] in a program with rapidly

mounting annual expenses. The $6200 cost for its first season increased to $12,500 by 1904 and doubled again eight years later. The Herald appealed for aid in sentimental yet concrete terms--a donation of only $3 would send an unfortunate tenement child to an idyllic country setting for ten days. Thousands of readers responded, occasionally even oversubscribing Montlawn's needs. During the years 1902-1904, for example, receipts exceeded expenses by more than $11,000. [26]

After the death of Louis Klopsch early in 1910, G. H. Sandison, managing editor of the Herald and associated with Montlawn "since the day it opened," continued Klopsch's close connection with the home. [27] Because Montlawn was perhaps Klopsch's favorite project, [28] the Herald soon established an endowment fund in his memory, in order to free the home from the burden of annual fund-raising efforts. The fund, tied as it was to income from new subscriptions, could not attain the size required by Montlawn's rising expenses, and soon passed quietly from prominence. [29] Montlawn itself continued to operate successfully throughout the decade, though the passing of Louis Klopsch and a changing national milieu were already numbering the years of the Christian Herald's large-scale philanthropic programs.

In 1897, three years after the opening of Montlawn, and more than a decade after the first organized camping in the United States, the Salvation Army began its initial "fresh-air camp" in Kansas City. Providing transportation as well as a week in tents for as many as twenty families, the officers took five women and their children the first day, adding a few more each day up to the camp's capacity. The Army occasionally used these facilities for other purposes, as when it housed several hundred Negro refugees there during severe flooding in 1903, and provided temporary facilities for a group of evicted tenement families three years later. [30]

The Army and the Volunteers of America established many other camps thereafter, until by the early 1920s the two organizations separately sponsored extended outings in almost every large city in the nation. [31] The Salvationist camp at Long Branch, N.J., opened June 20, 1902, with an initial contingent of thirty mothers and children. A year later the Army launched its "Spring Valley Fresh Air Camp" on a "magnificent property" near New York City. That same season the Volunteers transported shifts of about thirty

Chicago children seventy miles up Lake Michigan, and then
by rail and hayrack to a resort for a two-week stay. [32]
Among numerous other establishments begun during the next
few years was a camp at Highland, N. J. , where the Volunteers took children to the ocean for two weeks, and a combined summer home and "outing camp" the Army operated
at Glen Ellyn, Ill. , for children from the Chicago area. [33]

The rest homes sponsored by the Salvation Army, the
Christian and Missionary Alliance, and various individuals,
were often similar in intent and natural setting.   At Carrie
Judd Montgomery's "City of Refuge" near Oakland, Calif. ,
various institutions, including at least two homes of rest,
shared an attractive location.   Besides retreats for missionaries located in or near the mountains of India and
Colorado, the Alliance aided its people with homes by the
Hudson river at Nyack near New York City, and in numerous
other centers. [34]

A considerable emphasis on the beneficial results of
the out-of-doors accompanied camping and other fresh-air
activities.   The presence of medical personnel furthered this
healing influence at the Army's Camp Ramona near St. Louis,
and some institutions screened all applicants for contagious
diseases. [35]   In general, however, workers stressed the impact of sun, fresh air, and good food.   Here, they said, was
"Paradise for Slumdom's Victims. "   When the Army claimed
mothers and children would have "the time of their lives" at
Glen Ellyn, it expressed the expectation of all these camps.
Booth-Tucker, speaking of the Kansas City camp and the
fresh-air endeavors in general, stated that "Sick children at
the point of death have been restored to life and health in
an incredibly short time. "   His fellow-officer, William Peart,
who judged the summer outings one of the most valuable
Army charities, summed up both the claims and the sentiment often expressed about this branch of welfare:

> They come to us ... puny and half-starved, their
> lungs choked ... their faces pale....   They leave
> us plump and robust, their faces tanned by sum-
> mer suns and fresh breezes.   For ten days in the
> year, at least, the yearnings of their stomachs
> have been satisfied--meat, potatoes, and vegetables,
> fresh bread and butter, pure rich milk, fresh eggs;
> in fact, everything which growing boys and girls
> require.   The mothers can rest all day long, while

the children play and swim under safe supervision, eat, sleep, and are happy. [36]

The Assistance of Outsiders

When, for Christmas of 1901, Maud Booth wrote that "the girls of Vassar College" had once again sent the Volunteers a large box of gifts, [37] she touched on an important element in all the charities of gospel welfare groups. Their own resources made projects of this size possible only with large outside support. The Salvation Army also claimed extensive aid, including the San Francisco Examiner Fund in 1893, and the provision of expensive automobiles for outings after the turn of the century. In 1896, when the Army's National Headquarters served more than 1600 poor at a Thanksgiving dinner, New York's Metropolitan Restaurant roasted most of the turkeys, another common method of assistance. [38] Besides the backing city officials gave to fresh-air outings, politicians quite often participated in Christmas festivities; in 1911, for example, Commissioner Drummond of the New York City Department of Charities and Corrections opened the Salvation Army celebration there, and Mayor Fitzgerald presided over the Army's distribution of dinner baskets in Boston. [39]

V

THE GOSPEL OF HEALING

In the summer of 1885 the Rev. A. B. Simpson, a prominent American representative of "faith healing," attended an International Conference on Divine Healing and True Holiness in London.[1] That conference, broadly expressive of a burgeoning interest in faith healing and mind-cure during the late nineteenth century, was symbolic in particular of the renewed interest in healing among evangelicals of holiness persuasion. Central to that new interest was a physician, Charles Cullis, who had developed in Boston after 1860 a varied group of institutions which blended closely medical relief, evangelism, and holiness. Cullis was the leader of the "faith convention" at the Old Orchard assembly grounds on the Maine coast where A. B. Simpson experienced in 1881 what he believed to be a miraculous healing that established faith-cure as one of the cardinal doctrines of his Christian and Missionary Alliance. Cullis and Simpson, together with such other persons as Carrie Judd Montgomery and Emma Whittemore, made healing a significant element in the gospel welfare movement's mission among the poor in the United States and overseas.[2]

The paradox of a practicing physician's being a central figure in the faith healing movement was part of the larger conjunction of medical relief and faith healing within radical evangelicalism. For while gospel welfare organizations did not all place equal emphasis on divine healing, or on medical relief, they did all combine the two to some extent, and the larger movement heartily embraced both, just as it heartily embraced both complete dependence upon God and energetic activism. The paradox resolves partly from their belief that healing came largely as an accompaniment of the life completely "surrendered" to God morally and spiritually; the more limited resources of medicine operated on a different level among the needy. Moreover, almost all these workers were activists who believed that God wanted their every energy; he was using them as his instruments to redeem the world, and they in turn used every human resource at their command, including medical science.

Charles Cullis, the Alliance, and Faith Healing

Charles Cullis, a man who entered medicine partly because of his own sickly childhood, directed his efforts toward the cure of tuberculosis--then known as "consumption"-- after the death of his own wife from that disease. Her death also occasioned his conversion. Thereafter, a growing sense of religious and social mission gradually led him into his life work for invalids and other needy persons. The determinative event in that process was a request for help for a "homeless consumptive." This convinced Cullis of his "call"; two years later, in 1864, he opened his first home in a building housing twelve patients, a matron, and a nurse. The Children's Home, Deaconness' Home, and other buildings he gradually added soon overcrowded his first location. Cullis then secured land in the Grove Hall area of Boston's "highlands," and erected facilities for his medical mission, as well as for a Deaconness' Home, a church, and the Children's Cottage Homes. Cullis' Beacon Hill Branch elsewhere in Boston included several other endeavors. The Willard Tract Repository, begun in 1867, became a considerable publishing house by 1880. From it Cullis issued two monthly papers and a variety of books and pamphlets. In the Faith Training Cottage he prepared a "large" number of persons for Christian work, and his Foreign Missions Branch, begun in 1875, sponsored missionaries in Central India. He also operated a Cancer Home in the village of Walpole, fifteen miles from his Grove Hall center. [3]

Cullis' institutional work led him gradually into an enlarged spiritual ministry, as numerous persons sought his help in their quest for "salvation" or for "holiness." Moreover, in addition to his emphasis on divine healing, his was a work of "faith" similar to that of the evangelical British philanthropist, George Müller; the Christian Herald reported during 1880 that in fifteen years Cullis had received contributions of $386,977 for his institutions "in answer to prayer" and "without any solicitations from man."[4]

Among the thousands of persons Cullis and Simpson influenced was Carrie Judd, a young woman from Buffalo, N.Y., who became widely known in rescue circles. [5] A close friend of Simpson's from the early 1880s, she often addressed his congregation, as well as Alliance conventions. She became one of the first officers of the Christian Alliance, [6] and had Simpson officiate at her marriage to a young California businessman, George Montgomery, in 1890. When the Montgomeries joined the Salvation Army two years later, Simpson assured his followers that the young couple remained free to pursue the Alliance work "so dear to their hearts."[7]

For much of her life, Carrie Judd Montgomery combined the preaching of healing and holiness with rescue and welfare work. Active in a city mission and in slum visitation in Buffalo, she also opened first a room and then a "Faith Rest Cottage" there in 1882 for the physical and spiritual renewal of any who desired help. Soon after their move to California eight years later, the Montgomeries began a rescue mission in San Francisco and then literally a village of welfare institutions of "beneficence and faith." Later that summer Mrs. Montgomery reported to Alliance readers that Beulah was "already so filled with charitable institutions that I call it a 'City of Refuge'." Her city included a "Home of Peace" similar to her Buffalo "Faith Rest," the first of a proposed group of cottages for orphans, a Salvation Army rescue home for women, and a Rest Home for Salvationist officers. [8]

Alliance "homes" also placed strong emphasis on faith healing, and in general aimed at physical as well as spiritual renewal. The Philadelphia home thus welcomed anyone "weary or sick in body or mind." Simpson claimed "Berachah," the home at New York City and later at Nyack, was as "delightful" a place "of rest or spiritual blessing" as one could find anywhere. "A tired housekeeper" and a "tired and weary teacher" were among the many who professed continuing benefits from the "physical and spiritual uplift" they received there. [9]

Faith healing contributed to personal renewal in Alliance homes of rest; one report stated, in fact, that the homes had developed around this feature of the Alliance gospel. [10] Descriptions often included the faith-cure function, and reports from the homes appeared regularly in the "Divine Healing" section of the Alliance Weekly. [11] Berachah, the

most important Alliance rest home, claimed that in fifteen
years at least 10,000 guests were "transformed" in its atmosphere of "rest, quickening, and divine healing."[12]

The experience of A. B. Simpson, whose influence
was comparable to that of the Booths in the Salvation Army,
assured a continuing strong emphasis on divine healing within
the Alliance. Crippled in health as a young clergyman, he
attributed to healing his subsequent ability to simultaneously
pastor a large church, edit a weekly paper, head a multi-
phased system of schools, preach constantly across the
United States, author many books, and guide a world-wide
missionary movement. His healing, Simpson wrote, had
made his "life a luxury, and a labor a joy." In his Gospel
Tabernacle and in Alliance conventions, as a result, he
stressed the importance of this experience for all Christians.[13]

Henry Wilson, William S. Rainsford's associate at
St. George's Episcopal Church during the 1880s before becoming one of Simpson's closest co-workers, likewise professed he had been healed after two decades of "severe invalidism." Seventeen years later, when he was nearly seventy
years old, he wrote that his continually deepening spiritual
experience had made him "in every sense a younger, fresher
man" than he was at thirty. In God's strength, strength that
made his labor "a joy," he claimed to be doing "full twice
as much work" as he had ever done before.[14] Both Wilson
and Simpson thus believed that faith healing renewed the
whole person in all areas of life. "We need to get attached
to the Living One," Simpson affirmed, "and then it is more
than an act of healing, it is life."[15]

The conventions and local gatherings of the Alliance,
as well as its periodicals, featured a constant stream of
testimonials. One person wrote of being freed from mor-
phine and other troubles; another of deliverance from "nervous
prostration"; still another professed release from twenty-five
years of dependence upon drugs, besides insomnia and inability to take solids. The latter person credited her healing
to Simpson's book, The Gospel of Healing. "I have stopped
reading it again and again," she declared, with the kind of
reaction Simpson's writing and preaching often evoked, "to
weep and praise God for the blessing it has been to me."[16]

Because claims were sometimes bizarre--a woman

testified at Old Orchard, for example, that "God had filled a
tooth for her"[17]--Simpson and others cautioned against abuses
and misunderstanding. Despite their emphasis, they had, he
noted, "no set of professional healers ... and no claim of
special miraculous powers or miracle workers."[18] Their
most effective safeguard against misuse was probably their
union of healing with a greater stress on character and service for others. "God is much more concerned," Simpson
wrote, "to have you right than to have you well." He held
that many persons did not experience healing because they
wanted it "too cheaply." It could not be gotten for selfish
reasons, he told his people, but only through total commitment, only "for the glory of God and the good of our fellow
men."[19]

Healing related strongly, then, to helpfulness to sick
and suffering persons. Pointing out the sensitivity of Jesus
to human need, Simpson and others emphasized that love,
concern for others, was central to the infilling of divine life
which they believed healed and transformed human lives.
Responding with love to the needy, he affirmed, "brightens
and gladdens all our life and makes every duty a delight and
even every sacrifice a joy."[20] In one of the many testimonies
which reflected this quality, a woman wrote that her service
"among the sick" was a "joy" to her since her own healing.
Similarly, the periodical published by the Peniel missions
spoke in memory of a Mrs. Hollister who had carried on
extensive relief work among the poor after her "wonderful
healing" three years earlier.[21] In the largest sense this
connection of healing with service seemed true of Simpson,
Wilson, Montgomery, Whittemore, and others, for their
healing linked directly with the quality of their religious life,
and it was that quality which motivated and infused their lifelong work for the dispossessed.[22]

Medical Relief: Dispensaries and Hospitals

In addition to the thousands of persons who believed
themselves renewed in health through these rest and faith
healing ministries, many others benefitted from the varied
medical services offered by gospel welfare agencies. Urban
missionaries frequently provided medical assistance in the
course of slum visitation or in their rescue institutions.
Jerry McAuley and Emma Whittemore both arranged hospital
care for needy clients. Amelia Barnett, a member of Simpson's congregation in New York City for many years, was

one of a number of physicians who made their "medical knowledge and skill" available without charge to anyone in need. And the early reports of the Salvation Army "slum work," in common with most such efforts, all told of nursing the sick.[23]

Separate medical institutions appeared very early in the development of evangelistic welfare in the United States. Dr. M. B. Kirkpatrick, who in 1888 was considering serving in China under the Alliance, opened in Philadelphia nine years earlier what the Alliance Weekly called the first American medical mission. Within two years he started branch missions in Chicago and New York with the same object of aiding "the suffering poor in the most destitute neighborhoods." The mission, whose program also included gospel services, a Sunday School, temperance efforts, and literature distribution, gave medical treatment to 40,000 persons in nine years.[24]

Almost as early was George Dowkontt's dispensary, visitation, and education work in medical missions in New York City. While he engaged in combined religious and medical rescue from the mid-seventies, his formal medical relief apparently began with the establishment of his missionary training school in the early 1880s. His International Medical Missionary Society reported more than fifty students in training in 1891, by which time forty graduates were serving as medical missionaries overseas. Those trainees greatly enlarged the number of poor that Dowkontt could help in the New York area. Working in dispensaries and missions as well as in the tenements, they combined medical services for the poor with training for overseas missions. At the "anniversary exercises" in the autumn of 1889 the Society reported seven dispensaries and nearly 15,000 separate medical treatments. The Christian Herald, noting that Dowkontt's first dispensary had aided an average of fifty patients daily within a few weeks of its inception, stressed both the poverty of the patients and Dowkontt's cheerfulness and generosity toward them. Both the Herald and the Alliance-affiliated Berachah Mission in New York supported free dispensaries staffed by Dowkontt and his medical students.[25]

After 1890 rescue literature described an increasing number of free dispensaries, some within and others separate from the various institutions sponsored by gospel welfare organizations. A woman physician associated with the New York

Rescue Band's Industrial Home for women made 194 visits to
sick persons within the home as well as in its immediate
neighborhood during a period of several months early in 1896.
A few years later the Crittenton home in Detroit reported
that "one of the leading specialists of the city" directed its
free dispensary. That group's home in Washington, D.C.,
had access to nearly a score of physicians, giving its residents more adequate medical care, it claimed, than most
American women received. [26]

Other rescue organizations sponsored similar programs.
At the Volunteer clinic in Toledo, a dozen medically trained
persons assisted, while in Los Angeles the organization's dispensary averaged 93 free treatments a month during its first
twenty-seven months. [27] Salvation Army dispensaries included
those in St. Louis, Houston, Danville, and Chicago. [28] The
Christian Herald gave medical care to the men who came to
its Bowery Mission, as well as to the children it brought to
Montlawn, its summer home at Nyack-on-the-Hudson. It
eventually added a "thoroughly equipped hospital building" to
the latter institution, though one report claimed the hospital
was in little demand, so strong was the healing influence of
the home's other facilities and services. [29]

Similar services developed overseas as dispensary and
hospital care supplemented the medicine and informal nursing
care missionaries provided. The first Alliance missionary,
William Cassidy, like Dowkontt's students, served his "intern-
ship" among American poor, sailing for China after completing his medical training. Robert Hall Glover, another
prominent Alliance missionary, was also a medical doctor. [30]
For the Salvation Army, one writer claimed in 1908 that its exclusively medical missions in India were primarily the result of
Henry J. Andrews' "passion" for healing. He began there a
small dispensary which by the turn of the century developed
into the Catherine Booth Hospital. Together with another
Salvationist physician, Andrews eventually established several
hospitals and a medical school that was "recognized" by the
government. [31] In the Catherine Booth Hospital alone Army
personnel aided nearly a half-million out-patients and 14,114
resident patients during the first two decades of this century.
The hospital averaged, in addition, more than 1000 operations
a year between 1908 and 1921. [32]

In America as well, a number of full-scale hospitals

emerged, despite the great difficulty of funding such institutions.[33] Perhaps the largest was St. Gregory, located in a downtown industrial area in Brooklyn, and donated to the Volunteers of America in 1906. Established with "modern" equipment a year earlier, and open twenty-four hours a day, the hospital was treating 1500 to 2000 cases weekly at the time of transfer. Financial difficulties prompted the change of management to the Volunteers, whose response seemed enthusiastic despite Ballington Booth's later remark that "No branch of work was undertaken ... with more trepidation...."[34]

St. Gregory was soon an important part of Volunteer social work. The Gazette featured it regularly, perhaps more frequently than any other single institution the Volunteers operated during the following decade. While St. Gregory could accommodate at least forty-five or fifty resident patients, it was essentially a "downtown emergency hospital." The Board of Health sent all emergency cases of children in area schools to St. Gregory, the Gazette claimed. In addition, the hospital's report of nearly a dozen ambulance cases each day reflected the unusually high incidence of industrial accidents in its district near the Brooklyn Bridge. The Volunteers compared St. Gregory's statistics favorably with those of the largest hospitals in New York City. The combined volume and emergency character--caught in the phrase "A house of help in a neighborhood of need"-- elicited the comment that "perhaps no phase of Volunteer work" had "more forcibly demonstrated its need."[35]

A decade later, in 1916, the Salvation Army assumed operation of the Brooklyn Children's Nursery, Home, and Hospital, one of the largest gifts it had ever received. Begun in 1871, the institution's complex of buildings included a new hospital erected in 1907-08. A local paper found fresh hope for the financially troubled institution in the Army's record of efficiency and sympathy for the needy.[36]

Lesser "hospitals," often difficult to distinguish from dispensaries in size and function, were an increasingly common rescue institution. Dr. Alexander De Soto's "Wayside Mission and Floating Hospital" in Seattle, begun in 1897, consisted of a lodging house and a hospital for the "homeless and outcasts" in the "depths of Seattle's slums." By 1903 De Soto had in planning for his prospering enterprise a four-story building that would be the second largest hospital in Seattle. During the same period the Army sponsored a sixteen-bed hospital in Topeka, with the aid of a woman physician who donated her services. Its farm colony at Fort Amity, Colo., included a large sanitarium for the care of victims of tuberculosis. At Webb City, Mo., the Army's dispensary for injured miners developed into the community's only hospital. In contrast to its limited facilities, the War Cry later claimed that the organization's hospital and dispensary at Roxbury in greater Boston was "the biggest poor man's hospital, dispensary, and drug-store in any part of the world."[37]

The dispensary and hospital facilities necessary for maternity and infant care within rescue homes for women eventually gave additional impetus to the general hospital program. As Palmer pointed out in the case of the Salvation Army, pressures built up to use such facilities for the benefit of outsiders as well as inmates. The Crittenton home in Sioux City, Iowa, which in 1914 owned "the only incubator in the state," received private maternity cases as a result of similar outside inquiries.[38] The Army, after dedicating a hospital in connection with its New York Rescue Home in 1913, opened its large Booth Memorial Hospital at Covington, Ky., two years later. Salvationists dedicated the Evangeline Booth Women's Hospital and Home in Boston in 1920, by which time they had fourteen maternity hospitals in the Eastern United States.[39]

Trained Personnel

Expanding medical welfare programs demanded an increasing number of trained persons. To some extent outside volunteers filled this need. Maud Booth stated she could have "the best advice" in New York at a very few moments notice for cases requiring expert handling. Years later another Army writer asserted that the "splendid professional showing" of their hospitals was largely due to the capable doctors who donated their skills for little or no charge.[40] But needs were also met through the increasing number of medically trained members, including men and women like Barnett, Barrett, Cassidy, Cullis, Dowkontt, Glover, and Kirkpatrick. As Booth-Tucker commented for the Army, by the turn of the century rescue agencies included "a considerable number" of persons with "medical experience."[41]

The difficulty of attracting trained nurses into work in the slums or overseas at subsistence wages gradually led several rescue organizations and individuals into the field of

medical education on a limited scale. Dowkontt's training
school for medical missionaries, which began in the early
1880s, was probably the first such endeavor. More than a
decade later, in the autumn of 1894, the Peniel Mission in
Los Angeles offered a six-month "medical course" under the
supervision of Dean Widney of the Los Angeles Medical College. Taught by several physicians, the courses covered
"anatomy, physiology, hygiene, midwifery, ... the simpler
forms of disease and surgical injuries, and all points which
pertain to intelligent nursing." As a part of their training
the students, most of whom planned "to spend their lives in
mission work," gave free medical service to the poor. [42]

The Salvation Army, besides training its cadets in
"the most up-to-date methods of first aid ministration, "[43]
added nurses training under the pressure of needs in its increasing number of dispensaries and hospitals. Both the
Brooklyn Children's Hospital, and the Booth Memorial Hospital at Covington, Ky., graduated nurses during the second
decade of the new century. In early 1918, for example, the
former institution awarded diplomas to thirteen student
nurses. [44]

As Michael Harrington has pointed out, slum conditions, illness, inadequate medical care, unemployment, and
low wages reinforce each other in a "vicious circle" for the
very poor. Moreover, at any time, and particularly in the
event of serious illness, Harrington writes, the prospect of
the poor is to sink even lower and into a cycle of more
serious suffering. [45] If this is true in mid-twentieth century
America, it was more true in the decades after the Civil
War, if only because a less prosperous period lacked the
social insurance our century knows. As a result, food,
shelter, fuel, summer ice, and indeed almost all gospel
welfare programs, aimed to restore the poor to physical
health. "Sick children at the point of death," Booth-Tucker
thus wrote, had regained "life and health in an incredibly
short time" at the Army's fresh-air camp at Kansas City. [46]

Faith healing constituted one direct contribution rescue
workers made to the health of the very poor. Lacking adequate medical care, and with ailments often difficult to cure
in any case, thousands of the American poor professed to
find renewed health through the teaching of holiness and of
healing offered by Cullis, Montgomery, Simpson, Whittemore,
and others. And the acknowledged psycho-somatic character

of wholeness is relevant to a day when, as modern scholarship is pointing out, marginal existence impinged on the health of mind and spirit as well as of body.[47]

Rivivalistic welfare agencies thus embraced the resources of both medicine and faith. This was true of a physician like Charles Cullis, true of a group like the Alliance, and true of the larger rescue movement, even though the weight given to divine agency varied a great deal. Their healing efforts ranged from lay and professional visitation nursing through numerous dispensaries to full-scale hospitals and medical education, both in the United States and abroad. For these urban evangelists, salvation brought healing to soul and body alike.

VI

RESCUE HOMES FOR WOMEN

<u>The Story of the Homes</u>

Midway in Jerry McAuley's term in Sing Sing prison, and several years before William Booth entered the slums of East London, Charles Nelson Crittenton, who had been reared in upstate New York, began a modest drug business in New York City. Born in 1833 and having come to New York twenty-one years later, Crittenton launched out on his own in 1861. Like other self-made men in that age of rapidly expanding business, Crittenton parlayed a small initial investment into a fortune which approached a million dollars by the time he withdrew from active leadership more than two decades later. His business absorbed the main energies of a life he later decried as spent in worldliness and the pursuit of wealth and power. Yet his family background, as well as a number of incidents from his business years, indicate both an affectionate, emotional nature, and an undercurrent of religious feeling that was not difficult to arouse. When his third child, Florence, died in 1882, Crittenton's world collapsed. Apparently losing all interest in business and in life, his deep depression ended only with a gradually unfolding religious experience precipitated by what he thought was the voice of his dead child. Following an initial crisis alone at his home, Crittenton moved steadily into the fervent religion that characterized the remaining twenty-five years of his life. Leaving his business in other hands, he devoted almost all of his considerable energies to revivalism and welfare work, and with much of the same effectiveness that had marked his business career.[1]

At a prayer meeting not long after Crittenton's conversion, a friend invited him to join in rescue work in the saloon district; the outcome was the establishment of the

first Florence home for women. While exhorting two prostitutes to forsake their old lives, Crittenton realized the emp-
tiness of his words. There was no place for them to go. [2]
He immediately began pressing discussions of the situation,
with the result that he and interested friends soon launched
a mission on Bleecker Street, and named it after the daughter
whose death had prompted his conversion. [3] Opened April 19,
1883, the Florence Mission was soon overcrowded, and a
"surprising number" came to the mourner's bench at the
nightly meetings. During that first year the home received
176 girls; it averaged nearly 250 annually during its first
decade of existence. [4]

Charles Crittenton spent the next six years supervising
the activities of the Bleecker Street home, which eventually
became the "mother mission" of a large group of such institutions. His long hours of work, including daily gospel
services and a "rescue band" that combed the area nightly,
gradually undermined his health. He sought rest and re-
covery through a world tour, during which, however, he
plunged into rescue work in Great Britain and studied closely
the plight in other lands of prostitutes and unwed mothers. [5]
While on that trip, his plans matured for a chain of homes
across the United States in which unfortunate girls could make
fresh starts. [6]

Crittenton never returned to active work in the Bleecker
Street Mission. Landing in San Francisco in 1890, he became
so absorbed in revival meetings at the Y.M.C.A. in nearby
San Jose that he stayed day after day. He launched there a
second career as an evangelist, leading a tent revival in which
"San Jose was shaken from center to circumference. "[7] In
what became a pattern in California and then across the nation, Crittenton and his converts and other helpers organized
a Florence Crittenton Mission in July, 1890. Like its predecessor in New York, the San Jose Mission combined an ambitious program of public gospel meetings with a home for
"fallen" girls. [8]

During the following six years, Crittenton's admirers
claimed that he "held probably more services than any other
living evangelist. "[9] He remained in California more than
three years, holding "union" revival meetings at which "thousands" of converts were reported, and establishing Florence
homes and missions in San Jose, Sacramento, San Francisco,
and Los Angeles. [10] Leaders of the Woman's Christian
Temperance Union became permanent allies, first at San Jose,

where one of the workers at the home was the state president of the organization, then at Oakland and, soon thereafter, through Crittenton's gift of $5000 in 1892, at homes
in Denver, Fargo, Chicago, Portland, Ore., and Norfolk,
Va.[11] Frances Willard, the national president, gave him
the title, "Brother of Girls," which was his favorite, and
estimated that no other man had done as much in rescue
work for women. She granted him what Crittenton felt was
the distinction of being the first man invited to national office
in the W.C.T.U.[12]

The Crittenton chain of rescue homes for women organized nationally in 1895 and held its first general convention two years later.[13] The founder's large private income,
as well as funds raised through his evangelistic meetings,
supported the national organization and supplemented the
funds that local sponsors provided.[14] The twenty homes in
operation in 1895 grew to forty-five four years later. "A
home is no sooner opened than it is full," an official publication reported in 1897. "Today, if the means were at hand,
fifty homes could be opened...."[15] Several of the institutions, including, at Nashville, "one of the first organized
movements for rescue work in the United States," antedated
the national organization by many years.[16]

When Crittenton died in 1909, leadership passed to
Mrs. Kate Waller Barrett, a graduate of the Medical College
of Georgia and wife of an Episcopalian clergyman. During
her husband's early pastorates in Virginia and Kentucky, and
then in St. Luke's Cathedral in Atlanta, Mrs. Barrett experienced a growing concern for the needy, and particularly
for women in poverty and trouble.[17] When an abandoned
woman appeared with her baby in the Virginia manse, Mrs.
Barrett thought how much like herself the woman was except
in the men they had loved. She vowed that night, "by the
power of the God that ruled the universe," to spend her life
trying to help such girls.[18] In the summer of 1892 Mrs.
M. M. Wolfe called on the Barretts to interest them in the
work of her New Orleans rescue home. Later she joined
Mrs. Barrett in establishing a home in Atlanta in the face
of serious opposition from both clergymen and laymen who
did not want the peace and respectability of their own neighborhoods disturbed. In their difficulty, the two women appealed to Crittenton, who sent the manager of his San Francisco home to Atlanta, followed later by a check for $3500.[19]
Mrs. Barrett's subsequent contacts with Crittenton and his
work for girls led her, after her husband's death in 1896, to

join the Florence Crittenton Association of homes, a connection she maintained until her own death nearly three decades later. [20]

Meanwhile, Sidney and Emma Whittemore, a wealthy New York couple who were among Crittenton's early associates in that city, opened the Door of Hope missions. Converted in 1875 at Jerry McAuley's Water Street Mission, the Whittemores were thereafter active participants in mission work. Mrs. Whittemore experienced what she believed was the miraculous healing of a troublesome back ailment in 1884, partly under the influence of A. B. Simpson. The event helped direct her into extreme dependence upon divine intervention, as well as into a long relationship with the Christian and Missionary Alliance. [21] Her subsequent evangelistic efforts caused the Alliance in 1889 to "solemnly set [her] apart" for a special rescue ministry to girls. A year later, on October 25, 1890, she opened the first Door of Hope at 102 East 61st Street in New York City, in a house Simpson provided. S. H. Hadley and other prominent evangelical welfare leaders were present, with Simpson delivering the dedicatory address. [22]

The publicity which the Door of Hope received in the columns of the Alliance Weekly and the Christian Herald, as well as Mrs. Whittemore's increasingly effective speaking across the country, inspired many others to support similar rescue homes. As a result, by 1903 Mrs. Whittemore was managing a chain of sixty-one Doors of Hope in a national organization, which, like Crittenton's, enabled not only an exchange of information about spirit and methods, but the relocation of women who needed a fresh start in life. [23] Perhaps Crittenton's equal as a revivalist and inspirational speaker, she apparently lacked his business acumen as well as his ability to develop a close-knit organization and recruit able associates. But until her death in 1931, the missions she led brought hope to thousands of women.

Emma Whittemore eventually aligned several of her Door of Hope properties with a third chain of rescue homes for girls, operated by the Salvation Army. [24] Assistance to prostitutes and unwed mothers had been a growing part of the Army's social program since the mid-1880s, both in England and the United States. [25] By the time the Booth-Tuckers arrived in 1896, Salvationists maintained rescue homes in New York, Boston, Cleveland, Chicago, and San

Francisco.[26]   By 1900 Booth-Tucker had increased these to
fourteen homes, with accommodations for a total of 360
women, and an annual clientele almost three times that large;
during the next two decades the number doubled again.[27]   The
Booth women identified themselves closely with this work.
Mrs. Bramwell Booth supervised the first home in England,
and Maud Booth, Emma Booth-Tucker, and Evangeline Booth
actively promoted them in the United States.[28]

The Army inaugurated the League of Love in the summer of 1896 as a special phase of its program for "fallen"
girls.   Women in the various corps set aside time each week
for visitation, sought out girls to befriend in all Army meetings, and helped solicit support for the homes.   The new
organization reported that in a single month its members in
New York City had visited 212 "prisons, hospitals and saloons," contacted 264 women, and distributed both food and
$50 in cash.[29]

Probationary court work was another phase of the
Army's ministry to girls.[30]   Its officers appeared at municipal court sessions daily, prepared to assume the oversight
of any women the court would place in their care.   A report
for 1903 noted that 102 girls had been under the Army's probationary care that year, many of them in the rescue homes.
Nearly four years later Evangeline Booth wrote that such
work was assuming greater importance in her program; matrons of many homes had received appointment as special
police officers, and others were serving in the new juvenile
courts.[31]

Although the Alliance did not officially sponsor any
rescue homes for women, both its leaders and its lay members supported such institutions.   In addition to the close association A. B. Simpson had with the Whittemores and the
Door of Hope, a leading Alliance family in Fort Worth, Texas,
operated another of the early units of that chain of homes.[32]
Delia Collins, supported by her businessman son, Warren,
devoted her life to the "relief of suffering and charitable and
Christian work," particularly in the "Woman's Industrial
Home" there.   That home, begun in 1891, cared for 200
girls and "a large number of homeless babies" during the
next three years.[33]

Another Alliance leader, Henry Wilson, who had served
needy women while managing the mission that St. George's

Episcopal Church operated on New York's East Side during
the 1880s, became chaplain of the independent "Magdalene
Home" for women in 1894, three years after he joined Simpson's staff. [34]   Thereafter, at the annual "Rescue Day" the
Alliance sponsored in New York, Wilson and other gospel
welfare leaders regularly presented the cause of the Magdalene Home and similar institutions to an enthusiastic audience. [35]

The Doyer Street Mission and the New York Rescue
Band sponsored another cluster of welfare efforts which,
though organized independently, operated with the blessing
and support of the Alliance until 1902.   Formed in April,
1893, the Rescue Band provided temporary shelter for more
than 1300 girls during its first year.   In the summer of
1895 it opened a Girl's Club and Industrial Department in
two five-story buildings capable of lodging and training one
hundred girls. [36]

The Christian Herald publicized and supported fully
these interlocking programs for prostitutes and unwed
mothers.   Among instances of overlapping support its columns
reveal is that of the home which Margaret Strachan, a working woman of very limited means, began in New York City
in 1883.   Alliance literature attributes this home to the influence of the Gospel Tabernacle. [37]   Renting a house in an
area that "swarmed" with houses of prostitution, Miss Strachan held nightly gospel services, sheltered women who had
no place to live, and assisted them in finding employment or
coping with other needs.   In 1892, five years after her death,
the Herald reported that the home had sheltered 500 girls and
found employment for 267 the previous year.   A year later
the magazine announced a new lodging house for young women
in New York City, begun by one of Margaret Strachan's early
helpers, who had also served elsewhere in Door of Hope and
Florence Crittenton missions. [38]

Attitudes: Acceptance and Love

As important as the extent of their activity was the
attitude of gospel welfare workers toward prostitutes and unwed mothers and toward the society from which they came.
Although thoroughly orthodox in their doctrine of human de-
pravity, and committed to a supernatural "salvation" as the
only remedy, these evangelicals displayed toward the fallen

an attitude less of censure than of understanding and protection. Not naively blind to individual faults, they stressed
rather the terrible poverty and degradation they encountered,
believing they had gained through personal contact an awareness of the real conditions in American slums.

Rescue workers did not, however, pass lightly over
personal guilt and responsibility. The editor of the War
Cry concluded a plea for women with the note that "... when
Christ said ... 'Neither do I condemn thee', He also added,
'Go and sin no more'."[39] The London Times commented,
several years after William Booth's death, that though the
Salvation Army had "never let dirt dismay it or keep it at
arm's length," neither had it "tolerated dirt at close quarters." "It is difficult," the editor added, "to think of many
other human institutions of which as much can be said."[40]
Rescue leaders generally decried what Henry Wilson called
"weak sentimentality"; "fallen" women must be treated, he
said, with both love and strength. Charles Crittenton at
times professed himself "staggered" by the personal and
social evil he encountered. His co-worker Mrs. Barrett
urged their matrons to cultivate a cordiality that was not
"oppressive," a sympathy that did not blur judgment, and a
wise love that sought both to educate and to control.[41]

Yet rescue workers refused to place exclusive blame
upon the fallen, whether the person were a tramp, a criminal, a prostitute, or simply unfortunate. Booth-Tucker described them as "more sinned against than sinning," and his
successor termed them "sisters who have stumbled."[42] Mrs.
Barrett judged such girls "often not fallen but 'knocked down',
yet with like possibilities as myself."[43] The matrons thus
encouraged their clients to close the door on the past and its
sins.[44] Mrs. Whittemore had residents of the Door of Hope
in New York City to dress for the mission services in such
a way that outsiders would not be able to identify them. At
nearby Tappan the home had its own chapel, in order to protect the girls from what she judged to be the often critical
and harmful attitude of town and church folk.[45]

Leaders in work for women sought to make their missions "homes" rather than "institutions." Mrs. Barrett devoted several pages to this topic in her book of suggestions;
they were to give the girls the best of everything, to leave
doors unlocked, to plan creative diversions.[46] Workers cultivated informal associations and avoided inflexible regulations. Thus Mrs. Whittemore admitted one girl with her

baby against rules, and after other homes had refused to receive her unless she gave up her child.[47]

Indeed, rescue workers felt that the most significant factor in their efforts was "love," defined simply as personal affection and concern for the women they helped.[48] "It is all contained in the word love," Delia Collins said, when asked the secret of her success with troubled girls. "Love to God flows out to others, ... and a bond of affection binds them to us.... We do this work in His name and He returns and repays it to us in the affection of our dear girls...." In her estimate, only an "unselfish love" for the outcast and needy would assure good results.[49] Mrs. Whittemore declared that the Door of Hope not only welcomed some girls rejected by all other institutions, but readmitted them no matter how often they stumbled.[50] Crittenton asserted early in his career that the Florence Mission would "receive all comers," and with "no rule at all but the rule of love and Christian sympathy." Mrs. Barrett wrote that "when all other methods" failed, she had "seen the hardest heart melt beneath a caress and a whispered word of sympathy."[51]

In an address before the National Union of Women Workers in London in 1907, Mrs. Bramwell Booth declared that the most important lesson she had learned from twenty-three years of experience was "that the first and chief consideration in successful Rescue Work is the character, inspiration and qualifications of the workers." The qualities she wanted in her officers were "strength of principle," experience, unfailing love, faith in the very worst, and the inclination and ability to deal with people as individuals. Not all Salvation Army people embodied these traits in the degree she wished, but she believed that as a group they did, and that from this fact stemmed their power.[52] Similarly, at a time when white slavery investigations in New York made the topic a live one, Evangeline Booth remarked that the reason for the success of the Army--a success which, she claimed, puzzled experts--was the ability of its officers to establish meaningful relationships with the people they served. In Army homes, she said, they never spoke of "fallen women," only of sisters, never of "cases" but always of "our girls." Matrons displayed no "touch of patronage or condescension," no reproach. The "love and devotion" of such officers, Miss Booth declared, together with their strong faith in God, gave the Army its great optimism in an otherwise discouraging work.[53]

The Indictment of Society

When William Booth indignantly asserted that "our very souls boil" at the roadblocks society placed in the path of the fallen, [54] he highlighted another facet of the outlook of these revivalists: their desire to correct the situations that caused women to fall. Their most immediate goal was to change society's outlook. Any thoughtful person, Mrs. Barrett asserted, must "feel that society's attitude toward the fallen woman is illogical, unjust and short-sighted." Central to her program, therefore, was to "educate public sentiment." [55] In keeping with this conviction, the Florence Crittenton Purity and Prayer Circles aimed to cultivate among sponsoring church members a "broadening of sympathy" and a "development of charitableness," and to curb the "self-righteous, selfish" attitudes that often made "the fallen girl's attempt at right living such a thorny experience." [56] Thus Emma Whittemore was indignant when a church politely expelled a girl whom it discovered had been a resident of the Door of Hope, and Charles Crittenton expressed amazement at the harshness of "Christians." [57]

Crittenton and his fellow workers helped, then, to reverse the outlook under which unwed mothers and prostitutes bore the brunt of society's disapproval of sexual deviation. Though the urban missionaries seem to have avoided a sentimental whitewashing of such women, they directed their hostility largely toward other segments of society, including its respectable members; for them the cause and the cure of immorality was essentially "social." They explicitly attacked the double standard in sex. The War Cry expressed gratitude, for example, that Americans were awakening to the fact that men must share the blame for sex offences; the editor hoped society would eventually place "double" punishment on men. [58]

In another important part of the evangelical indictment, Booth-Tucker attacked the impossible wages that left women to "starve or sell their virtue." Mrs. Whittemore noted that a Brooklyn establishment paid a young Jewish girl a salary of $3 a week, forcing her into prostitution. "Better days have come," she said, but the "wretched wages" paid by greedy employers continued to result in tragedy for many girls. The same men, she charged, would self-righteously refuse to help those girls. She pled for American women to unite in efforts to correct both wages and attitudes. And Crittenton, speaking at the first general assembly of his

organization in 1897, described a factory which paid 300
women $1.50 per week. "About one-half of those girls were
wrecked and their lives ruined by this system of wages," he
declared. [59]

Claims of Success

Grounding their work, then, in sympathy and optimism
toward their clients, gospel welfare agencies reported unusual
success. [60] Under the characteristic caption, "Love's Con-
quering Power," Mrs. Whittemore asserted that the early
records of the Door of Hope showed a success ratio of about
80 per cent. [61] The Christian Herald recorded that during
the first six years of the Crittenton mission in New York,
"considerably more than half" of those received were reformed. [62] And for several decades after 1890, the Salvation
Army consistently claimed a success ratio ranging from 75
to more than 90 per cent. Evangeline Booth, for example,
cited three homes which during 1910 housed a total of 411
girls with only six cases of an unsatisfactory result. [63]

While those who advanced these remarkable claims
apparently used no consistent formal definition of good results, they were attempting, as a minimum, to restore girls
to society's norms. They had failed if a girl returned to
sexual deviation in any form, or if she could not retain employment. But their ideal was much more ambitious, to enable girls to enjoy, as one report put it, "lives of happy
usefulness." [64] And they wanted to impart their own concern
for other persons, particularly for anyone in need. The contributions many graduates later made to the homes, and the
willingness of residents to help others around them, seemed
proof of a degree of success. [65] Religious faith was also a
major criterion of success; in the last analysis, therefore,
gospel welfare workers did not think their task completed
unless conversion accompanied restoration. [66]

Many contemporaries commented both on the spirit
and the results of gospel welfare programs for women. Implicit in the hearty though g eneral approval of these organizations given by men like Lyman Abbott, Josiah Strong,
William T. Stead, and F. W. Farrar, this recognition found
explicit statement by numerous others. George S. Wilson,
for one, secretary of the Board of Charities of Washington,
D.C., indicated to Mrs. Barrett his "hearty sympathy" and
"cordial approval" on the basis of several years of careful
observation. [67]

The Traffic in Girls

Gospel welfare workers helped contribute to the belief, widespread by 1910, that a well-organized traffic in girls existed in the United States.[68] One evangelistic contemporary declared that the "commercial trade in girls" was as real as the trade in animals in the stockyards of Chicago.[69] Slum missionaries shared his view, as a part of their general transfer of blame from the problem woman to the larger society. While their literature contained numerous accounts of women abandoned by lovers and even by husbands, it also placed great emphasis on men and women who posed as friends or lovers in order to trick girls into prostitution. This kind of person, together with entrepreneurs of organized vice, perpetuated the "social evil."[70]

The most famous exposure in which these organizations took active part was also the earliest, London's Pall Mall Gazette episode of 1885. That exposure had its origin in accounts of traffic in girls that Bramwell Booth and his wife learned of in conversation with residents of the Army's first rescue home. At first doubtful of the stories, Booth and his family soon became convinced of their truth, and launched a determined effort in support of the Criminal Law Amendment Act which was under consideration by Parliament at that time. The elder Mrs. Booth addressed impassioned letters to the Queen, prime minister, and other prominent persons, while the General organized mass meetings throughout the land and secured over a third of a million signatures on a petition in support of the Act. Bramwell Booth, meanwhile, convinced the influential journalist, William T. Stead, with the same evidence that had so stirred his own family.[71]

Failing to secure satisfaction through other channels, Stead finally undertook his own investigation, fully utilizing Salvation Army personnel. The results of that effort, which included the purchase and abduction of a thirteen-year-old girl as a graphic demonstration of the traffic, Stead published in four articles in the Gazette. Those articles created a sensation that not only contributed importantly to passage of the Amendment Act, but also aroused determined opposition. Focusing especially upon the purchase and transportation of the girl, opponents of the reform legislation succeeded in prompting a cynical prosecution of Bramwell Booth and Stead by the British government under the very terms of the legislation for whose extension Booth and Stead had pressed. Although Stead was convicted on the abduction for immoral

purposes charge and served a short jail term, the disclosures and trial resulted in a great impetus for Salvationist
rescue work in England and abroad. [72] Moving accounts in
the American War Cry--"I could not sleep, " Bramwell wrote
in one letter, "I could not take my food. At times I could
not pray"[73]--stirred the sympathies of Salvationists in the
United States, and won much support for the rescue homes
that began springing up there within months of the Gazette
exposures. [74]

Rescue workers participated in agitation against white
slavery from this point. Two decades later, the Army played
a widely-publicized role in efforts to release slave-girls from
prostitution in Japan. Spurred by a request to help free a
girl, Salvationists finally secured the cooperation of the
police, and within a few months a revision of the laws liber-
ated the slave-girls. [75] The War Cry, meanwhile, after 1908
enlarged its agitation about the American traffic in girls.
An article in September of that year described Chicago's
white slavery as the worst in the nation, and commended the
Illinois law which a year earlier had tightened restrictions
on vice. [76] A later editorial praised efforts current in New
York and Chicago to catch the "vampires," and called the
trade the "... most damnable traffic of all the centuries. "[77]
And Charles Crittenton, observing the awakening of public
interest in the problem during those closing years of his life,
declared that the traffic was the same he had seen in operation for twenty-five years. [78]

VII

THE PROBLEM OF UNEMPLOYMENT

The introduction of industrialism into rescue missions, the Christian Herald reported after the first annual convention of the International Union of Gospel Missions in 1914, was the "outstanding note of the addresses by successful mission workers." J. B. McIntyre of the Whosoever Gospel Mission of Germantown, Pa., like many other speakers, stressed "employment as the basis for material relief." The Germantown institution maintained a $75,000 plant employing 125 persons daily on a "work-for-what-you-can-get plan." The Herald stated that reports of the work of this and other missions had "stimulated all the delegates and made a tremendous impression upon the audiences at the various meetings."[1]

McIntyre's mission had been carrying on this kind of program since the mid-1890s, and had become well-known in evangelical welfare circles. It was, for example, one of the missions regularly represented at the Alliance's annual Rescue Day, and news of its operations appeared from time to time in the Christian Herald and other journals. Its founder, William Raws, had been converted at a revival meeting in 1888, after which he and his wife began witnessing in the slums. As a result of that witnessing, Raws opened the Whosoever Gospel Mission in a former saloon in 1892, featuring only "gospel services." He soon became convinced that he must meet material needs also, and "Rescue Home, cheap meals, lodging-house, woodyard and various industries came by a very natural evolution." In little more than two years the Mission dispensed 92,000 meals, gave short-term lodging to 1174 persons, and began manufacturing brooms and producing kindling wood. By 1897 Raws claimed to have employed 8000 men in operations which by then included "broom-making, brushmaking, woodcutting, shoe-making, upholstering, printing, and chaircaning." He credited divine guidance for this development of one of the "most complete" missions in the United States. Meanwhile, as a writer in the Volunteers Gazette stressed, nightly evangelistic meetings continued as before, with numerous conversions. Late in 1897, when the Germantown venture was scarcely five years old, Raws departed to found the "Keswick Colony of Mercy" on a 400-acre tract of land near Whiting, N.J.[2]

The Problem of Unemployment

Unemployment, due partly to the peculiar problems of the poor and partly to the periodic recessions that gripped the nation's economy, was a growing spectre. The indigent often lacked the personal skills, mobility, and other qualities essential to obtaining jobs. In addition, alcoholism, prostitution, or criminal records kept many of them chronically unemployed. Among the latter group were many of the principal clients of evangelistic rescue institutions. During the winter following the panic of 1907, for example, the Volunteers of America reported that its stations had never had so many unemployed men seeking help; 35 or 40 men frequently applied at one of their eastern offices in a single day. At the same time the Salvation Army's War Cry noted great suffering among "appalling numbers of workless men." Statistics issued by organized labor, indicating more than 160,000 unemployed in New York City alone, prompted the editor to call for "special city, state and national legislation."[3]

Gospel welfare organizations sought to counter the problem of unemployment by supplying men with jobs, partly within their own institutions, and partly through the formal and informal "employment bureaus" they operated. And they attempted to train unemployables in new skills as well as in new attitudes and life patterns. For some, new skills sufficed; the alienation of others from society was so great that considerable personal change had to precede any attempt to obtain and hold employment.

The Provision of Employment: Woodyards

Many persons found jobs staffing rescue institutions and programs. The men who operated and serviced the Tibbals lodging houses in New York in 1895 had all first come there unemployed and seeking shelter, as had the cook

at the Salvation Army's New York "Lighthouse."[4] Indeed,
scores of men and women rescued "from the depths" became
officers and preachers within these groups. The first annual
convention of the Union of Gospel Missions was, the Christian Herald observed, "remarkable ... for the number of
superintendents who were themselves converted in Gospel missions." Many of the most important leaders--men like Jerry
McAuley, the Hadley brothers, and Mel Trotter--were, as we
have seen, among this number.[5]

Rescue institutions early began providing temporary
work for the unemployed. "Woodyards" were among the
simplest ways to exchange bed and board for labor, and so
avoid pauperizing the clients. The woodyard first operated
by the "Highway Mission" at Louisville, Ky., later passed
into the hands of the city Charity Organization. The Christian
Herald reported that between 1884 and 1893 the "Friendly Inn"
of Boston provided more than 275,000 meals and almost
120,000 lodgings for homeless men, most of whom earned
their keep in the woodyard while the organization helped them
to seek more permanent employment.[6] Salvation Army posts
operated major woodyards at Waterbury, Conn., Boston,
Houston, San Francisco, and Seattle.[7] There, for an average
of one or two hours of labor, a man could earn a day's food
and a night's lodging; sale of the resulting firewood contributed
to the institution's support.[8]

Evidence concerning actual profits from the woodyards
is mixed. Booth-Tucker thought them "one of the best and
simplest plans," but complained of financial difficulties in
various places. Edward Fielding, second only to the Booths
in Volunteer ranks, stressed the economic value of the woodyard in a paper he read before the council of officers in 1905.
The Patterson, N.J., rescue mission, which eventually became a Salvation Army post, estimated woodyard profits of
more than $3000 for 1895. However, the Army's Food and
Shelter Depot in Kansas City announced in 1897 that it had
curtailed its program because the unemployed were so numerous that the institution could not sell all the wood the men
sawed.[9]

The Farm Colonies of the Salvation Army

The Salvation Army, meanwhile, made a major attempt
to alleviate unemployment and other urban problems through
agriculture. As early as 1890 William Booth had declared in

his volume, In Darkest England and the Way Out, that any
ultimate solution of the problems of unemployment and poverty
would require the establishment of "farm colonies."[10] Though
Booth affirmed that his program was experimental and flexi-
ble, it developed along the lines he had laid out. The first
farm colony opened at Hadleigh, near London, in 1890, and
others soon followed in Australia, India, South Africa, and
Canada. The War Cry reported those developments to
American Salvationists, paying special attention to the migration of 40,000 persons to Canada by 1908.[11] During his visit
to the United States in 1894, Booth indicated that the Army
would also establish a farm colony in this land. Hopes had
mounted a few years earlier when a friend donated a large
farm near Lawrence, Kan., which seemed the potential "nucleus of a vast and important work of social reform." That
hope failed to materialize, however, until after Frederick
Booth-Tucker arrived in 1896.[12]

In the great expansion of social work which followed,
farm colonies received Booth-Tucker's special attention.
"The ultimate remedy for the social miseries in the city,"
he declared was to reverse the tide of migration back toward
the land. Accordingly, in addition to a "potato patch scheme"
for slum families in Chicago,[13] Booth-Tucker was able to
inaugurate three agricultural colonies by mid-1899. At Fort
Romie, 150 miles south of San Francisco, he purchased 520
acres of land for $26,000. At about the same time he se-
cured the 1760-acre Fort Amity site in Colorado's Arkansas
River Valley for $47,000. The third colony, at Fort Herrick
near Cleveland, bore the name of one of its donors, Myron
T. Herrick, governor of Ohio and ambassador to France
during the early twentieth century. Its 300 acres proved in-
sufficient for a farm colony, however, and when an industrial
farm and then a colony for inebriates also failed, the site
became one of the Army's growing number of "fresh-air"
camps.[14]

The farm colonies, which drew considerable national
attention during the years between 1898 and 1905, benefitted
from nearly a decade of prior Army experience as well as
from Booth-Tucker's personal leadership. Thoroughly familiar with the Army's overall operations as well as with
the General's agricultural plan, he popularized his program
with catch-phrases such as "Back to the land" and "The
landless man to the manless land."[15]

At the heart of Booth-Tucker's concern was what the

program would do for families. As it was, he said, families of the poor were first crushed by poverty and then scattered by prevailing attempts to deal with that poverty. The farm colonies would restore such families to wholeness by transferring them to profitable and meaningful work in healthier locales. For such reasons Booth-Tucker predicted that "the entire pauper system of the United States," and then that of the "civilized world," would soon yield to the operation of this principle.[16]

A number of outsiders shared Booth-Tucker's enthusiasm for the farms. The Sixth National Irrigation Congress, which met at Lincoln, Neb., in 1897, heard his plan "with great interest and pleasure," "unanimously" passing a resolution of "sympathy and support."[17] In the autumn of that year he reported offers of land from twenty-three states. By 1900 he could list more than a dozen prominent business and political leaders who "warmly advocated" and "cordially cooperated" in the project.[18] Industrial Commissioner John R. Davis of the Santa Fe railroad, on whose line Fort Amity was located, told a reporter from the New York Sun that his "knowledge of the worthlessness of other similar schemes" had made him reluctant even to investigate the site and plan. He had determined, he said, to turn the party back if his mind were not changed during the first evening. Booth-Tucker quickly won Davis' complete confidence: rough farmers who were at first unwilling even to talk with a Salvation Army officer, were soon "sitting ... on the very edge of their seat," the commissioner reported. The reason, he believed, was Booth-Tucker's "simple magnetic earnestness" as well as his grasp of the information necessary to answer every objection.[19] Others who endorsed Booth-Tucker's colonies included the Mayor and many civic leaders in San Francisco, who appointed a committee early in 1897 to work with the Army in establishing Fort Romie.[20] And at the height of the Army's efforts, Senator George F. Hoar of Massachusetts introduced "Booth-Tucker's bill" to create a colonization Bureau to assist settlers on the public domain.[21]

In 1905 the British government commissioned Sir Henry Rider-Haggard, novelist and student of society, to investigate the success of the Army's farm colonies in the United States and England. On the basis of an extended visit Rider-Haggard declared himself "on the whole extremely well satisfied" with Romie and Amity; in fact, he judged Booth's scheme so simple and workable he could "only wonder no one has propounded it before."[22] His report, based on personal contacts

with almost all the settlers, as well as on detailed examina-
tion of the financial status of both families and colonies,
found the settlers "almost without exception" prospering and
contented, despite many disappointments at the outset. The
first group of settlers at Fort Romie had quit under the
pressure of a prolonged drought. The second, arriving in
1901, benefitted from the new irrigation facilities as well as
from their own previous farming experience. At Fort Amity
the Army overcame serious problems of inexperience and
poverty, together with tough alkaline soil and lack of rain.
"It would be difficult," Rider-Haggard concluded, "to find a
better instance of the advantage of skillfully managed land
settlement for the benefit of persons without capital...."23

Citing the equally favorable judgments of President
Theodore Roosevelt, Prime Minister Sir Wilfrid Laurier of
Canada, and other officials, Rider-Haggard recommended
that the British government should establish similar colonies
throughout its Empire. Though he suggested working through
any approved organization, the Salvation Army clearly was in
a favorable position, as Booth-Tucker assured him it would
undertake colonization "to any extent" the British government
proposed. 24

Ironically, the farm colonies went into sharp decline
at this point, in part because of the departure of Booth-
Tucker late in 1904. Evangeline Booth's primary welfare
interests lay in the Army's other social programs; she gave
the farm colonies little attention after 1905.25

The Extension of Industrialism

"Industrial" missions, which combined the provision
of food and shelter with labor designed to produce usable
goods, became a more permanent solution to the problems
of the unemployed. This branch of the Salvation Army's
social work apparently originated in 1896 when an officer in
New York's Bowery district began going from door to door
with a push-cart gathering castoff items for homeless men to
repair at his shelter. 26 Soon salvage "brigades" appeared
in Brooklyn, Jersey City, Newark, Boston, and Chicago. 27
In Chicago the Army had four double teams of horses and
wagons in operation by mid-1898, picking up, among other
items, a ton of paper daily in the two wards the city had
opened to them. The officers took a five-year lease on a
spacious building that functioned as a dormitory, warehouse,

and workshop, and opened, in addition, a large store for a
retail outlet. Among the nearly 500 destitute men who found
temporary employment repairing castoff goods were a former
shoemaker and an upholsterer. The officers rejoiced that
these men were earning their own way as well as enabling
the poor to purchase necessary goods at low prices. By
early 1904 Salvationists operated seven salvage stores in
Chicago alone, though they complained that the relatively
heavy initial cost of buildings and equipment prevented the
more rapid expansion they desired. 28

Industrial homes grew naturally out of a combination
of shelter and salvage operations. Before 1900 major published Army reports contained no separate section on such
establishments. The volume Ten Talks on the Salvation
Army, however, published in the 1920s, described the industrial homes in some detail. Standing for the principle that
"hard work and simple religious truth" were the "cure for
human waywardness, " the homes characteristically included
a large room for handling waste paper, workrooms for renovating furniture, and other used articles, a retail store, a
relief department for the very poor, and various facilities
for those for whom the building was a residence as well as
a place of employment. 29

A similar combination of shelter with labor appeared
in all of the gospel welfare institutions, whether the unit in
question was identified primarily as a rescue mission, a
home for girls, a children's home, or a school. The Bowery
Mission, for example, invested heavily in industrial programs
after 1910, opening in May, 1911, a "Labor Settlement" which
furnished temporary work and lodging as well as training for
those who lacked special skills. The Herald requested readers to send almost any castoff items they had, in order to
supplement the material its workers were able to collect in
New York City. The men cooperated heartily, the superintendent reported; one of them, a "restored" drunkard, wrote
that "liberality and liberty" prevailed in the Settlement, with
"no spirit of surveillance, and none of the obnoxious fussing
about immaterial things" that he had come to associate with
institutional life. 30

In January, 1915, the Bowery Mission added to its
employment complex a 300-acre farm in Westchester County,
thirty miles north of New York City. The property contained
an orchard and buildings for 5000 chickens, and was located
in a "magnificent" natural setting that included a stream and

a waterfall. More than a dozen men set to work renovating the farm's two large houses of over twenty rooms each. The officers of the Mission intended the farm to function as a training school for prospective farm hands, as well as the site of experiments aimed at lessoning the seasonal character of agricultural work. Superintendent John Hallimond felt that the project made the Mission, with its gospel meetings, men's brotherhood, and industrial settlement, "one of the most complete converting and regenerating institutions in the world." The success of the farm during the next two years encouraged the Mission to relocate the labor settlement, by then known as the "Dunwoodie Industrial Department," in the nearby city of Yonkers. [31]

Rescue work with women also included industrial training. Mrs. Barrett of the Crittenton homes emphasized the contribution which such training made to character re-formation, both in securing employment and in instilling proper habits. The director of the Crittenton home in Boston, believing that "honest industry lies at the bottom of true character," wrote that their establishment had achieved almost total self-support through its industrial program. [32] The home the Alliance's Delia Collins sponsored in Fort Worth, Texas, as well as the one opened by the New York Rescue Band in 1895, were also industrial institutions. [33] Similarly, Mrs. Whittemore trained residents of the Door of Hope missions in homemaking, dressmaking and fancy sewing. The forty-three-acre estate she operated at Tappan, near New York City, enabled training in gardening and poultry care as well. On departure each girl received the amount credited to her for her labor, including a share in any profits. [34]

The educational institutions that evangelistic welfare agencies supported also made industrial training an important part of their program. The Christian Herald, for example, gave extensive publicity and financial aid to the Mayesville (S.C.) Institute for Negro youth. In 1910-1911 the "Christian Herald Scholarship Fund" supported at least twelve students in a program which included agricultural training as well as blacksmithing, metal work, and wheelwrighting. [35] Overseas, the Salvation Army taught useful skills in its schools and homes in India and China, as did the Alliance. On a foreign tour in 1893, A. B. Simpson found the Industrial School and Workshop in Akola, India, a flourishing enterprise. Severe famines during the following decade left the Alliance responsible for hundreds of orphaned children, greatly expanding its responsibility for elementary education and industrial training

as well as food and shelter. Under that pressure, the superintendent pled for additional funds for housing and tools,
noting the assistance "industrial" facilities and equipment
provided in financing the mission as well as in training
the children adequately.[36] A number of the famine orphans
later settled on the Alliance's 350-acre Industrial Farm in
Sanand, India, receiving a house, a pair of bullocks, a cart,
implements, and support for a year. Missionary assistance
also extended to such other spheres as selecting mates for
their charges in the tradition of Indian parents. The Farm
prospered; twelve dwellings were occupied in 1904, and the
mission appealed for funds for a dozen more. However, in
subsequent years the pressure of famine eased in India, and
the Alliance gradually discontinued the orphanage and industrial portions of its mission program.[37]

Industrial activities functioned, then, not only as a
device to provide temporary employment and to help finance
the institutions, but also to give needed training in useful
skills to many persons. Through it all, the managers maintained a sense of both the spiritual and the social importance
of their task. They believed their institutions were not
simply beehives of activity, but bridges to a brighter future.[38]

Employment Bureaus

Although a large number of people found work in these
institutional programs, the formal and informal employment
agencies that gospel welfare organizations operated helped a
far larger number secure regular jobs. "Each of our corps
and Social Institutions is practically a Labor Bureau," a
major review of Salvation Army activities declared; and the
same was true for many other rescue institutions.[39] The
jobs provided for transients housed in the institutions were
temporary, intended to help them bridge the gap to normal
life. The process was carefully structured for former
prisoners, "fallen" women, and broken, homeless persons,
who needed time and training before feeling capable of accepting jobs outside. Their subsequent regular employment
seemed to the sponsors the best measurement of successful
rehabilitation. Officers at the Army's New York Rescue
Home, for example, tried to retain its residents for at least
three months; they asserted that they never dismissed a girl
without a job "unless incorrigible, and we have found very
few such."[40] Although according to Mrs. Booth-Tucker ten
positions were available for every girl the Army trained,
placing them generally required a considerable effort.[41]

Employment bureaus operated on both national and local levels to obtain positions outside of rescue institutions. In San Francisco, for example, the Salvation Army bureau, established at its food and shelter depot during the winter of 1893, found work for 165 men. The commanding officer in New England instituted Boston's "Labor Exchange" in 1895, stressing the urgent need. Three hundred men applied for help in the Exchange's first three weeks of operation. [42]

When Booth-Tucker assumed the Army command early in 1896, his goals included a national employment bureau. The central bureau in New York City, established in January, 1897, received approximately 2600 applications for work during its first twenty months, and placed 1975 men. Placement percentages rose steadily, until by mid-1898 officers claimed their rate of success approached 100 per cent. Local and regional reports at the turn of the century indicated Army bureaus were placing a national total of nearly 4800 persons every month. [43] Careful investigation of each applicant included questions about religion. Officers denied any discrimination, however, explaining that some employers, including Roman Catholics, requested candidates of their own faith. [44]

On New Year's Day, 1905, the Christian Herald's Bowery Mission in New York City established a similar "Free Labor Bureau," formalizing activities it had been carrying on for some years for the men in its bread line. Because of the scarcity of available positions in New York, the bureau provided free transportation to locations as far as fifty miles away. Of 110 men placed during the first month, 74 received transportation to employment outside the city. By March 15 the bureau had placed 503 men, but "very heavy" expense in money and effort then prompted a return to the earlier, less formal system. [45]

Like the Salvation Army, the Bowery Mission carefully screened all applicants. In practice this meant seeking jobs for most of them, since rescue workers took an essentially sympathetic view of the potential of even the most difficult cases. During the first month "almost every man" placed gave satisfaction, the Herald reported. Six years later it asserted that the "splendid record" of the more than 10,000 men for whom the mission had found jobs proved what such persons could accomplish if given the opportunity. [46]

During the decade beginning in 1910 the Mission greatly

enlarged its employment service. By 1915, the officers
claimed to have found work for more than 27, 000 men.
Meanwhile the Mission's Labor Settlement, and later its farm,
gave temporary employment to those seeking jobs but needing
a period of training and personal readjustment. [47] Much of
the available work was seasonal: farm labor, lumbering, ice-
cutting, snow removal, and the like. Like other evangelical
welfare institutions, the Mission was prepared to assume the
added expense of filling seasonal labor needs. During "Blizzard Day" in January, 1905, for example, the Bowery Mission arranged snow removal jobs with the city street department for several hundred men. Similarly, the Salvation Army
reported it not unusual in snowstorms "for a rush order to
be received at our hotels in the early hours of the morning
for one to two hundred men. "[48]

Attitudes Toward the Unemployed

Gospel welfare workers displayed toward the unemployed the same attitude of acceptance and forgiveness that
characterized their work with prostitutes and unwed mothers.
The editor of the War Cry early called for generosity toward
beggars, rebuking the niggardliness and abuse often shown
them as rooted in selfishness rather than conscience. "It is
really only for what is in the fist that we keep it shut, " he
said. After one of his excursions into the slums of New
York City, T. DeWitt Talmage declared that the poor deserved
sympathy; in similar circumstances most people would fall. [49]
And Commander Booth-Tucker of the Salvation Army repeatedly emphasized that poverty was not a crime, that the poor
must not be branded as worthless. "What, " he asked, in an
allusion to Bryan's famous "cross of gold" campaign speech
in 1896, could be said "in defence of nailing honest poverty
to a cross of shame?" Booth-Tucker's own estimate was that
90 per cent or more of the unemployed were willing to work
if given the opportunity. In The Salvation Army in the United
States, published in 1899, he repeated that estimate, quoting
statements by police, penitentiary personnel, and public officials to refute the allegation that "any man who wants work
can find it. "[50]

Workers engaged in food, shelter, and employment
efforts shared with the organized charity workers of that
era[51] an eagerness to avoid pauperizing their clients. William Booth, for all his immediate and energetic response to
persons' sleeping without shelter on a winter night, cautioned

with equal vigor against any "coddling." And the War Cry editor who received food and lodging during his incognito visit to an Army shelter, reported with some satisfaction that the officer in charge first gave him "quite a neat little speech ... on the evils of indiscriminate charity," then informed him that he could work off his debt in the shelter's woodyard.[52] The officers tried in this way to foster strength and self-respect among the poor.[53]

In addition to a basic underlying attitude of acceptance and respect, several other factors eased the harshness that the fear of pauperization could breed. Rescue workers professed to meet extreme need as quickly as possible and without imposing conditions. Persons physically unable to work received food and shelter without charge, while able-bodied latecomers could satisfy requirements the following day. This experience in trusting the unfortunate reinforced the contention of the officers that such people were dependable and willing workers. One report from Boston affirmed that no one had departed without completing his obligations. That this was not always the case, however, is evident from the note an early-rising transient left at the Army's "hotel" in Nashville: "Just tell them that you saw me, but you never saw me saw."[54]

VIII

PRISON PHILANTHROPY

In early March of 1892 the Christian Herald reported
the death of Michael Dunn, known as "the convicts' friend,"
who had established homes for ex-prisoners in a half-dozen
cities across the nation. "His father was a thief; his mother
was a thief, and every member of the family, as far as I
can learn, was a thief," S. H. Hadley later wrote. In jail
in his native Ireland before he was ten years old, Dunn made
no improvement after he arrived in the United States, but
served term after term in Sing Sing prison until he had been
behind its bars for thirty-six years. Then, as Hadley related the story, Dunn visited the Water Street Mission in 1879
and believed that Jesus spoke to his "poor, hardened soul."
He came to the mourner's bench, and from that moment "to
the day of his death he never returned to the old life."[1]

Though without means other than his new faith and
enthusiasm, Dunn immediately opened a refuge for other
former prisoners in a nearby cellar. The place was soon
full, and Dunn moved by degrees to more adequate quarters,
then began opening homes in other cities. In 1883, on the
fourth anniversary of his "Home of Industry" in New York
City, a Christian Herald article reported that he had assisted
more than 1000 men that year. At that anniversary, twenty
of these former criminals expressed publicly their gratitude
for the help they had received.[2]

The Development of Salvationist and Volunteer Prison Work

Michael Dunn had counterparts in gospel welfare organizations all over the nation. One Salvation Army slum
post reported in 1896 that forty-seven of its forty-eight members had prison records.[3] William Booth and his followers

103

won many such converts from the Army's beginning.[4] Ballington Booth, upon his accession to the American command
in 1887, strongly emphasized the need for renewed efforts to
reach the criminal class. He expressed great enthusiasm
for prison work, and asserted that the Army in proportion to
its numbers was doing more for the criminal than was any
other group.[5] Three years later the editor of the War Cry
announced that Prison Gate Work, a program of providing
food, shelter, and other aid for discharged prisoners, would
commence soon in the United States.[6] Yet the first large
extension of that program came with Booth-Tucker's establishment of three prison-gate homes within a year after he arrived
in 1896. Though he proposed similar establishments for every
major American city, by the 1920s the Army no longer maintained separate institutions of this kind. It had not abandoned
the prisoners, however, as through its shelters, industrial
homes, and employment bureaus it continued to care for most,
if not all, of the ex-convicts who appeared.[7]

The program was fairly consistent during these years,
though the labels varied. During 1894 Salvationists began the
"Prisoner's Hope Brigade"; soon after Booth-Tucker's arrival this became the "Knights of Hope," and Evangeline Booth
later instituted the "Brighter Day League." Each of these, as
their names indicate, aimed to lift morale through kindness
and concrete help both during and after the time when the
prisoner was serving his sentence.[8] The "Lifer's Club," to
whose members the Army circulated the monthly The New Day,
had similar purposes of religion and morale.[9]

While Salvation Army prison operations expanded under
the Booth-Tuckers and Evangeline Booth, Ballington and Maud
Booth were carrying on similar efforts through the Volunteers
of America. Prison work became the most prominent part of
the Volunteers' social program, and Maud Booth was its inspiration and support. Described in one article as a woman
of "sanctified refinement," Maud Booth had the platform ability
and the personal magnetism common to her new family.[10]
The daughter of an Anglican clergyman named Charlesworth,
she had moved, while still a child, into a parish in the same
East London slums where William Booth had recently begun
his Christian Mission. The noise and color of the Booth
meetings, occasionally held in the Charlesworth family's
churchyard, guaranteed that the young girl would take notice.
In after years she recounted how her initial fascination
changed to disgust, and how still later she developed a new

and stronger interest as she began to realize the quality of
the Army's devotion and service. Despite her father's
strong disapproval, she moved increasingly into Salvation
Army circles, and in September, 1886, married Ballington,
the second son of William and Catherine Booth. Seven
months later Maud and Ballington Booth arrived in New York
City as the new commanders of the Salvation Army in the
United States.[11]

The earliest and most notable part of the developing
social program of the Volunteers was the prison work which
Maud Booth originated and directed. In the introductory issue of the Volunteers' Gazette, she described the pivotal impact of her visit to San Quentin prison two years earlier. It
was as if God had taken her into the lives of the prisoners
to feel their despair, she said, and enabled her for the first
time to realize what prison meant to the men. She determined to try to "burn in upon the hearts of the fortunate" her
conviction that society must not imprison and brand and then
abandon such men.[12] In a second important formative event,
Mrs. Booth visited Sing Sing prison late in May, 1896.
Nearly a thousand prisoners listened closely for an hour,
and more than fifty came forward for prayer at the end of
her talk. Three weeks later, the editor of the Gazette reported, the prisoners gave her a "rousing and unmistakably
affectionate" welcome back, and once again thirty-five or
forty sought "salvation." During ensuing weeks the Gazette
described numerous such meetings, and declared that prisoners were fast becoming her "favorite kind of an audience."[13]

Out of these efforts the Volunteer Prison League
emerged. Its broad program of support for the prisoners
and ex-convicts rested heavily on the initiative of the men
themselves. Converts at Maud Booth's first meeting at Sing
Sing banded together for mutual strength and growth in what
became the nucleus of the organization. It was for earnest
seekers and it centered in life, not in "creed or theological
belief." Members were to observe five rules: daily prayer
and reading of scripture from the Volunteers' "Day Book,"
avoidance of "bad language," faithful observance of prison
rules, and conscientious efforts to encourage others in "right
living." A certificate and a lapel button for each member
reminded them of this pledge and of the Volunteer motto,
"Look Up and Hope!"[14] Prisoners responded to the League's
developing program and the hope it offered, as well as to the
persons of Maud Booth and her fellow workers. A special
issue of the Gazette declared in 1904 that the League had

grown from twenty-five members in mid-1896 to 12,000 by
1902, and then doubled in the following two years. Later
in the decade the membership reached 50,000.[15]

The Hope Hall residences grew out of the awareness
of society's hostility to released convicts and of the need for
a network of general welfare institutions to receive them.
The first such home opened in Flushing Meadows, N.Y., in
the late summer of 1896. Mrs. Booth declared on that occasion that during the three months since her second visit
to Sing Sing, the project had filled her "thoughts by day and
... dreams by night." She would have quit preaching to the
prisoners, she said, if she could not also provide them this
assistance once they were released.[16]

Facets of Prison Philanthropy

Rescue workers unable to establish similar homes
often gave food and clothing to released prisoners, sometimes with makeshift arrangements for lodging. The Christian Herald helped support such a program for the Tombs
Prison in New York City,[17] similar to the prison gate work
which F. B. Meyer, an influential evangelical minister in
England, had conducted for a number of years. Meyer met
released prisoners at the Leicester jail nearly every morning, bought them breakfast at a nearby coffee house, and
supplied them with necessary help in finding clothes, shelter,
and employment.[18] Local corps of the Salvation Army and
the Volunteers also regularly aided discharged convicts in
this way.[19]

Gospel welfare workers provided both physical and
psychological support to the families of prisoners, the "real
sufferers," as one prominent Salvation Army officer put it.[20]
Maud Booth pointed out that by imprisoning a family's bread-
winner without making any effort to fill the void, the state
imposed upon innocent members of the family greater physical hardship than that which convicts had to endure. Even
those who were not originally from slum areas were quickly
impoverished. Officers encountered some such families in
the course of their ordinary work, but the prisoners themselves directed them to the greater number. Those prisoners,
Christian Herald readers learned, often "begged" the Volunteers to help their children.[21] Faced with that kind of need,
the Salvation Army questioned all the men who joined its
"Brighter Day League" about their families, and turned the

information over to a relief officer, who then visited them
and did everything possible to supply pressing needs. [22]

Rescue agencies also provided special holiday outings
and gifts for the wives and children of prisoners. In 1911,
and for several years thereafter, the Volunteers used a
friend's estate near Philadelphia as a retreat for such families. Accommodations there for as many as 75 children and
50 mothers included swings and other play equipment, as
well as clubrooms for the mothers. [23] Christmas gifts and
meals were for many years "a special feature" of the Volunteers' prison work. Officers secured home addresses from
convicts in the New York City area and compiled a book
which listed each child's sex, age, and size. They then
sent out by wagon from Hope Hall clothing, toys, and candy
for each child, and a gift for each mother, as well as money,
fuel, and a large amount of food. Their gratitude, Mrs.
Booth said, was "pathetic in its intensity."[24]

Employment was a significant part of programs to aid
former prisoners, just as it was in other phases of evangelical welfare work. Each mission and each worker became a
de facto employment agency, impelled by the conviction that
the ability to secure and hold a job was vital to the successful rehabilitation of their clients. As in the case of other
needy persons, various institutions offered training in new
skills to ex-prisoners, as well as temporary employment.
Eventually, however, they had to secure and hold positions in
the outside world under the full pressure of a prejudiced and
hostile society. Thus from the beginning of her prison work
Maud Booth actively sought assistance in finding employment
for her men. In a letter to The Churchman in 1908 she
grounded her appeal on Christian duty, and insisted on "fair"
wages. [25]

Rescue workers often provided literature for the
prisons. The Christian Herald placed a Bible in every cell
of the Tombs in New York City, and reported the plan of
evangelist Dwight L. Moody to supply Sing Sing with a thousand copies of one of his books. The Bible Institute Colpor-
tage Association of Chicago, which continued Moody's program after his death, distributed more than 8000 books to
prison inmates at Christmastime, 1904. [26] The Salvation
Army established a library of its publications in many of the
leading prisons, and donated song books for use in their
chapels. All the rescue groups, of course, distributed their
journals regularly to prison reading rooms. [27]

The Importance of Friendship and Understanding

Among the intangible strengths of successful welfare programs was always simple friendship and personal concern. One of the prison reports of the Salvation Army stated that the organization succeeded because of its "friendliness for the lost," a friendliness that had no selfish aim beyond the satisfaction of extending a helping hand. Maud Booth similarly pledged herself and her Volunteers to be real friends, to show prisoners that, as one of her letters put it, "Somebody Cares!"[28] Certainly her own success in establishing rapport at Sing Sing and other prisons reflected the willingness of the men to regard her "as their friend." Lorenzo Coffin, a philanthropist and reformer who accompanied Mrs. Booth on her second visit to the state prison at Anamosa, Iowa, declared that the cordial greeting she received displayed an almost worshipful affection.[29]

Maud Booth's evident affection for the prisoners helps explain that kind of response. In one letter to her "boys" at Sing Sing, for example, she wrote:

> I cannot tell you ... how deeply I feel the responsibility of the position which God has given me. It is indeed a sacred trust and I pray earnestly that he will give me the strength and grace to be to all of you that which I have promised to be--a friend in your hours of loneliness and need and a faithful representative to champion your cause with the outside world.[30]

On her own tenth wedding anniversary she requested tin showers for Hope Hall. Her holidays, as was often true of other gospel welfare workers, frequently found her there or in the prisons.[31] Mrs. Booth evidently maintained an extensive correspondence with individuals. Letters from the prisoners brought her "joy and comfort," she wrote, and the editor of the Gazette observed that she always dropped other mail when a letter arrived from "some prisoner friend."[32] A "graduate" of three years appealed from the Philippines for her to write "as early as possible, if you only say, 'I am well', I shall be satisfied"; another wrote that he prayed for her every day and spoke of his happiness in his "home," Hope Hall, and in his new faith.[33]

The personal attention which evoked such response was expressed in other ways also. Besides her continuing talks in prison chapels, Maud Booth spent much time visiting and counseling with individuals; one report spoke of sixty-seven personal interviews in one day. She spent long hours with hospitalized men. And she intended to make the Hope Halls "homes" in the fullest sense. She asked that the first one be "as unlike 'an institution' as possible--light, bright, and homelike, " so that men on their arrival would recognize the personal concern that inspired it. [34]

Friendliness, sympathy, and forgiveness, rather than a bare religious message of sin, repentance, and possible salvation, thus characterized evangelistic prison welfare. The men did not need "religious discourse and the reading of prayers, " Mrs. Booth wrote, but the "personal influence of goodness and purity."[35] She especially prescribed an attitude of acceptance and forgiveness. Her Volunteers must not condemn the prisoner for his fall, nor assume the existence of a "criminal class" destined by inborn defects of character to fall and fall again. They were ready to present many excuses for his plight, and as in the case of delinquent women, to direct blame and bitterness largely toward the society that had erected the stumbling-blocks and then coldly condemned those who fell. She wished always to "burn in" on the consciousness of her hearers that these men were not at fault to the degree society usually had judged. Rather, they deserved sympathy and help, for many of them had "never had a chance in life." A similar environment would have caused many "upright" people to fall. Moreover, despite good resolutions in prison, they came out as "marked men, surrounded by temptations, and with the world against them." Former prisoners thus returned to crime not because they wanted to, but "because they must live, " and because in many instances they had "no alternative."[36]

Whereas Mrs. Booth became an insider in the sense of understanding and sympathy, other workers shared these qualities because they had themselves once been imprisoned. Many Salvation Army officers were harassed and jailed by police during the first several decades of the Army's existence. Other rescue workers were converts who had been in prison for reasons that seemed often to have stemmed simply from their poverty. Still others, such as Jerry Mc-Auley and Michael Dunn, were reformed criminals.[37] The rank and file in most of these organizations contained at least a sprinkling of converts who knew the world of the prisoner from within.[38] In many of them this common if varied background produced understanding, sympathy, and a desire for reform.

The Success of Prison Efforts

Evangelistic rescue workers not only forgave the prisoner for his crime, but were sure that he could change. E. J. Parker, after two decades of experience with convicts, declared that they could become "the noblest of Christian characters."[39] Both the Salvation Army and the Volunteers repeatedly affirmed a success ratio of 70 per cent or higher. The Volunteers reported in 1901, for example, that 75 per cent of the 2000 "graduates" of the Hope Halls up to that time were "known to be doing well." Similarly, in 1896 the Army claimed that 70 to 80 per cent of the residents of its twelve prison gate homes in other lands were satisfactorily reformed. Bouyed by such results, Salvationists in 1916 declared themselves almost ready to "guarantee" a high percentage of reclaimed men.[40]

This kind of success stemmed in part from the demands rescue workers placed upon the prisoners. Though they welcomed men without regard to race, creed, nationality, or past offense, they discouraged those who were not serious about reforming: Maud Booth warned convicts "most emphatically" not to come to her for helpuunless they were "absolutely in earnest."[41] Her letters to her converts often stressed her belief that only serious effort on their part would assure success.[42]

Numerous prison wardens, chaplains and public officials spoke highly of the prison work of gospel welfare groups. Warden R. W. McClaughry of the United States Penitentiary at Leavenworth, Kan., wrote that Maud Booth's effectiveness in reforming convicts had completely allayed his wariness of women in prison work. Mayor James Gray of Minneapolis judged that the Volunteers were dealing more effectively with the prison class, and at less expense, than were the police "or any other agency."[43] And frequent letters from prison chaplains attested to the change Mrs. Booth's visits had brought to their institutions.[44]

Prison Reform

E. J. Parker, surveying in 1920 America's gradual transition from a punitive to a curative approach toward criminals, asserted that the Salvation Army had from the first spoken freely for "all of these phases of prison reform." Members of the Booth family pressed for reform in numerous statements. Maud Booth thus promised prisoners she would "champion" their cause, and Lorenzo Coffin, a man prominent in prison reform in Iowa, judged her book, After Prison, What? to be an historic document in that cause. In 1908, five years after its publication, he told prisoners that Mrs. Booth's writings and addresses had been responsible for a "mighty change" in Iowa, including a new law.[45]

IX

THE LIBERATION OF WOMEN

Catherine Booth and the Salvation Army

Late in 1859 Catherine Booth became greatly agitated
over a pamphlet written by a neighboring minister, A. A.
Reese, which attacked "violently" the right of women to
preach.   His attack, which focused on the well-known American evangelist Phoebe Palmer, then holding meetings in England, elicited a defense that distressed Mrs. Booth almost
as much as did the Reese pamphlet: "They make so many
uncalled-for admissions," she wrote to her mother, "that I
would almost as soon answer her defenders as her opponents."
She considered going into Reese's town to refute him: "I
really think I shall try, if he does not let us ladies alone!
... That subject would warm me up anywhere and before
anybody." But the direction her indignation finally took was
a pamphlet of about thirty pages on "Female Teaching." In
it she defended woman's right to preach and teach, using the
Bible as well as arguments she had long been developing. [1]

"Female Teaching" was neither Catherine Booth's first
nor her last spirited defense of her sex.   Convinced of feminine equality early in life by the relative qualities of her own
parents, she made her position clear to young William Booth
during their courtship.   This was, in fact, their "first serious
difference of opinion," for he felt that man, while inferior in
"heart," was woman's superior intellectually.   Catherine was
adamant, arguing that any disparity was the result of lack of
opportunity rather than of natural differences.   And she largel
carried the day with him, though to the end of his life William
Booth continued to feel that the balance was at least slightly
weighted in the direction he originally conceived. [2]

Catherine Booth directed similar arguments at other

antagonists. Disturbed by a sermon her pastor preached in 1853, she penned a lengthy challenge to him to make "the subject of woman's equality as a being, the matter of calm investigation and thought." She made it clear that she would admit no inferiority of nature: "I think the disparity is as easily accounted for," she wrote, "as the difference between woman intellectually in this country and under the degrading slavery of heathen lands." Furthermore, she judged that no argument could be made from a past that had been "false in theory and wrong in practice. Never yet in the history of the world has woman been placed on an intellectual footing with man."[3]

Not long after her defense of Mrs. Palmer, Catherine Booth made her own debut as a public speaker. William, she had written, "is always pestering me to begin giving lectures." She walked to the front abruptly in one of her husband's meetings and declared that henceforth she intended to witness publicly. Thus a woman who described herself as "one of the most timid and bashful disciples the Lord Jesus ever saved," began a preaching career of remarkable effectiveness. While Mrs. Booth complained that the press passed over the addresses of women with a belittling absence of attention, she and her daughters were seldom ignored.[4] In the United States, Evangeline, Emma Booth-Tucker, and Maud Ballington Booth joined Catherine Booth in rivaling the men of their family as charismatic speakers and leaders.[5]

Long discussions in person and through letters, the Phoebe Palmer incident, and Catherine Booth's own effectiveness in public ministry, had served to fully convince her and her husband of the fact of feminine ability and equality with men. She thus established the foundation from which the Salvation Army built in making increasing use of women. Given that foundation, the pressure of needs and the presence of willing and apparently competent women was sufficient to ensure their use, despite the strong opposition of some officers and soldiers. As Bramwell Booth later recorded, their women preached effectively, often more so than men: "Thus by degrees, and without any preconceived arrangement, though with the entire approval of the Founders," women began to take their place.[6]

By degrees the role of women in the Salvation Army expanded. With the steady growth of the Christian Mission into other centers came the question whether women should be placed in charge of a corps, with authority over men.

Both William and Catherine Booth hesitated and others opposed the step. But in July, 1875, Captain Annie Davis
went out in "sole charge" of the Mission's branch in Banking,
a suburb of East London. Her devotion and her "ability to
manage and control" made the appointment a "complete success." "From that time," Bramwell Booth continued, the
Mission felt "no serious hesitation" about appointing women
"to take charge of Corps." Increasing expansion soon resulted in sending women to establish new branches, as well
as to supervise other undertakings. Emma Booth commanded
the Women's Training Home, Evangeline Booth one of the
large corps in London, and Mrs. Bramwell Booth the rescue
work for women. Two other capable women paved the way
in the matter of larger commands. Bramwell's sister
Catherine, who pioneered Army expansion into France and
Switzerland in the early eighties, and Hannah Ouchterlony,
who guided in Sweden after 1883, each did so well that it
was "perfectly plain ... that there was no adequate reason
for withholding the higher commands...."[7]

In the United States Maud Ballington Booth and then
Emma Booth-Tucker functioned as co-commanders and were
apparently as highly esteemed and as skilled in communication and leadership as their husbands. With the split in
Army ranks in early 1896 Evangeline Booth temporarily assumed a command which became hers permanently when she
succeeded Frederick Booth-Tucker nearly a decade later.
The Christian Herald welcomed her arrival with the observation that for the first time in the history of religious movements in the United States, a woman, "young, talented, and
of undeniable ability," was at the head of a major organization.[8]

The Army felt that its greatest contribution to the
cause of feminine rights was not in theory but in the actual
use of women. In its ranks all positions were open, and in
its councils women had an equal voice.[9] "Every day is
proving more and more that God can use women ... in our
ranks at all sorts of work, exactly as He can men," one of
three feminine "Adjutants" wrote in 1889. They had learned
to "put aside the fastidiousness and the timidities and the
cut-and-dried notions" of what was "fitting" for them. Among
the "principles" of the Army that Booth-Tucker listed for the
Seattle Post-Intelligencer eight years later was the equality
of the sexes, a principle that Maud Booth asserted had "been
proved true in our ranks again and again." As the Army officially stated, "By an unalterable position of [its] ... Deeds

Pool [women] ... can hold any position of authority or power in the Army from that of local officer to that of General. "[10]

Frances Willard, president of the Woman's Christian Temperance Union and one of many contemporaries who noted this feature of Army life, wrote that the Army represented "the nearest approach to primitive Christianity" in modern times, partly because it had "placed woman side by side with man as a teacher, worker and administrator." It had struck down all barriers, she said, to the fullest investment of her efforts in the world's improvement.[11] William T. Stead's Pall Mall Gazette declared that, by contrast with many other organizations which kept women in obscurity, one key to the success of the Salvation Army was this "perfect recognition of the equality of the sexes." Stead judged that the Army, and particularly Mrs. Booth, had given an "immense impetus" to the recognition and use of women "in all kinds of public work." This quality, he wrote, first attracted his attention to the movement, and continued to be for him the Army's greatest fascination.[12]

Other Gospel Welfare Groups

Women were essential to the success of the larger evangelistic welfare movement as well. In one of many rescue journal articles which stressed their importance in the missionary task of the church, A. B. Simpson asserted that women were probably the "chief asset" of the Alliance.[13] Jennie Fuller of India, Delia Collins of Texas, Emma Whittemore, and Carrie Judd Montgomery were among the organization's prominent women. Another influential friend was Miss J. E. Dougall of Montreal. Responsible for the W.C.T.U. there, and important in its general Canadian development, she was active on other fronts also. The Alliance memorial sketch called the Canada Congregational Woman's Board of Foreign Missions "largely the fruit of her efforts," saw her as "equally active" in promoting mission work among Canada's foreign population, and being also "perhaps the pioneer of newspaper women in Canada." A wealthy woman, she made her group of cottages near the Alliance grounds at Old Orchard, Me., a retreat for "scores" who could not otherwise have afforded that kind of vacation.[14]

Women also generously staffed the rescue mission movement, figuring prominently in the origins and continuing operation of Five Points, Water Street, and numerous other missions. Despite the dangerous location of the Peniel Mission's branch in San Francisco, the workers in charge were largely young women, as was also true, the Christian Herald later observed, in Peniel's chain of twenty-six missions.[15] The Eighth Avenue Mission in New York City found its leadership through those decades in two women who were active participants in the Alliance; one of them, Sarah Wray, also held important posts in larger rescue mission circles.[16] Mrs. Jerry McAuley, Mrs. S. H. Hadley, and "Mother" Sherwood at the Water Street Mission, and Sarah Bird of the Bowery Mission, were among other important rescue mission workers. At the time of Mrs. Bird's death in 1914, the Mission noted that of the 24,000 men its labor bureau had placed across the years, everyone who had written back referred gratefully to her.[17] Moreover, like Sarah Wray of the Eighth Avenue Mission, a number of women held positions of leadership within the larger rescue mission movement. Mrs. Whittemore of the Door of Hope, for example, besides exercising leadership in the Alliance, the Salvation Army, and larger evangelism, presided over the International Union of Gospel Missions during the first several years of its existence.[18]

Women in Other Lands

As Catherine Booth anticipated in her forays on feminine equality, the concern of gospel welfare workers included the rights of women in other lands. Louise Creighton, writing during that era about the development of Christian missions, observed that the ignorance, neglect, and cruelties suffered by women around the world were "a powerful inducement" for their Western sisters to go to their aid. This motivation helped produce what a later historian of missions has judged one of the "revolutionary" changes of the nineteenth century, a change whereby overseas missions, once "almost exclusively a sphere ... for men," saw women come to constitute a "considerable majority."[19] Gospel rescue efforts, heavily staffed in Western urban slums by women, shared in this. One of Catherine Booth's daughters was a pioneer in Salvation Army work among the poor of India. And Jennie Fuller, among the most prominent of Alliance missionaries, wrote an account of the plight of women in that land which others echoed in scores of articles and letters.[20] The needs of women and children in other lands

did indeed constitute one of the strong and recurring sanc-
tions for gospel welfare missions; their aims, in this area
as in others, were moral as well as "spiritual."

The Salvation Army attempted to apply overseas its
distinctive principle of equality of the sexes in the distribution of its commands. "If our beginning is any indication,"
its first commissioner for China wrote in 1919, "the ...
Army is going to achieve its most notable triumph in this
difficult sphere of labor." Claiming that "every post ... is
open" and that "neither nationality [nor] sex is a bar to ad-
vancement either in rank or responsibility," Commissioner
Charles Jeffries felt that the six Chinese women enrolled for
the Army's second training session there were "forerunners
of the host" who would eventually come.[21]

The Suffrage Movement

Gospel welfare organizations lent support also to the
movement to increase women's political and economic rights
in the United States. The Christian Herald, which paid continuing friendly attention to the suffrage cause,[22] commented
in 1915 that despite recent setbacks in several states, proponents should feel gratified at the support they had gained;
in a short time, "probably ... five or possibly ten years,"
it accurately predicted, women would gain the vote. The
following summer the editor commented that the case for
suffrage was "founded on reasonableness and justice." When
in early 1918 the House of Representatives voted favorably
on the question, an article accompanying the report urged
reader support. Two years later the new editor, Charles
M. Sheldon, continued the Herald's stance by calling favorable
attention to the triumph of the suffrage movement.[23]

X

"OF ONE BLOOD": BLACK AMERICANS

'If ... [Negroes] lack in any particular the intellect and culture ..." of white men, the War Cry commented in 1885, "it is not their fault, but their misfortune, caused by the great and wicked selfishness of those who unjustly withhold from them what they abuse them for lacking." The Salvation Army, it continued, intended to lead the way in fighting that kind of evil.[1] That Salvationists were not alone in their aggressive sympathy appeared in numerous statements in rescue literature. "The race is sharply criticized on points of ignorance and immorality," wrote an Alliance worker in the South, "but how can virtue thrive in an atmosphere like this?" Stressing the Negro's appalling conditions and noting the large number of whites who ascribe to them an innate inferiority, the writer declared that her experience convinced her that "infant classes of colored children would put to shame many of their so-called betters."[2]

Anger at white prejudice as well as a larger concern for oppressed minorities appeared in rescue literature from its beginnings in the United States. "Our hottest indignation," declared one of the earliest issues of the Christian Herald, "is for the infernal politics which have allowed the perpetual swindle and exasperation of the red man." The Indians were justified in warring against whites, the writer implied, by "the outrages of the famous white man's Indian Bureau." And from its early opposition to the Chinese restriction bill to its censure of the "un-American" and "odious" literacy test for immigrants, the Herald took a sympathetic stance toward the least welcome of the foreign-born.[3]

Not unnaturally, an era noted both for the rise of "Jim Crow," and for what now seems a perplexing absence of concern even by progressive reformers,[4] found gospel

118

welfare groups marked by the same acceptance and openness toward blacks that characterized their attitude to other oppressed minorities. Taking the part of Oriental and "new" European immigrants and blaming society for the plight of the drunkard, the "fallen woman," and the unemployed, they naturally found "social" explanations for the Negro's condition. On issues ranging from violence to backwardness in participating in mixed meetings, rescue workers excused blacks on the basis of the wrongs they had suffered.

This acceptance was, moreover, part of a conscious emphasis on the equality of all persons before God, and the necessity of brotherly concern for all. Booker T. Washington thus expressed his high regard for the Salvation Army, particularly because it drew "no color line in religion." The Christian Herald demonstrated its similar spirit in editorializing that there was "nothing farther from the spirit and teaching of the Master than race prejudice." All "who believe in Jesus," the editor wrote, ought to be "brethren to all men, of whatever race, color, or condition...."[5] In this vein, evangelical welfare personnel repeatedly affirmed that they raised no bars of race or creed. "No difference of circumstance, or of race, or of sex, or of age, made any difference" for Catherine Booth, her husband stated. "If she had preference, it was where the need was greatest." The Army's Jersey City Rescue Home reported that it accepted women "irrespective of nationality, creed or color."[6] The Steele orphanages of the American South, which had financial and other ties to both the Alliance and the Christian Herald, welcomed children regardless of race. And the Herald more than once emphasized that it dispensed its charitable aid without regard for color, creed, or national origins.[7]

The Participation of Blacks:
Army, Alliance, and Christian Herald

These expressions of sympathy and support found reinforcement in the fact of Negro presence and participation in rescue organizations. How significant the proportion was is difficult to judge, since thorough-going integration was not as much at issue as it became for the mid-twentieth century. Nor had Negroes congregated in northern cities in anything like mid-twentieth century percentages. On the simple fact of participation, however, there is certainty.

"Our three colored drummers, " Major Moore affirmed
for the Salvation Army early in 1883, proved that God had
indeed made them "of one blood." Eighteen months earlier,
little more than a year after the Army's arrival in the United
States, one of the Pennsylvania corps had reported the testimony of "colored sisters."[8] Subsequent issues of the War
Cry quite regularly mentioned the presence of Negroes and
made plain the interracial character of numerous gatherings.
A number of black troops accompanied Ballington Booth to
an International Congress in London in 1894, receiving considerable attention from British Salvationists. Two years
later "fully one-fourth" of those in attendance at any Army
picnic in St. Louis were Negroes. And when William Booth
visited the United States in 1903 he preached to an enthusiastic audience in the largest black church in Mobile, Ala.[9]

The Army conducted at the same time a continuing
effort to win the Negro to fuller participation in its activities.
Avowing its intention to be the first organization to break the
barrier between the races, the War Cry announced a "Great
Colored Campaign" during the summer of 1885. Salvationists
felt confident that their music, as well as the liveliness and
"freedom" of their meetings, would be a great asset in this
effort. While the campaign took place largely in the South,
one result was the corps begun at the 24th Street barracks
in New York in midyear.[10] Despite other references during
the following months, however, the expedition was apparently
one of numerous abortive attempts to enlarge the work between 1885 and 1915. In 1888 and again in 1894 the Army
announced goals for this branch of the "war."[11] Yet soon
after the arrival of the Booth-Tuckers in 1896, General
Booth sanctioned the "commencement" of operations among
Blacks. The War Cry saluted Col. Holland, second in command in Canada before becoming American Social Secretary,
as "the friend of the colored man!" and as "Our New Apostle
to the Colored Race."[12] Despite this auspicious resumption,
however, both the "Fall and Winter Campaign" in 1898 and
the "Century Scheme" for 1899-1901 proposed to "inaugurate"
the "colored work." Through the ensuing years, as it had
been earlier, scattered items reported various efforts for
the Negro. Yet in 1913 an editorial again announced the beginning of regularly organized work among "America's
Colored Population."[13]

Such a succession of unsuccessful projects indicates
that this was one of the more difficult areas the Salvation
Army entered. For while isolated corps and individual

members existed from the early 1880s, the effort to organize
and extend the work with Blacks was apparently subject to
continuing frustration.

Like the Army, the Christian and Missionary Alliance
felt that the Negro was attracted by its meetings and particularly by its "warm spiritual life."[14] Notes in the Alliance
Weekly--on a former slave at an Atlanta Convention, a student at Nyack, Dr. Henry Wilson with black children[15]--
revealed the presence of individual Negroes. Articles more
fully describing their place in the Alliance occasionally supplemented these hints. Some of the "best" Alliance branches
in Ohio and Pennsylvania, an editorial stated in 1898, were
among blacks. Within a few years Negro members there
and in other states were supporting a number of missionaries.
And in 1908 Simpson welcomed to the annual council of the
leaders of the Alliance "some of our most gifted and faithful
colored brethren."[16]

Though one article commented that "because of past
oppression" Negroes felt "somewhat backward" and hesitant
in mixed gatherings,[17] they did apparently participate effectively in Alliance conventions and other sessions. Simpson
reported that Peter Robinson, a hotel waiter in Pittsburgh,
gave a "remarkable address" at the convention there in
1900.[18] On numerous other occasions Alliance leaders paid
tribute to Robinson, who was responsible for converting
many Negroes in the Pittsburgh area, as well as for beginning other Alliance branches. In 1900 one convention reported his effective participation as part of a larger series
of preaching missions. And at Robinson's death in 1911
Simpson expressed his "deep sorrow" over the loss of "a
man with real genius and extraordinary gifts, both naturally
and spiritually. He was a man of fervid piety," Simpson
wrote, "and one of the most loyal of our Alliance leaders....
[He was] a marked figure at the late council at Nyack ...
[and] we have no words to express our deep sense of his
value and of our loss."[19]

Other black members elicited similar admiration.
In 1906, Simpson expressed his deep regret at the death of
Mrs. Seneca Brown of Cleveland, a "well-known leader of
the Alliance work among the colored people." He noted this
washerwoman's "remarkable spiritual gifts" and "commanding
power" in leading meetings "where both white and colored
women were glad to sit at her feet." She was, he wrote,

the type of person who was "the richest heritage of the
Alliance."[20] After Robinson's death the most prominent
Negro leader within the Alliance was probably E. M. Collette, a man who had earlier conducted the organization's
work among the black population of North Carolina. During
1911 he and Robinson held an effective ten-week campaign
in Philadelphia; that same year Collette delivered "a most
impressive address" to an Alliance Council meeting.[21]

As these entries indicate, Alliance leaders held their
Negro members in high regard. "One of the most unique
and encouraging features of the Alliance work in Ohio and
Pennsylvania," Simpson wrote early in 1898, "is the successful organization of a number of strong branches of our beloved colored brethern." "Some of our best" groups, he
later commented, were among the blacks. And in a more
general statement he asserted that they numbered "many of
the most devout and intelligent Christians."[22] In fact,
Simpson's confidence that Negroes would be attracted by the
"truths and the deep spirituality"[23] of his movement strongly
indicated his positive estimate of their intelligence and insight.

Simpson's frequent references to "our beloved colored
brethren" reflect what apparently was mutual goodwill and
acceptance. He and other white Alliance leaders, including
Henry Wilson, Frederick Senft, and A. E. Funk, were among
those in attendance at the conventions their black members
regularly sponsored in Pittsburgh. Wilson, perhaps Simpson's
closest and most influential co-worker, and the Alliance
leader most closely identified with efforts for neglected groups,
was said by Simpson to have a "special delight" in the black
children. A. E. Funk served for a time as acting president
of an Alliance school for Negroes in the South.[24] The repeated expressions of respect and affection these men made
were apparently returned by their black colleagues. E. M.
Collette thus spoke of the value to him of the assistance and
fellowship of his white associates. And Robinson referred
to the Senfts as "our beloved friends" on an occasion when
they were with him in Pittsburgh for the dedication of a
building.[25]

Negro members shared the foreign missions outreach
so central to the Alliance, as well as its spiritual emphases.
Their branches made a special effort to recruit missionaries,
particularly for Africa where the organization was encountering severe health problems with its white missionaries. In

1904 a report from Pittsburgh affirmed that "several" black missionaries would soon depart for the Congo and other fields. Other entries in the Alliance Weekly indicated a continuing effort to enlist missionary volunteers. In May, 1905, for example, Miss Mary Mullen spoke to "several colored audiences" in Richmond, Va., "about the need of evangelical work" in Africa "by the colored people themselves."[26]

In connection with mission work overseas, as well as with general training, the Alliance supported educational institutions for blacks in the Southern states. In 1906 it announced the fruition of long planning in the opening of Lovejoy Missionary Institute in North Carolina where a friend had donated eight acres of land and a spacious building. Typically, the relatively unstressed humanitarianism of the Alliance operated strongly, both for the students who received industrial and religious education at a total cost of $4 each month, and for the poor of the community. The latter, black as well as white, benefitted from a weekly kindergarten and nightly Bible classes, as well as from the store that was the school's main source of support. At it they could buy at nominal prices clothing donated by the Alliance and other friends. One such friend had come from an Alliance group in Illinois to teach in a public school near the Institute. She and her companion were cheerful, a writer in the Alliance Weekly declared, despite their poverty, in what was for them a mission among the poor and needy.[27]

Besides ties with two or more other schools for Negroes in the South, the Alliance assisted programs and institutions elsewhere, including Peter Robinson's proposal in 1904 for a rescue home primarily for black women, but open to whites as well. Two years later it assumed responsibility for continuing the "extensive social work" Miss Joanna Moore of Nashville had conducted "for many years" among "colored families through her personal efforts and her widely circulated publications."[28] Perhaps more widely known was the interracial work of one of the "staunch friends" of the Alliance, Mrs. A. S. Steele of Chattanooga, for needy children. Beginning with "home mission" work in South Carolina in 1880, she soon became a city missionary in Chattanooga, where the need she encountered among the children prompted her to provide homes for them. Despite serious opposition, by 1899 she had "educated and trained" nearly 700 children, with more than 150 of both races then enrolled.[29]

The Christian Herald, which like other gospel welfare organizations apparently uttered little or no negative comment on the Negro, paid considerable friendly attention to programs for that race. Its numerous articles on notable philanthropists and reformers included both Frederick Douglass and William Lloyd Garrison.[30] It had high regard for Booker T. Washington and his Tuskeegee Institute, and praised the efforts of the social gospel novelist and clergyman, Charles Sheldon, to help the blacks of Topeka in the 1890s.[31] During that decade it also reported the program of the Industrial Missionary Association of Alabama to provide education as well as low-cost land and housing for the masses of plantation Negroes.[32] And when, in those same years, it began its own extensive philanthropic work, its aid to blacks ranged from individual families to numerous institutions, including an orphanage and a home for working girls.

The institution to which the Herald gave perhaps the largest aid and publicity was the Mayesville (S.C.) Institute. Mayesville, whose beginning, one writer said, was "largely enabled" by the Herald, centered on "industrial" training for Negro youth, including agriculture, metal work, and wheelwrighting. Called "a new Tuskeegee" in one issue, the school benefitted from continuing Herald support, including approximately $5000 between 1906 and 1910.[33] In 1910-11 the journal supported at least a dozen students at Mayesville in a scholarship program resulting from reader response to an appeal on its pages from one young Negro girl. Because readers were alerted periodically to the school's material needs, and were encouraged to send contributions directly as well as through the Herald, such appeals probably resulted in considerably more aid than the journal actually claimed.[34]

Support of Blacks in an Unfriendly Era

Supporters of these programs were aware of the larger racial problems and tensions emerging in the United States. In 1879 the Christian Herald discussed the developing exodus of Negroes from the South in a series of issues. During the mid-eighties the Steele orphanages in Chattanooga were destroyed by fire in circumstances suspicious of arson. Several decades later Kate Waller Barrett, seeking to expand the Crittenton Association's program for Negro girls, wrote that "many" of the group's homes in the South could not "receive colored girls because of the law against mixing colored and white people." And the frequent defense of blacks in rescue literature often explicitly mentioned white attacks and prejudice. [35]

Rescue workers reacted with particularly sharp feeling against lynching. "Pennsylvania savages," the Christian Herald's editor labeled participants in one "inexpressibly revolting and cruel" incident and on another occasion declared his belief that nearly all such victims were innocent. The War Cry reported the unsuccessful efforts of Salvationists to prevent a lynching at Frederick, Md., and the editor later condemned mob violence, judging that legal executions were bad enough. While he admitted that the victims of lynching often deserved some punishment, in his judgment the cruelties that southern Negroes suffered partially excused their occasional acts of violence. [36]

"Any race that can exhibit self-control like that...," the editor of the Christian Herald wrote of the reaction of blacks in Topeka to a Tulsa race riot in which Negroes had been killed, "is a race that has the highest possibilities in it."[37] In an age when social Darwinism seemed to lend considerable support to the popular dogma of Anglo-Saxon superiority, the stress of rescue literature was on the achievements and potential of the Negro. An Alliance member in the South could thus indignantly refute the common white contention of black inferiority. The Christian Herald saw the success of the Mayesville Institute as "a welcome vindication" of Negro character and ability. In the same spirit, the Herald featured an article by a Negro giving examples of successful blacks who were then attending a convention in New York. And it was to this theme that Ballington Booth of the Volunteers of America returned again and again in the Gazette. There the affirmation that the Volunteers raised no bars of color was supplemented both by a strong stand against race prejudice and a recurring apologetic for black progress and possibilities. [38]

"The Gazette had made frequent reference" to the progress and possibilities of Southern Negroes, its editor wrote in 1901, noting with pleasure a recent report corroborating that position in the New York Times. Explicitly and implicitly the Gazette had regularly defended the black man. "Is it not amazing," questioned the editor in one of its earliest issues, in reference to enforced segregation in Florida schools, "that a state like Florida ... should give expression to narrow, unChristian prejudices and race antipathies?"[39] Subsequent issues spoke of shameful mistreatment of the Negro in the United States, scored the "disgraceful action" of citizens of Eldorado, Ill., in driving out a school for Negroes, and asked "what is the matter" with Southerners who would criticize President Roosevelt for inviting blacks to the White House.[40] To the Booths and their officers such actions were not only unchristian but ignored the fact of the considerable progress the Negro was making. This progress, the editor wrote early in 1900, rebutted much that was being written against the race. Challenging the accuracy of those who used the Negro skull as evidence of inferiority, he asked the opinion of the Gazette's medically informed readers, meanwhile citing in opposition several examples of great achievement.[41] Through the remainder of the decade the Gazette returned on several other occasions to the topic of Negro progress. And as was the case in Ballington Booth's 1906 editorial against double legal standards--"Not One Law for the White Man and Another for the Colored!"[42]--the position of the Volunteers, while sympathetic to both sides, was firmly and comprehensively against racial discrimination. Charles M. Sheldon spoke, then, for the volunteers as well as for many other gospel welfare workers in a poem published in the Christian Herald:

> My brother, of whatever tongue or race
> Whatever be the color of thy skin
> Tho' either white or black or brown thy face
> Thou art in God's great family--my kin.[43]

XI

WORK WITH ETHNIC GROUPS

To "deal properly with the foreign population in America without raising the devil of national hatred," George Scott Railton declared in 1893, was a task only the Salvation Army could accomplish. Railton, the Army's first leader in the United States and second only to the Booths internationally across those decades, spoke in the context of his organization's increasing contact with the rising tide of immigrants and the resulting nativist response. Under the Army's banner immigrants could unite, he said, without arousing the same suspicions that would otherwise occur.[1]

Friendliness and Support

As in the case of the Negro, the renewal of mass immigration, especially from southeastern and central Europe, posed a major urban social problem about which the Progressive Movement generally was ambivalent.[2] Differences in education, language, appearance, and religion contributed to the distinctly alien character of this immigration and to the mounting hostility with which an influential segment of Anglo-Americans greeted it. Many of the newcomers settled in the mushrooming cities, where their intense poverty compounded the difficulty of adjusting to a new culture. Their manner of speaking, comportment and dress, and obvious poverty helped saddle them with suspicion; they became, as a result, one scapegoat for the frustrating problems the new America faced. The combined pressure of cultural adjustment, poverty, and hostility rendered many of the new immigrants among the most needy of the nation's poor.

Despite prejudice strong enough that Congress increasingly restricted any not in the white Protestant strain, gospel welfare workers maintained friendliness and a continuing effort for the immigrant. The Christian Herald informed its readers from its earliest issues about Chinese and Japanese Americans, [3] and protested the nation's hostility and developing policy of exclusion. In February, 1879, the Herald emphasized negative arguments in describing the Chinese restriction bill the Senate had just passed. During ensuing weeks the journal renewed that opposition and maintained its stance into later decades. In 1914, for example, the editor expressed his satisfaction with the House's rejection of an anti-Japanese amendment to an immigration bill. [4]

The Christian Herald extended a similar friendliness to other "aliens," a friendliness which expressed itself in such descriptions as "A Happy Russian Group," or "Sturdy Italian Stock." [5] The Herald also took a strong stand against discriminatory legislation. In 1913 its editor, while approving the proposed exclusion of anarchists and the criminal "class," expressed satisfaction at the failure of the "educational test" bill. He attacked, in addition, the prejudice and narrowness that in his judgment enabled the passing of the Burnett bill. A year later he again opposed a literacy test, judging its value "very doubtful" in deciding one's worth for citizenship. When, in 1916, proponents of the test attempted to secure its passage in the form of a rider, the editor again noted it, this time as "a distinctly unAmerican measure." Still later he condemned the "odious" literacy test. [6]

Use of Rescue Institutions

The very fact of the numbers, poverty, and urban concentration of the foreign-born insured their substantial use of rescue institutions. The War Cry, which on other occasions noted the "heavy concentrations of the foreign born" in the nation's slums, in 1891 called for redoubled Salvation Army efforts in response to the rising tide of immigration. Individual institutions indicated a considerable encounter. Maud Booth wrote in 1892 that the proposed New York Rescue Home would have special value for immigrant girls, five of whom were then awaiting the home's opening. And a count one night in the late nineties in the Army's Bowery shelter in New York revealed that forty of the 131 residents were foreign-born. [7]

Programs for Immigrants

Both the Salvation Army and the Christian and Missionary Alliance maintained separate programs for immigrants. Railton appealed late in 1887 for a special campaign for German-Americans. A German corps began soon thereafter in New York City, and Scandinavian operations commenced in a small store in Brooklyn at about the same time.[8] Both campaigns prospered. A Swedish edition of the War Cry began publication in February, 1891, and a German one twenty months later.[9] By the mid-nineties, the Scandinavian division claimed, more than 200 officers, cadets, and candidates directed thirty-one corps and training schools, the Swedish War Cry issued about 10,000 copies weekly, and 2000 conversions were reported that year.[10] When Commissioner Hannah Ouchterlony of Sweden visited these corps in 1892, crowds of over 2500 twice filled the Swedish Tabernacle in Minneapolis to hear her speak.[11] Samuel L. Brengle, the most important American-born Salvationist and the Army's foremost preacher of holiness during the early twentieth century, was of Swedish-Methodist background. He spoke with great success in Swedish centers in the United States, as well as in Scandinavian lands. In Denmark in 1907, for example, more than a thousand persons came to the penitent-form in four weeks of meetings. The Army estimated at least a million copies of his books had been published in many languages by his death in 1936.[12]

Both Army and Alliance evangelists also worked with Americans of Italian birth. In 1895 the British War Cry praised the establishment of the first "Italian corps" in New York City. A decade later Captain John Costagna claimed striking results among Italians on the East Side.[13] The Alliance opened a mission in 1890 in a tenement house in "little Italy." A "faith" work, the mission included by 1895 an Italian church on 112th Street as well as a home for girls at Tivoli-on-the-Hudson. Students and faculty at Nyack Missionary Institute held Italian services regularly at nearby towns, and conducted night school sessions three times weekly.[14]

Evangelist Michele Nardi, who attended the Gospel Tabernacle and the Alliance training school in New York City, was a lifelong friend of A. B. Simpson, who reported Nardi's activities in the Alliance Weekly and compiled his biography after his death.[15] A contractor of Italian labor before his conversion, Nardi conducted extended missions among his people in Pittsburgh, Chicago, New York City, and San Francisco, as well as engagements in a number of other cities in the United States and Italy. A. F. Stauffler, president of the New York City Mission Society, under whom the Nardis served for a number of years, wrote that Michele was effective, fervently evangelistic, and "incessant" in his visitation of Italian homes.[16]

Nardi's interests included welfare as well as missions and churches. During his early years in New York, he visited and helped Italians in hospitals, prisons, and other need. His mission in Chicago, which stood in one of the worst areas of the city, featured a vocational school for children, a morning kindergarten, a Sunday School, and a sewing school. A later mission on the city's southwest side likewise developed Sunday School and sewing classes, as well as evening classes in English that used the Bible as a textbook.[17] Similar projects in other centers seemed also to result naturally from Nardi's concern for poverty-stricken immigrants. In New York, his biographers wrote, he had "at once begun the study of bettering their conditions." The Waldensian minister in Pisa, Italy, similarly emphasized the Nardis' "goodness and charity towards the poor." They opened their home "to everybody," he said, and "lovingly fed and cared for" the needy.[18]

"All Ranks Open to Chinese," stated the Salvation Army's first commissioner in China in an article asserting that "every post ... is open." Stressing the Army's efforts to identify with the Chinese people, Commissioner Jeffries countered the "all too prevalent" idea of the identity of Christianity and Westernization partly by having Salvationists live among the people and wear their style of clothing. Apart from the externals of dress and housing, Army and Alliance missionaries shared the outlook of most missionaries, who, a recent scholar has stated, "almost always identified ... emotionally with the welfare of the country and its people." In its extreme form this identification expressed itself in striking disregard for their own welfare during famine and epidemic. Mrs. Jennie Fuller, a prominent Alliance missionary, thus wrote of the death of a fellow missionary who contracted cholera aiding a "poor, unknown, nameless famine widow." She soon sacrificed her own life under similar circumstances.[19]

The striking identification of missionaries with their people stemmed from the same spirit that motivated rescue workers in American slums, where many of the missionaries had once labored, to accept and aid the foreign-born Americans they encountered in increasing numbers. The kind of humane openness that welcomed drunkards, prisoners, and other outcast residents of those slums thus extended itself naturally and effectively to men and women with unfamiliar language, customs, and religion. When a chronicler of the Water Street Mission wrote that "The doors of the Mission are closed to none.... And no man is ever repulsed. Whether Christian or Jew, Protestant or Catholic, citizen or alien--it matters not at all," he spoke for the larger evangelistic rescue movement as well. [20]

XII

"THE CUP OF FURY"

"Both directly and indirectly," wrote George Pardington of the Alliance in a constantly recurring emphasis, "the
drink traffic probably touches at more points the life of humanity than any other single evil."[1] "The greatest evil of
this nation," the Christian Herald declared, while Ballington
Booth of the Volunteers called it the "most powerful" force
in "effecting the misery and ruin of men." Everywhere
there were "Human wrecks" and "one vice was key--drink!"
In the same spirit, the Peniel Herald urged "every man,
woman and child" to oppose the national curse, and marveled
that anyone could be "so demoralized as to sell the destroy-
ing cup."[2]

Strangely extreme as such words sound to a later
generation, they were in the main stream of progressive
thought. Despite the disrepute into which prohibitionist sentiment eventually fell, social reformers of the nineteenth and
early twentieth centuries believed that the liquor traffic was
an evil which contributed heavily to the nation's ills. James
Timberlake has recently shown how temperance advocates fit
naturally within the Progressive Movement, sharing both its
moral idealism and its basic response to the nation's urban
and industrial problems.[3]

Gospel welfare groups stood in that progressive tradition rather than with the evangelical Protestant sects of
the 1920's who, as Clarke Chambers notes, were in favor
of Prohibition and against virtually every other reform.[4]
Salvationists and allied workers opposed drink because of
the problems it introduced and compounded across the entire
range of the life of the poor. They shared the view of
Charles M. Sheldon, prominent social gospel novelist and
frequent contributor to the Christian Herald, who judged that

alcohol had "cost the world more in terms of money, disease, crime, family desertion, and loss than all the wars, pestilences, and commercial disasters known to history."[5]

Motivating Spirit: Concern for Persons

The religion of evangelicals in the slums was thus rooted in concern for persons rather than in the observance of moralistic codes. Although, like the evangelists of the pre-Civil War decades, they opposed the theater, gambling, dancing, and a variety of other amusements and pleasures,[6] their main emphasis was not on externals. A. B. Simpson told his Alliance followers that they needed a great guiding principle for their lives rather than rules. "The spirit of selfishness," William Booth declared, was the "true spirit of worldliness." His wife Catherine warned Salvationists that their energies must be devoted to serving God and other persons, that they should waste no time on frivolities. Maud Booth thus opposed tobacco as "self-indulgence," an expenditure that benefitted no needy person. The Christian Herald excused overburdened working men for using Sundays for diversions such as baseball, boating, or picnics, in an age when many religious men thought such activities a desecration of the Sabbath. Later its aim in attacking immorality in moving pictures seems to have been to regulate and purify rather than to outlaw attendance. "Bad movies ... MUST GO!" the editor wrote in a piece asserting that the Herald's "campaign for the moral cleansing of the movies" was beginning to bear fruit.[7]

This kind of outlook naturally permeated the temperance stance of gospel welfare groups. The acceptance with which they received the homeless man and the fallen woman marked their treatment of the victims of alcohol as well. Drink was, in fact, a substantial part of the problem for most of the persons they helped. As Commander Booth-Tucker of the Salvation Army noted, most fallen women were also heavy drinkers.[8] And the same was true for the clientele of the rescue missions and low-cost shelters for men.

The heavy orientation of rescue missions to alcoholism shows up clearly in the history of Jerry McAuley's Water Street Mission. There the problem and salvation of McAuley and S. H. Hadley, the mission's leaders from 1872 to 1906, found an echo in thousands of converts. Hadley blamed McAuley's earlier vices partly on beer, and traced back to his

own first drink the gradual but total change that left him a
hopeless alcoholic for many years. His story of the Water
Street Mission centered on similar converts from the "vast
army" of "helpless victims" of alcohol. [9]

When Hadley, who from the late eighties until his
death in 1906 was the most important leader among American rescue missions, wrote that he gladly welcomed even
men who abused his charity, he vividly illustrated the nature
of the evangelical concern for persons. The outcast man,
Hadley affirmed, was received without rules or exhortations:
"He is neither watched nor suspected.... He is treated as
a brother; as if he were the best man in the world. He
meets with unvarying kindness on every hand." When on one
occasion he violated that principle, rebuffing a professed
"convert" who had often before gotten religion at Water
Street, his harshness so bothered him that he had little
peace of mind for days until he found the man and carefully
made things right. [10]

Similar acceptance and concern by Salvation Army
lassies resulted in the conversion of a former newspaper
editor, Henry F. Milans, shortly after he was dismissed
from the alcoholic ward of New York's Belleview Hospital
as incurable. [11] He later recalled the profound impact of
their persistent kindly interest shown, for example, in repeated invitations to special Army meetings and in the notes
they sent to him on days they did not see him. From his
own experience, therefore, Milans could later affirm that
kindness, sympathy, and love formed "the one key" that
would "unlock all hearts, " and that "tenderness" was the
"sine qua non of the soul saver's work. "[12]

Mission homes for outcast women mirrored this spirit
as well as the problem which evoked it. Thus, when Delia
Collins of the Alliance was asked the secret of her success
with such girls, her answer was the "bond of affection"
created by the "unselfish love" of her workers. [13] Similarly,
Crittenton's sole rule for his homes was "love and Christian
sympathy, " and his colleague and successor, Kate Waller
Barrett, emphasized the same kind of generous treatment. [14]
For the Salvation Army, the qualities Mrs. Bramwell Booth
sought in her rescue workers included unfailing love, faith
in even the most hopeless outcasts, and the inclination and
ability to deal with the fallen as persons. [15]

The Crusade Against Drink

Permeated, then, by an attitude of acceptance and concern, gospel welfare organizations mounted an extensive and varied attack on drink. The substantial proportion of alcoholics and other problem drinkers among the people they served, coupled with an increasing national interest in temperance, made this one of their strong emphases. In part they worked in cooperation with the large and influential Woman's Christian Temperance Union, an organization which shared their progressivism, and which, in the tradition of the temperance movement,[16] combined much practical aid with its anti-drink crusade.

Begun in 1874, the Union's varied activities soon came to include homes for women, prison welfare, and general rescue,[17] activities which naturally brought it into contact with the Alliance, the Salvation Army, the Volunteers, and similar groups. The columns of their journals indicate mutual high regard, considerable interaction among national organizations, and, at the local level, joint use of meeting halls and exchanges of speakers.[18] Among the delegates to the Temperance Union convention in New York in 1888, the Alliance Weekly noted, were "many of the leading workers of the Christian Alliance." In the autumn of 1890 the War Cry reported Mrs. Ballington Booth's major address at the national convention of the Union in Atlanta.[19] A. B. Simpson for a time gave daily Bible lectures at the "World's W.C.T.U. Evangelistic Training School," which met in the Alliance-related Berachah Mission in New York City in the mid-nineties.[20] Delia Collins of the Texas Alliance, prominent in rescue work for women, was continuously active in temperance circles, as was Mrs. John A. Best of Pittsburgh, who served as both county and state president of the W.C.T.U., and whose husband was head of the strong Alliance group there. One of Simpson's friends in Canada, Miss J. E. Dougall of Montreal, was "the moving spirit" in the organization of the Union in that city, as well as influential in its larger Canadian development. President for many years of the unit in Montreal, and Dominion delegate to the World's Union on several occasions, she was Dominion vice-president when illness forced her resignation in 1903.[21]

Frances Willard, the well-known president of the Union in the United States, maintained cordial relations with the leaders of all the gospel welfare organizations. Though having reservations about some aspects of the program of the

Salvation Army, she termed it her generation's "nearest approach to primitive Christianity," and declared that the true
heroes and heroines of her time marched in its ranks. The
recipient of extensive aid from Charles Crittenton, she gave
him his favorite title, "Brother of Girls," and once invited
him to unite his chain of homes with the Temperance Union.[22]

Miss Willard's spiritual compatibility with the Alliance
and other holiness groups was evident from a letter to the
Alliance Weekly which related her earlier experience of sanctification at the Old Orchard, Me., assembly grounds where
the Alliance met annually. At her death in 1898 Simpson
wrote that her loss would be felt "as widely as any break in
the ranks of Christian workers during the century." Many
of her friends and fellow workers, he noted, were "loyal
friends and members" of the Alliance.[23] Both the War Cry
and the Volunteers Gazette printed lengthy memorial tributes.
The former described Miss Willard as a "diligent auxiliary"
of the Army, in whose passing "all lovers of souls and well-
wishers of man" had lost a sympathetic friend. Ballington
Booth's retrospective sketch in the Gazette lauded her as "a
foremost defender" of the Volunteers and other Christian
enterprises.[24]

Gospel welfare agencies were themselves de facto
temperance societies. The Crittenton homes, besides having
W.C.T.U. members on their boards in all cases, held frequent temperance meetings. Crittenton and his co-workers
generally spoke on this question at the Association's conventions as well as in his evangelistic campaigns. He contributed energetically, for example, to the achievement of a
"dry" vote in two Georgia towns. Prior to his evangelistic
career he had run for mayor of New York City on the Prohibition Party ticket.[25]

Despite A. B. Simpson's conviction that there were
plenty of other people "to run social reform and temperance
societies,"[26] his Alliance followers were prominent in the
W.C.T.U. and generally active in the cause of temperance.
The Alliance Weekly, which he edited, for years featured a
regular "temperance column," as did most rescue journals.
Students at his training school in New York City spent their
afternoons and evenings in tenement houses, saloons, and
rescue missions, claiming many converts from "drink."[27]
Simpson's influential colleague, Henry Wilson, was president
of a mission which stressed the abstinence "pledge."

Josephus Pulis, a convert from apparently hopeless drunkenness who became a spiritual leader in the Alliance in New
York, served on the staff of the Christian Home for Intemperate Men, where he had himself first found shelter. [28]

The Christian Herald, which regularly featured temperance advocates, worked continuously to rehabilitate drunkards through its Bowery Mission, one of the largest in the
nation. [29] F. B. Meyer, friend of gospel welfare groups
and widely influential evangelical whose work and writings
appeared frequently in the Herald, besought all the prisoners
and unemployed men whom he aided to sign and honor the
temperance "pledge." Stephen Merritt, the father-in-law of
the Herald's publisher and one of the Bowery Mission's incorporators, was a "prominent and active laborer" for temperance. During a period of several months in the early
1880s he lectured on the subject almost daily and persuaded
"hundreds" of people to sign the pledge. The Herald charged
in 1885 that Merritt's defeat in a campaign for the office of
state comptroller had resulted from his prohibitionist principles. [30]

The temperance crusade in the United States drew
much inspiration from the attitude of William and Catherine
Booth. Drink was for General Booth simply "a curse."
His Christmas address in 1886 listed "the drink fiend" first
among the many enemies the Army had to fight. His wife's
"life long antipathy to drink" began when, by the age of
twelve, she not only led in a Juvenile Temperance Society,
but "eagerly ... devoured all the Total Abstinence publications of her day." [31] The Army reflected the Booths' spirit,
both in its stated principles and in the attitudes of its members. In fact, its leaders ascribed to its militant temperance stand the violent opposition they had encountered during
its early history. In the United States the first Salvationist
convert was "Ashbarrel Jimmy," whom Commander George
Railton found draped over a barrel in a drunken stupor. A
few years later an editorial in the War Cry called "total
abstinence" one of the most "glorious" elements in the Salvation Army platform. Abstinence, as Booth-Tucker said in a
Chautauqua address in 1903, was a condition for membership
in the Army for both soldiers and officers. There would be
neither drink nor drunkards, another writer asserted, if
everyone had the Army's spirit. [32]

Special Salvationist crusades drew much public attention to the temperance cause. Besides its strong on-going

emphasis, the War Cry occasionally became a temperance
sheet with the special title, "Anti-Drink Cry." It annually
featured the "Siege," a nationwide evangelistic campaign
during Evangeline Booth's command, which included a week
programmed especially for "drunkards and notorious sinners."[33]
The Army also held area temperance campaigns, such as
Boston's "Drunkard-Saving Crusade" in 1892, and General
Booth's similar drive in London a decade later. The War
Cry carried frequent announcements of such efforts as well
as of Union campaigns in which the Army cooperated in the
United States.[34] An occasional "saloon ... census" publicized the frequent visits its evangelists made to taverns,[35]
as did numerous individual accounts. One officer happily
reported selling many copies of the War Cry to customers
who left a saloon in protest against her eviction.[36] The
Army's special efforts for drinkers also included, for example, an ambulance corps in Cleveland, as well as nearby
Fort Herrick, which was for a time a colony for inebriates.[37]

The Salvation Army's best-known single thrust against
drink was probably its "Boozers' Day," inaugurated in New
York City on Thanksgiving Day, 1909, because Officer William A. McIntyre believed that something "unusual and desperate" had to be done to rescue drunkards. The program
for the day included a parade at which a whole regiment of
Salvationists, bearing a walking whiskey bottle ten feet tall
and pulling a "water wagon" with "bonafide" outcast men
aboard, rounded up all the drunkards and ne'er-do-wells they
could find to attend "The Trial of John Barleycorn" and a
free Thanksgiving dinner.[38] Boozers' Day got such wide publicity that Commander Evangeline Booth directed all the
American posts to attempt such an annual event.[39]

Evangelist Wilbur Chapman, who said he knew "all the
famous converts of America," thought Henry F. Milans, who
was converted on Boozers' Day in 1910, "the greatest of them
all."[40] A former newspaper editor who, as we have seen,
had become a hopeless drunk, Milans attended that second
annual event. He returned evening after evening, experienced
what the Army called the new birth, then, after several
months of gradual restoration, found a job and rejoined his
wife. "From that moment to the present," Milans said nearly
two decades later, he had "never been tempted to take a drink
of anything with alcohol in it." He spoke at the celebration
the next Thanksgiving, and with increasing frequency in New
York and elsewhere as the years passed. Milans also became known in wider circles, eventually participating in the

city-wide revivals which such evangelists as Chapman and
Charles M. Alexander conducted. [41]

The Army claimed other striking results from its
continuing temperance crusade. Troops in Grand Rapids,
Mich., took credit for a 25 per cent decrease in arrests
for drunkenness and disorderly conduct during the year following their arrival in 1883. The War Cry quoted an otherwise critical clergyman that the Army was "doing more than
any other agency" to empty "saloons and gambling dens."
From St. Paul, Minn., came a report of "Five Hundred
Redeemed from Rum," and a review of 1899 claimed 7000
drunkards converted that year. [42] The Army estimated, in
fact, that 10 per cent of its annual conversions--the latter
figure ranging up to 60,000 in the United States and 250,000
or more on the world front--were from drink. In 1903,
Booth-Tucker told a Chautauqua audience in New York that
of two million converts won by the Army during the preceding
decade, 200,000 had been drunkards. [43]

William Booth's famous answer to the question, "Where
will you get your preachers?," had been, "Out of the saloons."
In part this proved true, as many of the thousands of restored
drunkards who marched in the Salvation Army were among its
preachers. [44] Similarly, numerous "fallen women" went on to
leadership as matrons or in other capacities in rescue agencies. [45] Moreover, as we have seen, some of the most capable evangelistic rescue leaders were converts from alcoholism, including Milans, Jerry McAuley, Josephus Pulis, S. H.
Hadley, his brother and convert H. H. Hadley, who organized
dozens of rescue missions, and Mel Trotter, whose missions
from coast to coast concentrated on inebriates. [46]

The Goal: Wholeness and Concern for Others

S. H. Hadley's assertion that he welcomed the worst
outcasts to his Water Street Mission with acceptance and
patience highlighted the nature of his own conversion and that
of many other reformed drunkards. Rather than just changing
a bad habit and thus often producing mean and unproductive
"dry drunks," gospel welfare workers sought and frequently
achieved a conversion to helpful concern for others. They
sought a new integrating center, new wholeness, rather than
just the negative change of abstinence from drink. This kind
of orientation explains why Hadley became deeply troubled
over his impatience in throwing a bothersome drunkard out of

his mission. His kindness in finding and helping that man resulted in a radically transformed convert who brightened Water Street, as Hadley reported, for the remaining thirteen years of his life. [47] Similarly, when Henry F. Milans returned to his wife, he treated her with great care in the increasing invalidism she suffered until her death. His continuing helpfulness to other alcoholics reinforces the impression of one whose life had gained a new and positive center. Like Hadley and others, he devoted his life to service for outcast persons. [48]

Both Milans and Hadley were widely influential after their conversions. Hadley left his imprint on a whole generation of rescue mission leaders during the formative period of the movement. And, as we have seen earlier, that impact included not only his evangelistic zeal, but his patient concern for needy persons. After Hadley's death in 1906, Mel Trotter of Grand Rapids, Mich., was probably the most important mission leader for more than three decades. Trotter, himself a converted drunkard who cited Hadley's life and message of love as a pivotal influence on his career, shared that kind of accepting concern for outcast men. [49] And in this both Trotter and Hadley reflected the central emphases of practical love and sacrifice, the others-centeredness, which was the moral hallmark of the larger gospel welfare movement. [50]

The Support of Prohibition

Besides their continuing efforts to reform individuals from drink, urban revivalists wholeheartedly supported the structural reform of society through prohibition of the consumption of alcohol. They were intemperate on the subject of drink and recognized no moderation in its use. The Peniel Mission's leaders pled with their supporters to "smite" this "curse" by "prayer, by word, by vote." In 1896 A. B. Simpson declared his support for any legislation that would "even restrict that most awful curse of our land."[51] Despite these sympathies, however, and despite several individuals who sought office as prohibitionists, gospel welfare groups did not officially give their support to the Prohibition Party which by the turn of the century was more than three decades old. [52] The War Cry thus made a special point of declaring Ballington Booth's political neutrality in the fall of 1892. [53]

Though all rescue groups kept their members informed

of developments in the prohibition movement, [54] the Christian
Herald probably followed most closely the "great fight against
liquor." The editor termed the Senate's favorable action in
mid-1917 "One of the most important moral events of any
country or century...." The following month he saluted the
final passage of the revised amendment by both House and
Senate as the writing of a "red-letter page" in history; no
action since Emancipation, he declared, had been "so laden
with moral, industrial and social potentialities."[55] Pressing
all the while for a war-time ban on alcohol, [56] rescue workers
turned at once to promoting state action. By early 1919 the
Herald happily reported that forty states had already ratified
the amendment, making prohibition the law of the land.[57]
One retrospective editorial made plain the implications of the
event for a broad range of progressive reform. "Property
is sacred, when rightly used," the editor wrote, "but man-
hood, womanhood and childhood are far more sacred, and to
be protected at any sacrifice of sin-tainted property."[58]

During the nineteenth century, Robert Bremner has
written, the idea was commonly held that drink was a very
important cause of poverty. With this traditional consensus
gospel welfare workers obviously agreed. But as Bremner
also pointed out, social scientists in the early twentieth
century attributed a less prominent role to alcohol.[59] Reaction against what seemed religious and moral fanaticism
no doubt accentuated this swing of the scholarly pendulum.
This reaction, however, has obscured both the relationship
of the prohibitionists to the larger reform and progressive
movements of the late nineteenth and early twentieth century
and the causal role of alcohol in the social problems of that
era.

Evangelical welfare workers opposed alcohol primarily
because of the human toll it took, and thus were, like many
other temperance advocates, in the mainstream of American
progressive thought.[60] Their hostility grew out of extended
close personal contact with the poor and in many cases out
of the experience of their own members; as Ballington Booth
wrote, slum missionaries had unsurpassed knowledge of the
evil results of the liquor traffic. The same desire to con-
serve human lives that informed their hostility to war and
other social evils thus prompted their crusade for temperance.
They held, moreover, that the nation should use legal action
to achieve both structural reform and changes in personal
habits and attitudes. This attempt to influence morality

through legislation, which, interestingly enough, many critics of prohibition willingly endorse in other difficult areas of social and economic life, carried rescue workers into prohibition as well as into other areas of progressive reform. Their endeavors against drink maintained the spirit of persuasion rather than coercion as they energetically pleaded the tragic effects on tens of thousands of lives. With their influential contemporary, the reformer and novelist Upton Sinclair, they believed that alcohol was indeed for the nation a "cup of fury."[61]

XIII

PHILANTHROPY ABROAD

Large Scale Beginnings: Famine in Russia

In 1891 a disastrous famine occured in Russia that inaugurated an era of overseas philanthropy among gospel welfare agencies.   While that philanthropy depended most heavily
upon hundreds of foreign missionaries who had learned the
habits of humanitarianism in American slums,[1] the Christian
Herald magazine became the major source of funds.   As a
result of the Russian famine, Louis Klopsch and T. DeWitt
Talmage, who had recently assumed control of the Herald,
began the large-scale relief efforts which within little more
than a decade made it one of the most influential religious
magazines in the world, known chiefly for its promotion of
a wide range of domestic and foreign charities.[2]

Neither Talmage nor Klopsch, however, anticipated
the potential response of their readers when they hesitantly
committed the journal to a small consignment aboard the
Conemaugh, one of several American vessels carrying relief
cargoes to Russia.[3]   Thereafter, stirring articles and photo-
graphs brought the famine to the attention of the magazine's
readers.   Included were accounts by and about the novelist
and philosopher Leo Tolstoy, who fed hundreds of victims in
the afflicted area daily at his own expense.   The editor,
meanwhile, termed the famine the worst calamity in modern
history, confronting twenty million people with starvation.
"We implore you," he wrote, "not only to be generous, but
to be quick."   The subsequent outpouring of gifts, often accompanied by emotional letters, indicated the effectiveness
of the Herald's religious and philanthropic appeals to readers
already well-aware of suffering in American cities.[4]

When the fund reached $20,000, Klopsch decided to

143

charter a relief ship under the exclusive auspices of the
Herald, the first of a succession that was to sail under its
banner. Decorated by an organization called King's Daughters, [5] the Leo left New York in mid-June with a cargo of
nearly 1500 tons of food. Talmage and Klopsch preceded the
Leo to Russia, and wrote home descriptions of its "intensely
enthusiastic" welcome there a month later. [6] Their own reception was also gratifying; Talmage reported with characteristic expansiveness his audience with the Czar, and his
meetings with other Russian leaders. In the weeks that followed the two wrote extensively about what had been for them
a "grand and glorious mission" of relief. As they had declared in closing the Fund with more than $30,000, it had
succeeded "beyond even our most sanguine expectations."
Both the response of their readers and their reception abroad
augured well for future excursions into philanthropy. [7]

Armenia

Opportunities for the Christian Herald and other rescue
organizations to provide relief for the victims of famine,
plague, and other calamities overseas came in ample number
in the decades that followed. The Salvation Army War Cry
first heralded "The Horrible Butchery of Armenians" early in
1895, and in succeeding months Army periodicals as well as
the Alliance Weekly and the Christian Herald reacted with intense indignation to a series of brutal massacres by the
Turks. [8] The Herald began to dispatch aid late in 1895, and
its gifts, Klopsch wrote, soon reached almost every mission
station "from Van [eastern Turkey] to the Bosphorus." Eyewitness accounts of suffering from the missionaries, as well
as from the magazine's own administrator of relief in Armenia, helped the fund reach a total of $65,000 by its closing
in 1898. Of this amount, the journal channeled $7,000 into
the support of orphans, thus initiating a project its readers
supported for a number of years. [9]

The Salvation Army meanwhile dispatched an officer
to aid Armenian refugees landing at Marseilles, France, and
opened a temporary home for those who arrived in London.
At the same time Commander Booth-Tucker, along with Louis
Klopsch of the Christian Herald, took the initiative in similar
relief measures in the United States. Booth-Tucker led a
large meeting in the Salvation Army's Memorial Hall, designed to rally support and attended by such dignitaries as
the mayor of New York City and the prominent social gospel

clergyman Josiah Strong. Aid included employment assistance as well as the provision of temporary quarters on a
Salvation Army farm near New York City. In a note in the
War Cry that December, fifty refugees thanked the Army; it
was not "an easy matter," they wrote, "to find words strong
enough" to express their gratitude for the help and kindness
they had received.10

Famine in India

For Christian Herald, Alliance, and Salvation Army,
the largest and most sustained crisis was in India, a land
racked by famines of unprecedented severity beginning in the
mid-1890s. Describing crop failures brought by long drought
and already accompanied by plague, A. B. Simpson wrote in
the Alliance Weekly in early December, 1896, that Alliance
missionaries were "compelled to receive many refugees and
helpless children" in order to ease their "terrible need."
The following issue featured a moving account by Mrs. Mark
(Jennie) Fuller, a graduate of Charles Finney's Oberlin College and, with her husband, among the most capable and
well-known Alliance missionaries. Meanwhile the War Cry
called the famine "An Unspeakable Calamity" and challenged
Salvationists with a relief plan which included free or cheap
grain, industrial schools, and loans, to be provided through
the Army's "India Famine Fund."11

Ensuing issues of both journals continued to plead for
aid to India. The Army, pressing its appeal under such
headlines as "The India Famine. Help! Help! Help!," announced early in May that its world-wide fund had reached
$36,000. A month later Booth-Tucker reported that 300
Indian orphans were under Army care, relief projects were
in motion for 500 adults, and fifty centers were distributing
free or inexpensive food.12 Simpson's journal detailed the
"awful distress and suffering" in editorials, articles, and a
stream of missionary letters. One of these described "homeless children, most of whom will soon die of starvation,"
and another asked if "the Lord's dear people at home" would
not help in relieving the sufferers. One missionary wrote
that he thought it "almost a crime to ... eat a meal" with
famine sufferers all around. "We have more than once given
them the last pice (cent) in the house," he said, "and then
asked the good Lord to supply our own needs." And he posed
a question that included readers: "What, as Christians ...
are we to do for these poor suffering people?" "What a

mockery ... to tell them of a merciful and loving Savior" if we cannot help.[13]

American branches of the Alliance responded to such appeals sufficiently to enable Simpson to transmit "considerable sums" for famine relief. By late summer Alliance missionaries were feeding thousands daily at their scattered stations, housing an increasing number of orphaned children, and nursing cholera victims with disregard for their own welfare. Mrs. Jennie Fuller lost her daughter and later her own life via this route, part of what Henry Wilson called the exertion of "every energy of soul and body, far exceeding the limits of their scanty supply of money," and what Simpson termed an "unusual burden of work and care."[14]

In extended crises of this sort the resources of the Christian Herald became most evident. Where the greatest strength of the Army and the Alliance was the service of their dedicated personnel, that of the Herald was the contributions of its large and responsive body of readers. Increasing its power to promote extended and large-scale giving was the magazine's historic emphasis on foreign missions and its many contacts with workers overseas. It distributed its funds, as a result, largely through missionary agencies. Indeed, the Herald contributed one-half of the American Salvation Army's India Famine Fund, as announced in early May. And Alliance members learned through editorials and missionary correspondence of money and supplies reaching their own personnel through the same source.[15]

Louis Klopsch channeled the bulk of Christian Herald funds, moreover, through a committee of missionaries of the kind that became a fixture in his charities. Headed by the Methodist Episcopal bishop, J. M. Thoburn, the committee had the responsibility of organizing relief and distributing the mounting gifts from the Herald. Those gifts, which completely dwarfed the journal's efforts for Russia and Armenia, rose by as much as $18,000 in a single week, eventually totaling more than $400,000. Many letters of thanks arrived from missionaries, who bore the emotional and physical burdens of distributing relief. In addition, Assistant Secretary of State William R. Day sent the editor communiques from the British ambassador and the Viceroy of India which expressed gratitude to the American government and people and singled out Klopsch and the Christian Herald for special recognition.[16]

India had barely recovered from the shock of the famine of 1896 and 1897 before one of even greater severity struck. Bishop Thoburn wrote with "wonderful relief" in late fall, 1897, that harvests were bountiful and the people hopeful once again, though many years would pass before the marks of the disaster would "wholly disappear from the country." Two years later both the Alliance Weekly and the War Cry published the news of a recurrence of the crisis, and appeals for aid began arriving at the offices of the Christian Herald with every mail. Close observers who had declared the preceding famine the most severe of the century, soon were describing the new one as an even worse calamity.[17]

In response to the renewed famine, A. B. Simpson declared that it was "the duty of God's children" to "plan for systematic gifts from month to month ... until this awful burden has been removed." In a world of "unpitied and unaided misery," he said, the Bible warned plainly of divine judgment upon the pitiless. And as he later stressed for relief to China, the gifts of his people should be over and above their regular donations for missions, for otherwise the missionaries would actually bear the added sacrifice.[18] Mrs. Fuller, whose letter, printed in early April, 1900, described the spreading cholera plague and mourned the passing of one of her colleagues, shortly fell victim to cholera herself. The widowed Mark Fuller, pleading for reinforcements and furloughs later that year, wrote that scores of missionaries from all societies "will never be able to do hard work again till they have had a thorough rest."[19]

American rescue groups again provided substantial aid,[20] with the Christian Herald undertaking what became perhaps the largest single relief effort in its history. Hesitant to commit his readers again so soon for the same land, Louis Klopsch finally bowed to continuing missionary appeals describing appalling conditions. Soon after requesting contributions he cabled $5000, followed quickly by $10,000 more. On May 10, 1900, the Quito, a ship secured under terms of an unused government authorization made during the earlier Indian famine, sailed with a cargo of 5000 tons of grain and other supplies. Valued at $100,000 in the United States, famine conditions tripled its worth in Bombay, where it arrived late in June. Meanwhile Klopsch cabled other donations, and the balance sheet finally published May 1, 1901, showed total receipts of more than $640,000. This amount included upwards of a quarter of a million separate remittances to the

Christian Herald, and an even larger number of individual
contributors, since several persons often combined in a
single donation. In a practice which Klopsch generally followed in his charities, the magazine printed names of all
donors, no matter how small their gift.[21]

The personal visit Louis Klopsch made to India in
May of 1900 gave impetus to the relief fund. At some risk
to his own life, he spent days touring famine and plague
areas, professing himself appalled at what he found. Klopsch
wrote that although he had kept in close contact with the missionaries since the beginning of the crisis, conditions in
India were far worse than he had ever imagined. His extensive accounts of suffering and relief supplemented editorial
comments and missionary appeals for aid.[22]

The Christian Herald again received official recognition for its assistance to India. When the Viceroy of India
informed the State Department of worsening conditions early
in the famine, the latter forwarded a copy to Klopsch, re-
calling the efforts his magazine had made in 1897. President William McKinley and Secretary of State John Hay each
contributed $100 to the relief fund Klopsch soon opened.
Later the British government expressed its appreciation
through Lord George Hamilton, cabinet member in charge of
Indian affairs. Consel-General Fee of Bombay, who included
letters from the Viceroy and the governor of Bombay, affirmed that the Indian people had been "deeply affected" by
the Herald's gifts and judged that "one of the bright spots in
this appalling struggle" had been "the heroic efforts of the
Christian missionaries."[23]

Homes for Children: India, China, and Japan

One immediate development from the great Indian
famines was the provision of aid for the increasing number
of orphaned children. The Salvation Army was caring for
nearly 1000 such children by 1902.[24] Alliance reports frequently referred to their orphans, a number which increased
steadily until their missions housed well over 1000 by the
conclusion of the second famine. The children, whose care
included an education with some vocational training, remained with the missionaries into young adulthood. Thus
500 orphans were still in the care of the Alliance a decade
later. During this time prominent American leaders, including Henry Wilson, energetically pursued their support.

All in all, in terms of time, number, and thorough involvement, the famine orphan work was perhaps the major philanthropy in which the Alliance officially engaged. 25

While the Alliance worked energetically to assure the
systematic support of these children, they also gratefully
acknowledged that 500 were underwritten by the Christian
Herald. The hard reality of increasing numbers of orphans
combined with Louis Klopsch's special concern for children
to produce that support. In response to appeals that came
immediately after the heaviest famine pressure eased in
1897, Klopsch sent a general letter to twenty-two missionaries, telling them of his decision to combine late famine
contributions with $13,000 in freight refunds into a fund for
orphans. Apportioning the fund among missionaries caring
for the children, Klopsch promised quarterly installments
for the following three years. He then invited readers to
contribute, making the project more concrete and meaningful
with the information that the sum of $15 or $20 would support one child for an entire year. 26

The Christian Herald thought it providential that this
fund was in operation when the famine of 1900 greatly
swelled the number of orphans. A member of the relief
committee estimated that missionaries had rescued more
than 20,000 children, straining available resources to the
breaking point. The missionary committee gladly accepted
Klopsch's proposition in the summer of 1900 to underwrite
5000 orphans for a year. In September he cabled $25,000
for the first four months. The following spring, encouraged
by the surplus of nearly $175,000 in the famine fund, Klopsch
extended the plan in a firm guarantee for three years and
$225,000. Even at his death in 1910, four hundred orphans
remained in a program to which the Christian Herald had
contributed more than one-half million dollars. 27

As large as the India orphan program was, it represented little more than half of the children the Herald underwrote in the Far East before 1910. For Louis Klopsch used
similar fund surpluses to care for the victims of a series of
severe famines in China and Japan during the first decade of
a new century. In Japan his Missionary Committee gathered
1200 children into two large orphanages at Sendai and Oka-
yama in 1906; the following year Klopsch applied $112,000
of famine relief money to the support of 3000 orphans in
China. When he died, nearly 2400 children remained in the
journal's care in the Orient, 2000 of them in China. The

Industrial Homes at Fukien, in China, which had about 200
children in 1910, tripled in size during the next decade, becoming one of the largest mission orphanages in that land.
And the Herald reported in 1919 that the British consul and
various high Chinese officials in that area had honored the
Homes' missionary founder, Miss Hartwell, in a way it
judged unique in the history of missions in China. [28]

Famine and Flood in China and Japan

As the orphanages make clear, India was not alone in
receiving famine relief. During the first decade of the twentieth century, Finland, China, and Japan were among areas
experiencing severe food shortages and extensive American
help. For both the Christian Herald and the Alliance, China
was an area of particularly heavy involvement after 1900.
The former organization, which dispatched a small amount
of aid in 1899, sent more than $125,000 in assistance during
a serious famine in 1901. Li Hung Chang, a prominent
Chinese government official, cabled information direct to the
Herald, as did E. H. Conger, American minister to China.
Telegrams from Secretary Hay and President McKinley again
helped prompt further contributions to the relief fund Klopsch
had now begun. In China a committee chaired by Acting
Minister Rockhill and composed mainly of American missionaries, organized the distribution of aid. When the crisis
was past, Governor Ts'en of Shensi province ordered a proc-
lamation hung in Christian churches and official places which
strongly contrasted the "true goodness" the missionaries had
shown with the treatment his own people had often accorded
foreigners. [29]

Even while that fund was underway, a major flood developed in the Yangtze Valley. The Christian Herald diverted
some money there for relief, and in 1902 sent an additional
contribution to allay the resulting famine. [30] The next spring
brought news of a severe food shortage in an area of South
China where Alliance missionaries claimed to be working almost alone. Their home board took measures to alert both
government and public to need severe enough that missionaries were buying and sheltering children whose parents were
selling them in order to keep alive. At one point their relief program supplied food to 3000 famine victims each day.
The Christian Herald, whose contacts relayed similar descriptions, forwarded remittances of at least $15,000. [31]

Famines continued to elicit the response of gospel welfare groups during the first decades of the new century. In the winter of 1902-1903 the Christian Herald sent aid to stricken areas of Scandinavia, with Louis Klopsch making a personal visit. [32] Three years later, crises in China and Japan resulted in Herald contributions totaling nearly $700,000. During that summer, Japan's northern provinces experienced famine too severe for the government adequately to relieve. Responding to missionary requests, Klopsch cabled aid in advance of contributions. By the time of the magazine's audited statement the following July, it had dispersed $241,000 through the Japanese famine fund. The Emperor of Japan presented the Order of the Rising Sun, at the time one of the two most important Japanese orders of distinction, to Louis Klopsch in New York City in May, 1907, in recognition of the Christian Herald's gifts. [33]

During the same period flood and famine in China called forth a major effort from Klopsch and his readers. He cabled $5000 in immediate response to President Roosevelt's appeal during the Christmas season in 1906, and inaugurated a fund as conditions worsened. Roosevelt and Secretary of State Elihu Root both sent contributions to a fund which by April had remitted $150,000 to China. By the time of the "usual certified, audited statement," the total had risen to more than $425,000 including the value of the cargo transported free on the Army troopship Buford. And, as we have seen, the famines of 1906-1907 occasioned the extended support of about 4200 famine orphans by the Christian Herald. [34]

Nor was the famine fund of 1907 the last which that journal provided for China. In late 1910, after the death of Louis Klopsch, the Herald's communications with the State Department and with missionaries convinced it that another major effort was necessary. As a result it sent money and supplies that included 10,000 sacks of flour. [35] A decade later, one of its largest single philanthropic projects resulted from the Chinese famine of 1920-1921. Soon after the Christian Herald opened its Chinese Famine Fund in November, 1920, President Woodrow Wilson expanded the Fund by appointing a national committee with headquarters at the journal's offices in New York. By mid-June readers of the Herald had contributed more than $560,000 toward a national total of $7 million. The editor expressed his satisfaction with the committee's enlistment of technical experts on famine prevention, as well as with the increased knowledge and goodwill the famine fund created. [36]

Relief for Italy

Shortly after the major famines of 1906-1907 in the Far East, a disaster of another sort devastated southern Italy. On the morning of December 28, 1908, an earthquake sent a huge tidal wave through the Straits of Messina, taking the almost unbelievable estimated toll of 200,000 lives, and leaving fearful wreckage over the entire area. Eyewitnesses reported that Messina lost more than two-thirds of its 150,000 people, as well as nearly all of its buildings. Klopsch cabled $20,000 to the American minister at Rome the next day, and soon sent $30,000 more in advance of reader contributions. As was his practice, he arranged to have a special representative visit the area, in this case the vacationing Rev. William Carter of the Madison Avenue Reformed Church in New York. Carter's eyewitness accounts were valuable aids in the campaign for funds. Besides general relief work, Klopsch supplied $1000 a day to support women and children bereaved by the earthquake, and sent $5000 in answer to an appeal from the Waldensian Church. The Fund for Italy closed early in March, showing total disbursements of more than $70,000. Klopsch visited Italy a short time later at the invitation of the Italian ambassador, and enjoyed an audience with King Victor Emmanuel III. [37]

XIV

WAR AND PEACE

"All the devilish animosity, hard hearted cruelty, and harrowing consequences of modern warfare" were not only sanctioned by the churches, Catherine Booth told a London audience in 1884, but held up "as an indispensable necessity of civilized life," and in times of war "patronized and prayed" for with such "impudent assurance" as to suggest that Jesus Christ taught the doctrine of an eye for an eye.[1]

Mrs. Booth's intense hostility to militarism characterized a group which in organization, garb, and language portrayed itself as the Army of the Lord. Its head was not a bishop but a general, its weekly magazine was the War Cry, and with unrelenting discipline it laid siege to all the forces of evil.[2] "At 10 A.M. precisely, we charged the enemy," one officer's report ran. Another described revival effort as "a week of incessant fighting." News of attempts to win converts appeared under captions such as "The War in Canada," "The Battle of Williamsburg," or "From the Front."[3] The editor of the War Cry switched to a naval metaphor one week, with a headline reading "The Battleship 'Salvation' Opens Fire on Fort Sin."[4] Thus Mrs. Booth's fierce attack on militarism, which was paralleled, as we shall see, in other gospel welfare leaders, reflected the martial spirit with which those groups joined battle against all the forces of evil.

At the same time, gospel welfare workers, like most progressive contemporaries,[5] found their pacifism seriously challenged by national interests in time of war. The sometimes noisy American patriotism of the Army, the Volunteers, and the Christian Herald[6] stemmed in part from an English derivation which might otherwise have made them suspect. Englishmen owned and controlled the Herald until Louis Klopsch

became its proprietor in 1890; the Salvation Army originated
in England, its International Headquarters there continued to
send officers and directives to the United States, and its
major ruptures in this land related both to that control and
to the question of adaptation to American ways. The Volunteers stressed their democratic and American character from
the beginning.[7] But more significant than their emphasis on
patriots and holidays was their confidence in American democracy and a sense of national mission that mingled patriotism and religion. As a result, though they maintained both
a genuine antipathy to war and a spirit of goodwill to all
nations, rescue groups occasionally compromised their ideals
of peace under the pressure of stronger national loyalties.

Pacifism and Patriotism, 1885-1920

The general hostility of rescue groups to war, along
with their patriotic compromises, appeared clearly by the
turn of the century in response to several international con-
flicts. General Booth, who in 1885 deplored the possibility
of Anglo-Russian hostilities, fourteen years later spoke
strongly in favor of the Czar's "Rescript" for peace and the
resulting first Hague Conference.[8] Like Booth, who declared "War with war!," the editor of the Christian Herald
during the nineties condemned war as a "relic of barba-
rism."[9] In contrast, the crisis with Spain in 1898 provoked
A. B. Simpson of the Alliance to extreme pro-American
judgments. Simpson, who two years earlier had rebuked
the "folly and haste" of both English and American leaders
in their Venezuelan dispute, called the war with Spain one of
"humanity" of which "no American need ever be ashamed."
If ever war was justified, he wrote, it was in this case of
a helpless race being crushed by a despotic nation.[10] His
own religious version of the doctrine of America's mission
prompted him to extend his approval to the acquisition of
the Philippines: "The principle of humanity that called for
the Cuban war," he declared, "as forcibly demands the protection of the oppressed Philippinos...." To have let the
"oppressors" keep the islands "would have been a crime
against humanity."[11]

Peace sentiment had free reign for two decades thereafter, until the United States was once again at war. In
1901, T. DeWitt Talmage, editor of the Christian Herald,
called war "the worst curse that ever smote the nations," but
admitted reluctantly that the United States must be armed.

Four years later Simpson devoted several editorials to the
Russo-Japanese conflict, asserting that Russia should apply
her energies "to the rights and wrongs of her suffering
people at home" rather than to war.[12] He and the editor of
the Herald both gave careful attention to the well-publicized
first National Peace Congress in New York in April, 1907,
and the second Hague Conference that summer and fall.[13]
The Herald's editor, noting that the world was amply convinced of the evil of war, expressed hope that practical steps
rather than theory would occupy the delegates at New York.
Simpson, who had more reservations about the value of such
conferences, commended the limited progress made by delegates at The Hague, but remarked that the preceding peace
talks at New York were marred by "much quarreling." For
him such performances, duplicated as they were in international politics, demonstrated a basic perversity in men
and in nations. War was but a symptom of a deeper ailment,
he said, for which secondary remedies would never suffice.[14]

Two events during 1910--President William Taft's full
support for arbitration, which by the summer of 1911 produced far-reaching treaties with England and France, and
Andrew Carnegie's $10 million "Endowment for International
Peace"[15]--resulted in a resurgence of sentiment for arbitration, particularly in the columns of the Christian Herald. In
April, 1911, the Alliance Weekly urged Alliance congregations
to support "Arbitration Sunday" wholeheartedly, and commended American churches for their broad backing for Taft's
negotiations.[16] The Herald once again proclaimed its belief
that every international dispute could be arbitrated. The
editor, who had commented almost weekly on the progress
of the treaties, praised their signing in mid-summer as one
of the greatest days in American history.[17]

To spread the ideals of peace and more effectively
support practical measures, the Christian Herald Peace
League began organizing local Peace Circles during the summer and autumn of 1911, reaching a total of 260 units by
late fall.[18] Meanwhile the editor presented in the magazine's
September issues an extensive symposium of national leaders,
including President Taft, on the subject of arbitration and
world peace. Though a few contributors disagreed, notably
the evangelicals R. A. Torrey and A. B. Simpson, the
Herald fully shared the Symposium's consensus that the world
was on the threshhold of a new era of universal peace. Even
the most skeptical person, the editor declared, must now ac-
knowledge that "the great transformation" was under way.[19]

The coming of war in Europe, while it shattered such
hopes, intensified the Herald's agitation for peace. The
editor termed the war a "tremendous indictment against Christianity, " and proof that armaments were a provocative rather
than a preventive force. [20] In September, with what became
characteristic moderation toward the Central Powers, he reported the "collapse" of early accounts of German "atrocities. "
The editor of the War Cry, meanwhile, despite the Army's
strong British ties, cautioned that Christians might pray, but
only for the cause of humanity, not for victory for their side.
Bramwell Booth, who later wrote that one of the worst features of the war was the "decay of the spirit of pity in so
many hearts, " denied in 1915 both the suggestion of a loss of
faith and the promise of a great gain for righteousness. His
diagnosis was "new boat, old rocks"; war was but an expression of man, and after the war the same "man" would remain. [21]

The editor of the Herald, who early called for an em-
bargo on all arms shipments, [22] joined strongly during 1915
and 1916 in the pacifist fight against the "militaristic mad-
ness" of "preparedness. "[23] He challenged President Woodrow
Wilson's use of the Bible in defense of arming, claiming that
nowhere did it support the "militarist gospel of preparedness. " Lyman Abbott's partial defense of war earned a similar categorical denial, while in a broader sweep the editor
scored the remarkable "elasticity ... of certain kinds of religion" that would permit the justification of war. [24]

In his opposition to preparedness the editor claimed
support from a number of influential contributors. In November, 1915, he printed an open letter from Charles M. Sheldon
to the President. Again asking "What would Jesus do?"
Sheldon answered that he would promote "justice and brotherhood" rather than spend money for armaments. Because of
this Sheldon declared his own full opposition to the President
and commended the Herald for its firm stand at a time when
most Eastern dailies and a number of religious journals were
"preaching war. " This, he said, "makes the Herald Christian. " Sheldon also noted a "powerful" article in that same
issue by Charles E. Jefferson, then pastor of New York's
Broadway Tabernacle and a prominent pacifist. "We must
cease to put America first, " Jefferson wrote in a plea for
"preparedness of spirit, " for an "international" conscience
and mind; "America is not first. Humanity is first. "[25]

The Herald maintained its anti-militarism as well as

its spirit of moderation toward Germany well into 1917.
During the increasing tension in January, 1917, it described
Allied rejection of a recent German peace proposal as "direct
and aggressive," and scorned those who held that the great
issues involved precluded stopping the war too quickly. A
few weeks later, the editor praised the President's call for
"peace without victory" as close to what the Herald had been
urging all along. [26] When Germany renewed its unrestricted
submarine warfare, he called for "calm councils." And a
few weeks later, shortly before Wilson's war message, he
played down the significance of the Zimmerman note, adding
that the American people remained "overwhelmingly" against
war. [27]

   After American entry in April, 1917, the Herald, like
an increasing number of erstwhile pacifists, called for united
support, "Now that the decision has been made." Evangeline
Booth, who had backed the President throughout the conflict,
justified his step and pledged the Army's continuing support. [28]
Like the English Salvationist Bramwell Booth, however, whose
statements had remained moderate despite the tensions of war,
the Herald's editor called for prayer "for the capacity to
render justice, to make peace in righteousness, ... in the
spirit of the Master who commanded us to love our enemies."
Charles Sheldon cautioned the magazine's readers that Americans should maintain the aim of world federation, with no
spirit of vengeance and no desire to acquire territory. [29]
Meanwhile, the editor vigorously opposed the Espionage Bill,
supported direct taxation to finance the war and prevent profi-
teering, and protested mistreatment of German-Americans. [30]

   At the same time, the Herald paradoxically embraced
elements of what it had formerly condemned. Like the Alliance writer who spoke of the "forces of liberty and righteousness," the journal referred to "a war of might against right,
of ruthless terrorism against justice and mercy." It praised
Lutheran schools for giving up the German language, urged
its readers to avoid "bondage to the Kaiser" by buying Liberty
Bonds, and enjoined strict enforcement of espionage laws. [31]
And when peace came, the editor expansively referred to the
downfall of autocracy in the "greatest war" and the "most de-
cisive peace" ever. Defeat, he asserted, was God's punishment for those who had broken the peace. [32]

   The postwar position of the Herald showed the enthusiasm for disarmament and internationalism it had held through

most of the war period. The magazine positioned itself strongly in favor of Wilson's policies, and particularly the League of Nations, in articles and editorials which included one by the administration's Senate leader, John S. Williams. Charles E. Jefferson, who had earlier urged that this nation must not put "America first," contributed a sermon strongly supporting the League.[33] A series of editorials also opposed any annexations or indemnities, spoke sharply against "provincial narrowness," and urged the nation not to detach and isolate itself from the rest of the world.[34] In this the editor repeated a point he had made as the war began, when he called for "A Broader Patriotism" of service to other nations. Such "international altruism" was a concept similar to the love of humanity that Sheldon had earlier written was the only valid base for patriotism.[35]

Christian Herald Wartime Philanthropy Abroad

In response to the intense suffering war brought to civilians and soldiers alike the Christian Herald and the Salvation Army mounted large-scale relief efforts. The Herald, which by 1914 had two decades of experience in overseas philanthropy, directed its funds largely to civilians. A prominent French journalist[36] provided its readers with detailed accounts, supplementing extensive editorial coverage.[37] Readers responded at once to the "Pitiful appeal of the women and children ... for American aid."[38] By early September contributions of nearly $3000 were already on hand for the magazine's "Relief Fund for Widows and Orphans." News of these gifts encouraged others, and readers sent in an average of nearly $9000 each week through the remainder of the year.[39]

By Thanksgiving of 1914 what the Herald later called "the first American relief to reach Belgium" was on the way.[40] Local committees in Holland, London, Paris, Berlin, and Vienna each received $10,000 through early January.[41] Twelve months later committees were distributing the Herald's funds in Lodz, Nish, Galicia, Constantinople, Jerusalem, and Armenia, as well. The Near Eastern committees usually worked through American missionaries or graduates of missionary schools, and depended heavily upon United States diplomatic officers. Ambassador Henry Morgenthau, Sr., was the chairman at Constantinople.[42]

Through editorials as well as through the appeals it

printed from its committees in Europe, the Herald continued
to stress the critical need.   A letter from Poland in the fall
of 1916 thus pleaded "with all urgency" for more funds to
relieve "very great" distress.   The editor reinforced such
communications, writing a week later that the spread of hostilities necessitated "redoubled vigor": "widows and orphans,
desolated homes, sickness, exile, hunger, cold, unspeakable
misery and death to all who have no helper. ...   Can we refuse
to give all we can spare ... in such a cause as this?"[43]
The Herald reduced the immense need to concrete and man-
ageable terms, informing its readers that $3 would support
one person for a full month.   It assured them, moreover,
of the dedication and efficiency of its agents.   The committee
in Austria, it pointed out, had handled more than $14,500
with an administrative expense of only $79.80.   And a re-
port late in the war noted that even after the fall of Poland,
the committee there managed to return remaining funds
safely to New York for use elsewhere.[44]

Reader response, while not maintaining the early rate,
did continue throughout the war.   The fund, supported by so
many small donations that the Herald had difficulty keeping
current in its acknowledgements, rose progressively from
$100,000 late in 1914 to $280,000 in April, 1917, and
$350,000 by May, 1918.[45]   The magazine called for Chris-
tian sympathy, but also urged its readers to organize monthly-
offering clubs to assure systematic giving.   By March, 1917,
the fund had nearly 300 club members pledging a total of
more than $400 in contributions each month.[46]

As the war dragged on, food shortages mounted in
Europe.   Early in the conflict the Herald expressed its fear
that Europe faced the worst famine in human history, and it
warned of crisis conditions in announcing its initial aid for
Belgium.   An editorial in April, 1916, cited efforts to insure
a milk supply for German and Austrian babies.   A few months
later a lead article described the daily mass feeding of
250,000 Berliners.   American orphans sacrificed their own
meals to "Feed the Hungry," readers learned.[47]   By 1918
attention centered even more fully on the food crisis in numerous articles and editorials.   The entire world hungered,
the Herald told its readers, and the United States must and
would supply out of her abundance.[48]

The era thus ended for the Christian Herald as it had
begun.   To this point at least, the journal continued to combine a conservative and revivalistic religion with active concern for other human needs.[49]

The Salvation Army: War Service and Postwar Popularity

The Salvation Army from the beginning confronted readers of the War Cry with the human tragedies the war brought, and with the Army's developing response. [50] "Pity all you like," Commander Evangeline Booth charged her readers in October, 1914, "but for God's sake give." Army social workers were already on the job, she wrote, in seven European military camps. They had supplied 10,000 pairs of socks to Swiss soldiers, given soup and shelter for the destitute in France, and furnished meals for hungry families in Holland. English corps early began providing for Belgian refugees, and sent Salvationist ambulances with drivers to the Western front. [51]

In the fall of 1914 American Salvationists began a major effort to collect used linen for military hospitals in response to what the War Cry called the worst crisis of supplies in the history of hospitals. The linen was sterilized under medical supervision in New York City, then packaged and shipped overseas. [52] Linking the campaign closely to Commander Evangeline Booth and emphasizing the urgent need, [53] the Army had on hand by early January material for more than a million bandages, far beyond what available officers could process. [54] It retreated, therefore, from its earlier pledge that there would be "absolutely no paid labor," [55] by hiring several hundred needy women and girls to assist its own personnel. [56]

War philanthropy, which did not occupy so large a place in the War Cry during 1916, [57] returned upon American entry into the conflict, centering once again on the presence of Salvation Army units among the troops. Commander Evangeline Booth wired President Wilson on April 2, 1917, immediately after his war message to Congress, offering her organization's assistance in any humanitarian work. [58] Charging her officers to prepare for a major effort, she renewed her offer to the President in a lengthy communication ten days later. She then reported the kinds of aid 30,000 Salvationists from Great Britain were already giving at the front, and proposed similar assistance from her own forces. They could provide ambulances and drivers, facilities for food and rest, and many other services for the soldiers, she said. On the home front her officers could make garments and assist in other ways. Secretary of War Baker responded with the President's "deep appreciation" and promised to contact Miss Booth as plans matured. [59]

Meanwhile Salvationists began implementing her promise of varied and energetic aid by calling for a half-million men and women to join their War Service League, "pledged to do all that can possibly be done to mitigate war's horror and minister comfort to the needy." The entrance fee of 50 cents would provide the nucleus of a large fund for war relief. The Army announced its first chaplain in early August, and Miss Booth commissioned the initial group to sail for France later that month. Selected for their knowledge, devotion, and loyalty, they were to bring comfort and encouragement to the troops, and to "live out salvation."[60]

By the time that first American party sailed, the Salvation Army was already hosting 300,000 soldiers and sailors weekly in more than 400 facilities in France and Britain.[61] Within two months American Salvationists opened seven "huts" of their own, and undertook a drive for a million dollars to erect scores of others. Probably the most important factor in the success of that drive, which dwarfed any previous Army campaign for funds in the United States, was the enthusiastic endorsement volunteered by "Pershing's Men," a group of sixty soldiers back from France to support the national Liberty Loan Drive. Their leader, Lt. J. J. Kassouf, asserted that New Yorkers would oversubscribe "ten times and more" if they "actually knew of the work" the Army was doing for American servicemen. It was, he said, "the most practical, gratifying, sensible, and 'close-up' service given to the men in France"; by the next Army fund drive, he predicted, news from the soldiers would carry it over any goal. In mid-June Commander Booth announced that the War Fund Drive had raised $2,370,000, with $324,000 of that from New York alone.[62]

With these resources, American Salvationists maintained a varied program at the front and in the camps, which by mid-1919 included more than 80 facilities, as well as thousands of women in the United States knitting for the military. Ambulance service was one of the earliest projects, with British officers working in that capacity from the beginning of the war. Evangeline Booth reported the formation of an American unit within the Red Cross during the spring of 1917. When General Bramwell Booth announced a contribution of $10,000 and twenty additional drivers a few months later, Sir Arthur Stanley, chairman of the British Red Cross, thanked him for that "most welcome news," and assured him that wherever Salvation Army officers were helping, he heard only good reports about their work. "Sir Ernest Clarke tells me," Stanley continued, "that your ambulance sections in France are quite the best of any in our service, and the more Salvation Army men you can send him, the better he will be pleased."[63]

As the special war correspondent of the Baltimore Journal noted in the summer of 1918, a prominent feature of Salvationist war service was its presence at or very near the front. One Salvation Army officer assured readers of the War Cry that their workers were holding up well despite the pressure of front-line service. James Hopper, war correspondent for Collier's magazine, reported that even the explosion of shells nearby did not disturb the young women in charge of a hut he visited. Similarly, Margaret Sangster wrote in the Christian Herald that Salvationists continued to bring food to the men despite the fact that their cook wagons were under fire.[64]

Doughnuts and pies, the subjects of numerous illustrations and poems in the War Cry,[65] were an important part of the Army's program. One Salvationist claimed that where he had been "the boys never cease talking about" the baked goods. Hopper of Collier's told of one young officer and her two helpers making fifty pies and 2000 doughnuts in a few hours, and a cable from France in October, 1918, reported officers serving 8000 doughnuts at the "extreme front" in one day. Accustomed to subsistence living themselves, and to dispensing food at prices the very poor could afford, Salvationists also provided other supplies to the soldiers for nominal charges. One of "Pershing's Men" stated that he could buy a "certain popular biscuit" from the Salvation Army for less than in New York, "and many times cheaper than any other organization will let us have it for over there." Another reported that the Salvation Army would serve men whether or not they could pay.[66]

Salvationists also wrote letters, furnished various supplies, made personal loans, sewed, and gave their time and friendship in other ways. For these many tasks and the spirit in which they were performed, Agnes Palmer used the term "mothering." The War Cry did repeatedly emphasize that its officers wished to bring as much of "home" to the soldiers as they could. Evangeline Booth wrote that the men must have bright spots, comfort, a sense of care. Hopper of Collier's, somewhat skeptical when "everyone" from all ranks went "out of his way" to praise the Salvation Army, wrote after his first visit that he could understand their enthusiasm. He was impressed with both the concern and the competence one officer and her two helpers showed. With limited facilities they turned out huge quantities of food near the front, earning, Hopper said, the obvious adoration of the men they served. "God help" anyone who would affront them, one serviceman wrote, while a returning Salvationist affirmed such wide regard for the women officers that he had not heard of a single disrespectful word to any of them. [67]

That the Salvation Army carefully screened its volunteers despite the pressing need, [68] helps explain this enthusiasm. Palmer's review of the early twentieth century asserted that Miss Booth hand-picked her personnel in the belief that it was "better to fall short in quantity than quality." In November, 1917, the editor of the War Cry noted the urgent need, but emphasized that only the most devoted persons were acceptable. Two months later the Commander called for willing, capable, and strong men and for "women of irreproachable character and ... reputation, free from romantic inclination and emotional weaknesses, and unencumbered by dependent relatives."[69]

Observers at the front confirmed the presence of these characteristics in Salvation Army personnel. Ball of the Baltimore Journal wrote of their "devotion to service"; one of "Pershing's Men" affirmed that Salvationists would "work themselves to the bone" for the soldiers; nothing, another person said after being at the front, would get any of them away from their posts. And that devotion was to the common soldier. As one worker remarked, officers in the armed forces had to line up with their men, since the Salvation Army had made it understood that it would show no preference. [70] In their work, as one soldier observed, Salvationists served the men "with a gusto and whole-heartedness that captures us all." Similarly, a Salvation Army officer noted that the almost staggering need, rather than causing despair, had "infused a great energy" in his comrades. [71]

One military officer from the front predicted during a Salvation Army fund drive in the spring of 1918 that when a little more time passed reports from overseas would suffice to oversubscribe any such drive. That spring 1918 effort for $1 million was itself exceeded by more than 100 per cent, [72] contributing to the Army's postwar decision to unify its fundraising efforts in one large annual campaign. Early in 1919,

therefore, the Army launched the Home Service Fund drive
to raise $13 million, a goal exceeded with apparent ease.
The most important factor in that success was no doubt the
groundswell of goodwill brought by the Army's service during
the war. As the editor of the War Cry noted in support of
the fund, "To countless Americans this organization ... was
practically unknown until our doughboys began to sing its
praises." Colorado, whose gubernatorial endorsement of the
Home Service Fund drive included prominent mention of Salvationist war service, attained 80 per cent of its $150,000
goal with the campaign barely underway. Numerous other
areas recorded similar success. [73]

Another indication of the Salvation Army's new popularity was the rapidly increasing circulation of the War Cry.
That magazine had expanded during its first fifteen years in
the United States to a figure of nearly 100,000 by the completion of Ballington Booth's command early in 1896. [74] The
War Cry lapsed some, however, in the confusion and temporary decline surrounding his resignation and had not again
reached that mark in regular circulation. Despite the Army's
energetic efforts, it settled near 70,000 until 1918. [75] But
following the war circulation began to rise steadily, reaching
130,000 by early autumn, 1919, and more than 150,000 by
the end of that year. The issue for May 29, 1920, reported
200,000 copies, and for Independence Day the War Cry ex-
ceeded that by 30,000, apparently with no special effort.
The total remained near 200,000 through the remainder of
1920, though an inflation-forced price boost in October contributed to a decrease in circulation later in the year. [76]

In an article in the New York American in February,
1919, Commander Evangeline Booth emphatically denied that
the Salvation Army's surge in popularity was the result of
new and more effective methods. On the contrary, she asserted, the war had simply focused attention on a veteran
organization employing methods and a spirit forged in sixty
years of helping the most needy persons in equally difficult
circumstances. The difference was that Salvationists had
now assisted not the anonymous and voiceless "submerged
tenth," but men from the mainstream of American life. For
the first time thousands of such families had been aided by
the Army and their response was not unlike that which
thousands of down-and-outs had long given. [77]

XV

CRITICS OF THE SOCIAL ORDER

In 1900, a decade after Catherine Booth's death, the reform journalist William T. Stead wrote a biography of his friend containing a chapter entitled simply "Socialist." A close friend of Mrs. Booth during her last years, though not a member of the Army, Stead declared that he knew her as "a Socialist, and something more"--one who was "in complete revolt against the existing order." Her "radical antagonism" to that order predisposed her, he said, "to regard with sympathy all schemes for remodelling society in accordance with humanitarian ideas." She regularly read the Standard, published by the well-known American reformer, Henry George, Stead had written in 1890, and was more intensely interested in the central issues George raised than any politician he had known.[1]

Though isolated comments have recognized the social and economic progressivism of many evangelistic welfare workers, scholarly opinion has probably more generally associated them with the "popular evangelists" whom Henry F. May describes simply as collectively a "stumbling block to social Christianity"; their emotional preaching, emphasis on individual conversion, and isolation from contemporary social thought, he argues, made them irrelevant.[2] True as that judgment may have been for many evangelists, Catherine Booth cannot be thus dismissed. Nor can many others. Mrs. Booth's importance in shaping the Salvation Army's social and religious outlook, and the almost unrivalled place in Army affections she continued to hold decades after her death, makes it not surprising that numerous Salvationists and others held similar views. "We must have justice--more justice," the New York Tribune quoted Ballington Booth, commander of the American Salvation Army forces, as saying. "To right the social wrong by charity," he had said, "is like bailing

the ocean with a thimble.... We must readjust our social
machinery so that the producers of wealth become also owners
of wealth...." The editor of the War Cry, in a spirit mind-
ful of the Booths, complained that laws giving "unbounded
power to the wicked and the strong to do evil and oppress
the weak are not liberty...." He later asserted that the un-
equal and unjust distribution of wealth" was chief among many
American social evils. Because of such statements he feared
"further" accusation "of having an abnormal amount of sympathy with our inflammatory neighbors the anarchists." Similarly taking issue with the establishment, the Christian Herald
condemned as "an inhuman principle" the laissez-faire idea
firmly held by "many employers" that they had a right to buy
labor, like other commodities, "in the cheapest market" that
competition would allow. Consistent with that emphasis, the
Herald in later years not only stressed the duties as against
the rights of property, but held that human rights were far
more important than property rights.[3]

Emphases like that indicate that what Stead termed
Catherine Booth's "radical antagonism to the existing order"
marked others in leadership positions within the gospel wel-
fare movement as well. That such statements did, in fact,
reflect the larger stance of the movement is evident from
William Booth's well-known In Darkest England and the Way
Out (1890), the Salvation Army's most significant social document. Embodying his wife's strong influence and written with
Stead's literary help, In Darkest England grew directly out of
the decades of first-hand experience in urban slums that
Booth and his organization had already had.[4] Although the
General's primary purpose was to awaken his countrymen to
the desperate plight of the very poor and to the support of
his program of immediate aid, his book contains numerous
statements that place him and his officers solidly on the side
of the dispossessed and in judgment upon the larger society
and its structures. Among such emphases were his sharp
criticism of industry and other established institutions, his
endorsement of reformers and their programs, his recognition of the social causes of poverty, his stress on the worth
and ability of the most destitute and outcast persons, and his
proposals for the creation of new programs and institutions
which if carried through on the scale he urged would effectively alter society's structures for the benefit of the lower
classes. Apart from these specific elements, moreover, the
larger tone of the book conveys not only the urgency Booth
felt, but also his close identification with the poor against
an oppressive society.[5]

Booth's identification with the lower classes showed itself in an attitude that was readily critical toward other classes and institutions. He thus repeatedly rebuked churches that, with the rest of a prosperous society, were "too busy or too idle, too indifferent or too selfish," to heed the continuing cry of the oppressed multitudes. "What a satire," he wrote, what "a ghastly mockery," to call churches Christian when they made little or no effort to help. [6] Challenging his fellow churchmen to "proclaim a Temporal Salvation ... full, free, and universal," he declared that men were not worthy of the name Christian until they had opened a door that included the most outcast of the poor. The Church must join in helping them out of their "present social miseries," or it would stand rejected both by the poor and by the God it falsely claimed to serve. [7]

As is evident, Booth directed these strictures at the larger prosperous "Christian" society as well as at the churches. It was that society which was "too indifferent or too selfish" to listen or to help the poor. Affluent enough to down rum in appalling quantities, England was unwilling even to provide adequate shelter for desperate persons whose chief offense was their inability to find the employment for which they pleaded. Commenting on society's intolerance toward any demonstrations by the starving unemployed, Booth declared for a day in which they, along with the "half-starved" workers, should proceed in all of their raggedness "through the main thoroughfares, past the massive houses and princely palaces of luxurious London." [8] Repeatedly noting the niggardliness of the wealthy toward the poor, he concluded in In Darkest England, placing the responsibility for social salvation squarely upon their shoulders: "If you give what you have the work will be done," Booth wrote. "If it is not done, ... the consequences will lie" at your door. [9]

Booth's critique found counterparts in the statements of other rescue leaders, who similarly denounced wealthy persons who were insensitive to injustice and poverty. [10] Where those denunciations touched on "tainted money," it is true, their decision concerning its use did not always parallel Washington Gladden's rejection of Rockefeller gifts; to use such money for worthy purposes could be acceptable. [11] But no matter how the rich attained their wealth, they had no right to lavish it on themselves when other persons were suffering in poverty. The Christian Herald thus protested extravagant social dinners on the basis of "common humanity," holding that to spend $10,000 on a meal for a few score guests showed "indifference to suffering worthy only of an animal."[12]

Contrasting sharply with their often caustic treatment of established classes was the approval Salvationists and other rescue leaders showed toward social reformers. William Booth, like his wife, displayed both knowledge and approval of the efforts of reformers. Declaring his intense sympathy for all such efforts, the General wrote that the evils reformers challenged were so formidable that they might well be correctable only by radical change, only by reform that turned everything "upside down."[13] Of a kind, then, with his wife's "complete revolt against the existing order," Booth's position was paralleled, as we have indicated, across the literature of the rescue movement. In addition, articles and briefer statements by influential reformers frequently appeared in rescue journals and generally found friendly reception. Henry George professed himself "immensely pleased" with William Booth's "Darkest England" proposals, and on other occasions also supported the Army. Eugene Debs, the prominent American Socialist, was likewise a friend of Salvationists. The Volunteers' Gazette cited Florence Kelley at length, while Jacob Riis, whose life story the Christian Herald featured in 1903, contributed articles to that journal and was a guest speaker at its summer children's home.[14] Charles M. Sheldon, the social gospel preacher and author of the well-known novel, In His Steps, published many sermons and stories in the Herald, and became its editor for a brief period after the First World War.[15] In 1913 the Herald supported Scott Nearing during the controversy that resulted in his ouster from the University of Pennsylvania on accusations of social and economic radicalism. The following year the editor cited Nearing in support of the Herald's call for improved conditions for coal miners.[16]

That kind of interest prompted gospel welfare groups to support reform across a wide range of issues and institutions, including legal and financial matters, industrial conditions, and consumer protection. On the latter front, numerous articles kept Christian Herald readers informed of abuses and abreast of protest on behalf of the American public. An early antagonist of food adulteration and unfit meat, the Herald followed closely the controversy surrounding Harvey Wiley, the pioneer champion of pure food laws in the Department of Agriculture.[17] During the "coal famine" of 1902-1903, the editor blamed the "outrageous" human suffering on the "tactics" of operators and dealers. He supported the widespread household boycott of meat and other foodstuffs in the winter of 1910, calling for "some radical reform" to protect the public from "inordinantly high prices."[18]

While registering some skepticism about the effectiveness of government as an instrument of social righteousness,[19] William Booth and other leaders generally appeared to favor governmental participation in social and economic life for humane purposes. Booth reacted intensely against the fiercely competitive extreme of nineteenth-century individualism[20] and, in contrast, suggested intervention at various points in his discussion of urban social woes.[21] Others called for legislation to protect the public from impure or overpriced food.[22] The Christian Herald strongly favored direct taxes to finance American participation in the World War, partly as a means to prevent excess profits.[23] On other occasions it endorsed regulation of the trusts, praised the Interstate Commerce Commission for blocking railroad rate increases, and supported legislation to outlaw the seven-day work week, protect children in industry, compensate injured workmen, and aid farmers through mortgage and price supports.[24] Several articles in the War Cry and the Herald indicated that compulsory jurisdiction ought to replace the "barbaric" method of strikes and lockouts.[25]

The plight of the laboring class, and the church's responsibility for it, constituted one of the central foci of the social problem for William Booth and his In Darkest England. While his solution especially sought to deal with the problems of the unemployed, the allied problem of oppressive conditions for the working poor also evoked his most intense reaction. Salvationists were, Booth wrote, pledged to a "war to the death" against every form of the "sweatshop." "What liberty is there," he asked, "for the tailors who have to sew for sixteen to twenty hours a day, in a pest-hole, in order to earn ten shillings a week?" In his opinion there could be "no discipline so brutal ... no slavery so relentless" as that.[26]

In the judgment of Booth and other rescue leaders the church was heavily implicated in the responsibility for the plight of the working class as well as for their rescue.[27] "One of the most grievous faults of the church," the editor of the Christian Herald wrote in 1916, was that she had "so often misunderstood and neglected and alienated the laborers," allowing society to "oppress and wrong" them.[28] Catherine

Booth illustrated a similar combination of sympathy for labor
and criticism of the churches in her account of a gentleman
telling her about "the great amount of love there is for the
Saviour" in the churches. "Yes, for their idealistic Saviour,"
she retorted. "But suppose Jesus was to come to your chapel
as He went about Palestine, with a carpenter's coat on, or
as He sat upon the well, all over perspiration and dust with
travel, where would your chapel steward put him to sit?"[29]

During decades of industrial conflict, rescue workers'
attitudes thus stood in sharp contrast to the hostility many
Protestant churchmen expressed toward labor.[30] William
Booth's reaction to the harsh treatment generally characteristic of the establishment's reaction, "in the name of law and
order," to peaceful demonstrations by the poor, was that the
destitute and oppressed indeed ought to march! Their march,
he indicated, ought to point up the contrast between their
poverty and the extravagant luxury of the wealthier classes.[31]
With similar spirit the Christian Herald responded to the railroad strike in New York City during the turbulent spring of
1886 by scoring the many employers who were operating on
the "inhuman principle" that they had the right to buy labor
in the cheapest market that competition could afford. A week
later the issue of May 6 declared workmen "ripe for a re-
bellion. They have been oppressed and cheated out of their
earnings,"[32] the Herald affirmed. And William Booth, while
proposing to solve the social problems by peaceful means,
reinforced his repeated statements about the terrible plight
of the poor with the acknowledgment that perhaps nothing
would be "put permanently right until everything has been
turned upside down," until "radical change" had been
achieved.[33]

As William Booth's protest against "sweatshops" indicated, rescue workers criticized hours, wages, and other
aspects of working conditions. The editor of the Christian
Herald argued for better pay and working conditions for
miners, and denounced the seven-day work week in the steel
industry. The War Cry supported a statement by President
Wilson calling for the humanizing of industry through legislation providing reduced hours, the right to organize unions,
and protection against industrial accidents. On the latter
question, an editorial in the Herald late in 1913 observed
that the United States remained "far behind" Europe in compensation for injured employees. The recent amendment to
the New York State Constitution would, he hoped, help set a
higher standard; it made possible, he wrote, what had long

been imperative, "the enactment of a compulsory workmen's compensation law."[34]

Abuses in child labor evoked most intense protests.[35] A series of articles in the Christian Herald during 1902 gave an "inside" picture of the life of coal miners and other laborers, concentrating on children.[36] Those revelations had been instrumental, the editor thought, in producing a wide demand for legislation. Noting the child labor law New York enacted in October, 1903, he urged that other states should follow that legislature's lead to end "this national reproach." In 1916, on the eve of passage of the first national law limiting and regulating child labor, the editor asked indignantly "just what kind of a man" would obstruct such legislation. Upon its passage a few weeks later he called the law, which he judged had originated in the Herald's earlier exposures, a "splendid victory for humanity," one which almost equalled the freeing of the slaves. When in 1918 the courts declared the bill unconstitutional, the editor urged its reworking for another attempt.[37]

While the Salvation Army's own industrial establishments resulted in part from the hard necessities of providing work for the poor, they were also intended to demonstrate what ought to be. Booth judged that the Army's small bookbinding "factory," where eighteen women were supporting themselves on wages almost double the norm for that kind of work, was based on principles that could be followed in a wide variety of other endeavors.[38] The Army also had in operation an "industrial factory" employing ninety men at the time of Booth's announcement of the "Darkest England" plan in 1890. That factory, which like other Army industrial establishments tried to fill the time before permanent employment was secured elsewhere, featured an eight-hour day in return for food, shelter, and wages of up to five shillings each week. The Army's general complaint against industrial evils was compounded in the matchmaking industry by the use of phosphorus, an element that caused a cancerous condition of the facial bones known as "matchmaker's leprosy." In 1891 Salvationists opened what the War Cry claimed was the first factory in the world making only safety matches, and using no phosphorus.[39]

In this and other Salvation Army efforts, Booth repeatedly expressed his concern that he do nothing that would jeopardize the larger well-being of labor. "While assisting one class of the community," he wrote, "... we must not

thereby endanger ... those who with difficulty are keeping on
their feet."[40] Aware that the leadership of the trade unions
had the "liveliest feelings" of uneasiness lest cheap labor and
low-priced goods undercut their position, Booth took special
care to demonstrate that his proposals would benefit rather
than damage their situation. "The most experienced Trades
Unionists," he affirmed, would be the first to admit that any
plan dealing adequately with the problem of unemployment
would be "most beneficial" to labor. Booth reinforced that
general contention with a variety of specific arguments, including the pricing of Army-produced goods, the increased
market for labor's products among the people rescued, and
the effect of the Army's colonization projects at home and
overseas on an overstocked labor market.[41] Consistent with
the urgent note of moral obligation in his writing, however,
Booth added that he did not see "how the skilled worker
could leave his brothers to rot in their present wretchedness" even if their rescue "might involve the sharing of a
portion of his wages."[42]

These kinds of programs and statements lend credence
to the thankfulness rescue workers expressed about improvements in the condition of the working classes,[43] and help to
explain the support they received from organized labor. In
mid-1891 the "Pacific Coast Laborers' Union No. 1" unanimously endorsed the Army's new rescue home for girls.
Praising the organization's general friendliness to labor and
the poor, the letter urged all unions to extend to it "their
moral and financial aid." A few years later a Labor Day
issue of the War Cry included notes of commendation from
the secretary of the United Mineworkers of America, as well
as from the Socialist leader, Eugene Debs. "In its main
purposes," Debs wrote, the Army "has my unqualified approval and my hearty sympathy." Although he hoped the
necessity for its work would not always exist, it was fortunate, he added, that while conditions were bad for the poor,
the Salvation Army was there with its "tenderness, sympathy,
and unceasing patience."[44]

"Society," Booth declared in many different ways in
his discussion of England's submerged masses, had "greased
the slope" down which the poor slid; society must, therefore, "seriously take in hand their salvation." Indeed, Salvationist support for labor, as well as its general identification with the dispossessed, resulted in considerable part
from this recognition of the social causes of poverty and its
attendant ills. Whether for the working poor, the unemployed,

the drunkard, the prostitute, or the criminal, forces were
at work that inexorably dragged them down. Those forces
"shattered and disorganized" the poor, Booth wrote, and
created a "general wreck" from which those at society's
lower levels had no possibility of escape. He and his officers launched their social program to create an avenue of
escape. [45]

This is not to say that Booth and other rescue leaders
did not recognize personal causes behing the plight of the
poor. Booth wrote, in fact, that "the first essential" for
success was, in many instances, to change the individual.
"No change in circumstances, no revolution in social conditions," he added, could possible "transform the nature of
man."[46] There was, Booth said, "an immense lack of
common sense and of vital energy on the part of multitudes";
his was in part, therefore, a war against ignorance. But,
he added, how could one scorn the poor judgment of the disadvantaged when so little sense was shown by the prosperous
classes who had so many advantages. "Placed in ... similar
circumstances," Booth asked, "how many of us would have
turned out better...?"[47] Whatever the need for personal
change, therefore, no real amelioration could take place
without substantial change ín the attitudes and institutions of
an oppressive society.

Booth's strong conviction that the social causes of
poverty were the determining factor in the plight of the poor
expressed itself in many ways in his writings. That conviction appeared in his strictures upon an industrial system that
offered low wages, long hours, and the constant threat of
unemployment that could drop its victims into the quagmires
of destitution, crime, or alcoholism. [48] It appeared also in
the recognition that business built its prosperity out of the
labor of the poor and that society's financial and legal institutions protected the prosperous classes while compounding
the problems of the needy. [49] And the same society which
had thus deprived the poor of their footing then placed the
fallen in charitable and penal institutions, which added still
further injury. The poor law treated its beneficiaries like
criminals and pauperized them, frequently landing them in
prisons where conditions were, Booth declared, outrageous.
He called for thorough-going prison reform, particularly
necessary since, in his judgment, society placed pressures
upon ex-convicts that virtually forced them back into crime. [50]

"At present," Booth wrote, in words that highlighted

his goals in the "Darkest England" programs as well as his emphasis on the social causes of poverty, society was organized "far too much on the principle of giving to him who hath..., and taking away from him who hath not...." It is not surprising, therefore, that the General proposed programs and institutions that would help to correct at least some of the environmental causes of poverty. The broadly social nature of the solutions he proposed has been partially obscured by the fact that they have been incorrectly equated with the Army's emergency care for the most destitute, and therefore dismissed as merely ameliorative. The fact is, however, that whether in the case of the shelters that provided the bare essentials of life for the outcast, or in the case of the more obviously corrective programs ranging through the legal and financial aid that even the relatively sturdy poor desperately needed, all did form part of a large attempt to secure a practical and permanent solution to the problem of urban poverty. [51]

That Booth did not propose an even more ambitious restructuring was due in considerable part to the immediate urgency of the needs he faced. "What," he asked proponents of what he judged to be "Utopian" schemes, "is to be done with John Jones," unemployed, penniless, and hunting in vain for work, who appeared nightly at the Army's shelters by the multiplied hundreds? "In the good time coming," Booth conceded with some sarcasm, whether in the religious or the socialist kingdoms, there might be no more John Joneses. But they were here now in appalling numbers, and their desperate and socially inflicted needs must be met. On the living John Joneses Booth chose to concentrate his organization's main efforts. [52]

If a utopianism offering no promise of immediate practical assistance was one of the dangers that threatened contemporary efforts to help the poor, the other was a philanthropy that was largely ameliorative. Booth intended Salvationist programs to be permanent and preventive as well as practical. To accomplish that goal the "Darkest England" plan aimed at the great mass of the most destitute, working within principles, or "laws," Booth thought to be essential for success. The principles he outlined included that the efforts deal with both personal and environmental solutions, and that they be large-scale, permanent, "immediately practicable," and without harmful effects on either the direct beneficiaries or on other segments of society, including labor in particular. [53] While Booth repeatedly stressed the immense difficulties of his task and the relatively limited, "Cab Horse" level of success that could be expected, even that level would make a major difference in the condition of the oppressed masses. [54]

Because the "Darkest England" program aimed thus at the most destitute of the poor--those who, as Booth put it, had "no helper"--the provision of such simple necessities of life as food and shelter was basic to it. Because he also aimed at permanent solutions, however, restorative services such as employment bureaus and "industrial homes" played an important role. The former would help them find the jobs that the General and his officers considered essential to the relief of poverty. The latter not only gave them food, shelter, and other immediately urgent assistance, but also employed them temporarily, often providing training in some useful skill. [55]

The restorative measures Booth planned for the unemployed and outcast persons his officers rescued also served a preventive social function for others. Since unemployment often produced homelessness, family disintegration, and alcoholism, employment exchanges and Salvationist factories provided urgently needed temporary help for the laborers. Other proposed institutions and programs aimed similarly at a more friendly environment for the working poor. Rejecting "the vast, unsightly piles of barrack-like buildings," as well as lodging houses and tenement apartments, as being unsatisfactory solutions "of the burning question of the housing of the poor," Booth urged the provision of model surburban villages with "decent, healthy, pleasant homes."[56] His "Household Salvage Brigade" were to function not only for the collection of discarded materials, but also as "a universal Corps of Commissionaries, created for the service of the public and in the interests of the poor." Each an "Ubiquitous Servant of All," its members would carry messages and see to the provision of all sorts of needed services for the poor. [57] Booth hoped his agricultural colonies would lead the way in providing food of high quality for the poor, in contrast to the inferior fare they so often endured. [58] Low-cost excursion trips to the seaside promised to enable multitudes of slum-dwellers to enjoy at least some of the pleasures that otherwise only the prosperous could afford. [59] Thousands of Salvationist officers in most of the world's major cities would, meanwhile, assist the Army's "Inquiry Bureau" in its searches for missing persons, thus giving the poor a form of aid available nowhere else. [60]

Among the most significant of Booth's proposals for aiding the destitute were the legal and financial aid programs he suggested in the form of a "Poor Man's Bank" and a "Poor Man's Lawyer." Salvationists wished the needy to enjoy the considerable advantages the prosperous classes gained from the credit system, without the exorbitant rates and ruthless treatment they suffered at the hands of the loan agencies currently operating in the slums.[61] The indignation Booth expressed about the financial oppression poor people endured was equalled in his deploring the fact that no agency in all of London offered the lower classes legal assistance. He proposed the establishment of a "Court of Counsel or Appeal" to which anyone in need of legal aid could come. Without it, he felt, many innocent persons would be sentenced and imprisoned simply because they could not afford legal counsel. Booth thought this program also would play a preventive role. "The [potential oppressor's] knowledge that the oppressed poor have in us a friend able to speak for them," he affirmed, "will often prevent the injustice" that would otherwise occur.[62]

An important result of the recognition of the social causes of poverty is a changed attitude toward the destitute. If the causes of poverty are social rather than personal, the grounds for blaming the poor are removed. Moreover, because prejudiced attitudes contribute significantly to injustice, their reshaping is probably as important to social reform as is the reshaping of unjust social and economic structures. And at this essential point of attitude, gospel rescue workers were most notable, not only in accepting the dispossessed with compassion and optimism, but in energetically proclaiming their worth to all who would hear.[63]

Partly as a result of the extensive first-hand experience that made gospel welfare workers understand clearly the social causes of poverty and crime, and partly because concern for others was at the heart of their religious experience and teaching, rescue groups accepted the destitute as worthy and capable persons. Ranging from the simple recognition of the common humanity and brotherhood of all to the assertion that "some of the brightest" and most capable people in the land were among the unemployed,[64] Booth repeatedly affirmed the worth of the poor. Their "infinite potentiality" was apparent from the fact that, as he said, some of his "best officers" had come from their ranks. The unemployed persons working in Army "factories," moreover, validated that high estimate by their willing and competent performance.[65] In such affirmations, as well as in his criticism of the upper classes, his support of organized labor, and his attention to the social causes of poverty, Booth's high estimate of the dispossessed was persistently evident. That kind of acceptance was one of the moral and social hallmarks of the evangelistic welfare movement. [66]

This perspective permeated every facet of their rescue programs, no matter how wretched or troublesome the beneficiaries. Prostitutes, ex-convicts, and drunkards were all excused on the basis of the economic, social, and personal pressures of their environment. All of them deserved acceptance and a second chance, rescue workers asserted; given that, the overwhelming majority would become happy and useful citizens. Nor should the poor be blamed or punished for their poverty. Assistance ought to be gracious and prompt, providing much-needed help without offense or pauperization. Rescue personnel generally agreed with William Booth that the large majority of the unemployed would work willingly and capably if given the chance; it was to provide that chance that they established employment bureaus, industrial training institutions, and farm colonies. Moreover, since the poor needed more than the barest physical assistance, rescue agencies provided holiday meals and gifts as well as picnic and camping outings. And they envisioned their evangelism as bringing inner as well as formal religious salvation, peace and joy as well as rescue from the curse of future punishment. [67]

The "brotherhood" to which William Booth frequently alluded[68] and which was a concept implicit in much evangelistic welfare literature, embraced all mankind. Largely the result of a deep-rooted, inward concern for people, the breadth of their sympathies placed them in sharp contrast with most of their contemporaries, progressives as well as conservatives. Then as now, such factors as race, sex, and ethnic origin compounded the plight of the lower classes. Rescue workers accepted black persons and the foreign-born with the same kind of warmth with which they greeted others of the very poor. Opposing restrictive immigration laws, they apparently received the "new" immigrant as they had the "old." In a day when progressives as well as other national leaders paid little attention to the plight of blacks, the Salvation Army and kindred organizations defended them and welcomed them into their institutions and programs for assistance or as fellow workers. Finally, these groups opened their highest offices to women, using them to preach and administer in numbers and with a freedom far in advance of most of their clerical and secular contemporaries. For them there did seem to be little distinction of persons, whether male or female, slave or free, rich or poor. [69]

Far from being a hindrance to social Christianity, then, the revivalistic and holiness faith of these people produced extensive social programs and close identification with the needy. Entering the slums in pursuit of the evangelism that remained their chief concern, they gained there an almost unparalleled knowledge of the conditions in which the poor had to live. Encountering that kind of need, they responded with energy and with growing sympathy and indignation. The extensive first-hand experience of rescue workers in the slums taught them both the worth of the poor and the heaviness of the environmental pressures that weighed upon them. It taught them also that society bulwarked the prosperous and oppressed the helpless. Awareness of such facts was not enough, however. Not everyone with first-hand knowledge of slum conditions responded to the victims with the acceptance and practical helpfulness of these workers. Their awareness was clarified and translated into action by their pervasive commitment to expressing "love" in practical, sacrificial, and helpful ways--a commitment which stemmed directly from their religious experience and teaching. Often that commitment was expressed in terms that revealed their debt to Methodism, at other times in a stress on the "brotherhood" that marked the teachings of the social gospel movement, but always in an experiential as well as a theoretical sense. And it was this central thrust in their teaching and experience that produced so consistent an identification with such a wide range of needy persons. For gospel welfare workers did not limit their concern and their aid to the industrially oppressed, but extended it to those who were dispossessed because of race, sex, drink, or other reasons. Other factors, including a knowledge of reformers and reform literature, also played a part. But the combination of extensive personal knowledge of the slums with a teaching and experience that centered on the Biblical meaning of love as practical helpfulness was primarily responsible for the philanthropy and the reform emphasis that marked the gospel welfare movement.

NOTES*

INTRODUCTION

1. Ernest Fremont Tittle, "Liberal Protestantism," Varieties of American Religion, ed. Charles S. Braden (New York, 1964, c1936), 52-53.

2. See, for example, the activities and institutions of the Woman's Christian Temperance Union (pp. 135-36, above), as well as those sponsored by Charles Cullis (p. 69, above) and Carrie Judd Montgomery (p. 70, above).

3. Timothy L. Smith, Revivalism and Social Reform in Mid-Nineteenth-Century America (New York, 1957).

4. See Carl F. H. Henry, The Uneasy Conscience of Modern Fundamentalism (Grand Rapids, Mich., 1947).

5. Charles Loring Brace, Gesta Christi; or, A History of Humane Progress Under Christianity (New York, 1887); Francis Herbert Stead, The Story of Social Christianity (London, 1924).

6. The large body of literature which has explored this question includes the following volumes: J. Wesley Bready, England: Before and After Wesley; The Evangelical Revival and Social Reform (London, 1938); L. E. Elliott-Binns, The Early Evangelicals: A Religious and Social Study (Greenwich, Conn., 1953); Earle E. Cairns, Saints and Society; The Social Impact of Eighteenth Century English Revivals and its Contemporary Relevance (Chicago, 1960); and, most recently, Anthony Armstrong, The Church of England, the Methodists and Society, 1700-1850 (London, 1973). Although these and other studies do not arrive at identical positions, the overall conclusion, in this writer's judgment, is that of a strong social concern and impact.

---

*The following abbreviations are used throughout:

AW	Alliance Weekly	TF	Triumphs of Faith
CH	Christian Herald	WC	War Cry
FC	Florence Crittenton Magazine	WC (L)	War Cry (London)
G	(Volunteers') Gazette	WWW	Word, Work and
LT	Living Truths		World

7. David O. Moberg, The Great Reversal; Evangelism Versus Social Concern (New York, 1972), 28.

8. See, for example, Bernard Sternsher, Consensus, Conflict, and American Historians (Bloomington, Ind., 1975), 1-2, 8-9, 14, 211, 369; John Higham, "The Historian As Moral Critic," The American Historical Review, April, 1962 (67:3), 609-16; and Edward C. Kirkland, "The Robber Barons Revisited," The American Historical Review, October, 1960 (66:1), 68-73.

9. See the standard early work by Charles H. Hopkins on the social gospel movement, The Rise of the Social Gospel in American Protestantism, 1865-1915 (New York, 1940), as well as the treatment of revivalists in Henry F. May, Protestant Churches and Industrial America (New York, 1963, c1949), 83, 190 (cf. 69-72), even though the latter book does note the absence of direct correlation between theology and social stance (80, 87, 230); for a continuing similar evaluation of evangelicals, see Donald R. White, "The New 'Old Time Religion'," Theological Markings; a UTS Journal, spring, 1973 (3:1), 35-42, and Robert S. Ellwood, One Way; The Jesus Movement and Its Meaning (Englewood Cliffs, N.J., 1973), 35-37.

10. James Dombrowski, The Early Days of Christian Socialism in America (New York, 1966, c1936), 18 (cf. 28, 30); Hopkins, Social Gospel, 171, 233, 323; May, Protestant Churches, 223, 235-36.

11. Washington Gladden, "What to do with the Workless Man," National Conference of Charities and Correction, Proceedings ... 1899, 141-42; for other examples of an emphasis on pauperizing, see earlier issues of the Proceedings, as 1878, 67-69, 117-23, 151-64, 1883, 144, 149-50, 1890, 43, and 1893, 269, 273-74, 276-77.

12. Jane Addams, "Social Settlements," National Conference of Charities and Correction, Proceedings ... 1897, 345.

13. E.g., Benjamin C. Marsh, "Notes of an Amateur Wayfarer," Charities, March 7, 1903, 224 (cf. Charities, August 1, 1903, 118-19, where Marsh concluded from his own experience that unemployed men could obtain work if they really wanted it); Editorial, War Cry, February 20, 1897 (803), 8; cf. War Cry, September 4, 1897 (831), 5.

14. Robert Bremner, From the Depths; The Discovery of Poverty in the United States (New York, 1956), 65-66.

15. For Booth-Tucker, see p. 101 above.

16. See the presidential address to the National Conference of Charities and Correction in 1897 by Alexander Johnson, editor of the Conference Proceedings from 1905 to 1912: Proceedings, 5, 7, 12;

see also Hopkins, Social Gospel, 171, 233, and Dombrowski, Christian Socialism, 28, 30.

17.   Edward T. Devine, "The Dominant Note of the Modern Philanthropy," Charities and the Commons, June 2, 1906, 344.

18.   See Chapter XV, above.

19.   Robert T. Handy, ed., The Social Gospel in America: Gladden, Ely, Rauschenbusch (New York, 1966), 354-55; Dores R. Sharpe, Walter Rauschenbusch (New York, 1942), 60, 79, and 59-79; Bremner, Poverty, 65-66, cf. 55-57.

20.   See pp. 30-34, above.

21.   See p. 32, above.

22.   Bremner, Poverty, 66, 69, 92-93.

23.   On pp. 38-44, above, is discussed the relationship of their teaching and experience to their social concern and action.

24.   See above, especially chapters 9-11.

I.   URBAN REVIVALISM, 1865-1920

1.   Important treatments of this period include: Robert Bremner, From the Depths; The Discovery of Poverty in the United States (New York, 1956); A. Abell, The Urban Impact on American Protestantism, 1865-1900 (London, 1962, c1943); C. H. Hopkins, The Rise of the Social Gospel in American Protestantism (New Haven, Conn., 1940); A. Abell, American Catholicism and Social Action: A Search for Social Justice, 1865-1950 (Notre Dame, Ind., 1960); Henry F. May, Protestant Churches and Industrial America (New York, 1963, c1949); from that period see, for example, Francis Greenwood Peabody, Jesus Christ and the Social Question (New York, 1900), and Walter Rauschenbusch, Christianity and the Social Crisis (New York, 1907).

2.   For a consideration of shifting historical interpretation, see Bernard Sternsher, Consensus, Conflict, and American Historians (Bloomington, Ind., 1975), 1, 2, 8, and John Higham, "The Historian as Moral Critic," The American Historical Review, April, 1962 (67:3), 609-16; for neglect of blacks, for example, during that era, see P. N. Williams, "The Social Gospel and Race Relations; A Case Study of a Social Movement," in Toward a Discipline of Social Ethics; Essays in Honor of Walter George Muelder.   Paul Deats, Jr., ed. (Boston, 1972), and David M. Reimers, White Protestantism and the Negro (New York, 1965), 53-54; cf. Herbert

Shapiro, "The Populists and the Negro; A Reconsideration," in
August Meier, ed., The Making of Black America (New York, 1969),
v. 2, 27-36.

3.   Sydney A. Ahlstrom, A Religious History of the American People (New Haven, Conn., 1972), 733, 765; for one significant
group that began during this era, see Stephen Gottschalk, The Emergence of Christian Science in American Religious Life (Berkeley,
Calif., 1973).

4.   See the accounts in George S. Railton, The Authoritative
Life of General William Booth (New York, 1912), 55-56; F. Booth-
Tucker, The Life of Catherine Booth (New York, 1892), I, 564,
538-40; and Charles Booth, Life and Labour of the People of London
(London, 1891).

5.   For Booth's early years, see his In Darkest England and
the Way Out (London, 1890), Preface; William Booth, "Principles of
Social Work," International Social Council Addresses, 1911 (London,
1912), 2; Harold Begbie, The Life of General William Booth (New
York, 1920), I, 70-104; Railton, William Booth, 16-24; Booth told
of his "miniature" Army in the WC, October 9, 1886 (262), 1; cf.
WC, May 11, 1889 (397), 6-7; for the period after 1852 see Booth-
Tucker, Catherine Booth, I, 456, 198, 223 (cf. William Booth's
account in WC, May 11, 1839 (397), 6-7); for Catherine Booth, see
Booth-Tucker, Catherine Booth, I, 412, 416-18, 564. This two-
volume biography (cover title: Memoirs of Catherine Booth), as
well as the biographies of William Booth by Railton and Begbie, reprinted letters, speeches, and other documents; for treatments of
Catherine Booth by eminent contemporaries, see William T. Stead,
Life of Mrs. Booth (New York, 1900), and F. W. Farrar, "The
Salvation Army," Harper's Magazine, May, 1891 (82:898); the ties
of the Booths with Methodism had been strong: WC, May 11, 1889
(397), 6.

6.   Partly reprinted in Booth-Tucker, Catherine Booth, I,
620-23; the Mission's name was, successively, East London Christian Revival Society, East London Christian Mission, and Christian
Mission: Ibid., 655-56, and Railton, William Booth, 67.

7.   Booth-Tucker, Catherine Booth, II, 81-82.   Cf. 107 for
the year 1875.

8.   F. Booth-Tucker, William Booth, the General of the
Salvation Army (New York, 1898), 26-28; Begbie, William Booth, I,
403-05; Booth-Tucker, Catherine Booth, II, 18-19, 172-80; Railton,
William Booth, 72-74; Bramwell Booth, Echoes and Memories (New
York, 1925), 43-48.

9.   See Booth-Tucker, Catherine Booth, II, 276-78 (Australia,
1880-81), 330 (France, 1881), 383 (India, Sweden, and Canada, 1882),
434 (Switzerland, 1883), to name the earliest.   The WC recorded

this expansion, as April 3, 1884 (130), 4. For the American contingent see CH, March 11, 1880 (3:11), 166-67. The CH paid close and friendly attention for many weeks, and inserted occasional articles for the next two years, including sketches of the Booths and Railton.

10. See Christian Mission Magazine, April, 1873, 63-64, and November, 1873, 168, for letters from Jermy, reprinted in Booth-Tucker, Catherine Booth, II, 35-40. Cf. WC, September 27, 1902 (1095), 3; see also Herbert A. Wisbey, Jr., "A Salvation Army Prelude: The Christian Mission in Cleveland, Ohio," Ohio Historical Quarterly, (64:1), January, 1955.

11. Booth-Tucker, Catherine Booth, I, 625-27, reported the first issue of the East London Evangelist published October, 1868. Rechristened the Christian Mission Magazine the following year, and the Salvationist in 1879, Booth's magazine finally became the War Cry late in 1879. When Booth-Tucker chronicled the life of Catherine Booth a decade later, the combined circulation of various national War Cry versions had reached nearly a million copies each week.

12. Ibid., II, 268-76; Railton, William Booth, unfortunately did not detail his own important story; in the WC, July 9, 1881 (10), 2, Captain Eliza Shirley described those early days. Years later, as Mrs. Eliza Symmonds, she recounted those events in greater detail in "Pioneering the Work in the United States," WC, November 28, 1908 (1417), 11, and December 5, 1908 (1418), 7, 16.

13. See Herbert A. Wisbey, Soldiers Without Swords; A History of the Salvation Army in the United States (New York, 1955), 1-95, for a detailed and well-documented history of these early years; "Salvation Army Stations in America," WC, August 6, 1881 (14), 4, listed seven corps; CH issues in 1880 reporting Army activities included April 22 (3:17), 262, May 27 (3:22), 348, June 10 (3:24), 380, September 2, (3:36), 569, and September 23 (3:39), 616-17; see the general historical survey in the WC, March 19, 1887 (285), 1, 4.

14. Wisbey in his books Soldiers, 106-17, and History of the Volunteers of America (New York, 1954), 18-31, describes this break and the pressures leading to it; WC, March 7, 1896 (753), 8, 9; War Cry Supplement, May 2, 1896 (761), reprinted letters the Booths exchanged, as did The Resignation of Commander and Mrs. Ballington Booth. The Correspondence Involved. Letters from the General, the Chief and the Commanders (New York, 1896).

15. Editorial, G, June 4, 1896 (8); Wisbey, Volunteers, 56; publicly reported totals did not increase greatly during the next two decades: e.g., The New International Encyclopedia (2nd ed., New York, 1917), XXXIII, 243, for 1915; cf. U.S. Bureau of the Census, Census of Religious Bodies, 1926 (Washington, D.C.), 5-6.

16. G, April 8, 1899 (156), 1; G, November 7, 1903 (395), 8; G, January, 1909 (658), 6-7.

17. See pp. 47-48, 56, 60, 62, 104-06, above, passim; also general articles in the G, as Basil C. Brooke, "Volunteer Philanthropy: Our Social Work," December 2, 1899 (190), 6-7, and "Our New Philanthropic Work," December 29, 1900 (246), 8, and November 30, 1901 (294), 5; Wisbey, Volunteers, 67-75, discusses the social program, and 40, 43-50, 151-57, the personnel; cf. CH, November 27, 1901 (24:48), 1013.

18. For a discussion of personnel and progress, see Wisbey, Soldiers, 76-80, 85, 118-22, 140-42; on Booth-Tucker, see his Muktifauj, or Forty Years with the Salvation Army in India and Ceylon (London, n.d.), as well as F. A. Mackenzie, Booth-Tucker, Sadhu and Saint (London, 1930), and occasional sketches in the WC, as "Commander Booth-Tucker," March 5, 1904 (1170), 9. Booth-Tucker left the United States for service in international operations and in India following the death of his wife in a railroad accident in October, 1903. See "The Beloved Counsul," WC, November 14, 1903 (1154), 1. Much of that issue was devoted to the story of her life and death; for an earlier presentation see "The Consul," Harbor Lights, July, 1899, 199-202.

19. WC, April 17, 1886 (237), 4; Ballington Booth, "To Friends and Sympathizers," WC, August 13, 1887 (306), 8, claimed Army presence in 318 towns and cities; for Booth-Tucker, see "Grand Call to Arms," WC, January 16, 1897 (798), 8, reviewing 1897, WC, October 4, 1902 (1096), 9, surveying the years 1898-1902, and "Commander Booth-Tucker," loc. cit.

20. WC (L), July 6, 1895 (989), 6; WC, March 12, 1904 (1171), 8; Booth-Tucker, Catherine Booth, II, 502, reported 1322 corps in 1885, an increase of 412 during that year.

21. Agnes L. Palmer, 1904-1922; The Time Between (New York, 1926), 15.

22. Josiah Strong, The New Era; or, The Coming Kingdom (New York, 1893), 268; cf. his Christianity's Storm Center; A Study of the Modern City (New York, 1907), 108-111.

23. WC, December 31, 1898 (900), 5.

24. George Railton, "Soldier of Jesus Christ," WC, June 18, 1881, 1; on the latter incident, see WC, April 22, 1893 (603), 1, 4, December 21, 1895 (742), 10-11, and April 1, 1905 (1226), 1; cf. Ten Talks on the Salvation Army (New York, 1926?), 11-12.

25. WC, April 11, 1891 (497), 8; cf. Ballington Booth, "Tide Marks in the Salvation Advance of 1888," WC, January 7, 1888 (327), 8.

26. WC, August 27, 1904 (1195), 8; "A History-Making Command," WC, September 3, 1904 (1196), 8; WC, October 15, 1904 (1202), 8; WC, October 22, 1904 (1204), 8, 9.

27. WC, April 29, 1899 (917), 5.

28. William T. Stead, "General Booth," WC, April 22, 1911 (1542), 9; "Jubilee Messages from Archdeacon Farrar...," WC (L), April 7, 1894 (924), 7; cf. F. W. Farrar, Letters, WC, January 24, 1891 (486), 8, and January 31, 1891, (487), 4.

29. William Booth, "From the Banks of the River," WC (L), January 11, 1890 (703), 8-9.

30. See WC, October 29, 1910 (1517), 8; Booth-Tucker, Catherine Booth, II, 671.

31. WC, April 13, 1912 (1593), 8; William Booth, Letter, WC (L), April 21, 1894 (926), 9; WC, April 3, 1884 (130), 1, "People say '... too enthusiastic--too hot!' My own impression is that we are not half hot enough. Oh, Lord, fire us up!"; for other examples see WC, March 27, 1884 (129), 1, February 14, 1885 (176), 1, March 24, 1888 (338), 16, June 30, 1888 (352), 5, and January 20, 1912 (1581), 9.

32. WC, March 12, 1904 (1171), 8; Ballington Booth, Letter, WC, April 23, 1892 (551), 9; "The Plan of Campaign," WC, January 16, 1897 (798), 8; Commander Miss Booth, "Looking Backward Through 1907," WC, January 4, 1908 (1370), 9; "Our 1909 Advance," WC, January 1, 1910 (1474), 9; Salvation Army, Yearbook (London, 1964), 1, 6, cited 108,000 converts the preceding year and more than 1,100,000 during the decade previous.

33. "Siege of 1910," WC, February 12, 1910 (1480), 8, claimed 11,245 conversions during this campaign in 1909; WC, June 21, 1913 (1655), 8; "Fruits of the Siege," WC, December 5, 1914 (1731), 8, editorially reported 103,973 conversions during the preceding ten years of the Siege.

34. "Tremont Temple Packed. 3,000 People Present...," WC, April 4, 1891 (496), 11; WC, January 12, 1895 (693), 3, claimed 7000 persons heard William Booth at "Apostle's Tabernacle," Salt Lake City; WC, July 6, 1907 (1344), 1, 9, 12; WC, October 15, 1904 (1202), 8; see Wisbey, Volunteers, 93-97, for Ballington Booth.

35. WC: May 30, 1908 (1391), 3 (Kilbey); December 11, 1909 (1471), 13 (Cadman); March 9, 1912 (1588), 9 (Brengle); January 26, 1918 (1895), 8 (Brengle). The WC often listed specific goals. During the winter of 1889-1890, for example, the goal was 20,000 "souls," with progress charted regularly in each issue. See January 4, 1890 (431), 9.

36. Strong, New Era, 351-52; cf. Lyman Abbott, Reminiscences (Boston, 1915), 479.

37. F. W. Farrar, "The Salvation Army," Harper's Magazine May, 1891 (82:899).

38. WC (L), November 9, 1889 (694), 8; cf. Staff Captain Caroline Welsh, "A Day with Our Probationary Officer," WC, November 23, 1901 (1051), 3: "a terrible fallacy" to deny this possibility.

39. William Booth, "Some of the Things I Want to See in 1912," WC, January 20, 1912 (1581), 9; cf. Editorial, WC, August 19, 1916 (1820), 8, on his continuing impact.

40. Ballington Booth, Letter, WC, October 22, 1887 (316), 8; Ballington Booth, "Out of the Depths; Reaching the Submerged," WC, February 6, 1892 (540), 9; cf. William Booth, "In Darkest England...," WC (L), November 15, 1890 (747), 9.

41. "Strike at the Root!" WC, January 13, 1894 (641), 8.

42. William Booth, "The Serious Condition of Our Funds," WC (L), May 14, 1892 (825), 9; cf. William Booth, "In Darkest England...," WC (L), November 15, 1890 (747), 9.

43. WC, March 25, 1899 (912), 4; cf. The Local Officer, December, 1919 (1:3), 4.

44. WC, May 2, 1896 (761), 2; WC, December 31, 1898 (900), 4; C. W. B., "'Naked and Clothed Me Not'," WC, January 6, 1917 (1840), 2: "a much-vexed question that is also a source of much argument in Salvation Army ranks"; General Bramwell Booth, "Shall Our Social Work Continue?", WC, April 6, 1918 (1905), 16; cf. the Alliance periodical, LT, November, 1902, 404, for a judgment that the Army's priorities had indeed changed.

45. G, November 8, 1902 (343), 9; G, November 7, 1903 (395), 8, 9; G, November 5, 1904 (447), 9; G, November 11, 1905 (500), 9; G, January, 1909 (658), 7; cf. Wisbey, Volunteers, 141.

46. Edward Fielding, "Philanthropic Work," G, November 14, 1903 (396), 9, 12; cf. G, January, 1910 (670), 12-13, Fielding presiding at a territorial council, with "Times of Spiritual Power and Blessing for All."

47. R. M. Offord, ed., Jerry McAuley, An Apostle to the Lost (New York, c1885), 27-31; see Arthur Bonner, Jerry McAuley and His Mission (New York, 1967), for a helpful recent history.

48. Offord, McAuley, 112, 138, 227, 255, 303; S. H. Hadley, "Jerry McAuley Mission," Record of Christian Work,

March, *1898 (17:3), 120; within the later literature of the rescue mission movement, see W. E. Paul, Miracles of Rescue (Minneapolis, n. d.), 9, 13-14, W. E. Paul, Romance of Rescue (Minneapolis, 1959, c1946), 13, 18-28, and C. F. H. Henry, The Pacific Garden Mission (Grand Rapids, Mich. , 1942), 27, 51.

49. Offord, McAuley, 9-31. Pages 13-22 relate the prison crisis and witnessing. Pages 27-28, and 157-61 detail the "John Allen excitement," with the later pages constituting part of the contribution McAuley's banker friend, A. S. Hatch, made to the Offord volume. According to Hatch, Oliver Dyer's article about Allen, "The Wickedest Man in New York," Packard's Monthly, July 1868, precipitated the "excitement."

50. Offord, McAuley, 31, 36-39. Hatch had purchased this property next door to John Allen's notorious place at the time of the "excitement," subsequently lending it to the New York City Mission and Tract Society until McAuley began his mission in 1872. Lewis E. Jackson, Gospel Work in New York City; A Memorial of Fifty Years in City Missions (New York, 1878), 112-13, described the earlier use of the property.

51. Offord, McAuley, 45-49, 74-76. Cf. 88, 183-208; later writings about the Mission also centered on converts: S. H. Hadley, Down in Water Street; A Story of Sixteen Years Life and Work in Water Street Mission (New York, 1902); Philip I. Roberts, The Dry Dock of a Thousand Wrecks; The McAuley Water Street Mission (New York, 1912).

52. Offord, McAuley, 45-47.

53. Ibid. , 5, 109, 135; on the funeral, see also Abell, American Protestantism, 37.

54. Offord, McAuley, 43-45, 213-15, 226-41, the latter pages reprinting a pamphlet describing the farewell meeting. During those years the CH frequently presented McAuley and his missions: e.g., April 5, 1883 (6:14), 209-11, and October 2, 1884 (7:40), 625-27, both feature articles, and December 13, 1883 (6:50), 793.

55. For the "newspaper," noted, e.g., in CH, November 13, 1883, 793, see Offord, McAuley, 110, 294-95, and J. Wilbur Chapman, S. H. Hadley of Water Street (New York, 1906), 154-56; Offord, McAuley, 255, included Wyburn's statement; for McAuley's impact on the Sidney Whittemores, see above, 21.

56. Hadley, Water Street, 59-71; Chapman, Hadley, 27-63, 72-80; William James included Hadley in his The Varieties of Religious Experience (New York, 1902), 198-99, 262.

57. Hadley, Water Street, 75-80, 87; Chapman, Hadley,

64-69. Chapman, 73, 203, said he had heard Hadley's story "hundreds of times"; CH, April 2, 1890 (13:14), 209-11, featured the Hadley story, based on a personal interview with him.

58. Abel, American Protestantism, 37, briefly discusses McAuley's effectiveness; and that effectiveness was an implicit and often explicit theme in much of the literature by and about gospel welfare personnel. For contrast with noted "institutional church" clergymen, see E. Clowes Chorley, The Centennial History of St. Bartholomew's Church in the City of New York, 1835-1935 (New York? 1935), 180-81; cf. Madele Wilson and A. B. Simpson, Henry Wilson, One of God's Best (New York, 1909?), 62-63, on W. S. Rainsford of St. George's Episcopal Church, New York.

59. Hadley, Water Street, 85-88.

60. "Samuel H. Hadley, the Soul Winner," The Missionary Review of the World, April, 1906 (29:4), 295-96; "A Most Notable Death," The Missionary Review of the World, March, 1906 (29:3), 166; Editorial, AW, February 17, 1906, 89; LT, March, 1906, 182-88; in CH, November 8, 1911 (34:45), 1118, John Wyburn of the Water Street Mission claimed 5000 converts there each year; cf. "To Save the Bowery Mission," CH, March 27, 1895 (18:13), 193, 197.

61. Chorley, St. Bartholomew's, 178-192; Hadley, Water Street, 215-20; Chapman, Hadley, 43; "A Temple of Rescue. St. Bartholomew's Rescue Mission," CH, June 10, 1891 (14:23), 353, 356.

62. Melvin E. Trotter, These Forty Years (Grand Rapids, Mich., 1939), 73-78, 119; Chapman, Hadley, 134-37; see "A His Interview. Paul Beckwith," His, November, 1974, 21, for comments on Trotter by a contemporary. Another prominent mission leader, William Bruce of Louisville, termed Hadley's influence on him "deeper ... than that of any other man." Ibid., 139; see also LT, March, 1906, 182-88.

63. Chapman, Hadley, 130; cf. Trotter, Years, 65; on Monroe and the Pacific Garden Mission, another important center of influence, see Trotter, Years, 15-17; Chapman, Hadley, 130, 129-39; Henry, Mission, 19, 25, 39-40, 49-52; "Sounded Ten Thousand Calls to Sinners. Twenty-Three Years Work of the Pacific Garden Mission," CH, June 19, 1901 (24:25), 549; "A Great Rescue Mission," CH, November 2, 1910 (33:44), 1014 (about Trotter and Grand Rapids); Orin E. Crooker, "Chicago's Best-Known Mission," CH, June 11, 1913 (36:24), 568.

64. Chapman, Hadley, 131-32; CH, May 10, 1893 (16:19), 305, 307; CH, October 28, 1891 (14:43), 673, 685; Charles Crittenton, The Brother of Girls; The Life Story of Charles N. Crittenton (Chicago, 1910), 175-76; AW, November 3, 1893, 273; AW,

November 24, 1893, 321; see also Abell, American Protestantism, 95-98, 1914 (37:23), 564; "Gospel Missions Convene," CH, June 9, 1915 (38:23), 606, briefly reported the second annual convention; cf. Paul, Romance of Rescue, 88-91.

69. "Gospel Missions Union Celebrated," loc. cit.; cf. "Mission Workers in Convention," loc. cit., for similar revivalism.

70. A. B. Simpson, "Memorial Address: at the Dedication of the Gospel Tabernacle," AW, March 21 and 28, 1890, 200-02; "The Christian Alliance," CH, March 30, 1892 (15:13), 193, 195; George P. Pardington, Twenty-five Wonderful Years, 1889-1914; A Popular Sketch of the Christian and Missionary Alliance (New York, 1914), 21-26; A. E. Thompson, The Life of A. B. Simpson (New York, 1920), 85-90. Simpson, in his "Memorial Address," and as quoted by Thompson, emphasized the "neglected masses" and "publicans and sinners," as he did in an interview featured in the CH: "The Christian Alliance," March 30, 1892 (15:13), 195.

71. Simpson, "Memorial Address," loc. cit.; Pardington, Alliance, 26-28; Thompson, Simpson, 90-91, 95-96.

72. Pardington, Alliance, 18-19; Thompson, Simpson, 41-45, 50-52.

73. Thompson, Simpson, 19-23, reprinted the Covenant, along with Simpson's renewals. Cf. 63-71, 119, 163 for spiritual crises previous to the New York pastorate.

74. Thompson, Simpson, 152. Cf. 122, quoting Harlan P. Beech, professor of missions at Yale University, in praise of Simpson's missionary journals.

75. On the years in Louisville, see Pardington, Alliance, 19-20, and Thompson, Simpson, 53-62; for New York, see Pardington, Alliance, 21-24, and Thompson, Simpson, 82-85; A. W. Tozer, Wingspread; Albert B. Simpson (Harrisburg, Pa., 1943), 68.

76. Pardington, Alliance, 21, 6, the latter from Simpson's Introduction; Thompson, Simpson, 73-77, quotes Simpson at length (cf. 81, 108, 119-20). Pages 63-71, 163, discuss two earlier crises building to this turning point; see also A. B. Simpson, The Gospel of Healing, rev. ed. (New York, 1915), 155-74.

77. Thompson, Simpson, 104-06.

78. Ibid., 106-12; WWW, July-August, 1885, 220, and September, 1885, 251, announced the second annual convention, which November, 1885, described; other journals gave friendly and even enthusiastic attention to these conventions: TF, November, 1885 (5:11), 241-42, and 250, reported Simpson's convention in Buffalo and announced a similar gathering in Chicago; CH, November 19,

1885 (8:47), 745, October 21, 1886 (9:42), and October 12, 1892 (15:41), 645; "The Christian Alliance Convention," G, September 25, 1897 (76), 5.

79. Thompson, Simpson, 108-09; Pardington, Alliance, 34-35; cf. Editorial, AW, August 22, 1903, 155, which referred to the "greatest" Old Orchard convention ever, and called it "the most remarkable rallying and radiating point of the Alliance movement" to that date.

80. Thompson, Simpson, 128-32. Pages 118-27 describe the development of Simpson's "Missionary Vision." Gospel Taber-nacle members organized "The Missionary Union for the Evangeliza-tion of the World" several years earlier, in 1883; WWW, January, 1885, 10, April, 1885, 102-04, and July-August, 1885, 220, re-ported an early missionary effort in the Congo; WWW, August-Sep-tember, 1887, 110-12, and passim, reported the 1887 convention; "The Christian Alliance," AW, January, 1889, 3-4.

81. See Thompson, Simpson, 86-87, 133-35; Pardington, Alliance, 92-94, 55.

82. Pardington, Alliance, 37-39, quoting at length; cf. Thompson, Simpson, 131-33.

83. A. B. Simpson, "The World for Christ," AW, April 23, 1897, 388; cf. AW, December 7, 1894, 531, October 16, 1895, 241, July 4, 1896, 85, and September 11, 1896, 238.

84. Simpson, "The World for Christ," loc. cit.; AW, May 13, 1905, 289; "Annual Report of the President," AW, June 9, 1906, 353-55, 357; see Mrs. Josephine Princell, Frederick Franson, World Missionary (Chicago, n.d.), 51-58, on the question of a large group of Scandinavian volunteers Franson secured for the Alliance.

85. In Thompson, Simpson, 232-33; cf. Editorial, AW, May 22, 1909, 128.

86. After Fifty Years (Harrisburg, Pa., 1939), 24, 48, 56, 82, reported 519 branches, 543 missionaries, and a total of nearly $18 million for missions, 1891-1938.

87. Pardington, Alliance, 25, 29-31; Thompson, Simpson, 96-103; see Simpson's plan in WWW, September, 1885, 252, to open three or four missions in New York City that winter; WWW, December, 1885, 350, noted several opened; for the training college see WWW, May, 1885, 160, September, 1885, 251, and October, 1885, 270-72; see editorial, CH, June 30, 1887 (10:26), 409, and CH, August 4, 1887 (10:31), 481-83, as well as WWW, July, 1887, 22-26, for sketches of the Berachah Mission, opened in 1885, and of the Henry Naylors who began and operated the mission. The Naylors shared Simpson's "faith healing" as well as his larger spiritual emphasis.

88. "Reports of the Home Work Given at Old Orchard," AW, August 17, 1894, 160; Frederic William Farr, "The Gospel Tabernacle and Related Work," AW, March 9, 1907, 111-12, 118; on Farr, see Thompson, Simpson, 98, 209-10, 143.

89. Wilson and Simpson, Wilson, 111, 114; "Rescue Mission Day at the New York Convention," AW, October 16, 1895, 253; AW, October 20, 1897, 404-06.

90. A. B. Simpson, "An Ideal Church," AW, October 7, 1899, 292; "The Gospel Tabernacle," AW, January 20, 1900, 41; cf. AW, February 24, 1900, 125, and May 1, 1896, 457.

91. AW, April 17, 1896, 373; "Varieties of Christian Work," AW, November 24, 1893, 334; WWW, November, 1885, 304-14, reported this kind of emphasis at the second annual convention in New York City.

92. A. B. Simpson, "The World for Christ," loc. cit.; "The Work at Home," AW, January 1, 1895, 11; "Annual Report of the Secretary of the Christian Alliance," AW, November 6, 1895, 300; for welfare in Denver, see "Editorial Correspondence," AW, June 6, 1895, 360-61; Mrs. Delia Collins, "Texas Work. The Woman's Industrial Home," AW, March 30, 1894, 351-52; Anna Prosser, "The Work of the Christian Alliance in Buffalo," TF, October, 1890, 227-28, and cf. July, 1890, 168; see LT for news about mission work, e.g., September, 1902, 157-62, November, 1902, 259-65, and January, 1903, 46-50.

93. Farr, loc. cit.

94. Editorial, AW, October 21, 1911, 34; Editorial, AW May 20, 1911, 120; cf. A. B Simpson, "An Earnest Life," AW, October 2, 1896, 303.

95. Thompson, Simpson, 106, 109, 110; cf. After Fifty Years, 35; for example from AW, see May 26, 1906, 324 (Robert Speer).

96. Thompson, Simpson, 97, spoke of "Simpson's closest friend and most trusted associate." On 209 Thompson reprinted a note from Wilson to Simpson.

97. In TF, April, 1892, 85-87, Wilson related his Kingston experience; WC, January 3, 1884 (117), 4, reprinted Wilson's defense of the Army in the Toronto Mail; Wilson and Simpson, Wilson, 11-12, 36-40, 43-58, 65-67. William Booth and other Salvationists retained cordial feelings for Wilson, whose daughter and biographer joined the Army about 1890 (e.g., 62, 67-69, and WC, March 7, 1908 (1379), 8, 13); Pardington, Alliance, 227-28.

98. On the mission see WWW, September, 1885, 227; Wilson and Simpson, Wilson, 58-59, 60-62, 75-78, 148-52, the

latter section reprinting a tribute from Rainsford; Pardington, Alliance, 228-29; Simpson referred to him as the first President of the International Missionary Alliance, Wilson and Simpson, Wilson, 76, 122, though cf. Pardington, Alliance, 236; for Rainsford's early fervent evangelistic emphasis, see A. J. Gordon's paper, Watchword, October, 1878 (1:1), 10-15, and WWW, November, 1885, 312-14. See also entry no. 105 below.

99. Wilson and Simpson, Wilson, 76-77, 90-91, 109-11; Pardington, Alliance, 229-31.

100. See Wilson and Simpson, Wilson, 111, 114.

101. Ibid., 63, 92-104, 14-15; Pardington, Alliance, 232; Henry Wilson, Bible Lamps for Little Feet (New York, 1902).

102. Editorial, WWW, July, 1887, 2-3; "Christian and Missionary Alliance Convention, " AW, October 6, 1900, 188; Pardington, Alliance, 51-61, elaborated on these elements.

103. Pardington, Alliance, 50-53.

104. [A. B. Simpson] "The Mission of the Christian Alliance, " AW, October 2, 1895, 216; Pardington, Alliance, 74-75; A. B. Simpson, "The Second Coming of Christ, " WWW, November, 1885, 316: "an intensely practical truth ... intimately associated with holiness.... "

105. Wilson and Simpson, Wilson, 26-27, 77; cf. the article in The Watchword, produced by Simpson's friend, A. J. Gordon: "The Second Coming of Jesus as the Working Man's Hope, " November 1878 (1:2), 19, 20.

106. This term, not entirely accurate, and unfortunate in the reaction it will evoke in some readers, has at least two strengths which support its use. It was the term these groups chose as embodying important elements in their viewpoint. And, in contrast to "unwed mother" or "prostitute, " it is inclusive of the rather wide range of needy women their homes served.

107. Emma Whittemore, Records of Modern Miracles (Toronto, 1931), 19-20; Henry Varley, Jr., Henry Varley's Life Story (London, n.d.), 113-19; Thompson, Simpson, 91, notes that Varley appeared frequently at A. B. Simpson's Gospel Tabernacle, and at Alliance Conventions, following a "most successful" six week "campaign" in the Tabernacle in 1885; see Simpson's journal, WWW, September, 1885, 251; Varley also spoke at T. DeWitt Talmage's Brooklyn Tabernacle, CH, August 6, 1885 (8:32), 499.

108. Offord, McAuley, 237-38, 242-44, included the Whittemore account; Whittemore, Miracles, 21-24; "A Life of Christlike Service, " CH, February 25, 1914 (37:8), 192; Henry Varley developed

close ties with McAuley: Henry Varley, An Evening of Happy Memory ... at Water Street Mission (London, 1875?).

109. Whittemore, Miracles, 24-25, 32, 64, 72, 94, 97, 102-03, brought out this relationship with the McAuleys and their missions; Offord, McAuley, 234, 237-38; Hadley, Water Street, 239-42, reprinted the "Certificate of Incorporation"; "A Life of Christlike Service," loc. cit.

110. Whittemore, Miracles, 24-25, 32-36, 94, 97, 103.

111. "Work in the Slums," AW, April 11, 1890, 233-34, reported her address at Simpson's Gospel Tabernacle; Whittemore, Miracles, 61-64, 150-54, discussed the first two homes.

112. "The Opening of Door of Hope, No. 2," AW, June 23, 1893, 398; E. M. Whittemore, "Now Sixty-One 'Doors of Hope,'" CH, September 9, 1903 (26:36), 750; Whittemore, Miracles, 237-38, reported 73 homes within 18 years and 97 before her death; CH, March 22, 1893 (16:12), 189, 191, gave the early story; see also E. M. Whittemore, "A Word from the Door of Hope," AW, February 2, 1894, 132.

113. Whittemore, Miracles, 236-37; Whittemore, "Now Sixty-One 'Doors of Hope,'" loc. cit.

114. For some of these connections, see Whittemore, Miracles, ix, 99-101, 105, 111-12, 248-49, 252, and 277; "A Life of Christlike Service," loc. cit.; "Good Work Among the Fallen Ones," CH, October 25, 1905 (28:43), 901.

115. "Mission Workers in Convention," CH, June 10, 1914 (37:23), 564; "Gospel Missions Convene," CH, June 9, 1915 (38:23), 606; John C. Goode, "Gospel Missions in Convention," CH, July 3, 1918 (41:27), 805; Paul, Romance, 88-91, lists the officers and meeting places from the beginning.

116. For Chapman's tribute see the editor's introduction to Whittemore, Miracles, xii. Pages viii, ix, and 112 bring out her connections with the Army; E. M. Whittemore (Staff-Captain), "To My Comrades in the Salvation Army," WC, December 29, 1917 (1891), 14; cf. WC, March 13, 1897 (806), 9, and October 1, 1910 (1513), 6; the Whittemores were officers in the Alliance and close to A. B. Simpson during that group's formative years: AW, February, 1889, 24; AW, September 29, 1893, 193; "Books and Tracts Published by the Christian Alliance Pub. Co.," AW, July 28, 1893, 64, included Emma Whittemore's "The Door of Hope Series" of twenty-one tracts.

117. E. M. Whittemore, "A Word from the Door of Hope," loc. cit.; Whittemore, Miracles, 238, 82; cf. Sidney Whittemore, AW, October 20, 1893, 251, speaking at the New York Convention

of the Alliance, where he "pleaded most powerfully and tenderly" for his listeners to surrender to Christ.

118. Emma Whittemore, Delia (New York, 1893), 33-39, 42-44, 69-71, 74-76, etc.; Whittemore, Miracles, 128-30, 167-68, illustration opposite 145; Offord, McAuley, 244-45; the CH published the story of Delia, with great reader response. See "The Door of Hope," March 22, 1893 (16:12), 189, 191; in AW, June 10, 1892, 379-80, Mrs. Whittemore reported Delia's address at Sing Sing prison.

119. "Work in the Slums," loc. cit.; Whittemore, Miracles, 17-18, 26-30; other incidents of healing occurred later, as in Whittemore, Delia, 120-21; for her observations soon after her healing, see WWW, March, 1885, 91-92, October, 1885, 276-78, and December, 1885, 343-44.

120. Whittemore, Miracles, 34.

121. Ibid., 48-53, 84, 87, 216-17, 218-21; most articles by her and others about the Door of Hope stressed its "faith" emphasis: "The Door of Hope," loc. cit.; "Enlarging the 'Door of Hope,'" loc. cit.

122. Whittemore, Miracles, 56, 144-49, 236-37, 105-09, 115-18, 206-09, 83-84; as an example of the wide publicity given this kind of supernaturalism, see AW, August 18, 1893, 102-03; cf. Samuel Brengle, The Way of Holiness (New York, 1918), 104, for an example of similar supernaturalism by a prominent officer of the Salvation Army.

123. See pp. 79-82, above.

124. Crittenton, Brother, 175-76; Crittenton gave the date as 1896, but the Barretts had been in Washington, D.C., for approximately two years by that date, and Mr. Barrett died in September, 1896. The Convention of Christian Workers that was held in the autumn of 1893 apparently occasioned his visit to Atlanta, as indicated by his letter in the CH, September 12, 1894 (17:37), 585, reviewing his activities of the past year. See also Otto Wilson, Fifty Years Work with Girls, 1883-1933; A Story of the Florence Crittenton Homes (Alexandria, Va., 1933).

125. K. W. Barrett, "Some Reminiscences--Part II," FC, June, 1899 (1:4), 86.

126. See Crittenton, Brother, 178, for his tribute to her.

127. See the Barrett Papers in the Library of Congress for documents relative to these honors and functions; National Florence Crittenton Mission, Report for the Year 1918-1919 (Washington, D.C., 1919), 11; Who Was Who in America (Chicago, c1943), I, 61; Wilson, Crittenton Homes, 174, 178, 181-203.

128. "Report of the First General Convention of the National Florence Crittenton Mission," Fourteen Years' Work Among 'Erring Girls' (Washington, D.C., 1897?), 163; K. W. Barrett, Some Practical Suggestions on the Conduct of a Rescue Home (Washington, D.C., 1903?), 30-34, 51, 61, 68, 91, 99 (most of the book was published earlier in FC as "How We Conduct Our Rescue Home," September 1900 (2:7), 151-58, and October, 1900 (2:8), 177-86); in "Sixteenth Anniversary of the 'Mother Mission,'" FC, May, 1899 (1:3), 59-60, she stated that no "matter how good people are," if they were not active Christians they could not serve on the boards of Crittenton homes.

129. "What Has the National Association Done for the Homes," FC, March, 1899 (1:1), 6.

130. "Report of the First General Convention...," Fourteen Years' Work, 99-100.

131. Ibid., 159-176, 197; Fourteen Years' Work, 71, 121, 157, 159-60, 197 (reports from the homes); FC, March, 1899 (1:1), 13; "The Formal Opening of the Seattle Home," FC, January, 1900 (1:11), 235-37; "A Haven for Outcasts," CH, November 13, 1895 (18:46), 749.

132. "A Word About Ourselves. What 'The Christian Herald' Has Accomplished in the Last Five Years," CH, December 5, 1894 (17:49), 771; "Dr. Klopsch's Life in Outline," CH, March 16, 1910 (33:11), 256; "Thirty-Five Years of Christian Service, 1878-1913," CH, October 22, 1913 (36:43), 969-72, 983; on circulation, see also CH, June 5, 1901 (24:23), 515, January 26, 1910 (33:4), 72, and November 23, 1910 (33:47), 1082.

133. "A Word About Ourselves," loc. cit.; "Dr. Klopsch's Life in Outline," loc. cit.; "Thirty-five Years of Christian Service," loc. cit.; see the Herald's seventy-fifth anniversary issue, September, 1953, passim, and especially Kenneth L. Wilson, "Compassion's Strong Right Arm," 46-50, 147, for a review.

134. William H. Taft, Letter, CH, March 23, 1910 (33:12), 278; CH, April 27, 1910 (33:17), 415; CH, November 30, 1910 (33:48), 1116; Charles M. Pepper, Life-Work of Louis Klopsch (New York, 1910), 361-63; cf. Who's Who in America, 1901-02 (Chicago, 1901), 644.

135. CH, July 7, 1881 (4:27), 424, and July 3, 1879 (1, 2:37).

136. CH, April 30, 1902 (25:18), 378; cf. "His Glorious Life-Work Ended," CH, April 23, 1902 (25:17), 351; for variation in dates for the Klopsch-Talmage beginning, see "A Word About Ourselves," loc. cit., and Who's Who in America, 1901-02, 644; see also T. DeWitt Talmage, "The Bible Proving Itself from God," Homiletic Review, January, 1901 (41:31-37).

137.   Preface to the bound volume of the CH for 1878-79; CH, July 3, 1879 (1, 2:37); for articles by Blackstone, see CH, October 23, 1884 (7:43), October 30, 1884 (7:44), and June 4, 1890 (13:23), 358; George Müller, "Speedy Return of Christ," CH, August 7, 1879 (1, 2:42), 661-63; CH, March 31, 1881 (4:13), 204-06; cf. George Müller, "Waiting for His Return," AW, March 2, 1898, 202; for Tyng, see CH, February 27, 1879 (1, 2:19), 289-91, and September 17, 1885 (8:38), 593-95.

138.   CH, December 18, 1879 (1, 2:61), 968; CH, October 2, 1884 (7:40), 625-27; CH, April 2, 1890 (13:14), 209-11; see Bonner, McAuley, 79, on Talmage's role in beginning McAuley's Cremorne Mission.

139.   Charles H. Spurgeon, Autobiography; Compiled from His Diary, Letters, and Records, by his wife and private secretary (Philadelphia, n.d.), III, 173-77; CH, June 19, 1879 (1, 2:35), 550-51, reviewed Spurgeon's twenty-five year pastorate; "The Stockwell Orphanage," CH, October 31, 1878 (1, 2:2), 32; Chas. H. Spurgeon, "Appeal for a Girl's Orphanage," CH, August 14, 1879 (1, 2:43), 677; two prominent clerical advocates of social Christianity were among Spurgeon's biographers: Russell H. Conwell, Life of Charles Haddon Spurgeon, the World's Great Preacher (n.p., 1892), see chapters 10, 13-15; George C. Lorimer, Charles Haddon Spurgeon (Boston, 1892); see the valuable recent doctoral study by Albert R. Meredith, The Social and Political Views of Charles Haddon Spurgeon, 1834-1892 (Ann Arbor, Mich., c1973) for an overview of Spurgeon's philanthropy as well as of his social and political views: 79 (war), 69, 64-70 (Liberal), 8, 161, 173-89.

140.   "Dr. Klopsch's Life in Outline," loc. cit.; Pepper, Klopsch, 1-7, 358-59; Who's Who in America, 1901-02, 644.

141.   May, Protestant Churches, 95 (cf. 198), notes "one of his few references to worldly events," in Talmage's autobiography; see, however, "Current Events," CH, December 19, 1878 (1, 2:9), 131-33, which promised a widening of his series of sermons into a consideration of "moral conditions and prospects of this country." That series had already touched on urban and moral problems, as November 28, 1878 (1, 2:6), 84-86, December 12, 1878 (1, 2:8), 116-17, and December 19, 1878 (1, 2:9), 136. See Talmage's books, such as The Abominations of Modern Society (New York, 1872), 104-05, and Evils of the Cities (Chicago, 1895), 128-30, 162-63, for example. His autobiographical writings reveal wide contacts with political and business figures and a continuing interest and comment on their world, as in T. D. Talmage, T. DeWitt Talmage As I Knew Him (New York, 1912), 56, 92, 112, 158, 187, 236-41, 261, 332-33, etc. As to his interest in and response to human need, see T. D. Talmage, "Hunger in Ireland," CH, January 22, 1880 (3:4), 52; "A Bread and Beef Charity," CH, January 10, 1894 (17:2), 19; and "Dr. Talmage's Philanthropies," CH, August 6, 1902 (25:32), 652; cf. "Twelfth Annual Report of the

F. C. Hope and Help Mission, Washington, D.C.," FC, March, 1900 (2:1), 7, which listed Talmage as one of the "Incorporators and officers of the National Society."

142. Pepper, Klopsch, 324-25; "A Great Bible Revival," CH, January 10, 1894 (17:2), 17, 29.

143. See p. 1, above.

144. See "A Word About Ourselves," loc. cit.; "Dr. Klopsch's Life in Outline," loc. cit.; "Thirty-five Years of Christian Service, 1878-1913," loc. cit.; and Pepper, Klopsch, passim.

145. Frank Talmage supplied the Herald's "American Pulpit" sermon weekly for some time after his father's death, and frequently for a number of years. "In His Father's Footsteps," May 7, 1902 (25:19), 397. F. DeWitt Talmage, "Lukewarm Christianity," August 30, 1905 (28:35), 716-17; April 19, 1911 (34:16), 399, reported the first sermon of John H. Jowett in his pastorate in New York City as a "clear, simple, forceful exposition of the orthodox gospel," and yet one which emphasized "institutional work" as "the foundation" which "should be the future path of the church's development." Before Jowett's coming, William Durban, a friend in London, spoke of his ministry of sixteen years in Birmingham, England, as a "marvelous local work, sociological and philanthropic as well as spiritual." And the editor reinforced the "spiritual" in calling Jowett "simply an earnest soul-winner." "The Passion for Souls," March 15, 1911 (34:11), 272; another frequent contributor from England, F B. Meyer, whose books remain influential in revivalist and fundamentalist circles, shared Jowett's "sociological and philanthropic" orientation. See his The Bells of Is; or, Voices of Human Need and Sorrow (London, n.d.), as well as his introduction to Hadley's Water Street, and his interest in rescue work for women as shown in Whittemore, Miracles, illustration opposite 224. Both Jowett and Meyer contributed regularly to "Daily Meditations" in 1915. "Talks on the Golden Text," e.g., December 29, 1915 (38:52), 1338, was another regular feature by Meyer. Wilbur Smith, ed., Great Sermons on the Resurrection of Christ (Natick, Mass., 1964), 255-56, estimates five million copies of Meyer's publications to his death in 1929, indicating his popularity and influence.

146. CH, June 28, 1911 (34:26), 656-57, July 20, 1910 (33:29), 652-53, and August 17, 1910 (33:33), 728; the editor earlier (February 16, 1910 (33:7), 148) strongly urged readers to follow this series; Pepper, Klopsch, 314, referred to Moody as "one of Dr. Klopsch's most valued and appreciative friends"; earlier, Moody's associate, Ira D. Sankey, regularly supplied music for the CH: see December 6, 1893 (16:49), 795.

147. A recurring early CH entry was "Anecdotes" from recent evangelistic meetings, as December 20, 1888 (11:51), 803;

on Torrey, see the lead article, "Australia's Pentecostal Wave,"
September 3, 1902 (25:36), 715, 729, as well as "Wales Aflame
with Revival," January 4, 1905 (28:1), 6; "Another Town Yields to
Christ. A Remarkable Revival at Hiawatha, Kansas...," March 6,
1901 (24:10), 209; February 22, 1905 (28:8), 168, 177; "Billy Sunday's Philadelphia Tabernacle," January 6, 1915 (38:1), 11; "New
York Awaits Billy Sunday," March 28, 1917 (40:13), 355-56; for a
Stelzle-Biederwolf campaign see "Among the Workers," January 6,
1915 (38:1), 21.

148. "An Evangelistic Vacation," CH, July 5, 1893 (16:27),
433, 437.

149. E. O. Guerrant, "The Soul-Winner's Revival Year,"
CH, May 15, 1901 (24:20), 449; CH, November 8, 1911 (34:45),
1118.

150. CH, June 20, 1894 (17:25), 389. Klopsch and Talmage
each contributed $100. The article noted that students at the Moody
schools were active in missions, "homes," industrial schools, and
other institutions as well as in exclusively "religious" work; see
Bernard R. DeRemer, Moody Bible Institute; A Pictorial History
(Chicago, 1960), 26, for the incorporation papers of the "Chicago
Evangelistic Society" in 1887; cf. feature article, CH, January 25,
1893 (16:4), 49, 53.

151. "May Yet Bring Her Unevangelized Millions to Christ,"
CH, June 3, 1903 (26:22), 467, referring to India and the journal's
5000 orphans there; "Christian Herald Gospel Hall," CH, March 6,
1901 (24:10), 208, a permanent memorial to the famine sufferers
in India; "The Food Fund's Soul-Harvest," CH, April 11, 1894 (17:
15), 229; Z. Chas. Beals, "Our Mission House-Boat in China," CH,
August 9, 1905 (28:32), 670; George Sandison, "Famous Christian
Personalities," CH, February 28, 1920 (43:9), 253, went into some
detail on the "Christian Herald Gospel Fleet" of boats around the
world; "A World-Survey of the Spiritual and Benevolent Work of the
Christian Herald Family Circle During 1915," CH, December 29,
1915 (38:52), 1334.

152. "Our Own Missionary," CH, April 6, 1892 (15:14),
216; "Grateful Flood Sufferers," CH, October 19, 1892 (15:42), 673;
"Christian Herald Evangelism," CH, September 20, 1916 (39:38),
1053.

153. E.g., CH, October 3, 1894 (17:40), 629.

154. "To Save the Bowery Mission," CH, March 27, 1895
(18:13), 193, 197, noted the fifteen-year history of the Mission, as
well as the participation of its founder in rescue work "long" before
that; cf. CH, November 19, 1885 (8:47), 745.

155. CH, October 14, 1896 (19:42); cf. "The Lost Boys of

the Bowery, " CH, April 17, 1895 (18:16), 249, with "Mother" Sarah Bird affirming she had "no hope for the Bowery but in the Gospel of the Lord Jesus Christ"; "A Beacon Light to the Lost, " CH, April 3, 1895 (18:14), 217, stressed that none were so fallen that they "cannot be reached by the love of Christ. " "By God's mercy, " the article continued, many were cast up to the Bowery's door.

156. "To Save the Bowery Mission, " loc. cit., claimed 60, 000 "inquirers" for "salvation" in fifteen years, with a daily average attendance of 300 persons at the evening gospel service; "Montlawn's Helpers, " CH, October 10, 1900 (23:41), 833; "The Bowery Mission in War Time, " CH, October 17, 1917 (40:42), 1086, 1103; "Brought Up From the Depths, " CH, January 30, 1907 (30:5), 93.

157. CH, December 20, 1905 (28:51), 1094; for comment on reader response, see CH, May 1, 1901 (24:18), 406; cf. also CH, April 13, 1892 (15:15), 225, 229, May 4, 1892 (15:18), 278, and "Closing the Relief Fund, " CH, May 25, 1892 (15:21), 326.

II.   HOLINESS SLUM WORK

1. In F. Booth-Tucker, The Life of Catherine Booth (New York, 1892), I, 622-24; see Christian Mission Magazine, February, 1873, 26-27, 30-31, and April, 1873, 57; William Booth, "Principles of Social Work, " International Social Council Addresses, 1911 (London, 1912), 3; William Booth described his boyhood concern for the needy in his Preface to In Darkest England and the Way Out (New York, London, 1890); on "soup kitchens" see Booth-Tucker, Catherine Booth, I, 658-59; cf. Harold Begbie, The Life of General William Booth (New York, 1920), I, 352.

2. See pp. 79-80, above.

3. R. M. Offord, ed., Jerry McAuley, An Apostle to the Lost (New York, c1885), 45, 48, 50.

4. Robert Bremner, From the Depths; The Discovery of Poverty in the United States (New York, 1956); Charles H. Hopkins, The Rise of the Social Gospel in American Protestantism, 1865-1915 (New Haven, Conn., 1940); A. Abell, The Urban Impact on American Protestantism, 1865-1900 (London, 1962, c1943).

5. Ballington Booth, "A Retrospect of 6 Years' Work, " G, March 29, 1902 (311), 2; Maud Ballington Booth, "Salvation Army Work in the Slums, " Scribner's Magazine, January, 1895 (17:1), 109 (italics hers); Ballington Booth, "The Review Column, " WC, February 21, 1891 (490), 6.

6. E.G., "Voices from ... Boston Slums," WC, February 27, 1892 (543), 3; "Dispossessed," WC, February 1, 1902 (1061), 1.

7. See William Booth, "The Week of Self-Denial and Prayer," WC (L), September 6, 1890 (737), 2; Evangeline Booth, "The War Without Truce," WC, December 12, 1914 (1732), 8.

8. Christian Mission Magazine, August, 1873, 127; cf. Booth-Tucker, Catherine Booth, II, 102.

9. See pp. 2, 9-15, 17, 20-21, 23, 26, above.

10. WC, January 26, 1889 (382), 8-9; Ballington Booth, "Review Column," WC, April 4, 1891 (496), 8; WC, July 18, 1891 (511), 2-3; the issues for August 1 (513), 4, and August 29 (517), 3, also reflected that concern; Ballington Booth, New York's Inferno Explored (New York, 1891); cf. "Commr. Booth-Tucker As a Slummer," WC (L), May 9, 1896 (1033), 8.

11. "Our Yankee Slum Leader," WC (L), August 31, 1895 (997), 7; Ballington Booth, "Out of the Depths; Reaching the Submerged," WC, February 6, 1892 (540), 9; cf. "A Few Startling Statistics from 'Ocean to Ocean,'" WC, June 20, 1891 (507), 13.

12. WC (L), May 14, 1892 (825), 7; cf. "Indorsing Gen. Booth's Plan," WC, February 13, 1892 (541), 3.

13. WC, January 3, 1891 (483), 16, included many excerpts from the press.

14. "The Army Helps the Chicago 'Mail' in the Free Bread Distribution," WC, September 30, 1893 (626), 2; "Cleveland's Poor," WC, April 27, 1895 (708), 5.

15. "Alliance Notes," AW, July 6, 1898, 17; "Mrs. Mattie H. White," G, December 12, 1896 (35), 5; cf. G, June 21, 1902 (323), 2, August 2, 1902 (329), 3, and July 30, 1904 (433), 4; for the Alliance, see also AW, February 12, 1897, 160, and March, 1899, 124. The latter entry described Miss Kate White, a woman who "threw herself, body and soul, into the work of caring for, feeding and clothing the poor and needy, worthy and unworthy, of this Tabernacle neighborhood."

16. Booth-Tucker, Catherine Booth, I, 331 (cf. II, 301).

17. "New Castle, Pa.," AW, January 17, 1903, 39; "Field Notes at Home," AW, January 31, 1896, 115.

18. Editorial, CH, May 17, 1893 (16:20), 326; repeated, as May 31 (16:22), 358.

19. AW, April 24, 1896, 406; cf. March 20, 1896, 282, 283,

and F. L. Spindler, "Springfield, Mo.," December 26, 1903, 53;
for the Gospel Tabernacle in New York City, see January 30, 1908,
300-01, and Editorial, February 15, 1908, 332; cf. CH, July 3,
1918 (41:27), 809, for help to a black family.

20. Emma Whittemore, Records of Modern Miracles
(Toronto, 1931), 115-16, 155-58, 165-66; AW, April 11, 1890,
233-34.

21. In Whittemore, Miracles, 284-87, a chapter written by
the volume's editor, F. A. Robinson.

22. "Bella Cooke's Life Work," CH, September 3, 1890
(13:36), 561, 564-65; "Thanksgiving With God's Poor," CH, November 23, 1892 (15:47), 749; CH, January 3, 1894 (17:1), 1; "Many
Good Causes Helped," CH, November 7, 1894 (17:45), 207; "Charity
Balance Sheet," CH, January 16, 1895 (18:3), 38; "Charity Balance
Sheet," CH, March 4, 1896 (19:10), 188; cf. reprint of an article
from the London Christian: J. W. Thirtle, "A Prisoner of the Lord;
the Story of Bella Cooke," AW, March 20, 1909, 419-20.

23. Booth, Darkest England, 159, 158-69; for earlier similar statements, see The Salvation War, 1884 (London, 1885?), 141,
and Salvation Army, Calendar, 1887 (New York, 1887), 12; cf.
William Booth, "Principles of Social Work" International Social
Council Addresses, 1911 (London, 1912), 2-7.

24. "London Letter," WC, March 23, 1889 (390), 9.

25. WC, February 23, 1889 (386), 8.

26. Editorial, WC, May 24, 1890 (451), 8; WC, July 11,
1891 (510), 8 (Boston); E. Bown, "Scouting in Philadelphia Slums,"
WC, November 28, 1891 (530), 8; E. Bown, "Chicago's Slums At-
tacked," WC, July 30, 1892 (565), 3; "In Darkest Philadelphia,"
WC, October 29, 1892 (578), 6 (begun in December, 1891); F.
Booth-Tucker, The Social Relief Work of the Salvation Army in the
United States (Albany, N.Y., 1900), 19.

27. See Maud Booth, "Salvation Army Work in the Slums,"
op. cit., 104; "The Consul in the Slums," WC, July 18, 1896 (772),
4.

28. Harriet C. Lamb, "With the 'Slum Angels,'" CH, September 6, 1905 (28:36), 742; WC, December 17, 1898 (898), 3.

29. "The Slummers at Dr. Stone's Church," WC, February
28, 1891 (491), 2; "Mrs. Booth and the '400,'" WC, May 2, 1891
(500), 7; WC, December 15, 1894 (689), 1.

30. "Slum Angels," WC, November 25, 1893 (634), 2,
credited Ballington Booth with this term; WC, March 28, 1896 (756),
13; "Our Slum Lasses," WC, February 23, 1895 (699), 1; cf. "With

the 'Slum Angels,'" CH, September 6, 1905 (28:36), 742; Ballington Booth, "A Retrospect of 6 Years' Work," G, March 29, 1902 (311), 2, called the Volunteer tenement work "perhaps the most Christ-like" of their programs.

31. WC, December 15, 1894 (689), 1.

32. E. J. Bown, "Dive, Garrett and Tenement Work," WC, October 12, 1889 (419), 9.

33. Ballington Booth, From Ocean to Ocean; or, The Salvation Army's March from the Atlantic to the Pacific (New York, 1891), 60; Bown, "Dive, Garrett and Tenement Work," loc. cit.; "What Does America Think of the Salvation Army?" WC (L), December 31, 1891 (858), 11 (34,534 families visited); "The Slum Brigade," WC, March 23, 1895 (703), 6 (44,014 visits); Ballington Booth, "Out of the Depths; Reaching the Submerged," WC, February 6, 1892 (540), 9; Salvation Army, Buffalo, N.Y., Annual Report, 1898, 7, reported that four slum sisters had visited 3638 families.

34. Maud Booth, Letter, WC, June 30, 1888 (352), 5; Maud Booth, "Salvation Army Work in the Slums," op. cit., 110, noted 15,782 families visited during the preceding six months; Maud Booth, Letter, G, June 4, 1896 (8), 9.

35. WC (L), June 18, 1892 (830), 2; cf. AW, April 11, 1890, 233-4.

36. E. J. Bown, "The Nursery," WC, March 20, 1897 (807), 1.

37. WC, October 6, 1900 (992), 4, quoting the Commerical Tribune; cf. WC, September 29, 1900 (991), 8, and October 13, 1900 (993), 4-5.

38. "Staff Capt. Bown Speaks," WC, November 29, 1890 (478), 7; Emma Bown, "In the Slums," WC, June 20, 1891 (507), 7; cf. "our hearts ache," in "Street Work in the Slums of New York," Social News Supplement, WC (L), March 5, 1892 (815), 7.

39. "Slum Angels," WC, November 25, 1893 (634), 2; cf. WC, November 28, 1891 (530), 4; WC, January 26, 1895 (695), 7, reported 500 garments distributed in the slums of Brooklyn and New York.

40. See the CH's "Montlawn" summer home for tenement children: July 15, 1896 (19:29), 521; August 26, 1903 (26:34), 705; cf. S. H. Hadley, Down in Water Street; A Story of Sixteen Years Life and Work in Water Street Mission (New York, 1902), 108, for that mission.

41. "The Army Creche. A New Departure," WC, December

21, 1889 (429), 12; "News From Our Slum Nursery," WC, July 18, 1891 (511), 7; "The Slum Creche and Its Inmates," WC, October 22, 1892 (577), 3; "Angels of the Slums," WC, August 30, 1890 (465), 6, taken from The Illustrated American; "Frank Leslie's Weekly. A Day Nursery of the Slums," WC, October 21, 1893 (629), 7; "In Sin's Stronghold. The Brave Work ... by the 'Salvation Army' Lasses...," CH, August 12, 1891 (14:32), 497; Maud Booth, "Salvation Army Work in the Slums," op. cit., 113-14.

42. WC, December 24, 1904 (1212), 12; Harriet C. Lamb, "With the 'Slum Angels,'" CH, September 6, 1905 (28:36), 742; "Commander Dedicates Cherry Hill Settlement," WC, June 2, 1906 (1287), 11.

43. Hugh Redwood, God in the Slums (New York, 1931), passim; see his autobiographical Residue of Days; A Confession of Faith (New York, 1959), 22-26.

44. The Volunteers of America claimed 20,000 hours of visitation during the year in which they announced their formal Tenement Work. G, November 3, 1900 (238), 9; Florence I. Bush, "Florence Crittenton Mission Work," AW, August 5, 1911, 301; Sister Charlotte, "Work on the Street and in Houses of Ill-fame," Fourteen Years' Work Among 'Erring Girls' (Washington, D.C., 1897?), 35; H. B. Gibbud, "All-night Missionary Work in New York City," ibid., 46-51; the Peniel Mission in Los Angeles, which later had branches across the country, asked in 1895 for six or eight full-time "devoted and competent women" to extend the "good deal of ... visiting, and looking after the rich and poor" already being done. Peniel Herald, May, 1895 (1:8), 2. Cf. February, 1895 (1:5), 3, 4, and "The Peniel Missions," CH, February 4, 1903 (26:5), 105; the rescue missions for men or for women employed missionaries, all-night rescue brigades, and other measures to increase their contacts with the needy. See the Crittenton references in this note, as well as AW, May 8, 1896, 446-47 (New York Rescue Band), and Hadley, Water Street, 232-34; Editorial, CH, March 29, 1883 (6:13), 200, announced the addition of an all-night missionary to the staff of the Florence Crittenton Mission in New York.

45. WC, May 11, 1889 (397), 6; George S. Railton, The Authoritative Life of General William Booth (New York, 1912), 17, reprinted an address containing similar words; William T. Stead, Life of Mrs. Booth (New York, 1900), 56-57; Booth-Tucker, Catherine Booth, I, 381-82; see the emphasis on "sanctification" in U.S. Bureau of the Census, Report of the Statistics of Churches in the U.S. at the Eleventh Census: 1890 (Washington, D.C., 1894), 751.

46. Booth-Tucker, Catherine Booth, I, 387 (cf. 382-83, 400).

47. Railton, William Booth, 68-70.

48. "All Nights of Prayer," "Three Hours at the Cross,"

"Two Days of Pentecost," etc.: Railton, William Booth, 68; Booth-Tucker, Catherine Booth, I, 656; WC, June 4, 1892 (557), 2; "Waves of Power," WC, May 27, 1893 (608), 8; Begbie, William Booth, I, 373-92, discussed holiness meetings during the late 1870s.

49.   WC, May 7, 1887 (292), 1.

50.   WC, March 14, 1914 (1693), 15; cf. WC, June 10, 1882 (37), 1.

51.   WC, March 14, 1914 (1693), 15; S. Brengle, "The Holiness Standard of the Salvation Army," WC, July 3, 1915 (1761), 3; Editorial, WC, July 27, 1901 (1034), 8, stated that there was "no question but that ... holiness has been, is now, and will increasingly be ... the very backbone and strength of the Army"; Clarence W. Hall, Samuel Logan Brengle; Portrait of a Prophet (New York, 1933).

52.   E.G., S. H. Hadley of rescue missions, in "Reports of the Home Work Given at Old Orchard," AW, August 17, 1894, 160; one plea by Simpson typified the aim of most of these workers: "Intense earnestness, a whole heart for Christ, the passion sign of the cross, the enthusiasm of our whole being for our Master and for humanity ... oh for men God possessed....," AW, March 27, 1896, 300-01.

53.   See "Address by the Rev. Dr. Wilson, St. George's Church," AW, March 21, 28, 1890, 181; also, George P. Pardington, Twenty-five Wonderful years, 1889-1914; A Popular Sketch of the Christian and Missionary Alliance (New York, 1914), 56.

54.   A. B. Simpson, "Not I But Christ," AW, September 25, 1896, 277; cf. Salvation Army, Calendar, 1887, 16, for Herbert Booth's statement that officers in training at his Clapton school "are taught and continually reminded that true religion consists in pure, unselfish love towards God, their comrades, and a dying world," with "the utmost and constant self-denial" their rule of life.

55.   "Christian Work and Workers," AW, August 19, 1899, 188.

56.   William Booth, "The Spirit of Christ," WC, August 7, 1886 (253), 1; WC, October 27, 1894 (682), 8.

57.   A. B. Simpson, "The Life of Love," AW, October 13, 1900, 204; WC, October 10, 1896 (784), 9; William Booth, "Mrs. Booth's Promotion to Glory," WC (L), October 11, 1890 (742), 1: "... no difference of circumstance, or of race, or of sex, or of age, made any difference to her. To be ... in any sort of need ... commanded her sympathy. If she had any preference it was where the need was greatest"; Bramwell Booth, "After Seventy Years," WC, March 7, 1903 (1118), 11. "His greatest power," Bramwell said, "lies in his sympathy."

58. "Theoretical Religion," WC, July 18, 1885 (198), 1; cf. A. B. Simpson, "Fervor and Fanaticism," AW, December 22, 1906, 390-91. In a kind of emphasis that permeated much of what Simpson wrote, he held that authentic Christian experience "melts the heart into tenderness and inspires the soul with love."

59. "Our Colored Alliance Brethren," AW, March 2, 1898, 228; Editorial, AW, July 6, 1898, 12-13; Mrs. L. Kristensen, in "Correspondence," AW, June 5, 1896, 549-50, wrote "These dear children," "the dear Chinese," and "our hearts long" to do good for them.

60. Editorial, AW, December 16, 1899, 461; "Dr. Wilson and the Children," AW, March 31, 1906, 195; AW, August 11, 1906, 91; Madele Wilson and A. B. Simpson, Henry Wilson, One of God's Best (New York, 1909?), 63, 92-104, 116.

61. WC, September 28, 1912 (1617), 8; cf. letters reprinted in Booth-Tucker, Catherine Booth, I, 199-200, 243, 371-72, II, 40-41, 132, 460-62; William Booth, "Mrs. Booth's Promotion to Glory," WC (L), October 11, 1890 (742), 1; Booth-Tucker wrote with equal affection and emotion after his wife's death, WC, November 14, 1903 (1154), 13, 16; though note the element of calculation in both William and Evangeline Booth as discussed in St. John Ervine, God's Soldier (New York, 1935), II, 894; cf. Carrie Judd Montgomery, active in Alliance, Salvation Army, and rescue missions, on her father in her magazine, TF, July, 1890, 144-45.

62. Whittemore, Miracles, 41, 43-45, 225-30 (cf., e.g., 191, 211-12); cf. CH, March 22, 1893 (16:12), 191.

63. Hadley, Water Street, 100-02; cf. Charles Crittenton in "A Haven for Outcasts," CH, November 13, 1895 (18:46), 749; though see "Beware of this Girl," WC, January 4, 1890 (431), 7.

64. Maud Booth, "Our Rescue Work; or, A Home of Love," WC, July 30, 1887 (303), 9; "Love's Power," G, December 12, 1896 (35), 8; Mother Prindle, "How Shall We Reach the Street Girls?" Fourteen Years' Work (Washington, 1897?), 40; Salvation Army, Calendar, 1887, 5.

65. "Mrs. Booth at Harlem," WC, November 21, 1891 (529), 8; William Booth, "Husbands and Wives Alike," August 18, 1900 (985), 2, in a series which centered on the family for weeks following, as February 16, 1901 (1011), 7 (cf. August 3, 1901 (1035), 2); his Letters to Salvationists on Religion for Every Day (London, 1902), 2 volumes, reprinted his "Letters" from the WC; for Bramwell Booth's article, see WC, January 29, 1910 (1478), 6, and September 11, 1915 (1771), 7, as well as WC (L), December 23, 1882; Mrs. Herbert Booth, "A Passionate Appeal ... Against ... Evil Speaking," WC, October 21, 1899 (942), 5; Evangeline Booth, "Thinketh No Evil," WC, August 17, 1901 (1037), 11; Mrs. Samuel Brengle, "Freedom from Unholy Tempers," WC, October 3,

1908 (1409), 6; General Bramwell Booth, "Kindness," WC, August 8, 1914 (1714), 7; cf. "Stifle ... Slander," G, September 5, 1896 (21), 8, "perhaps no sin more cruel, vile, or venomous."

66. A midpage, bold-type "motto," WC, March 3, 1894 (648), 7; A. B. Simpson, "The Life of Love," AW, June 20, 1903, 31; cf. others: K. W. Barrett, Some Practical Suggestions on the Conduct of a Rescue Home (Washington, D.C., 1903?), 16; Redwood, Slums, 42; Maud Booth, "Hope Hall," G, September 12, 1896 (22), 9, 12; G, November 14, 1903 (396), 9.

67. Redwood, Slums, 67-68.

68. Bramwell Booth, Echoes and Memories (New York, 1925), 4-5; Begbie, William Booth, II, 58, 124, 125; cf. Emma Booth-Tucker as a child, in Booth-Tucker, Catherine Booth, II, 125; ibid., I, 25-29; Agnes Palmer, 1904-1922; The Time Between (New York, 1926), 114, termed Evangeline Booth a "passionate lover and defender of all dumb animals"; cf. Begbie, William Booth, II, 61, 131.

69. Charles Crittenton, The Brother of Girls; The Life Story of Charles N. Crittenton (Chicago, 1910), 115-16; McAuley used force effectively for other purposes also, as in maintaining order in his mission: Offord, McAuley, 65-68.

70. "Archdeacon Farrar Speaks," WC, May 16, 1891 (502), 8; Farrar's sympathy for and defense of the poor and "fallen" classes is apparent in his articles about the Salvation Army and in his other writings. For the latter, see, for example, F. W. Farrar, The Messages of the Books (London, 1885), 81-87.

71. A. B. Simpson, "Making Jesus King," AW, April 9, 1896, 342; A. B. Simpson, "The Spirit of Love," AW, January 3, 1896, 5; "All About the Salvation Army," WC, August 14, 1897 (838), 3.

72. WC, August 9, 1913 (1662), 8, also stressed Railton's notable strength of will, as did Ten Talks on the Salvation Army (New York, 1926?), 8-9; Maud Booth, Beneath Two Flags (New York, 1891, c1889), vii; WC, November 2, 1895 (735), 11.

73. F. Booth-Tucker, "The Altar of Sacrifice," WC, March 4, 1899 (909), 8; the centrality of selflessness is indicated by William Booth's indictment of the selfish spirit as the "true spirit of worldliness," in his "Two Excellent Rules," WC, November 23, 1907 (1364), 11; cf. Christian and Missionary Alliance, Annual Report, 1916-17 (New York, 1917), 24, which asserted the world was "corroding through selfishness."

74. Barrett, Suggestions, 11-17; published earlier in FC as "How We Conduct Our Rescue Home," September, 1900 (2:7), 151-58, and October, 1900 (2:8), 177-86.

75. Otto Wilson, Fifty Years Work with Girls, 1883-1933; A Story of the Florence Crittenton Homes (Alexandria, Va., 1933), 133-34, quoting Mrs. Barrett at length.

76. "Missionary Correspondence," AW, February, 1888, 31; AW, April, 1888, 63-64, included an extract from his correspondence which revealed his tenderness toward his wife and children and his sorrow over his separation from them; cf. earlier death in the Congo of John Condit, WWW, July-August, 1885, 220 (cf. January, 1885, 10, and April, 1885, 102-04).

77. AW, June 29, 1894, 696; AW, September, 1888, 144, noted three graves overseas at that early date; AW, April 22, 1911, 61, reported 100 such deaths; "In Memoriam," AW, April 13, 1894, 387; Henry Wilson, "Our Honor Roll in India," AW, June 18, 1897, 577-79; Editorial, AW, June 22, 1894, 669, reported nine deaths on the difficult Sudan field alone by that date; Pardington, Alliance, 161-226, included sketches of most of these missionaries.

78. See p. 36, above.

79. AW, September 2, 1899, 220.

80. A. B. Simpson, "Words in Season," AW, November 5, 1898, 413; cf. the probable income of between $500 and $600 annually for "adult male workers in the leading industries," as discussed in Bremner, Poverty, 153-54; see the article by A. B. Simpson, "Why Our People Give So Much for Missions," LT, November, 1905, 634-44.

81. Charles Crittenton, "A Plea for the Friendless Girls," FC, April, 1899 (1:2), 30; "Self-Denial Week," FC, June, 1900 (2:4), 82; "Self Denial Week," FC, March, 1900 (2:1), 5-6; Hope and Help Mission, Washington, D.C., pamphlet (n.d.); National Florence Crittenton Mission, Report for the Year 1919 to 1920 (Washington, 1920), 47.

82. Mrs. Booth-Tucker, "Our New Industrial Home for Women," WC, January 5, 1901 (1005), 12; cf. WC, February 23, 1901 (1012), 9; cf. Union Gospel Mission, St. Paul, Annual Report, 1913, 13.

83. For their persistent and strong orientation to the Bible, see Maud Booth, Beneath Two Flags, 131; WC, May 24, 1883 (85), 2; "Sketch of Chas. N. Crittenton," Fourteen Years' Work, 5; and Booth-Tucker, Catherine Booth, II, 301.

84. War Cry Supplement, May 2, 1896 (761), 2, 3; General Bramwell Booth, "Shall Our Social Work Continue?" WC, April 6, 1918 (1905), 16; cf. the struggle of Walter Rauschenbusch, and the combined social and biblical emphasis he held as in, e.g., Robert T. Handy, ed., The Social Gospel in America; Gladden, Ely,

Rauschenbusch (New York, 1966), 255; see Walter Rauschenbusch, The Social Principles of Jesus (New York, 1916).

85. WC, March 15, 1883 (75), 1; WC, December 29, 1894 (691), 1; WC, February 7, 1914 (1688), 1; WC, October 10, 1914 (1723), 1.

86. "A Real Banquet--Salvation Army Methods in Olden Times," WC, March 15, 1883 (75), 1; Commissioner Booth-Hellberg authored a WC series on the "Social Wing in the Early Christian Church": September 10, 1904 (1297), 4; September 17, 1904 (1298), 5; and September 24, 1904 (1299), 2-3.

87. Matthew 25:31-46; John 8:1-11; Mark 6:34-44; Hosea 6:6; etc.

88. Hadley, Water Street, 51; J. Wilbur Chapman, S. H. Hadley of Water Street (New York, 1906), 39, 181; cf. Charles Crittenton in Charlton Edholm, Traffic in Girls and Florence Crittenton Missions (Chicago, 1893), 116.

89. A. B. Simpson, "Aggressive Christianity," AW, November 27, 1895, 345; presented in A. B. Simpson, The King's Business (New York, 1900), 9-23, as one of the "first sermons" he preached in New York City; cf. A. B. Simpson, "The Parables of the Son of Man," AW, December 23, 1905, 806; also used, e.g., in Mrs. Delia Collins, "Texas Work. The Woman's Industrial Home," AW, March 30, 1894, 351.

III. FOOD AND SHELTER

1. "Tenement Houses in New York City," CH, March 6, 1879 (1, 2:20), 311; CH, March 20, 1879 (1, 2:22), 344; CH, April 3, 1879 (1, 2:24), 377; T. D. Talmage, "The Poverty of the Very Poor," CH, November 14, 1878 (1, 2:4), 58-60; T. D. Talmage, "The Night of Theft," CH, November 28, 1878 (1, 2:6), 84-86.

2. R. M. Offord, ed., Jerry McAuley, An Apostle to the Lost (New York, c1885), 69-73. McAuley described them as "terrible dens" without windows or plumbing, in which eight to ten persons lived and paid, to his astonishment, $30 to $40 in rent each month.

3. William T. Stead, Life of Mrs. Booth (New York, 1900), 203-04.

4. Roy Lubove, The Progressives and the Slums; Tenement House Reform in New York City, 1890-1917 (Pittsburgh, 1962), 39, 47-48, and passim; Arthur Mann, Yankee Reformers in the

Urban Age (Cambridge, Mass., 1954), 3, 4-6; cf. Robert Bremner, From the Depths; the Discovery of Poverty in the United States (New York, 1956), 205 (see also 81-83), who reports "general agreement that the tenement house was the nexus of all the evils associated with the slum."

5. Bremner, Poverty, 204-06.

6. Ibid., 204-12; see Michael Harrington, The Other America; Poverty in the United States (Baltimore, 1963, c1962), and William Stringfellow, My People Is the Enemy (New York, 1964), for current descriptions of the housing of the poor; Lubove, Progressives, 251-56, discusses the complexities and difficulties of achieving social change through housing reform.

7. Bramwell Booth, Echoes and Memories (New York, 1925), 1-2; cf. St. John Ervine, God's Soldier (New York, 1935), II, 675.

8. On Crittenton, see pp. 79-80, above; Maud Booth, "Hope Hall," G, September 12, 1896 (22), 9.

9. E.G., "Certificate of Incorporation (as amended) of the Florence Crittenton Home of the State of Delaware," Social Welfare History Archives, University of Minnesota: "the object ... to afford and maintain a temporary shelter ...''; cf. E. M. Whittemore, "Now Sixty-one 'Doors of Hope,'" CH, September 9, 1903 (26:36), 750.

10. CH, May 29, 1879 (1, 2:32), 503; CH, October 9, 1879 (1, 2:51); CH, January 12, 1882 (5:2), 17-19; George Müller, "The Story of Ashley Down," CH, September 8, 1887 (10:36), 573-74, part of a series on Müller extending from July 21 to December 8, 1887; A. T. Pierson, "George Muller's Centennial," CH, October 11, 1905 (28:41), 841; for a larger historical perspective, see Kenneth Scott Latourette, A History of Christianity (New York, 1953), 248, 896, 980-81, 1185, 1270, 1335; for evangelical contemporaries of Müller with programs of similar spirit, see Alexander Gammie, William Quarrier and the Story of the Orphan Homes of Scotland (London, n.d.), as well as LT, May, 1905, 289-94, June, 1905, 367-72, and November, 1905, 688-96.

11. See p. 26, above.

12. See pp. 148-50, 62-64, above.

13. Caroline E. Shultz, "Berachah Orphanage," AW, June, 1888, 75, spoke in detail about divine guidance for the home; her article, "Berachah Orphanage," AW, May 29, 1895, 348, gave her background as superintendent and the story of Berachah's origin, noting its regular publication, Echoes from the Valley of Blessing; AW, December, 1888, 190-91; Editorials in the AW, December 9,

1899, 445, and December 30, 1899, 492, referred to the removal of the home to Nyack; George P. Pardington, Twenty-five Wonderful Years, 1889-1914; A Popular Sketch of the Christian and Missionary Alliance (New York, 1914), 96-97; A. E. Thompson, The Life of A. B. Simpson (New York, 1920), 101.

14. For the home in Boone, Iowa, see AW, December 14, 1907, 185, and June 12, 1909, 185; for others, see AW, June 24, 1899, 61, August 12, 1899, 173, and October 12, 1907, 32.

15. See p. 145-46, 148, above.

16. Among many articles in the WC, see: "The Cherry Tree Home," March 13, 1897 (806), 1, 9; "Prairie Homes for City Children," November 24, 1900 (999), 9; the issue for December 8, 1900 (1001), was the "Cherry Tree Home Number"; "Great Children's Home and Hospital Donated to the Salvation Army," December 30, 1916 (1839), 12, 16; for a brief general sketch, see "Cherry Tree Homes of the Salvation Army," CH, May 6, 1903 (26:18); The Salvation War, 1884 (London, 1885?), 148-49, notes the beginning of an orphanage two or three years earlier; for the Volunteers, see the G, October 24, 1903 (393), 1, December 26, 1896 (37), 1, 8, August 3, 1901 (277), 1, 8, and November 14, 1903 (396), 8; for rescue homes for women, see pp. 76, 83, 85-86, above.

17. Offord, McAuley, 50, 45-59; S. H. Hadley, Down in Water Street; A Story of Sixteen Years Life and Work in Water Street Mission (New York, 1902), 35, 225; CH, February 5, 1896 (19:6), 103; Philip I. Roberts, The Dry Dock of a Thousand Wrecks; The McAuley Water Street Mission (New York, 1912), 29-30; cf. statistics for the Canal Street Mission in Buffalo, N.Y., in 1881, given in TF, September, 1881, 139.

18. CH, October 16, 1895 (18:42), 687.

19. Hadley, Water Street, 114, 106-09; cf. Melvin E. Trotter, These Forty Years (Grand Rapids, Mich., 1939), 88-91, and Charles Crittenton, The Brother of Girls; The Life Story of Charles N. Crittenton (Chicago, 1910), 115-16; on the response of the Door of Hope, see "The Door of Hope," CH, March 22, 1893 (16:12), 189, 191; Ballington Booth, "Reflections at My Desk," G, December 10, 1898 (139), 10, defended the habitual tramp as almost always "positively driven" into that kind of life.

20. Hadley, Water Street, 100; cf. CH, December 5, 1894 (17:49), 771, which claimed the "Food Fund" (see p. 50, above) personnel worked "so quietly and in such kind fashion, that even the recipients did not feel that they were eating the bread of charity."

21. Hadley, Water Street, 100, 101, 230.

22. Ibid., 100, 102, 113-14; Roberts, Water Street, 24-25,

reprinted a poem from the American Magazine which had this theme of men "working" a mission; on Hadley's "love," see also J. Wilbur Chapman, S. H. Hadley of Water Street (New York, 1906), 134-37; cf. Arthur Bonner, Jerry McAuley and His Mission (New York, 1967), 91-92, on the patience of John Wyburn, Hadley's most notable successor during this era.

23. Roberts, Water Street, 29-31.

24. "An Uptown New York Mission," CH, February 22, 1905 (28:8), 166.

25. Among similar establishments not mentioned here were the following: the Whosoever Mission of Germantown, Pa., and its sister institution, the Keswick Colony of Mercy, described, e.g., in November 6, 1897 (81), 6-7; for the Good Samaritan Home for Friendless Men, see "A Unique Washington Charity," CH, November 29, 1905 (28:48), 1025; CH, April 5, 1893 (16:14), 225, 227, presented the Friendly Inn of Boston; "How a Western Mission Grew," CH, May 20, 1903 (26:20), 438, described the Seattle Wayside Mission; "Washington's Gospel Mission," CH, May 3, 1911 (34:18), 450; and Mrs. Whittemore of the Door of Hope homes for women arranged for shelters for outcast men, related in her book Delia (New York, 1893), 122-23.

26. For the Central Union Mission see the Alliance journal, LT, March, 1904, 157-64, and CH, February 8, 1893 (16:6), 93; "Editorial Correspondence," AW, June 6, 1897, 360, described Peck's Denver mission; for the Bowery Mission, the CH, June 12, 1895 (18:24), 377, mentioned a newly acquired "mammoth restaurant" feeding 2000 persons daily, besides the enlargement of the Mission's sleeping quarters; CH, March 11, 1896 (19:11), 203; "Christian Philanthropy. The Christian Herald," G, March 12, 1898 (100), 20; CH, October 6, 1915 (38:40), 995.

27. Agnes L. Palmer, 1904-1922; The Time Between (New York, 1926), 57, 54-58.

28. "The Traveller's Club," CH, January 11, 1893 (16:2) 17, 26; "The Rev. Stephen Merritt, the Philanthropic Preacher of New York," CH, September 10, 1885 (8:37), 577-79; CH, December 5, 1894 (17:49), 771; for an additional indication of Merritt's earnest religion and wide influence, see WWW, November-December, 1887, 202, as well as Lindley J. Baldwin, March of Faith (New York, n.d.), 26-28, 42-57, 85-86.

29. CH, January 24, 1894 (17:4), 49, 53.

30. "Our Food Fund at Work," CH, January 31, 1894 (17:5), 65, 67; CH, February 21, 1894 (17:8), 113, 116-17; CH; March 14, 1894 (17:11), 161, 164; CH, March 28, 1894 (17:13); the Fund apparently was touched off by Editor T. DeWitt Talmage. See "A Bread and Beef Charity," CH, January 10, 1894 (17:2), 19, which

provided "immediate and unconditional relief" in the distribution of 3000 "boneless" pounds of meat and 2000 loaves of bread. This began the morning of December 26, 1893, with each adult receiving two pounds of meat, each child one; cf. F. Booth-Tucker, The Social Relief Work of the Salvation Army in the United States (Albany, N.Y., 1900), 25-26, for another example of large-scale winter relief. He related that during one winter in the late 1890s the Army channeled $200,000 worth of food and clothing to 7000 needy families in Detroit.

31. CH, January 24, 1894 (17:4), 49, 53; CH, March 28, 1894 (17:13); cf. CH, February 7, 1894 (17:6), 84; for a Salvation Army food and shelter program that professed to spring spontaneously out of the needs of the homeless, see WC, January 6, 1894 (640), 5, 8.

32. CH, March 29, 1905 (28:13), 277; cf. description in CH, December 17, 1913 (36:51), 1175, 1178; CH, December 7, 1910 (33:49), 1148.

33. CH, December 17, 1913 (36:51), 1175, 1178; cf. CH, December 7, 1910 (33:49), 1150, and May 10, 1911 (34:19), 471; for similar assistance two decades later, see "A Trip Through the Bowery Mission," CH, January, 1932 (55:1), 18-19.

34. CH, December 17, 1913 (36:51), 1175, 1178.

35. CH, February 8, 1905 (28:61), 123; WC, February 11, 1905 (1219), 4.

36. WC, February 20, 1897 (803), 1, 7; WC, February 25, 1899 (908), 5, 8.

37. WC, October 23, 1897 (838), 8; WC, January 25, 1908 (1373), 12; WC, February 1, 1908 (1374), 8; WC, February 8, 1908 (1375), 3.

38. William Peart, "Seasonal Social Work," Social Problems in Solution; Papers Read at the International Social Council, London, ... 1921 (London, 1923), 85, included the flood in Johnstown, Pa., in 1889, among the calamities to which the Army extended "effective aid of large proportions"; "A Word About Ourselves. What 'The Christian Herald' Has Accomplished in the Last Five Years," CH, December 5, 1894 (17:49), 771; "Flood Sufferers Relieved," CH, August 3, 1892 (15:31), 485; "Grateful Flood Sufferers," CH, October 19, 1892 (15:42), 673; WC, June 18, 1892 (559), 1, 4; "A Great Western Calamity," CH, September 12, 1894 (17:37), 589; CH, September 26, 1894 (17:39), 613, reported a committee which included the governor of Minnesota, as well as Klopsch and Sandison of the Herald.

39. WC, September 22, 1900 (990), 8; WC, September 29,

1900 (991), 9; WC, October 6, 1900 (992), 1, 9; F. Booth-Tucker, "1900," WC, December 22, 1900 (1003), 2.

40. WC, September 29, 1900 (991), 9; "Dr. Talmage's Philanthropies," CH, August 6, 1902 (25:32), 652; see CH, October 10, 1900 (23:41), 839, and June 5, 1901 (24:23), 522, for totals.

41. WC, June 27, 1903 (1134), 12; WC, July 11, 1903 (1136), 5.

42. G, July 18, 1903 (379), 4, 6; G, August 1, 1903 (381), 3.

43. CH, June 17, 1903 (26:24), 511.

44. AW, April 28, 1906, 249; AW, May 5, 1906, 365.

45. G, May 5, 1906 (525), 9; WC, May 19, 1906 (1285), 13; WC, June 16, 1906 (1289), 4.

46. Ballington Booth, Editorial, G, July 21, 1906 (536), 9; cf. G, May 12, 1906 (526), 1, July 14, 1906 (535), 7, and July 28, 1906 (537), 4-5.

47. Ten Talks on the Salvation Army (New York, 1926?), 77-78.

48. WC, May 5, 1906 (1283), 1, 8, 9, 12.

49. WC, May 19, 1906 (1285), 8; WC, June 2, 1906 (1287), 4; WC, June 16, 1906 (1289), 4; WC, June 23, 1906 (1290), 8, 12; WC, June 30, 1906 (1291), 4.

50. Cf. the mid-twentieth century, with Harrington, Poverty, 30, describing winter as "a most bitter enemy of the poor."

51. Peart, "Seasonal Social Work," Social Problems, 85.

52. WC, February 25, 1899 (908), 5, 8; WC, November 8, 1902 (1101), 1, 8.

53. "Cheap Coal for the Multitude," WC, November 15, 1902 (1102), 4; "The Dreadful Coal Famine," WC, January 3, 1903 (1109), 9, 12; "The Coal Situation," WC, January 31, 1903 (1113), 5.

54. WC, February 7, 1903 (1114), 4; WC, March 21, 1903 (1120), 10; cf. Peart, "Seasonal Social Work," Social Problems, 85.

55. WC, February 14, 1902 (1115), 5.

56. G, February 28, 1903 (359), 1, 9; cf. G, September 3, 1904 (438), 5, for the winter of 1903-04.

57. Booth-Tucker, Social Relief Work, 27; reprint, "How the Penny Ice Brings Joy to the Poor," WC, September 24, 1898 (886), 9. Cf. Editorial, 8, quoting the Kansas City Star.

58. "Chicago's Free Ice for the Poor," WC, August 31, 1901 (1039), 9, 12, reprinted from the Chicago Herald Record; WC, July 20, 1901 (1033), 9, 12.

59. WC, September 9, 1911 (1562), 9; "Our 1909 Advance," WC, January 1, 1910 (1474), 9.

60. WC, September 5, 1908 (1405), 8; WC, September 10, 1910 (1510), 1, 8.

61. WC, September 10, 1910 (1510), 1; WC, August 3, 1901 (1035), 1; WC, August, 5, 1905 (1244), 1; WC, July 29, 1911. (1556), 1; Kansas City Post article reprinted as "Lives of Babies Are Saved by Ice," WC, November 15, 1913 (1676), 5; Editorial, WC, September 24, 1898 (886), 8, quoted the editor of the Kansas City Star on spoilage; cf. Peart, "Seasonal Social Work," Social Problems, 79.

62. See Booth-Tucker, Social Relief Work, 27, 28, 21, 22.

63. "Chicago's Free Ice for the Poor," loc. cit.

64. On pauperizing, see editorial, Kansas City Star, cited in WC, September 24, 1898 (886), 8; cf. reprint from a Pittsburgh newspaper, "The Salvation Army's Penny Ice Philanthropy," WC, August 23, 1902 (1090), 9; WC, September 24, 1898 (886), 9, from the Kansas City Star.

65. "The Army and the Slums," WC, May 3, 1890 (448), 4; cf. earlier articles about the British shelters, e.g., "A Day in the Food and Shelter Home," WC, June 8, 1889 (401), 1, 2.

66. "The Commander Returns to America," WC, June 20, 1891 (507), 9; "Our First Food and Shelter," WC, December 12, 1891 (532), 8; "At the Lighthouse," WC, February 6, 1892 (540), 1, 4-5.

67. "Social Work in San Francisco," WC, March 18, 1893 (598), 11; cf. WC, November 18, 1893 (633), 8.

68. "'The Ark' Food and Shelter Depot, Buffalo, New York," WC, August 26, 1893 (621), 1, 4; cf. "The 'Out-o'-Works'. The People of Seattle Help the Poor Through the Army," WC, January 6, 1894 (640), 5; the WC featured these shelters with front-page sketches of Salvationists rescuing men floundering in a sea of hunger

and want. Cf. William Booth, In Darkest England and the Way Out (New York, London, 1890), for a similar but more elaborate illustration.

69. F. Booth-Tucker, "May Lift up the Lowly, " WC, May 23, 1896 (764), 10, described the situation at his arrival; WC, August 29, 1896 (778), 5; Booth-Tucker, Social Relief Work, 11-12; F. Booth-Tucker, The Salvation Army in the United States (New York, 1899), 17, reported 47 shelters with capacity for 4800 men, and three with capacity for 200 women; "Our Fortieth American Shelter, " WC, October 29, 1898 (891), 9; "A Year's Survey of the Social Work, " WC, April 18, 1903 (1124), 4.

70. G, November 7, 1896 (30), 6 (Council Bluffs, Iowa); G, December 12, 1896 (35), 4 (Syracuse, N. Y.); G, January 15, 1898 (92), 25 (Erie, Pa.); G, February 5, 1898 (95), 23 (Akron, Ohio; G, February 12, 1898 (96), 4 (Butte, Mont.); G, February 26, 1898 (98), 4 (Minneapolis); G, March 18, 1899 (153), 3-4 (Chicago); G, May 5, 1900 (212), 6 (Chicago); G, June 22, 1901 (271), 8 (general statistics).

71. Booth-Tucker, Social Relief Work, 10-11; cf. "A Glimpse at the Chicago Social Work, " loc. cit. , and "At the Lighthouse, " loc. cit.

72. "Dry Dock Hotel, " WC, October 24, 1896 (786), 1, 12.

73. Booth-Tucker, Social Relief Work, 14; "Metropoles for Clerks and Artisans, " in Booth-Tucker, Salvation Army in the United States, 25; cf. G, March 18, 1899 (153), 3-4; although these facilities constituted a distinct effort within the shelter program, the statistics, and often the descriptive articles, did not carefully isolate them from the general shelter work; the "Mills Hotels, " the first of which had 1500 rooms renting for 20 cents a night, with an "excellent" meal for 15 cents, had similar aims. A ten-story building, it claimed "immense reading and lounging rooms, " larger than in any other hotel in New York City. See "The Mills Hotel No. 1, " G, February 5, 1898 (95), 4; see Union City Mission, Minneapolis, Annual Report, 1904-05, 13, for its St. James Hotel, acquired three years earlier.

74. Booth-Tucker, Social Relief Work, 14; Booth-Tucker, Salvation Army in the United States, 25.

75. G, December, 1908 (657), 3; G, January, 1911 (682), 3.

76. Booth-Tucker, Social Relief Work, 14; WC, April 18, 1899 (914), 5; cf. K. W. Barrett, Motherhood a Means of Regeneration (Washington, D. C. , n. d.), 3.

77. "A Woman's Shelter, " WC, August 31, 1895 (720), 8; WC (L), December 7, 1895 (1011), 6, 8; F. Booth-Tucker, "May

Lift up the Lowly, " WC, May 23, 1896 (764), 10; Booth-Tucker, Social Relief Work, 13, 15; Booth-Tucker, Salvation Army in the United States, 17.

78. WC, June 15, 1901 (1028), 8; see WC, April 8, 1899 (914), 5, for description at its opening.

79. "The Salvation Army's Rest Home for Working Girls at Tappan, New York, " WC, August 18, 1906 (1298), 1; cf. "Enlarging the 'Door of Hope,'" CH, May 14, 1902 (25:20), 435, and E. M. Whittemore, Records of Modern Miracles (Toronto, 1931), 154.

80. WC, March 7, 1914 (1692), 12; for the Volunteers' program for "working girls, " see "Helping Hand Home for Young Women, " G, February 28, 1903 (359), 3. Similar entries in the G included August 22, 1903 (384), 5, October 10, 1903 (391), 12, November 7, 1903 (395), 6, December 3, 1904 (451), 1, 4, March 17, 1906 (518), 4, and August 11, 1906 (539), 6. See also, "Real Homes for Working Girls, " CH, March 15, 1905 (28:11), 243; cf. "Working Girl's Home, N.Y. City, " FC, June, 1899 (1:4), 98, a home designed to give protection and aid to "small-salaried, self-respecting, self-supporting young women. "

81. "Real Homes for Working Girls, " loc. cit.

82. Ibid.; G, August 11, 1906 (539), 6; "Helping Hand Home for Young Women, " loc. cit.; WC, April 8, 1899 (914), 5; Booth-Tucker, Social Relief Work, 12.

83. Booth-Tucker, Social Relief Work, 12, 13; G, August 11, 1906 (539), 6; cf. Mrs. General Bramwell Booth, "True Rescue Work, " WC, January 9, 1915 (1736), 10-11.

84. "Real Homes for Working Girls, " loc. cit.; cf. "Shall We Turn Them Away?" FC, May, 1900 (2:3), 55-56; Kate Waller Barrett, "Twelfth Annual Report of the F. C. Hope and Help Mission, Washington, D.C., " FC, March, 1900 (2:1), 8, reported that the mission was "always full, " and that "only the privilege of sending girls to other homes" prevented them from turning many away.

85. "Real Homes for Working Girls, " loc. cit.

86. WC, October 29, 1898 (891), 7; cf. G, February 28, 1903 (359), 3, and January, 1911 (682), 3.

87. Hadley, Water Street, 100; see similar assertion for the Army farm colonies in H. Rider-Haggard, The Poor and the Land; Being a Report on the Salvation Army Colonies in the United States and at Hadleigh, England (London and New York, 1905), 43; cf. "Transients Won't Sing; Boycott Mission, " Sioux City (Iowa)

Journal, March 24, 1967. The superintendent of the Marysville, Calif., mission asserted that "if the transients are not interested in hearing the gospel, we're not interested in feeding them."

IV.   HOLIDAY AND FRESH-AIR PROGRAMS

1.   William Peart, "Seasonal Social Work," Social Problems in Solution; Papers Read at the International Social Council, London, ... 1921 (London, 1923), 83.

2.   R. M. Offord, ed., Jerry McAuley, An Apostle to the Lost (New York, c1885), 45, 48; WC, December 20, 1883 (115), 1; WC, December 23, 1893 (638), 8, 9; see Christian Mission Magazine, February, 1873, 26-27, 30-31, for earlier holiday meals.

3.   WC, January 20, 1894 (642), 1, 4-5.

4.   WC, January 18, 1896 (745), 4, 1, 5, 13; for mounting totals see WC, December 16, 1899 (950), 8, January 13, 1900 (954), 1, 8, 9, December 27, 1902 (1108), 8, January 14, 1905 (1215), 8, 9, January 11, 1908 (1371), 6, 7, January 8, 1910 (1475), 8, January 6, 1912 (1579), 9, January 16, 1915 (1737), 3-6, January 11, 1919 (1945), 8, and January 10, 1920 (1997), 8, 9.

5.   "Newsboys' Thanksgiving Dinner," G, December 12, 1896 (35), 1, 5; "Thanksgiving Day in Orange Valley, N.J.," G, December 12, 1896 (35), 6; "A Thanksgiving Dinner; The Poor of Topeka Fed...," G, December 19, 1896 (36), 7; G, December 26, 1896 (37), 10.

6.   G, November 19, 1898 (135), 19; G, January 15, 1898 (92), 3-4; cf. G, January 19, 1901 (249), 1, 4-5, January 17, 1903 (353), 1, 7, and January 21, 1905 (458), 6.

7.   WC, January 26, 1895 (695), 7; "Our Great Christmas Tree," WC, January 9, 1897 (797), 1, 12; Mrs. Brigadier Perry, "Rescue Notes," WC, January 25, 1896 (747), 5; Peart, "Seasonal Social Work," Social Problems, 84.

8.   WC, January 11, 1908 (1371), 1, 12; Maud Booth, "Christmas Among the Very Poor," CH, December 23, 1903 (26:51), 1131; Jennie V. Hughes, "Mrs. Booth's Christmas Work for the Poor," G, January 13, 1900 (196), 4; Maud Booth, "How Santa Went Forth and What Santa Accomplished," G, January 7, 1905 (456), 4. The Bethany Church group took its name from Maud Booth, who was known as the "Little Mother" of the prisons.

9.   "Our Fresh-Air Venture in Kansas City," WC, August 24, 1895 (725), 6, with Star reprint, 10; Salvation Army, Buffalo,

N.Y., Annual Report, 1898, 7, reported a July excursion to Lake Erie for 1200 mothers and children.

10. G, July 11, 1896 (13), 6-7; facsimile of Harrison's note, G, December 2, 1899 (190), 4; "Chicago's Great Day for the Poor Children," G, July 11, 1903 (378), 1, 4-5; for other years, see G, July 2, 1898 (116), passim, July 8, 1899 (169), 1, 3, 5, July 13, 1901 (274), 2-3, 7, and July 18, 1908 (640), 1-3.

11. WC, August 23, 1902 (1090), 2; WC, July 31, 1909 (1452), 1; G, September, 1909 (666), 3.

12. For the fifth of a series of evangelistic campaigns by car, see WC, July 25, 1908 (1399), 8, and August 1, 1908 (1400), 1; G. S. Railton, The Authoritative Life of General William Booth (New York, 1912), discussed these trips in chapter 21 ("Motoring Triumphs"); W. P. Ryan, The Romance of a Motor Mission; With General Booth on His White Car Crusade (London and New York, 1906).

13. "Chicago Slum Outing," WC, July 25, 1908 (1399), 3; "More Automobiles," WC, August 15, 1908 (1402), 8; WC, August 22, 1908 (1403), 7; WC, September 12, 1908 (1406), 5; see also later outings, as WC, August 6, 1910 (1505), 1, 8.

14. CH, June 6, 1894 (17:23), 358; "A Children's Paradise. Opening the Christian Herald Children's Home," CH, June 13, 1894 (17:24), 369, 383; "The Story of Montlawn," CH, February 22, 1911 (34:8), 192-93; for an account of the Food Fund, see p. 50, above.

15. John A. Ledlie, editor, Managing the YMCA Camp (New York, 1961), 21, indicates this precaution was not common in the early days of camping; two of the initial applicants for Montlawn were temporarily rejected for medical reasons.

16. "The Story of Montlawn," loc. cit.; "A Children's Paradise," loc. cit., promised a ratio of one counselor for every fifteen children and an avoidance of large "institutional" sleeping rooms; CH, September 25, 1894 (17:39), 621.

17. CH, June 20, 1894 (17:25), 395; CH, June 27, 1894 (17:26), 401; "The Children's Paradise," CH, June 29, 1910 (33:26), 602; cf. "Our Children's Paradise at Spring Valley," WC, June 3, 1905 (1235), 1.

18. "The Story of Montlawn," loc. cit.; Vera L. Connolly, "Mont-lawn As a Stranger Sees It," CH, July 17, 1918 (41:29), 837; "Paradise-on-Earth," CH, July 18, 1917 (40:29), 766; cf. CH, August 13, 1902 (25:33), 665, and August 27, 1902 (25:35), 597.

19. CH, July 19, 1905 (28:29), 609, 618-20; CH, July 20, 1910 (33:29), 654-55; Charles M. Pepper, Life-Work of Louis Klopsch (New York, 1910), 304-06.

20. CH, June 8, 1910 (33:23), 551; Pepper, Klopsch, 295-96; CH, March 6, 1907 (30:10), 215, discussed Christ and children, relating to the then well-known picture by Fleming Williams, "Christ and the Child-Waif."

21. "A Children's Paradise," loc. cit.; "A Consecrated Band," CH, September 23, 1896 (19:39), 691; CH, June 26, 1907 (30:26), 571, referred to Miss Collins as Montlawn's "Housemother of twelve years standing"; AW, November 3, 1906, 285.

22. "Montlawn's Helpers," CH, October 10, 1900 (23:41), 833; CH, July 10, 1895 (18:28), 445; CH, June 28, 1905 (28:26), 555.

23. CH, September 4, 1895 (18:36), 569, 571; "A Conse-crated Band," loc. cit.; CH, July 25, 1917 (40:30), 799.

24. CH, September 12, 1894 (17:37), 577, 589; "A Word About Ourselves," CH, December 5, 1894 (17:49), 771, reported 1,124 children at Montlawn in 1894, though "A Children's Paradise," loc. cit., had projected "nearly two thousand"; CH, June 19, 1895 (18:25), 397-400; CH, June 26, 1907 (30:26), 571, reported 2,000 in 1906; CH, June 19, 1907 (30:25), 548, predicted the same for 1907; CH, May 25, 1910 (33:21), 509.

25. CH, June 18, 1913 (36:25), 576; cf. CH, September 9, 1896 (19:37), 661.

26. CH, April 10, 1895 (18:15), 234; Pepper, Klopsch, 291, noted a $1000 deficit for 1894, supplied by Klopsch; CH, April 22, 1896 (19:17), 328; CH, May 24, 1905 (28:21), 458; CH, November 12, 1913 (36:44), 1060; readers also provided much clothing and other supplies: June 13, 1894 (17:24), 369, 383; July 15, 1896 (19:29), 521, 536; June 22, 1898 (21:25); August 13, 1902 (25:33), 665; August 26, 1903 (26:34), 704; Pepper, Klopsch, 299; most donations were small, as indicated in October 11, 1911 (34:41), 1009-16, which listed hundreds of contributors on each page.

27. "The Children's Paradise," CH, June 29, 1910 (33:26), 602; cf. CH, July 13, 1910 (33:28), 638.

28. CH, November 25, 1896 (19:48), 878; CH, March 16, 1910 (33:11), 256; Pepper, Klopsch, 298; cf. the Episcopalian clergy-man, Henry Wilson of the Alliance, in Madele Wilson and A. B. Simpson, Henry Wilson, One of God's Best (New York, 1909?), 63, 92-96.

29. CH, January 11, 1911 (34:2), 32, 35; "Memorial to Dr. Klopsch," CH, January 25, 1911 (34:4), 74; CH, February 1, 1911 (34:5), 98, 104; CH, March 1, 1911 (34:9), 219; CH, March 8, 1911 (34:10), 250, 271; CH, November 12, 1913 (36:44), 1060, listed en-dowment income for the preceding year as $800.

30. "A Fresh-Air Camp," WC, August 14, 1897 (828), 7; F. Booth-Tucker, The Social Relief Work of the Salvation Army in the United States (Albany, N.Y., 1900), 27; "The Kansas Floods," WC, June 27, 1903 (1134), 12; WC, September 29, 1906 (1304), 4.

31. See Peart, "Seasonal Social Work," Social Problems, 81.

32. WC, July 19, 1902 (1085), 11; G, September 12, 1903 (387), 6.

33. G, August 15, 1908 (644); WC, June 10, 1905 (1236), 1, 3; WC, July 29, 1905 (1243), 1; WC, August 11, 1906 (1297), 1, 3; for other camps, see G, July 28, 1906 (537), 7, August 25, 1906 (541), 3, September 1, 1906 (542), 6-7, and January, 1909 (658), 6 and WC, August 4, 1906 (1296), 9, September 29, 1906 (1304), 4, 11, August 13, 1910 (1506), 4, July 20, 1912 (1607), 9, and September 27, 1913 (1669), 1, 9.

34. See pp. 70-71, above.

35. "Camp Ramona," WC, August 10, 1907 (1349), 4; Peart, "Seasonal Social Work," Social Problems, 81; CH, June 20, 1894 (17:25), 383.

36. WC, September 4, 1909 (1547), 8; F. A., "Preparation for Summer Guests," WC, June 6, 1908 (1392), 3 (Glen Ellyn); Booth-Tucker, Social Relief Work, 27; Peart, "Seasonal Social Work," Social Problems, 82.

37. G, January 11, 1902 (300), 9.

38. "The Thanksgiving Banquet," WC, December 12, 1896 (793), 13; "Christmas in Chicago," WC, January 18, 1896 (745), 4.

39. WC, January 6, 1912 (1579), 9, 12; WC, January 13, 1912 (1580), 12; cf. WC, January 8, 1908 (1372), 14; for other instances of support see WC, September 28, 1901 (285), 4, and July 25, 1903 (380), 3.

V. THE GOSPEL OF HEALING

1. See WWW, February, 1885, 63, as well as Carrie Judd Montgomery's magazine, TF, January, 1885, 24, for the letter of invitation sent out by W. E. Boardman, convener and host. The gathering was also known as the "Bethshan Conference," after the auditorium which was the center of Boardman's activities in London; WWW, July-August, 1885, 192-219, contained addresses and "testimonies" from Bethshan, with Simpson (220) describing his

forthcoming October convention in New York City as in a sense a
sequel; A. E. Thompson, The Life of A. B. Simpson (New York,
1920), 112-13; Carrie Judd Montgomery, "Under His Wings"; The
Story of My Life (Oakland, Calif., 1936), 120-22.

2. For that era see Sydney E. Ahlstrom, A Religious
History of the American People (New Haven, Conn., 1972), 1019-
33, on "Harmonial Religion," Stephen Gottschalk, The Emergence
of Christian Science in American Religious Life (Berkeley, Calif.,
1973), Robert Peel, Christian Science; Its Encounter with American
Culture (New York, 1958), and Raymond J. Cunningham, "From
Holiness to Healing: The Faith Cure in America, 1872-1892,"
Church History, December, 1974 (43:4), 499-513; cf. Grant Wacker,
Jr., "Dowie's Zion: A Case of Charisma and Commitment" (un-
publ. ms., 1975) for an important but relatively unknown practi-
tioner of healing, especially 4-7; see also the pp. 14-15, above.

3. Consumptive's Home, Boston, Annual Report, 1864-65,
6-18, and passim, and other annual reports until Cullis' death in
1892; W. H. Daniels, ed., Dr. Cullis and His Work (Boston, 1885),
25-38 and passim, made extensive use of Cullis' writings; "Dr.
Cullis of Boston. His Wonderful Work of Faith," CH, April 29,
1880 (3:18), 273-75; "A Wondrous Work of Faith. The Late Charles
Cullis, M.D.," CH, July 27, 1892 (15:30), 469; other journals also
contained portions of his annual reports, e.g., The Watchword,
March 1897 (1:6), 110-11, and TF, February 1881, 28; A. J. Gordon,
The Ministry of Healing, or Miracles of Cure in All Ages (Boston,
1883), 170-73, also referred to "city mission work" and "schools
among the freedmen," as part of Cullis' outreach; Montgomery, My
Life, 106, 123.

4. "Dr. Cullis of Boston," loc. cit.; "A Wondrous Work of
Faith," loc. cit.; this was a major theme in his annual reports.

5. For Cullis' influence see TF, April, 1881, 63-64, December, 1883, 286, and December, 1884, 265-66. Carrie Judd's
wider sphere of influence included rescue missions, among them
the Peniel Missions in California, and the Door of Hope and Crittenton mission homes for women: Montgomery, My Life, 89, 106-
07, 131, 135, 144, 149. Emma Whittemore, Records of Modern
Miracles (Toronto, 1931), 18; Charles Crittenton Letter, CH, September 12, 1894 (17:37), 585; she carried extended reports of Crittenton's activities for many months in TF, beginning June, 1891,
131-33.

6. See WWW, November, 1885, 288, 301-02, for her participation in the second annual convention in New York; she reported, e.g., the Old Orchard convention in TF, September, 1887,
203-04, and as recording secretary of the Alliance in 1890 included
her annual report, TF, April, 1890, 82-84; Anna W. Prosser,
"Wedding Bells," TF, June, 1890, 121-23; in TF, July, 1890, 166,
she referred to Simpson as "the kind friend whom we always think

of as our pastor"; on her husband, see TF, December, 1892, 265-67, 269; Montgomery, My Life, 98-102, 186-87.

7. Montgomery, My Life, 132-33, 144-46; AW, April 22, 1892, 257; TF, May, 1892, 108-10, and October, 1892, 217-20.

8. Montgomery, My Life, 83-84, 89-91, 140, 144-47, 149-50, 157-58; TF featured Buffalo's Alliance-supported Canal Street Mission regularly, as, e.g., in the first issue, January, 1881, 14; cf. TF, October, 1890, 227-28; on San Francisco, see TF, October, 1890, 227-28; for the "Faith-Rest Cottage" see TF, February, 1882, 19-20, December, 1882, 186-87, March, 1885, 88, and February, 1892, 35, 36; Editorial, AW, June 19, 1895, 392-93; AW, August 21, 1895, 124; the rest home was one of several the Army operated. Besides its inclusion at Beulah, and the presence in Army ranks of such persons as the Montgomeries and Emma Whittemore, occasional friendly references in the WC indicated its openness to healing during much of this era. For other homes see WC, July 11, 1891 (510), 1-2, and August 8, 1891 (514), 10; Salvation Army, Orders and Regulations for Field Officers (London and New York, 1917), 53, affirmed that faith-healing was "in perfect harmony with the views of the Salvation Army," with "numerous" such cases; for the Crittenton homes, see "Report of the First General Convention of the National Florence Crittenton Mission," Fourteen Years' Work Among 'Erring Girls' (Washington, D.C., 1897?), 111.

9. "Philadelphia Home and Work," AW, November 4, 1905, 700; Editorial, AW, May 4, 1898, 420; "Berachah, Nyack-on-Hudson," AW, November 7, 1908, 100; AW, September 18, 1909, 411; for other homes in various cities see: AW, May 14, 1904, 361; A. E. Funk "The Homes and Institutions of the Alliance," AW, April 23, 1897, 373; cf. Montgomery, My Life, 84-85, and TF, January, 1881, 12-13, and February, 1882, 19-20.

10. AW, May 14, 1904, 361.

11. E.G., "Jottings from Berachah Home, Nyack Heights," AW, November 3, 1897, 447.

12. AW, April 23, 1897, 387; cf. "The Past Year at the Berachah Home," WWW, May, 1885, 158-59.

13. WWW, July-August, 1885, 203-05, 208-10; AW, May 21, 1904, 371; A. B. Simpson, The Gospel of Healing, rev. ed. (New York, 1915), 155-74.

14. Madele Wilson and A. B. Simpson, Henry Wilson, One of God's Best (New York, 1909?), 40-41; Wilson related his experience at the first "national" convention of the Alliance in 1887, WWW, November-December, 1887, 228; see Carrie Judd Montgomery's very similar words in TF, December, 1884, 269.

15. "Old Orchard Convention," AW, September 2, 1905,

556-57; cf. AW, December 2, 1899, 429, "Divine healing is divine life..."; see also WWW, May, 1885, 154-58.

16. "Divine Healing," AW, October 27, 1897, 423; AW, March 1, 1908, 365; "Testimony," AW, May 19, 1906, 299-300; see George P. Pardington, Twenty-five Wonderful Years, 1889-1914; A Popular Sketch of the Christian and Missionary Alliance (New York, 1914), 58-59, on the large numbers of Alliance members healed; cf. Montgomery, My Life, 54-83, for response to her writing on healing.

17. AW, August 31, 1898, 208-09; cf. AW, November 11, 1911, 87; see James Rogers, "Divine Healing in Mission Work," India Alliance, January, 1906, 82-83.

18. Editorial, AW, August 13, 1910, 320.

19. Editorial, AW, December 2, 1899, 429; Editorial, AW, May 28, 1904, 383; Simpson, "Phases, Facts, and Fallacies," AW, May 21, 1904, 371; cf. The Gospel in All Lands, September, 1881, 138, in relation to Charles Cullis.

20. Editorial, AW, May 18, 1894, 527-28; Editorial, AW, September 3, 1904, 209; A. B. Simpson, "A Message for the Last Times," AW, September 10, 1904, 227 (the quote).

21. "Testimonies," AW, March 13, 1896, 262; Peniel Herald, February, 1895 (1:5), 4.

22. "The Past Year at the Berachah Home," WWW, May, 1885, 158-59, placed emphasis on conversion and Christian holiness.

23. R. M. Offord, ed., Jerry McAuley; An Apostle to the Lost (New York, c1885), 98-99; Emma Whittemore, Delia (New York, 1893), 35, 70-71; AW, January 26, 1898, 89; for the slum work, see pp. 32-37, above.

24. "Medical Missions," AW, May, 1888, 76.

25. CH, November 29, 1888 (11:48), 754-55; "Progress of Missions," Missionary Review of the World, September, 1889 (12:10), 719-20; CH, December 30, 1891 (14:52), 817, 825-26; CH, July 5, 1893 (16:27), 433, 437; "Christian Philanthropy. The Christian Herald," G, March 12, 1898 (100), 20; "Berachah Mission," AW, May, 1888, 78; "Berachah Mission," AW, October 25, 1889, 203-04; cf. WWW, February, 1882, 78, for other similar medical operations within the Alliance, see AW, June 6, 1895, 360-61, and June 8, 1898, 544.

26. "The New York Rescue Band and Its Industrial Home Department," AW, May 8, 1896, 447; National Florence Crittenton Mission, Report [1914] (Washington, D.C., 1914?), 133; The Girl

Problem As Handled by the Florence Crittenton Hope and Help Mission of Washington, D. C. (Washington, D. C. , 1920), 5.

27. G, December 24, 1904 (454), 4; G, March 14, 1908 (622), 2-3; for others, see G, December 2, 1899 (190), 6-7, September 3, 1904 (438), 4-5, and April 6, 1907 (573), 5.

28. WC, December 8, 1906 (1314), 3; WC, April 6, 1907 (1331), 1; WC, May 18, 1907 (1337), 2; WC, August 3, 1907 (1348), 2, 4; WC, December 20, 1913 (1681), 5; cf. "Camp Ramona," WC, August 10, 1907 (1349), 4.

29. CH, June 20, 1894 (17:25), 395; "Close of Season at Montlawn," CH, September 19, 1917 (40:38), 991; cf. WC, September 5, 1903 (1144), 12.

30. "Memorial of Rev. Wm. Cassidy, Missionary to China," AW, March, 1888, 33; Robert H. Glover, "Parting Words," AW, November 30, 1894, 516-18; Glover, later associated with Moody Bible Institute and the China Inland Mission, wrote a popular survey and text of world missions that remains in use: The Progress of World-Wide Missions (New York, 1960); like Cassidy, George Dowkontt's student, William Summers, was an early casualty to missions overseas: CH, November 29, 1888 (11:48), 754-55.

31. "The Salvation Army Officer As Doctor," WC, September 5, 1908 (1405), 10; F. Booth-Tucker, Muktifauj, or Forty Years With the Salvation Army in India and Ceylon (London, n. d.), 187-93; British Medical Journal, September 18, 1920, 456, recorded the award of the Victoria Cross to Andrews; Ten Talks on the Salvation Army (New York, 1926?), 83; WC, April 5, 1913 (1644), 8-9, presented General Bramwell Booth's appeal for a Self Denial Week fund which was to include $250,000 each for overseas hospital programs and service for lepers.

32. Booth-Tucker, Muktifauj, 190.

33. For contemporary Protestant groups, see A. Abell, The Urban Impact on American Protestantism, 1865-1900 (London, 1962, c1943), 30, 52-55, 158; Lucy Meyer, Deaconesses and Their Work (Chicago, 1897), passim; L. R. Elliott, ed. , Centennial Story of Texas Baptists (Dallas, 1936), 179-82; as Kenneth S. Latourette, A History of Christianity (New York, 1953), 247, 538, 558, 569, 980, indicates, healing ministries for the needy had continued in almost uninterrupted fashion from the numerous healings recorded in the New Testament.

34. G, September 29, 1906 (546), 1, 8, 16; Ballington Booth, "Our Tenth Anniversary," G, November 17, 1906 (553), 9; G, November, 1908 (656), 2; cf. G, November 9, 1907 (604), 9.

35. "A House of Help in a Neighborhood of Need," G, January, 1909 (658), 3; "Why the Hospital Is All-Essential," G, March,

1910 (672), 10; "The Volunteer Hospital," G, June 15, 1907 (583), 1, 6-7, stated a daily average of 200 medical treatments; "Volunteer St. Gregory Hospital," G, August 1, 1908 (642), 5, claimed 1020 cases in one week; G, November 9, 1907 (604), 9; G, February, 1911 (683), 6.

36. "Great Children's Home and Hospital Donated to the Salvation Army," WC, December 30, 1916 (1839), 12, 16; Brooklyn Eagle editorial reprinted in War Cry, January 13, 1917 (1841), 8; WC, February 24, 1917 (1847), 9.

37. "How a Western Mission Grew," CH, May 20, 1903 (26:20), 438; "A Thrilling Branch of the War," WC, November 27, 1897 (843), 2; "The Salvation Army Sanitarium. Amity, Colorado," WC, August 5, 1905 (1244), 13; on the sanitarium, see also the reprint from the New York Herald in the WC, September 7, 1901 (1040), 5; "Splendid Hospital Service at Webb City, Mo.," WC, October 19, 1907 (1359), 1, 4; WC, January 31, 1920 (2000), 5; WC, March 6, 1920 (2005), 11.

38. Agnes L. Palmer, 1904-1922; The Time Between (New York, 1926), 59-60; WC, November 22, 1913 (1677), 13; National Florence Crittenton Mission, Report [1914], 25, 133.

39. WC, February 20, 1915 (1742), 8; "The History of the Booth Memorial Hospital, Covington, Ky.," WC, May 1, 1915 (1752), 11; "The Booth Memorial Hospital," WC, June 26, 1915 (1760), 9, 16; "The Evangeline Booth Womens Hospital and Home in Boston," WC, March 20, 1920 (2007), 1, 12-13; Margaret Bovill, "Importance and Significance of Our Hospital Work," Social Problems in Solution; Papers Read at the International Social Council, London, ... 1921 (London, 1923), 224; the WC frequently noted developments overseas: August 3, 1912 (1609), 8; December 20, 1913 (1681), 11; March 7, 1914 (1692), 9.

40. "United States Auxiliaries," WC (L), December 1, 1894 (958), 3; Bovill, "... Hospital Work," Social Problems, 225; the same was true for the other organizations, as we have seen on p. 74, above.

41. Booth-Tucker, Social Relief Work, 27, 15; other examples include WWW, October, 1887, 171-72, TF, February, 1892, 37-39, TF, August, 1891, 187, and India Alliance, December, 1908, 68.

42. "Peniel Mission School for Nurses," Peniel Herald, October, 1894 (1:1), 2; cf. Peniel Herald, January, 1895 (1:4), 3, and November, 1895 (1:14), 1; see the Salvation Army's unsuccessful effort to place a resident nurse at each slum post during the autumn of 1897, in "Care of the Destitute Sick by Salvation Army Nurses," WC, March 19, 1898 (859), 1, 4.

43. Ten Talks, 74; see also WC, May 16, 1914 (1702), 4.

44. "Nurses of Brooklyn Nursery Receive Diplomas," WC, February 23, 1918 (1899), 12; WC, July 26, 1919 (1973), 4; Palmer, 1904-1922, 59; Booth-Tucker, Muktifauj, 188-89; the Crittenton Association, meanwhile, had training schools for nurses in at least two of its homes, Detroit and Sioux City, with the latter in operation "for many years" by 1914. See National Florence Crittenton Mission, Report [1914], 133. See also FC, October 1899 (1:8), 169-74.

45. Michael Harrington, The Other America; Poverty in the United States (Baltimore, 1963, c1962), 22.

46. Booth-Tucker, Social Relief Work, 27; cf. CH, September 4, 1895 (18:36), 569, 571, and September 23, 1896 (19:39), 691.

47. Robert Bremner, From the Depths; The Discovery of Poverty in the United States (New York, 1956), 124-28; cf. Harrington, Other America, 17; Ralph H. Gabriel, The Course of American Democratic Thought, 2nd ed. (New York, 1956), 469-70, discusses Eric Fromm and the "laws" of the inner life; cf. Fromm, The Sane Society (New York, 1955), chapter 5, "Man in Capitalistic Society."

VI.   RESCUE HOMES FOR WOMEN

1. Charles Crittenton, The Brother of Girls; The Life Story of Charles N. Crittenton (Chicago, 1910), 22-78; Life Sketch and Work of Evangelist Charles N. Crittenton (Washington, D.C., 1899?), 1-4, 6, 7; Charlton Edholm, Traffic in Girls and Florence Crittenton Missions (Chicago, 1893), 109-16.

2. "Report of the First General Convention of the National Florence Crittenton Mission," Fourteen Years' Work Among 'Erring Girls' (Washington, D.C., 1897?), 173, reported a Crittenton speech; "A Haven for Outcasts," CH, November 13, 1895 (18:45), 745, 749; Crittenton, Brother, 84-86; Edholm, Traffic, 117.

3. Crittenton, Brother, 86-89; Edholm, Traffic, 117-18.

4. "Mr. Chas. N. Crittenton--The Rescue Work of the Florence Mission in New York," CH, January 2, 1889 (12:1), 2; Edholm, Traffic, 301-02, also reported 27,000 "requests for prayer" by residents and visitors; see also the brief early reports in TF, March, 1884, 63-65, and WWW, November, 1885, 307.

5. While both descriptive writings and statistics tended to blur the distinction between types of "fallen women," partly by invariably blaming lovers, producers, and an unjust society, hardcore prostitutes apparently constituted only a small percentage of the clientele served by Crittenton and other rescue workers.

6. Crittenton, Brother, 128, 138-39, 142-54, 168-72; "Sketch of Chas. N. Crittenton," Fourteen Years' Work, 4; "Mr. Chas. N. Crittenton," loc. cit., indicated the beginning of this plan as early as 1888; see Crittenton's account of his tour and subsequent activities in Carrie Judd Montgomery's monthly, TF, beginning June, 1891, 131-33, and continuing for many months (e.g., April, 1892, 78-80); see also earlier issues, as TF, September, 1890, 213, 215.

7. Edholm, Traffic, 214; "To Rescue the Fallen. Mr. Charles N. Crittenton's Effort to Establish a Chain of Missions," CH, December 2, 1891 (14:48), 762; Crittenton, Brother, 164-65.

8. Edholm, Traffic, 216-18, 223; as is evident in S. H. Hadley's remarks in J. Wilbur Chapman, S. H. Hadley of Water Street (New York, 1906), 144, these institutions were "missions," with evangelistic meetings open to the public; AW, May 26, 1893, 332, and TF, August, 1891, 187-88, reported men converted in the Florence missions; "Homes vs. Missions," FC, March, 1899 (1:1), 23-24, contended, as eventually happened, that the functions should be separated, although each of the homes was "a Mission, in the truest sense"; cf. "The Door of Hope. A Rescue Mission in New York...," CH, March 22, 1893 (16:12), 189, 191.

9. "Sketch of Chas. N. Crittenton," Fourteen Years' Work, 5; see "Revival Echoes," CH, September 12, 1894 (17:37), 585, for Crittenton's schedule.

10. Edholm, Traffic, 219-41; Carrie Judd Montgomery reported these meetings in TF, e.g., September, 1890, 213, 215, and October, 1890, 233.

11. Edholm, Traffic, 3-5, 215, 283, 293, 266-85.

12. FC, April, 1899 (1:2), 38; Crittenton, Brother, 196-98, 200-03.

13. "Report of the First General Convention," Fourteen Years' Work, 95; Crittenton, Brother, 187-90.

14. Crittenton, Brother, 44-45, 95; "Sketch of Chas. N. Crittenton," Fourteen Years' Work, 7; Edholm, Traffic, 220 [308]; "The National Florence Crittenton Mission," FC, March, 1899 (1:1), 4; National Florence Crittenton Mission, Report for the Year 1928 (Washington, 1929), 4, reported that during his lifetime Crittenton had contributed more than $500,000 to the work; Life Sketch and Work, 6-7, stated an annual income of $60,000.

15. "A Haven for Outcasts," CH, November 13, 1895 (18:46), 749; FC, March, 1899 (1:1), 12; "Hints and Suggestions," Fourteen Years' Work, 206; cf. later but undated pamphlet, The Florence Crittenton Hope and Help Mission (Washington, D.C.), which claimed 71 homes in the United States, and five abroad.

16. FC, December, 1899 (1:10), 218; reports of the homes, in Fourteen Years' Work, 80; cf. The Girl Problem As Handled by the Florence Crittenton Hope and Help Mission of Washington, D. C. (Washington, D. C. , 1920), 3.

17. Kate Waller Barrett, "Some Reminiscences, " FC, May, 1899 (1:3), 62-66; National Florence Crittenton Mission, Report for 1918-1919 (Washington, D. C. , 1919), 11; Otto Wilson, Fifty Years Work With Girls, 1883-1933; A Story of the Florence Crittenton Homes (Alexandria, Va. , 1933), 155-61.

18. Kate Waller Barrett, Motherhood a Means of Regeneration (Washington, D. C. , n. d.), 8-9; see also Barrett, "Some Reminiscences, " loc. cit. , 63-64, and "Report of the First General Convention, " Fourteen Years' Work, 163.

19. Edholm, Traffic, 249-58; Barrett, "Some Reminiscences, " loc. cit. ; Kate Waller Barrett, "Some Reminiscences--Part II, " FC, June, 1899 (1:4), 84-85.

20. See p. 24, above.

21. Emma Whittemore, Records of Modern Miracles (Toronto, 1931), 18, 26-31 (cf. 27, 32f, 41, 48-49); for her early writing on healing, see WWW, October, 1885, 276-78, and December, 1885, 343-44; see "The Christian Alliance, " CH, March 30, 1892 (15:13), 195, which included the Door of Hope among the Alliance institutions listed.

22. Whittemore, Miracles, 61-64 (see 59-60 for the origin of the name).

23. Mrs. E. M. Whittemore, "Now Sixty-One 'Doors of Hope, '" CH, September 9, 1903 (26:36), 750, also claimed 3800 women cared for by that date; Whittemore, Miracles, 237-38, claimed 73 homes begun by 1908, and 97 by 1931; ibid. , 236-38, discussed the national organization.

24. Whittemore, Miracles, viii, xv, illustration opposite 112, 154; cf. WC, March 13, 1897 (806), 9, October 6, 1906 (1305), 13, November 14, 1908 (1415), 12, January 16, 1909 (1424), 8, October 1, 1910 (1513), 6, and December 29, 1917 (1891), 14.

25. F. Booth-Tucker, The Life of Catherine Booth (New York, 1892), II, 466; WC, October 9, 1886 (262), 1; WC, October 23, 1886 (264), 1; WC, April 28, 1888 (342), 12; WC, October 20, 1888 (368), 13; The Salvation War, 1884 (London, 1885?), 143, "For many years ... a great deal of rescue work through individual efforts"; for an example, see The Salvationist, June 1, 1879, 162.

26. F. Booth-Tucker, "May Lift Up the Lowly, " WC, May 23, 1896 (764), 10; Ballington and Maud Booth also operated Volunteer

rescue homes by 1899: Herbert A. Wisbey, History of the Volunteers of America (New York, 1954), 71; "The Newark Home of Refuge," G, January 26, 1901 (250), 2, G, November 30, 1901 (294), 5.

27. WC, July 11, 1896 (771), 12; WC, January 8, 1898 (849), 8; F. Booth-Tucker, The Social Relief Work of the Salvation Army in the United States (Albany, N.Y., 1900), 17; WC, January 4, 1908 (1370), 9; WC, May 1, 1915 (1752), 11; Ten Talks on the Salvation Army (New York, 1926?), 57-58.

28. Booth-Tucker, Catherine Booth, II, 466-67; for Maud Booth see "Rescue Workers Wanted," WC, August 20, 1892 (568), 10; Evangeline Booth, "Manifesto for Nineteen-Eleven," WC, December 31, 1910 (1526), 8-9.

29. WC, September 5, 1896 (779), 5; WC, September 4, 1897 (831), 6; WC, March 19, 1898 (859), 11; Emma Booth-Tucker, The League of Love (New York, 1896).

30. Cf. other organizations: Whittemore, Miracles, 132-38; G, January 26, 1901 (250), 2; AW, May 8, 1896, 446 (New York Rescue Band); Kate Waller Barrett, "Report of the Hope and Help Mission," Fourteen Years' Work, 89.

31. WC, November 23, 1901 (1051), 3; WC, May 14, 1904 (1180), 11; WC, January 4, 1908 (1370), 9; cf. WC, December 1, 1906 (1313), 10.

32. On the ties with the Door of Hope, see Whittemore, Miracles, 27-28, 56-57, 61-64, 237, as well as her Delia (New York, 1893), 97; AW, June 19, 1892, 370, and March 9, 1894, 273, show the place of the Collins family in the Texas Alliance; see also India Alliance, March, 1915, 218-19, February, 1915, 172, and April, 1916, 237-40, for the Bethany Rescue Home, opened in November, 1913.

33. AW, March 30, 1894, 351; AW, January 22, 1897, 89; cf. "The Delia Collins Rescue Home, from Fort Worth, Texas," AW, September 2, 1899, 220, and Warren Collins, "The Work of the Lord in Fort Worth, Texas," TF, April, 1891, 107-10; Warren Collins' subsequent support also included the Berachah Orphanage in New York: AW, August 5, 1899, 157, and December 30, 1899, 492.

34. AW, March 19, 1896, 280; Madele Wilson and A. B. Simpson, Henry Wilson, One of God's Best (New York, 1909?), 109-10, 60-62, 76.

35. AW, October 20, 1897, 405; "Days of Blessing," AW, October 16 and 23, 1896, 346, described a "magnificent" presentation to an "immense" audience that included about 500 persons standing through an entire evening; AW, October 21, 1899, 336; FC,

October, 1899 (1:8), 185, reported a "cordial" Alliance invitation, and the participation of Mrs. Barrett and other Crittenton personnel; WWW, November, 1885, 307, included a report on the Florence Mission at the second annual New York convention.

36. AW, May 8, 1896, 446-47; Editorial, AW, March 29, 1902, 178, recorded Simpson's break with S. E. Furry, the leader of the Rescue Band, because of allegedly questionable stock-selling practices; for numerous ties of local Alliance branches and individuals with rescue homes, see AW, November 30, 1894, 519, June 8, 1898, 544, November 18, 1899, 400, and July 2, 1904, 76-77; cf. CH, April 12, 1893 (15:14), 245.

37. See A. E. Thompson, The Life of A. B. Simpson (New York, 1920), 100, who also credited the origin of the "Catherine Street Mission" to the "ladies of the Tabernacle."

38. CH, July 9, 1890 (13:28), 436-37; CH, April 27, 1892 (15:17), 261; CH, June 21, 1893 (16:25), 405; for other evidence of its support of rescue homes, see CH, December 5, 1894 (17:49), 771, March 4, 1896 (19:10), 188, and October 7, 1896 (19:41), 725, 730; cf. FC, June, 1899 (1:4), 94, which stated that "The 'Christian Herald' has always been a friend of our work...."

39. WC, February 22, 1908 (1377), 7; similar entries by Maud and Ballington Booth and others included June 4, 1887 (296), 8, July 23, 1887 (303), 8, and July 30, 1887 (304), 9.

40. In T. H. Kitching, "The Relationship of the Press to the Army and its Social Work," Social Problems in Solution; Papers Read at the International Social Council, London, ... 1921 (London, 1923), 123.

41. AW, March 19, 1897, 280; Crittenton, Brother, 168-69; K. W. Barrett, Some Practical Suggestions on the Conduct of a Rescue Home (Washington, D.C., 1903?), 16-17, 56, 82-83; Barrett, "The National Florence Crittenton Mission," Fourteen Years' Work, 28.

42. Booth-Tucker, Social Relief Work, 16; Evangeline Booth, "Manifesto for Nineteen-Eleven," WC, December 31, 1910 (1526), 8-9.

43. Barrett, "Some Reminiscences," loc. cit.; cf. Kate Waller Barrett, "Maternity Work--Motherhood a Means of Regeneration," Fourteen Years' Work, 58-59, and "Report of the First General Convention," ibid., 163.

44. Barrett, "The National Florence Crittenton Mission," Fourteen Years' Work, 26; cf. Barrett, Suggestions, 53, and Whittemore, Miracles, 124.

45. Whittemore, Miracles, 120, 235.

46. Barrett, Suggestions, 7-15, 104-5; "Homes vs. Missions," FC, March, 1899 (1:1), 23-24; cf. Evangeline Booth, "Rescue Work," WC, June 11, 1910 (1497), 8-9.

47. Whittemore, Miracles, 93 (cf. 206-09).

48. See pp. 38-40, above, on "love"; while personal concern was central, freely expressed emotion was also important. Evangeline Booth spoke of her "precious sisters," and Emma Whittemore related a number of instances where her tears or an embrace won over a particularly difficult girl. Yet emotion generally seemed to be the product of their deeper concern: Evangeline Booth, "Manifesto for Nineteen-Eleven," loc. cit., and Whittemore, Miracles, 225-30, 211-12.

49. AW, March 30, 1894, 351.

50. Whittemore, Miracles, 46 (cf. 43-45).

51. "Mr. Chas. N. Crittenton--The Rescue Work of the Florence Mission in New York," CH, January 2, 1889 (12:1), 2; Barrett, "Report of the Hope and Help Mission," Fourteen Years' Work, 90.

52. Mrs. General Bramwell Booth, "True Rescue Work," WC, January 9, 1915 (1735), 10-11.

53. Evangeline Booth, "Rescue Work," WC, June 11, 1910 (1497), 8-9; cf. WC, February 27, 1909 (1430), 6; for their optimism see, for example, WC, November 23, 1901 (1051), 3, and FC, May, 1900 (2:3), 56.

54. His "Preface" to Selected Papers on the Social Work of The Salvation Army (London, 1907), xiii.

55. FC, May, 1900 (2:3), 57; FC, March, 1900 (2:1), 1.

56. "Should Young People Do Rescue Work?" FC, March, 1900 (2:1), 2.

57. Whittemore, Miracles, 269-75 (cf. 120-21, 258-68). Formerly in partial charge of a house of prostitution, this girl, whose husband was also converted at the Door of Hope, subsequently made her home a shelter for fallen girls, and did "salvation work in the slums" of a southern city; Charles Crittenton, "A Plea for the Friendless Girl," FC, April, 1899 (1:2), 29; LT, November, 1905, 699, noted the unwillingness of George Müller to admit illegitimate children to his homes, in contrast to the similarly evangelical Barnardo homes on which the article centered.

58. "The Work of Rescue," WC, April 28, 1894 (656), 8; for an extension to other rights within marriage, see K. W. Barrett, The Sanctity of Marriage (Washington, D.C., 1912), 6-9.

59. Booth-Tucker, Social Relief Work, 14; Whittemore, Miracles, 182-84, 249-64; "Report of the First General Convention," Fourteen Years' Work, 174; cf. T. DeWitt Talmage, in CH, November 28, 1878 (1, 2:6), 85; on preventive institutions, see p. 57, above.

60. A part of the reason resides, of course, in the apparently low percentage of hardened prostitutes these groups served. Other negative considerations include possible exaggeration (see Charles C. Cole, The Social Ideas of the Northern Evangelists, 1826-1860 (New York, 1954), 231, 112, for this trait in earlier revivalists), the question of permanence of cure, and bias in admissions toward persons genuinely desiring change (though see S. H. Hadley, for example, on pp. 48-49, above).

61. Whittemore, Miracles, 46; cf. E. M. Whittemore, "A Word From the Door of Hope," AW, February 2, 1894, 132.

62. CH, January 2, 1889 (12:1), 2; CH, November 13, 1895 (18:46), 749; cf. undated pamphlet, The Florence Crittenton Hope and Help Mission (Washington, D.C., n.d.), and National Florence Crittenton Mission, Report for the Year 1918-1919 (Washington, D.C., 1919), 36.

63. Evangeline Booth, "Rescue Work," WC, June 11, 1910 (1497), 9; among numerous other claims, see: WC (L), August 5, 1893 (889), 7; WC, June 23, 1894 (664), 9; WC, September 24, 1898 (886), 4; WC, November 25, 1911 (1573), 5; WC, March 20, 1920 (2007), 1, 12-13; Booth-Tucker, Social Relief Work, 17; H. Rider-Haggard, Regeneration; Being an Account of the Social Work of the Salvation Army in Great Britain (London, 1910), 119-20; Palmer, 1904-1922, 77; cf. similar claims for prisoners and other difficult groups: CH, July 13, 1892 (15:28), 437; WC, July 21, 1894 (668), 10; G, November 30, 1901 (294), 5; LT, November, 1905, 695.

64. The Florence Crittenton Hope and Help Mission; on employment, see WC, March 20, 1920 (2007), 1, 12-13.

65. See p. 43, above.

66. Another criterion for the Crittenton homes, as well as an important contribution to success, in their judgment, was that unwed mothers should keep their babies, becoming true "mothers": Kate Waller Barrett, Motherhood a Means of Regeneration (Washington, D.C., n.d.); Barrett, "Maternity Work--Motherhood a Means of Regeneration," Fourteen Years' Work, 52-62; The Florence Crittenton Hope and Help Mission.

67. In The Florence Crittenton Hope and Help Mission; Charles Lore, Chief Justice of the Supreme Court of Delaware, wrote similarly in November, 1903, in a letter on file in the

Crittenton Association offices in Chicago; cf. H. W. Lewis, Super-
intendent of the Board of Charities in Washington, D. C., Letter,
FC, April, 1899 (1:2), 42; Maud Morlock and Hilary Campbell,
Maternity Homes for Unmarried Mothers, A Community Service
(Washington, D. C., 1946), 9.

68. On the larger situation, see Roy Lubove, "The Progressives and the Prostitute," The Historian, May, 1962 (24:3),
313.

69. S. C. Rees, Miracles in the Slums (Chicago, 1905),
13; see reference to Rees' book in G, August 5, 1905 (486), 3.

70. WC, April 28, 1888 (342), 12; WC, February 10, 1894
(645), 4; "Hints and Suggestions," Fourteen Years' Work, 204; WC,
September 27, 1913 (1669), 12; cf. Rees, Miracles, 21, 136-37,
143, 147, 154-60, 185-86.

71. Booth-Tucker, Catherine Booth, II, 466-83; see William
Booth, "Principles of Social Work," International Social Council Addresses, 1911 (London, 1912), 102.

72. WC, July 25, 1885 (199), 1 (from the New York Sun);
WC, August 29, 1885 (204), 1; WC, October 17, 1885 (211), 1;
WC, November 14, 1885 (215), 1 (acquittal); WC, December 26,
1885 (220), 8 (Henry George); cf. Booth-Tucker, Catherine Booth,
II, 490-98.

73. WC, October 24, 1885 (212), 1; Booth-Tucker, Catherine
Booth, II, 479, quoted Mrs. Booth that she had not "known anything
take such hold of Bramwell for years." (Cf. 470-82 for other indications of their intense feeling on this matter.)

74. On the homes, see pp. 82-83, above; WC, February 5,
1887 (279), 8; WC, August 11, 1888 (358), 12; WC, January 21,
1893 (590), 8.

75. WC, September 3, 1904 (1196), 5, 12; WC, January 9,
1909 (1423), 10; for similar Crittenton efforts in China, see "Rescue
of Chinese Girls," Washington Post, October 8, 1905.

76. Harry Miller, "White Slave Traffic in Chicago," WC,
September 19, 1908 (1407), 2; cf. Lubove, op. cit., 312, on the
increasing nation-wide attention paid the question beginning about
this time.

77. WC, November 28, 1908 (1417), 8; cf. WC, May 21,
1910 (1494), 4, 8, and June 3, 1911 (1548), 3; Mrs. General Bramwell Booth, "The White Slave Traffic; An Article Contributed by
Request to Cassell's Magazine, July, 1911," Social News, January,
1915, 2-3, 12, 13.

78. Crittenton, Brother, 116; for other Crittenton and Door

of Lope efforts, including Mrs. Barrett's articles in the Washington Times during 1914, see Whittemore, Miracles, 277-82, and Wilson, Work With Girls, 53-58, 179-81.

VII. THE PROBLEM OF UNEMPLOYMENT

1. "Mission Workers in Convention, " CH, June 19, 1914 (37:23), 564; cf. W. E. Paul, Miracles of Rescue (Minneapolis, n.d.), 15-18, on McIntyre.

2. CH, June 5, 1895 (18:23), 361; AW, April 16, 1897, 376; G, November 6, 1897 (81), 6-7; AW, December 18, 1896, 570, reported Raws' leadership in "Rescue Day" in 1896; on Rescue Day, see also AW, October 19, 1898, 377, and October 20, 1900, 225.

3. G, February 1, 1908 (616), 8: WC, February 1, 1908 (1374), 8; WC, February 29, 1908 (1378), 8; cf. WC, January 18, 1908 (1372), 11, February 8, 1908 (1375), 3, and March 7, 1908 (1379), 1, 12.

4. CH, October 16, 1895 (18:42), 687; WC, February 6, 1892 (540), 4.

5. "Mission Workers in Convention, " loc. cit. ; see pp. 9-13, above, for McAuley, the Hadleys, and Trotter; other leaders included Harry Monroe of the Pacific Garden Mission in Chicago from 1880 until about 1910, e.g., CH, September 13, 1916 (39:37), 1014; AW, October 20, 1900, 225, noted Crittenton personnel; cf. WC, June 9, 1888 (349), 1, for William Booth's well-known prediction that he would get his preachers "out of the saloons. "

6. J. T. Burghard, "Work in Louisville, " AW, January, 1888, 15; on Burghard, the Alliance, and "wayside" missions, see TF, October, 1890, 228; CH, April 5, 1893 (16:14), 225, 227; for other references to woodyards in the CH, see, e.g., June 17, 1891 (14:24), 369, 372, and January 15, 1896 (19:3), 47.

7. F. Booth-Tucker, The Social Relief Work of the Salvation Army in the United States (Albany, N.Y., 1900), 24; WC, December 17, 1898 (898), 12; WC, April 30, 1898 (865), 8; cf. WC, February 6, 1892 (540), 4, and April 24, 1897 (812), 2.

8. CH, June 17, 1891 (14:24), 372; CH, January 15, 1896 (19:3), 47; WC, May 22, 1897 (816), 3.

9. Booth-Tucker, Social Relief Work, 23-24; G, March 4, 1905 (464), 6; CH, January 15, 1896 (19:3), 47; WC, April 24, 1897 (812), 2; cf. Burghard, loc. cit. , WC, May 22, 1897 (816), 3, and WC, June 4, 1898 (870), 7.

10. William Booth, In Darkest England and the Way Out (New York, London, 1890), 90-93, 124-55; cf. F. Booth-Tucker, "The Housing of the Poor in the City of New York," WC, October 10, 1896 (784), 2.

11. WC, March 10, 1906 (1275), 10; WC, April 7, 1906 (1279), 1, 10; WC, May 9, 1908 (1388), 9.

12. WC, November 24, 1894 (686), 9; WC, October 17, 1891 (524), 8; The War Cry reported other farms of which little or nothing was subsequently heard: October 17, 1891 (524), 8; October 24, 1896 (786), 12; June 12, 1897 (819), 6-7.

13. WC, October 10, 1896 (784), 2; WC, March 27, 1897 (808), 14, and May 8, 1897 (814), 10-11, present the potato patch scheme.

14. H. Rider-Haggard, The Poor and the Land; Being a Report on the Salvation Army Colonies in the United States and at Hadleigh, England (London and New York, 1905), 38-39, 45, 67, 73-74, 115-16; WC, September 17, 1898 (885), 9; WC, September 27, 1913 (1669), 1, 9.

15. WC, December 18, 1897 (846), 2-3; WC, March 5, 1904 (1170), 9; F. Booth-Tucker, The Salvation Army in the United States (New York, 1899), 32; Booth-Tucker, Social Relief Work, 30-31; cf. his other publications: Prairie Homes for City Poor (New York, 1901?); A Review of the Salvation Army Land Colony in California (New York, n.d.); Farm Colonies of the Salvation Army (U.S. Bureau of Labor Bulletin No. 48, September, 1903).

16. Booth-Tucker, Social Relief Work, 29-30; WC, September 10, 1898 (884), 9; cf. WC, December 18, 1897 (846), 3, and October 18, 1902 (1098), 4, and Rider-Haggard, Colonies, vii.

17. Reported in Booth-Tucker, Social Relief Work, 36.

18. WC, October 16, 1897 (837), 12; Booth-Tucker, Social Relief Work, 35-36; cf. WC, April 30, 1898 (865), 13.

19. WC, December 11, 1897 (845), 9.

20. WC, October 16, 1897 (837), 4; Rider-Haggard, Colonies, 46; cf. WC, September 7, 1901 (1040), 5.

21. WC, April 9, 1904 (1175), 8; for comments from various newspapers, see WC, April 23, 1904 (1177), 5, and May 14, 1904 (1180), 5.

22. Rider-Haggard, Colonies, vii, viii.

23. Ibid., 68, 71-72, 54, 62-66, 102-03, 41; on the difficulties, see 46-47, 53-54, 67-99.

24. Ibid., vi, xv, xix, 123.

25. Miss Booth did contribute a paper on the colonies to the N. Y. State Conference of Charities and Corrections. Editorial, WC, December 2, 1905 (1261), 8; for sustained interest in colonies elsewhere, see WC, August 20, 1910 (1507), 8; see F. Booth-Tucker, Muktifauj, or Forty Years with the Salvation Army in India and Ceylon (London, n.d.), 170-77, for the decade after 1915.

26. See Ten Talks on the Salvation Army (New York, 1926?), 60-61; Robert Sandall, The History of the Salvation Army (London, 1947-55), III, 127, gives October, 1897, as the date of origin, though see WC, August 14, 1897 (828), 12.

27. WC, August 14, 1897 (828), 12; WC, March 26, 1898 (860), 4; WC, December 9, 1899 (949), 3.

28. WC, June 4, 1898 (870), 7; WC, April 16, 1904 (1176), 7; cf. WC, November 4, 1899 (944), 3, and Booth-Tucker, Social Relief Work, 23.

29. Ten Talks, 62-63; for earlier surveys, see Booth-Tucker, Salvation Army in the United States, and Booth-Tucker, Social Relief Work.

30. CH, June 14, 1911 (34:24), 616; CH, August 16, 1911 (34:33), 807; cf. earlier efforts presented as "industrial," CH, May 20, 1903 (26:20), 435.

31. CH, October 6, 1915 (38:48), 995; CH, October 17, 1917 (40:42), 1086, 1103.

32. K. W. Barrett, Some Practical Suggestions on the Conduct of a Rescue Home (Washington, D.C., 1903?), 107-09; FC, March, 1899 (1:1), 22.

33. AW, March 30, 1894, 351-52; CH, December 4, 1895 (18:49), 823; cf. TF, July, 1890, 168, and October, 1890, 227, for an Alliance-related "Industrial School" for girls in Buffalo.

34. CH, March 22, 1893 (16:12), 189, 191; CH, May 14, 1902 (25:20), 435; cf. G, August 11, 1906 (539), 6, and WC, January 5, 1901 (1005), 12.

35. CH, August 16, 1905 (28:33), 686; CH, November 6, 1907 (30:45), 955; CH, May 4, 1910 (33:18), 445; CH, September 28, 1910 (33:39), 885; Charles M. Pepper, Life-Work of Louis Klopsch (New York, 1910), 356.

36. WC, July 16, 1910 (1502), 1; Ten Talks, 82; AW, April 28, 1893, 261; AW, May 3, 1902, 241-42; see India Alliance for frequent articles: September, 1902, 26-27, December, 1902,

67-68, April, 1903, 115-16, May, 1904, 129-30, and July, 1907, 11-12.

37. AW, November 19, 1904, 392; AW, February 15, 1908, 332; the India Alliance generally was very positive on the value of the orphanages: October, 1905, 44, 47-48, July, 1907, 11-12, February, 1908, 92, October, 1908, 43, and July, 1913, 6 (reported 70 orphans at Dholka where the Alliance had had several hundred); cf. CH, February 15, 1905 (28:7), 139, 141, for the Foreign Missions Industrial Association, which began in evangelism in Peru in the 1890s.

38. See WC, December 16, 1905 (1263), 5.

39. Booth-Tucker, Salvation Army in the United States, 16; cf. the statement of officials of the Peniel Mission in Los Angeles that they were "all the time trying to get work for the men who are around Peniel Mission and are out of work," in Peniel Herald, February, 1895 (1:5), 4; see also AW, December 1, 1900, 309.

40. WC (L), August 22, 1896 (1048), 10; on the temporary nature of "industrial" positions, see Booth-Tucker, Social Relief Work, 23.

41. WC, January 5, 1901 (1005), 12; on the difficulty, see William Booth, In Darkest England, 190; cf. Maud Booth on placing prisoners, G, July 11, 1896 (13), 9, June 7, 1902 (312), 7, and April 18, 1908 (627).

42. WC, March 18, 1893 (598), 11; WC, June 22, 1895 (716), 11.

43. WC, May 23, 1896 (764), 10; WC, October 22, 1898 (890), 4; Booth-Tucker, Salvation Army in the United States, 16; Booth-Tucker, Social Relief Work, 24; WC, October 26, 1907 (1360), 4, claimed 1500 placements by the Army's Labor Bureau in St. Paul, Minn., during the preceding twelve months.

44. WC, March 6, 1897 (805), 4-5.

45. CH, January 4, 1905 (28:1), 5; CH, February 15, 1905 (28:7), 158; CH, March 29, 1905 (28:13), 277.

46. CH, February 15, 1905 (28:7), 158 cf. March 29, 1905 (28:13), 277; CH, May 10, 1911 (34:19), 471, set the Bureau's beginning as January, 1907, a date repeated or implied in later articles also.

47. CH, November 26, 1913 (36:48), 1096; CH, October 6, 1915 (38:48), 995; CH, October 17, 1917 (40:42), 1086, 1103.

48. CH, February 8, 1905 (28:6), 123; William Peart,

"Seasonal Social Work, " Social Problems in Solution; Papers Read at the International Social Council, London, ... 1921 (London, 1923), 82.

49. WC, January 15, 1887 (276), 8; CH, November 14, 1878 (1, 2:4), 58-60; CH, November 28, 1878 (1, 2:6), 84-85.

50. WC, October 10, 1896 (784), 2; Booth-Tucker, Salvation Army in the United States, 13; WC, April 26, 1902 (1073), 9, quoted the New Haven Evening Register on his estimate of 95 per cent; cf. E. Fielding's similar judgment, G, June 29, 1901 (272), 2; although the Alliance's LT, April, 1903, 217-18, contained a friendly statement, in AW, January 30, 1909, 300, F. Marsh, for a time on the staff of A. B. Simpson's Gospel Tabernacle in New York, stated that 95 per cent of outsiders wanting help were in the "beggar's business" and would "neither work nor want!"; for reports from their institutions, see: WC, April 24, 1897 (812), 2; WC, May 22, 1897 (816), 3; CH, February 15, 1905 (28:7), 158; CH, March 29, 1905 (28:13), 277; CH, August 16, 1911 (34:33), 807; CH, October 6, 1915 (38:48), 995.

51. See National Conference of Social Work, Proceedings ... 1897, 345, where Jane Addams remarked on "that great fear of pauperizing people which many of you seem to have"; cf. Proceedings ... 1878, 67-69, 117-23, 151-64, Proceedings ... 1883, 144, 150, Proceedings ... 1890, 43, and Proceedings ... 1899, 141, 151, 411.

52. Bramwell Booth, Echoes and Memories (New York, 1925), 2; WC, February 6, 1892 (540), 4.

53. The practice of sending holiday baskets to individual homes replaced great public feasts for the same reason: CH, March 15, 1905 (28:11), 243, G, May 3, 1902 (316), 3, WC, February 20, 1897 (803), 8, and WC, February 8, 1908 (1375), 3.

54. WC, May 22, 1897 (816), 3 (Boston); WC, April 15, 1899 (915), 5.

VIII. PRISON PHILANTHROPY

1. "The Convicts' Friend Dies, " CH, March 2, 1892 (15:9), 131; S. H. Hadley, Down in Water Street; A Story of Sixteen Years Life and Work in Water Street Mission (New York, 1902), 126-27; for the prison work of rescue missions, see, e.g., Union City Mission, Minneapolis, Annual Report, 1904-05, 30-32, and Union Gospel Mission, St. Paul, Annual Report, 1913, 10-11.

2. "The Convicts' Friend Dies, " loc. cit., listed New York, Detroit, San Francisco, Chicago, Brooklyn, and Philadelphia; CH, February 1, 1883 (6:5), 72; Hadley, Water Street, 127-28.

3. WC, May 23, 1896 (764), 10; cf. E. J. Parker, "Our Opportunities and Responsibilities for Prison Populations, " Social Problems in Solution; Papers Read at the International Social Council, London, ... 1921 (London, 1923), 113, 115.

4. See The Salvation War, 1884 (London, 1885?), 150: "A great many ex-convicts have been saved in connection with our meetings. "

5. WC (L), September 14, 1889 (686), 6; WC, April 23, 1887 (290), 1; WC, August 13, 1887 (306), 8; WC (L), August 5, 1893 (889), 7; for the beginning, see WC, January 22, 1916 (1790), 8, and Robert Sandall, The History of the Salvation Army (London, 1947-1955), III, 10.

6. WC, September 6, 1890 (466), 8; cf. WC, June 16, 1894 (663), 11, and "Social Plans for 1895, " WC, February 2, 1895 (696), 13.

7. WC, May 23, 1896 (764), 10; WC, October 24, 1896 (786), 13; WC, January 16, 1897 (798), 8; the prison report, WC, November 11, 1916 (1832), 9, noted rescue homes for women and industrial homes for men; Parker, "Our Opportunities, " Social Problems, 109-10, 113.

8. WC, June 16, 1894 (663), 11; WC, July 11, 1896 (771), 12; Parker, "Our Opportunities, " Social Problems, 104; Ten Talks on the Salvation Army (New York, 1926?), 65-68; for other discussions and reports on the prison work see Social News, December, 1911, 3-5, January, 1912, 3-5, November, 1914, passim, January, 1916, 1, 15, and October, 1916, 2-14.

9. Parker, "Our Opportunities, " Social Problems, 112; Ten Talks, 65-66.

10. WC, April 23, 1887 (290), 1; Lorenzo Coffin, active in prison work in Iowa, wrote that one of her gospel sermons at Fort Dodge held the large audience of prisoners spellbound: Reprint of a letter to the editor of the Fort Dodge Messenger, G, March 21, 1903 (362), 6; cf. report of the Miami Valley, Ohio, Chautauqua in G, August 26, 1899 (176), 3-4.

11. Maud Booth, Beneath Two Flags (New York, 1891, c1889), v-vii; F. Booth-Tucker, The Life of Catherine Booth (New York, 1892), II, 529-32.

12. G, April 11, 1896 (1), 6; Maud Booth, "The History and Purpose of the Volunteers' Prison League, " G, June 1, 1907 (581), 9.

13. G, June 4, 1896 (8), 8, 9; G, June 11, 1896 (9), 9; Editorial, G, June 25, 1896 (11), 8; Editorial, G, July 4, 1896 (12), 8.

14. Maud Booth, "The History and Purpose of the Volunteers' Prison League," loc. cit.

15. G, June 4, 1904 (425), 13; G, November 9, 1907 (604), 9; cf. CH, November 27, 1901 (24:48), 1013.

16. G, September 12, 1896 (22), 9, 12; for other early Hope Halls, see G, November 21, 1896 (32), 8 (San Francisco), and December 17, 1898 (140), 8-9 (Chicago).

17. CH, January 25, 1905 (28:4), 89; CH, August 2, 1905 (28:31), 662.

18. CH, September 9, 1891 (14:36), 569; F. B. Meyer, The Bells of Is; or Voices of Human Need and Sorrow (London, n.d.), 28-49; note his ties with gospel welfare leaders in the United States, as in Hadley, Water Street, [12], and E. M. Whittemore, Records of Modern Miracles (Toronto, 1931), illustration opposite 223.

19. WC, February 26, 1898 (856), 6; G, September 26, 1896 (24), 4.

20. Parker, "Our Opportunities," Social Problems, 104.

21. CH, November 1, 1911 (34:44), 1090; cf. Ten Talks, 67-68.

22. Ten Talks, 67-68; see also Parker, "Our Opportunities," Social Problems, 104; cf. G, August 19, 1899 (175), 4, for the Volunteers.

23. See CH, November 1, 1911 (24:44), 1090; cf. G, June, 1909 (663), 9.

24. Maud Booth, "Christmas Among the Very Poor," CH, December 23, 1903 (26:51), 1131; cf. G, December 17, 1904 (453), 7; for the Salvation Army's holiday program, see Parker, "Our Opportunities," Social Problems, 104; cf. WC (Chicago), December 24, 1966 (86:52), 12-13, for the Army's mid-twentieth century plan.

25. G, July 11, 1896 (13), 9; her letter to The Churchman reprinted in G, April 18, 1908 (627); cf. her letter, G, June 7, 1902 (321), 7.

26. CH, December 4, 1895 (18:49), 810; for Moody, see CH, December 30, 1896 (19:53), 992; CH, January 18, 1905 (28:3), 63.

27. Parker, "Our Opportunities," Social Problems, 103-04, 114; WC, April 8, 1893 (601), 13; G, May 14, 1896 (5), 8.

28. WC, November 11, 1916 (1832), 1; Maud Booth, Letter, G, April 4, 1908 (625), 4.

29. G, September 5, 1896 (21); see the report of her visit to the prison at Auburn, N. Y., G, August 1, 1896 (17), 8, 9, 12, as well as the letter from its chaplain, G, August 15, 1896 (18), 9; G, March 21, 1903 (362), 6 (Coffin).

30. G, April 4, 1908 (625), 4.

31. "Showers of Tin for Hope Hall," G, October 10, 1896 (26), 6-7; G, December 31, 1904 (455), 6; cf. G, September 12, 1896 (22), 9, and October 17, 1896 (27), 13.

32. G, August 15, 1896 (18), 9; G, May 14, 1896 (5), 8.

33. G, June 15, 1901 (270), 6.

34. G, May 11, 1901 (265), 6; Maud Booth, Did the Pardon Come Too Late? (New York, 1897); Maud Booth, "Hope Hall," G, September 12, 1896 (22), 9; cf. G, June 15, 1901 (270), 6, for a prisoner's response.

35. Maud Booth, "The Prisoners and How the Volunteers Can Help Them," G, April 11, 1896 (1), 6.

36. Ibid.

37. Hadley, Water Street, 20-21, 26, 66-71, 99, 125-32, 144, 149 (chapter nine is titled "Refuge of Crooks"); R. M. Offord, ed., Jerry McAuley; An Apostle to the Lost (New York, c1885), 52-61, 70-71, presented McAuley's claim of harassment by the police; CH, May 24, 1893 (16:21), 339; CH, June 4, 1913 (36:23), 541; Charles N. Crittenton, The Brother of Girls; The Life Story of Charles N. Crittenton (Chicago, 1910), 109-11.

38. WC, June 18, 1881, 3; WC, December 26, 1885 (220), 2; WC, April 16, 1887 (289), 6; WC, May 5, 1888 (344), 6; WC, May 23, 1896 (764), 10; Salvation Army, Buffalo, N. Y., Annual Report, 1898, 2.

39. Parker, "Our Opportunities," Social Problems, 114-15; cf. WC, July 26, 1890 (460), 10, and F. Booth-Tucker, The Salvation Army in the United States (New York, 1899), 24.

40. CH, November 27, 1901 (24:48), 1013; WC, May 23, 1896 (764), 10; WC, November 11, 1916 (1832), 9; cf. Ballington Booth in G, November 11, 1905 (500), 9.

41. G, April 4, 1908 (625), 4; cf. G, June 1, 1907 (581), 9, and CH, January 25, 1905 (28:4), 89.

42. G, May 25, 1901 (267), 2; cf. G, September 12, 1896 (22), 9.

43. G, June 1, 1907 (581), 12 (McClaughry); cf. G, September 7, 1907 (595), 4; G, August 19, 1899 (175), 1; cf. G, June 7, 1902 (321), 9, and June, 1909 (663), 15; for the Army, see the very favorable comment of Chief of Police P. Crowley of San Francisco in WC, November 18, 1893 (633), 8.

44. G, June 11, 1898 (113), 7-8.

45. Parker, "Our Opportunities," Social Problems, 97-99; Father Coffin, Letter, G, December 19, 1903 (401), 5, a reprint from the Fort Dodge (Iowa) Daily Chronicle; Father Coffin, Letter, G, May 23, 1908 (632), 3; cf. the Christian Herald's opposition to capital punishment, October 25, 1905 (28:43), 888-90, 886, and March 15, 1911 (34:11), 272; William Booth's principles included punishment, but without revenge or long sentences and always with the aim of reclamation: William Booth, "Principles of Social Work," International Social Council Addresses, 1911 (London, 1912), 136-40, 145; William Booth, In Darkest England and the Way Out (London, 1890), 57-61, 173-79.

IX. THE LIBERATION OF WOMEN

1. F. Booth-Tucker, The Life of Catherine Booth (New York, 1892), I, 343-49.

2. Ibid., I, 16-17, 116-17; General Booth, "Mrs. Booth As a Woman and a Wife," WC, October 28, 1911 (1569), 7; for his early position, see letter reprinted in Harold Begbie, The Life of General William Booth (New York, 1920), I, 236; William T. Stead, and some others, felt that she was also the pivotal figure in the Army's larger development, especially in its stress upon intense and charitable religion: William T. Stead, "The Late Mrs. Booth," WC (L), October 11, 1980 (742), 8; George Railton, The Authoritative Life of General William Booth (New York, 1912), 26-27, noted and denied the extreme form of this view; cf. such works as The New Schaff-Herzog Encyclopedia of Religious Knowledge (Grand Rapids, Mich., 1951, c?), II, 233, which allocated Mrs. Booth twice as much space as her husband received.

3. Booth-Tucker, Catherine Booth, I, 117-23.

4. Ibid., I, 344, 358-62.

5. On Evangeline Booth, see "Dr. Wilbur Chapman's Introduction," WC, March 4, 1911 (1535), 12 (cf. 8 on Catherine Booth); cf. "Salvation Army Night at the Chapman-Alexander Mission," WC, February 25, 1911 (1534), 8.

6. Bramwell Booth, Echoes and Memories (New York, 1925), 166-67.

7. Ibid., 167-72.

8. "Evangeline Booth," CH, February 15, 1905 (28:17), 144; the Herald ignored Mary Baker Eddy, who had written Science and Health three decades earlier and founded the Church of Christ, Scientist in 1879.

9. See "Staff Council: 1895," WC (L), July 27, 1895 (922), 6-7.

10. "Adjutant Isa Cartner, of the Slum Work," WC (L), July 13, 1889 (677), 3; "Planned for the Poor," WC, June 12, 1897 (819), 7; "Mrs. Ballington Booth Conducts a Rescue Meeting in Association Hall," WC, March 18, 1893 (598), 4; Orders and Regulations for Field Officers (London and New York, 1917), 309; cf. WC, July 6, 1895 (718), 11.

11. Frances Willard, Letter, WC (L), May 5, 1894 (928), 3; "Miss Frances Willard on the Salvation Army," WC, January 10, 1891 (484), 7; cf. WC, June 18, 1887 (298), 12.

12. Article reprinted in WC (L), October 11, 1890 (742), 7; William T. Stead, Life of Mrs. Booth (New York, 1900), 85-86; see William Booth's writing, as WC, May 11, 1889 (397), 6-7, and September 19, 1903 (1146), 8; cf. Mrs. George Railton, "Our Pathfinder, Women's Thanksgiving for the Life of William Booth," WC, August 22, 1914 (1716), 7.

13. A. B. Simpson, "The Conservation of the Forces and Resources of Our Work," AW, April 13, 1912, 20; cf. AW, September 8, 1906, 154; for similar statements in the CH, see August 7, 1879 (1, 2:42), 569-60, and April 6, 1892 (15:14), 214; for a series about and to women, see CH, January 12, 1888 (11:2), 20-21.

14. "Death of Miss Dougall," AW, April 23, 1904, 312; for grudging acquiescence in female leadership, see J. Hudson Ballard's "Spiritual Clinic," AW, June 10, 1911, 173 (cf. 167), and August 19, 1911, 333.

15. Peniel Herald, November, 1894 (1:2), 2; "The Peniel Missions," CH, February 4, 1903 (26:5), 105; see also "Deaconness Work," Peniel Herald, May, 1895 (1:8), 2.

16. Editorial, AW, December 2, 1899, 429, noted May Agnew's "long and successful experience in rescue work"; Editorial, AW, November 1, 1902, 246, the marriage and residence in Toronto, Canada, where she and her husband headed a city mission as well as the local work of the Alliance; "Eighth Avenue Mission," AW, November 15, 1902, 274, described Sarah Wray as "long and favorably

known as a most successful rescue worker"; on Miss Wray, see also W. E. Paul, The Romance of Rescue (Minneapolis, 1959, c1946), 77.

17. S. H. Hadley, Down in Water Street; A Story of Sixteen Years Life and Work in Water Street Mission (New York, 1902), 232-33; "In Memory of 'Mother Bird'," CH, May 13, 1914 (37:15), 492, which also included a tribute from the well-known clergyman, Lyman Abbott.

18. See the listing of officers in Paul, Romance, 89. He also discusses important leaders, 42-43, 71-72, "The Place of Women...," 50-52, and the Sidney Whittemores, 33-34, 52; "Gospel Missions Union Celebrated," CH, November 19, 1913 (36:47), 1082, referred to Sarah Wray as vice-president of the New York district of the I.U.G.M.; "Rescue Mission Workers to Meet," CH, April 16, 1913 (36:16), 376, listed Mrs. Whittemore and Miss Wray on the Executive Committee of the National Federation of Gospel Missions, with Miss Wray also a vice-president.

19. Louise Creighton, Missions, Their Rise and Development (New York, 1912), 120 (cf. 112-27); Stephen Neill, Christian Missions (Baltimore, 1964), 255-56.

20. For Emma Booth-Tucker, see F. Booth-Tucker, The Life of Catherine Booth (New York, 1892), II, 534-38; Mrs. Marcus B. Fuller, The Wrongs of Indian Womanhood (New York, 1900); A. B. Simpson, "The Claims of India," AW, January 12, 1894, 42-45; R. H. Glover, "Paul's Missionary Creed, or the Church's Obligation to the Heathen," AW, February 14, 1896, 146-48; Mrs. J. Fuller, "Widows in India," AW, April 17, 1896, 361-65; Miss Jennie Gilliland, "The Christian Woman's Debt to Her Heathen Sister," AW, November 5, 1898, 424; "Commencement Day at the Missionary Institute," AW, May 4, 1898, 409-10, 413, reported a paper with a title identical to that of Miss Gilliland's article; Mrs. R. H. Glover, "The Sorrows of China's Women," AW, November 4, 1905, 697-98; for the CH, see September 23, 1903 (26:38), 787, 789, March 15, 1905 (28:11), 250, and July 15, 1914 (37:28), 664.

21. Charles H. Jeffries, "The Salvation Army in China," The China Mission Year Book, 1918 (Shanghai, 1918), 307-08.

22. CH, April 13, 1910 (33:15), 367; CH, May 4, 1910 (33:18), 431, 436; CH, February 12, 1913 (36:7), 140, 154; cf. Margaret Sangster, "Woman's Right to Wage-Earning Work," CH, May 15, 1901 (24:20), 456.

23. "Not Yet," CH, November 17, 1915 (38:46), 1158; Editorial, CH, July 26, 1916 (39:30), 876; CH, January 23, 1918 (41:3), 92, 109; CH, February 14, 1920 (43:7); cf. WC, October 2, 1920 (2035), 8; some comments were rather innocuous, relative to concrete "rights": CH, March 19, 1885 (8:12), 180-81; WC, January 9, 1904 (1161), 4.

X. "OF ONE BLOOD": BLACK AMERICANS

1. "Christ or Color," WC, July 18, 1885 (198), 1; WC, April 3, 1886 (235), 1, attributed the Negro's difficulties to his heritage of slavery.

2. Frances Naylor Henck, "Open Doors," AW, January 24, 1896, 86.

3. CH, February 6, 1879 (1, 2:16), 48; on the restriction of Chinese and Japanese, see CH, February 27, 1879 (1, 2:19), 296, March 6, 1879 (1, 2:20), 312, March 20, 1879 (1, 2:22), 344, and February 18, 1914 (37:7), 156; for the literacy test, see CH, August 23, 1916 (39:34), 954, and February 14, 1917 (40:7), 170.

4. For social gospellers, see, e.g., P. N. Williams, "The Social Gospel and Race Relations; A Case Study of a Social Movement" in Toward a Discipline of Social Ethics: Essays in Honor of Walter George Mueller, ed. by Paul Deats, Jr. (Boston, 1972), Rayford W. Logan, The Betrayal of the Negro from Rutherford B. Hayes to Woodrow Wilson (New York, 1965), 170-73, Charles H. Wesley, The Quest for Equality; From Civil War to Civil Rights (International Library of Negro Life and History) (New York, 1968), 72-73, and David M. Reimers, White Protestantism and the Negro (New York, 1965), 53-54; Herbert Shapiro, "The Populists and the Negro: A Reconsideration," in August Meier, ed., The Making of Black America. V. 2 (New York, 1969), 27-36, sees the Populist interest as largely rooted in expediency; among numerous other comments see Allan H. Spear, Black Chicago; the Making of a Negro Ghetto, 1890-1920 (Chicago, 1967), 7-8, Dwight W. Hoover, comp., Understanding Negro History (Chicago, 1969), 124-25, and Gilbert Osofsky, The Burden of Race (New York, 1967), 164.

5. "A Kind Letter from Principal Washington," The Conqueror, October, 1896, 475; "The Evil of Race Prejudice," CH, March 22, 1911 (34:12), 296.

6. William Booth, Letter, WC (L), October 11, 1890 (742), 1; WC, June 5, 1915 (1757), 13; see also Maud Booth, Letter, G, April 4, 1908 (625), 4, and CH, February 28, 1920 (43:9), 252, and October 22, 1913 (36:43), 92.

7. "The Work Among the Children of the South," AW, June 24, 1899, 61, mentioned several times the absence of any color line in the Steele orphanages; cf. Harry E. Neale, The Hallelujah Army (Philadelphia, 1961), 161, 164, who reports his "casual conversation" with an aged Negro officer, Lambert Bailey, who indicated some "soldier" prejudice during the period between the world wars. Bailey emphasized, however, that Commander Evangeline Booth and other officers would have "quickly remedied" the situation had they known.

8. WC, February 8, 1883 (70), 1; WC, August 6, 1881 (14), 2.

9. "Arrival of Commander Ballington Booth and a Troupe of Coloured Soldiers....," WC (L), June 30, 1894 (936), 7; "A Page of Apostolic Reading. The Americans," WC (L), July 6, 1894 (937), 3 (cf. 10); "Sights and Sounds from the States," WC (L), September 5, 1896 (1050), 6; "A Colored Meeting," WC, February 21, 1903 (1116), 8; cf. WC, October 31, 1903 (1152), 2.

10. "The Great Southern Expedition Fund," WC, July 11, 1885 (197), 1; "Christ or Color," WC, July 18, 1885 (198), 1; "The Colored Work," WC, June 9, 1894 (662), 15; cf. "A Lively Army," WC, August 6, 1881 (14), 1, which compared Salvationists favorably to Negro camp meetings for freedom and noise; WC, August 1, 1885 (200), 2.

11. WC, September 26, 1885 (208), 2; WC, November 28, 1885 (217), 1; WC, January 23, 1886 (225), 1; WC, April 3, 1886 (235), 1; WC, July 14, 1888 (354), 8; WC, August 25, 1888 (360), 12; WC, June 23, 1894 (664), 9; WC, July 6, 1894 (666), 11.

12. WC, July 11, 1896 (771), 12; WC, July 18, 1896 (772), 13; "Colonel Holland, Our New Apostle to the Colored Race," WC, August 22, 1896 (777), 1-2; on Holland, see also "A Thrilling Branch of the War," WC, November 27, 1897 (843), 2; cf. "Salvation Among the Blacks," Full Salvation, December, 1896, 380.

13. WC, September 10, 1898 (884), 9; WC, April 1, 1899 (918), 8, with Booth-Tucker listing American goals; "The Colored Work Inaugurated," WC, December 14, 1901 (1054), 14; WC, November 30, 1901 (1052), 7, stressed the urgent need for candidates; WC, June 27, 1903 (1134), 12; WC, October 31, 1903 (1152), 2; WC, September 12, 1908 (1406), 5; "Salvation Army Work to Be Started Among America's Colored Population," WC, April 19, 1913 (1646), 12; see Christian and Missionary Alliance, Annual Report, 1917-18 (New York, 1918), 50-51, for expression of disappointment over the lack of progress of their efforts among blacks.

14. Editorial, AW, September 23, 1899, 264-65; "Our Colored Alliance Brethren," AW, March 2, 1898, 228.

15. "Atlanta Convention," AW, September 23, 1899, 269; AW, September 9, 1899, 232-33; AW, November 17, 1906, 318; Madele Wilson and A. B. Simpson, Henry Wilson, One of God's Best (New York, 1909?), 94-95.

16. "Our Colored Alliance Brethren," AW, March 2, 1898, 228; cf. Editorial, AW, September 23, 1899, 264-65, and "Annual Report," AW, June 28, 1902, 369; AW, June 6, 1908, 157.

17. "Work Among Colored People," AW, July 13, 1898, 41; cf. spirited participation, as in AW, March 23, 1898, 281.

18. "The Pittsburgh Convention," AW, March 3, 1900, 136; cf. AW, February 6, 1904, 133.

19. "Rocky Springs Park Convention," AW, September 15, 1900, 155; Editorial, AW, July 8, 1911, 232; on Robinson, see also AW, August 10, 1912, 297.

20. AW, June 6, 1908, 157; AW, August 25, 1906, 113.

21. Editorial, AW, January 14, 1911, 264; Editorial, AW, June 17, 1911, 184.

22. AW, March 2, 1898, 228; AW, September 23, 1899, 264; AW, March 2, 1898, 228.

23. AW, March 2, 1898, 228; cf. Editorial, AW, September 23, 1899, 264-65.

24. See AW, November 28, 1903, 363-64, February 6, 1904, 133, and August 10, 1910, 302, for Pittsburgh; Wilson and Simpson, Wilson, 94, 96; AW, June 5, 1915, 158, 168 (A. E. Funk).

25. E. M. Collette, "Evangelistic Work Among the Colored People," Christian and Missionary Alliance, Annual Report, 1910 (New York, 1911), 79; "Pittsburgh, Pa.," AW, June 6, 1908, 168.

26. AW, July 2, 1904, 76-77; AW, May 20, 1905; see also AW, January 13, 1906, 35.

27. AW, January 13, 1906, 35; AW, June 9, 1906, 354; AW, May 2, 1908, 83-84; Editorial, AW, October 27, 1906, 257, mentioned two additional schools; AW, June 17, 1911, 178, announced the Institute's transfer to the campus of Boydton Bible School, the gift of whose property the Alliance had just accepted.

28. AW, July 2, 1904, 76-77; AW, June 9, 1906, 354, also mentioned Miss Moore's "widely circulated publications."

29. AW, June 24, 1899, 61; Charles M. Pepper, Life-Work of Louis Klopsch (New York, 1910), 354.

30. CH, June 12, 1879 (1, 2:34), 529-31 (Garrison); CH, October 11, 1883 (6:41), 651-52, and December 13, 1883 (6:50), 792 (Douglass); "The Apostle of the Negro," CH, December 1, 1915 (38:48), 1218 (Booker T. Washington); for philanthropies, see pp. 98 and 123-24, above, for example.

31. On Washington, see Editorial, CH, December 1, 1915 (38:48), 1218; CH, January 16, 1907 (30:3), 46, and November 29, 1905 (28:48), 998, cover Sheldon's efforts; cf. "Mayesville; A New Tuskeegee," CH, August 16, 1905 (28:33), 686.

32. CH, March 8, 1893 (16:10), 165; CH, May 27, 1896 (19:22), 421.

33. Pepper, Klopsch, 353, 356; CH, August 16, 1905 (28: 33), 686; CH, November 6, 1907 (30:45), 955; CH, September 28, 1910 (33:39), 885.

34. CH, May 4, 1910 (33:18), 445; Pepper, Klopsch, 356.

35. CH, April 24, 1879 (1, 2:27), 425, May 15, 1879 (1, 2:30), 472, and May 29, 1879 (1, 2:32), 505; AW, June 24, 1899, 61; for the Barrett contribution see her communication in the Crittenton Association Papers, Social Welfare History Archives, University of Minnesota (Box 3, Envelope 13-14).

36. "Pennsylvania Savages," CH, August 30, 1911 (34:35), 848; Editorial, CH, June 5, 1918 (41:23), 696; WC, December 28, 1895 (743), 1, 2; "Lynching Craze," WC, May 20, 1899 (920), 8; see Ida Wells, Crusade for Justice; the Autobiography of Ida B. Wells (Chicago, 1970), 201-10, for a black woman's critique of Frances Willard of the W. C. T. U. for what seemed to her a soft stand on lynching.

37. CH, June 25, 1921 (44:26), 456.

38. AW, January 24, 1896, 86; "A Model of Self-Help in the South," CH, November 6, 1907 (30:45), 955; Gilson Willets, "After Forty Years of Freedom; Examples of Negroes Who Have Risen," CH, September 27, 1905 (28:39), 802-03.

39. G, March 30, 1901 (259), 8; G, May 14, 1896 (5), 13.

40. "Is Not This a Shame?" G, September 14, 1901 (283), 8; "Disgraceful Action Toward Colored People," G, July 5, 1902 (325), 8; "The Race Question in the South," G, February 14, 1903 (357), 8.

41. G, January 6, 1900 (195), 8; "Does the Negro Skull Delay Advance?" G, March 26, 1904 (415), 8.

42. G, October 13, 1906 (548), 8.

43. CH, November 29, 1905 (28:48), 998.

XI. WORK WITH ETHNIC GROUPS

1. "Our Weekly Interview," WC (L), November 4, 1893 (902), 5; "George Scott Railton," CH, June 10, 1880 (3:24), 380.

2. See, for example, Richard Hofstadter, The age of Reform; From Bryan to F. D. R. (New York, 1955), 8-9, 176-86.

3. CH, February 27, 1879 (1, 2:19), 296; CH, May 8, 1879 (1, 2:29), 456; CH, April 24, 1901 (24:17), 380-81; "New York's Japanese Colony," CH, December 16, 1903 (24:50), 1094-95; E. R. Johnstone, "The Japanese in America--How They View Our Nation," CH, January 9, 1907 (30:2), 26-27.

4. "Current Events," CH, February 27, 1879 (1, 2:19), 296; CH, March 6, 1879 (1, 2:20), 312; CH, March 20, 1879 (1, 2:22), 344; Editorial, CH, February 18, 1914 (37:7), 154.

5. Frances A. Kellor, "Citizens or Aliens," CH, July 1, 1914 (37:26), 629.

6. "Good and Bad Immigration," CH, March 5, 1913 (36: 10), 226; "The Literacy Test Again," CH, March 11, 1914 (37:10), 246; Editorial, CH, August 23, 1916 (39:34), 954; "The Odious Literacy Test," CH, February 14, 1917 (40:7), 170.

7. "The Tide of Immigrants," WC, July 25, 1891 (512), 8; Minnie B. Brewer, "In the Slums of Our Western Cities," WC, February 24, 1900 (960), 12; Maud Booth, "To the Rescue," WC, April 23, 1892 (551), 8; F. Booth-Tucker, The Salvation Army in the United States (New York, 1899), 17.

8. "The Marshall Appeals for German America," WC, October 29, 1887 (317), 9; WC, December 10, 1887 (323), 13; on the Swedish branch, see WC, April 14, 1888 (341), 15, and "The Scandinavian Work in America," December 30, 1893 (639), 17; the Alliance also operated among German immigrants from the late 1880s: AW, November 6, 1895, 300; AW, February 7, 1903, 76; AW, June 6, 1908, 157.

9. WC, March 21, 1891 (495), 12; WC, October 22, 1892 (577), 8; WC, December 3, 1892 (583), 1, featured the German and Swedish editions; for the regular Swedish column in earlier issues, see, for example, WC, February 9, 1889 (384), 4.

10. WC, January 5, 1895 (692), 12; cf. "The Scandinavian Work in America," loc. cit.; for statistics and goals for German-American Salvationists, see WC, September 22, 1894 (677), 1-2.

11. "The Scandinavian Work in America," loc. cit.; the Booths also visited Scandinavian branches and other gatherings: WC, April 21, 1894 (655), 12 (Ball:ngton and Maud Booth); WC, October 31, 1896 (787), 1 (the Booth-Tuckers); WC, May 7, 1898 (866), 4 (William Booth); WC, February 4, 1905 (1218), 9 (Evangeline Booth).

12. Clarence W. Hall, Samuel Logan Brengle; Portrait of a

Prophet (New York, 1933), 175-76, 227; WC, December 13, 1919 (1993), 4; WC, September 23, 1899 (938), 7.

13. WC (L), November 23, 1895 (1009), 8; R. E. Holz, "Scandinavian, German and Italian Department," WC, December 12, 1896 (793), 3; "Little Italy," WC, March 17, 1906 (1276), 6; WC, December 18, 1909 (1472), 14-15.

14. AW, November 27, 1895, 348; Christian and Missionary Alliance, Annual Report, 1910 (New York, 1911), 117.

15. Editorial, AW, April 14, 1906, 217; AW, November 3, 1906, 285; A. B. Simpson, comp., Michele Nardi, The Italian Evangelist; His Life and Work (New York, 1916), 12-23; pages 5, 41, 95, and 100 list individual contacts with such other gospel welfare workers as the Montgomeries of Oakland, Calif., and leaders of the Whosoever Gospel Mission of Germantown, Pa.

16. Simpson, Nardi, 7-10, 24-30.

17. Ibid., 22, 24, 28-30.

18. Ibid., 3, 33, 143, 51.

19. Charles H. Jeffries, "The Salvation Army in China," The China Mission Year Book, 1918 (Shanghai, 1918), 308, 304-05; R. Pierce Beaver, "Nationalism and Missions," Church History, March, 1957 (26:1), 26; on Mrs. Fuller see pp. 146, 147, above.

20. Philip I. Roberts, The Dry Dock of a Thousand Wrecks; The McAuley Water Street Mission (New York, 1912), 17.

XII. "THE CUP OF FURY"

1. George Pardington, "Woes of Intemperance," AW, November 11, 1899, 382; Pardington, friend of Simpson and chronicler of the early history of the Alliance, wrote the weekly Sunday School lesson column, which included frequent temperance studies.

2. "A National Evil," CH, April 24, 1901 (24:17), 378; Editorial, G, December 8, 1900 (243), 8; "The Curse," Peniel Herald, May, 1895 (1:8), 2; cf. Ballington Booth, "Drink Wreckage," G, August 15, 1896 (18), 10-11, and WC, November 26, 1887 (321), 1.

3. James H. Timberlake, Prohibition and the Progressive Movement, 1900-1920 (Cambridge, Mass., 1963), 1-2; cf. Arthur Mann, Yankee Reformers in the Urban Age (Cambridge, Mass., 1954), 11, 17, 80, 93, 105-07; Paul A. Carter, The Decline and

Revival of the Social Gospel: Social and Political Liberalism in American Protestant Churches, 1920-1940 (Ithaca, N.Y., 1954), 32-34, indicated the progressive character of prohibitionism a decade before Timberlake's book.

4. Clarke A. Chambers, Seedtime of Reform: American Social Service and Social Action, 1918-1933 (Minneapolis, 1963), 138, also 120-21.

5. CH, February 21, 1920 (43:8), 207.

6. See Charles C. Cole, The Social Ideas of the Northern Evangelists, 1826-1860 (New York, 1954), 112-16; "Beware of the Socials, Parties, and Dances," G, November 18, 1899 (188), 10; "The Gambling Curse," WC, March 16, 1901 (1015), 4; "Christians and Cards," CH, March 12, 1902 (25:11), 220; "Crusade Against Swearing," CH, April 26, 1905 (28:17), 379; William Booth, Letters to Salvationists on Religion for Every Day (London, 1902), I, 100; Evangeline Booth, "Manifesto," WC, February 10, 1906 (1271), 1, cited "fashion" as a stronghold of the devil; cf. G, October 6, 1900 (234), 1, on the "Sporting Life."

7. A. B. Simpson, "Christian Consecration in Relation to Our Civil and Social Duties," AW, June 29, 1894, 699; Editorial, AW, January 11, 1908, 248; William Booth, "Two Excellent Rules," WC, November 23, 1907 (1364), 11; WC, February 2, 1889 (383), 8 (Catherine Booth); Mrs. Ballington Booth, "Notes," G, September 19, 1896 (23), 9; "Our Mail Bag," CH, October 3, 1900 (23:40), 802; "Reforming the Movies," CH, September 25, 1920 (43:38), 990; cf. Kate Davis, "Regulating the Movies," CH, October 15, 1913 (35:42), 937.

8. F. Booth-Tucker, "The Temperance Side of Salvation Army Work," WC, August 22, 1903 (1142), 8.

9. S. H. Hadley, Down in Water Street; A Story of Sixteen Years Life and Work in Water Street Mission (New York, 1902), 24, 63-64, 199.

10. Ibid., 100, 104-09.

11. Clarence Hall, Out of the Depths; the Life-Story of Henry F. Milans (New York, 1935), 3, 100-06.

12. Ibid., 118, 121, 123, 138-42.

13. AW, March 30, 1894, 351.

14. "Mr. Chas. N. Crittenton--The Rescue Work of the Florence Mission in New York," CH, January 2, 1889 (12:1), 2; K. W. Barrett, Some Practical Suggestions on the Conduct of a Rescue Home (Washington, D.C., 1903?), 11-17.

15. Mrs. General Bramwell Booth, "True Rescue Work," WC, January 9, 1915 (1735), 10-11; cf. Evangeline Booth, "Rescue Work," WC, June 11, 1910 (1497), 8-9.

16. See John Allen Kraut, The Origins of Prohibition (New York, 1925), 15, 214.

17. W. C. T. U., Minutes of the Convention, 1874, 21, 26-27; W. C. T. U., Minutes ... 1892, 6-10; The Union Signal, May 24, 1894, 8; CH, October 14, 1896 (19:42), 755; CH, November 25, 1896 (19:48), 880; CH, March 25, 1903 (26:12), 243; AW, March 5, 1904, 206; AW, December 8, 1906, 365; Charles Crittenton, The Brother of Girls; The Life Story of Charles N. Crittenton (Chicago, 1910), 201; Charlton Edholm, Traffic in Girls and Florence Crittenton Missions (Chicago, 1893), 286-94.

18. AW, January 27, 1906, 53; AW, February 7, 1896, 139; "Peoria's Unique Gospel Mission," CH, April 15, 1903 (26:15), 329.

19. AW, September, 1888, 129; cf. AW, January 3, 1896, 19; WC, November 29, 1890 (478), 8; cf. Frances Willard, Letter, WC, September 10, 1892 (571), 5; see W. C. T. U., Minutes ... 1892, 34, 50-51 for participation by Charles N. Crittenton.

20. AW, April 24, 1896, 403; cf. CH, March 23, 1910 (33:12), 301.

21. AW, January 22, 1897, 89; "Mrs. John A. Best," AW, April 11, 1903, 205; "Death of Miss Dougall," AW, April 23, 1904, 312; cf. AW, December 8, 1906, 365, and March 5, 1904, 206.

22. "Loving Letters," WC (L), May 5, 1894 (928), 3; "Miss Frances Willard on the Salvation Army," WC, January 10, 1891 (484), 7; Crittenton, Brother, 196-98, 201; FC, April, 1899 (1:2), 38; W. C. T. U., Minutes ... 1892, 34, 50-51.

23. J. G. Harvey, Letter, AW, March 12, 1895, 172 (Harvey was an official at Old Orchard); Editorial, AW, May 22, 1896, 492-93; "The Late Miss Frances Willard," AW, March 2, 1898, 204-05.

24. WC, March 19, 1898 (859), 4 (cf. March 5, 1898 (857), 4, 8); G, March 5, 1898 (99), 16, 4, 8, 13; cf. G, March 12, 1898 (100), 25, and March 19, 1898 (101), 21.

25. Crittenton, Brother, 203-04, 126-27, and Chapter 42, "A Temperance Crusade."

26. AW, October 27, 1897, 417.

27. "The Home School," AW, May, 1899, 182; AW, March

10, 1900, 157; for the temperance column, see AW, February 2, 1894, 137, and April 9, 1897, 353.

28. "A West-Side Sailors' Bethel," CH, June 29, 1892 (15: 26), 405; A. B. Simpson, From the Uttermost to the Uttermost; The Life Story of Josephus Pulis (New York, 1914), 11, 31, 65; New York Christian Home for Intemperate Men, Annual Report, 1881-82, 26-29, 1884, 24, 1885, 25, and 1886, 18; for articles concerning the home, opened in 1877, see the CH, February 10, 1881 (4:6), 88, and April 15, 1891 (14:15), 225, 228-29. Both articles claimed a cure rate of more than 60 per cent.

29. E. G., CH, November 28, 1878 (1, 2:5), 81-84, and February 13, 1879 (1, 2:17), 257-58; for the Mission see CH, March 27, 1895 (18:13), 193, 197, and January 30, 1907 (30:5), 93.

30. F. B. Meyer, The Bells of Is; or Voices of Human Need and Sorrow (London, n. d.), 41-42, 77-81; "The Rev. Stephen Merritt, the Philanthropic Preacher of New York," CH, September 10, 1885 (8:37), 577-79; cf. CH, May 25, 1892 (15:21), 331, 335.

31. WC, December 25, 1886 (273), 1; F. Booth-Tucker, The Life of Catherine Booth (New York, 1892), I, 22-23; cf. WC, May 11, 1889 (397), 7; Christian Mission Magazine, July, 1873, 111, reported large attendance and response for a temperance lecture by Mrs. Booth.

32. For the early opposition see Harold Begbie, The Life of General William Booth (New York, 1920), I, 441-46, and Bramwell Booth, Echoes and Memories (New York, 1925), 25, 28-29; cf. WC, October 31, 1885 (213), 1; on "Ashbarrel Jimmy," see Ten Talks on the Salvation Army (New York, 1926?), 11-12; WC, November 7, 1891 (527), 8; WC, August 22, 1903 (1142), 8; WC, November 6, 1884 (161), 4; cf. WC, June 27, 1908 (1395), 7, and August 20, 1910 (1507), 8.

33. WC, December 12, 1896 (793), 1; cf. CH, February 21, 1920 (43:8), 207-11; for the "Seige," see WC, February 12, 1910 (1480), 1.

34. WC, December 31, 1892 (587), 15; WC, March 8, 1902 (1066), 12; WC, January 27, 1906 (1269), 1; WC, April 6, 1918 (1905), 2; WC, November 7, 1891 (527), 8, notified officers to obtain signatures for a petition sponsored by the W. C. T. U.

35. "Saloon War Cry Census," WC, April 3, 1884 (130), 4; WC, May 15, 1884 (136), 4; WC, November 26, 1887 (312), 1.

36. WC, January 13, 1894 (641), 13; cf. F. Booth-Tucker, The Social Relief Work of the Salvation Army in the United States (Albany, N. Y., 1900), 19.

37. "Ambulance Work in Cleveland," WC, September 26,

1908 (1408), 11; H. Rider-Haggard, The Poor and the Land; Being a Report on the Salvation Army Colonies in the United States and at Hadleigh, England (London and New York, 1905), vii.

38. "Great Drunkards' Convention, " WC, December 11, 1909 (1471), 12; Hall, Milans, 107-11; the WC described numerous other temperance parades in which the Army participated: WC, October 31, 1908 (1412), 1, 8; WC, October 23, 1909 (1464), 1, 3.

39. Hall, Milans, 107-08; Evangeline Booth, "Manifesto for Nineteen-Eleven, " WC, December 31, 1910 (1526), 8-9.

40. Hall, Milans, 6.

41. "Saved Boozers' Demonstration, " WC, February 28, 1914 (1691), 8, described Milans; Hall, Milans, 100-06, 115-23, 174-76; cf. WC, December 27, 1919 (1995), 3.

42. WC, November 29, 1884 (165), 2; WC, August 16, 1883 (97), 1; WC, January 28, 1888 (330), 14 (St. Paul); WC, December 30, 1899 (952), 9.

43. WC, August 22, 1903 (1142), 8; the War Cry carried numerous other accounts of results: June 18, 1881, 3; June 10, 1882 (37), 3; May 10, 1883 (83), 2; May 23, 1903 (1129), 3; December 10, 1910 (1523), 9; December 16, 1916 (1837), 9.

44. Booth-Tucker, Catherine Booth, II, 89; WC, June 9, 1888 (349), 1; WC, August 22, 1903 (1142), 8.

45. Crittenton, Brother, 106-07, 109-11; Sister Charlotte, "Work on the Street and in Houses of Ill-fame, " Fourteen Years' Work Among 'Erring Girls' (Washington, D.C., 1897?), 32-36.

46. Hadley, Water Street, 215-21; "A Temple of Rescue; St. Bartholomew's Rescue Mission, " CH, June 10, 1891 (14:23), 353, 356; Melvin E. Trotter, These Forty Years (Grand Rapids, Mich., 1939), 72-78, 119; Orin E. Crooker, "Chicago's Best-Known Mission, " CH, June 11, 1913 (36:24), 568, referred to Trotter's "chain of rescue homes for inebriates ... from Boston to San Francisco. " This apparently was based on Trotter's influence in opening and staffing scores of missions.

47. Hadley, Water Street, 106-09.

48. Hall, Milans, 145-67; Henry F. Milans, God at the Scrap Heaps (New York, 1945), 5-7, and passim.

49. Trotter, Years, 73-78, 119; J. Wilbur Chapman, S. H. Hadley of Water Street (New York, 1906), 134-37.

50. See pp. 38-43, above.

51. WC, July 3, 1909 (1448), 2-3; "The Curse," Peniel Herald, May, 1895 (1:8), 2; Editorial, AW, March 6, 1896, 229.

52. Crittenton, Brother, 126-27; cf. Editorial, AW, September 11, 1909, 398.

53. "The Salvation Army and Politics," WC, September 3, 1892 (570), 8; cf. David L. Colvin, Prohibition in the United States (London, 1926), 277, 290, for the early support given the Prohibition Party by Frances Willard and the W. C. T. U.

54. "History of Temperance Movements in America," G, April 30, 1898 (107), 16; AW, May 27, 1905, 333, called attention to a "history" of temperance in the Alliance's Living Truths magazine for June, 1905; WC, January 17, 1920 (1998), 11; "Forty Years' Temperance Work," CH, January 25, 1905 (28:4), 87.

55. CH, Editorial, March 21, 1917 (40:12), 336; "Demanding a Prohibition Amendment," CH, January 7, 1914 (37:1), 5; "Majority Vote for Prohibition in Congress," CH, January 6, 1915 (38:1), 9; "Senate Passes National Prohibition Amendment," CH, August 15, 1917 (40:33), 856; "The Prohibition Outlook," CH, November 7, 1917 (40:45), 1174; "The Prohibition Amendment," CH, January 2, 1918 (41:1), 12.

56. WC, June 2, 1917 (1861), 9; Editorial, CH, June 6, 1917 (40:23), 638; "Let's Drum Booze Out of Camp," CH, September 12, 1917 (40:37), 952-53.

57. "Prohibition's Day of Triumph," CH, January 29, 1919 (42:5), 107-09; cf. CH, February 15, 1919 (42:7), 167-68; WC, January 10, 1920 (1997), 8.

58. CH, February 22, 1919 (42:8), 200.

59. Robert Bremner, From the Depths; The Discovery of Poverty in the United States (New York, 1956), 80.

60. Timberlake, Prohibition, 1-2 and passim, developed the thesis which Carter, Social Gospel, 32-34, earlier suggested, namely the liberal and humanitarian character of the temperance movement before and during the Progressive Era.

61. Upton Sinclair, The Cup of Fury (Westwood, N. J., 1965, c1956).

XIII. PHILANTHROPY ABROAD

1. See, for example, the training schools operated by A. B. Simpson, Charles Cullis, and George Dowkontt (on pp. 17, 69, 73, 77, above).

2. The Herald had ventured into overseas famine relief on a small scale more than a decade earlier: T. DeWitt Talmage, "Hunger in Ireland," January 22, 1880 (3:4), 52-53; February 12, 1880 (3:7), 104; February 19, 1880 (3:8), 120; April 15, 1880 (3: 16), 248.

3. "Russia's Cry for Bread," CH, March 23, 1892 (15:12), 177, 181; "Russia's Cry Heard," CH, April 13, 1892 (15:15), 225, 229; CH, April 20, 1892 (15:16), 248; CH, April 27, 1892 (15:17), 264; CH, June 15, 1892 (15:24), 368; Charles Pepper, Life-Work of Louis Klopsch (New York, 1910), 16, 21.

4. Pepper, Klopsch, 18-20; "Russia's Cry for Bread," loc. cit.; CH, April 13, 1892 (15:15), 230 (cf. 225, 229).

5. CH, June 15, 1892 (15:24), 368; see A. Abell, The Urban Impact on American Protestantism, 1865-1900 (London, 1962, c1943), 219-20, for a general sketch of this organization. For its ties to gospel welfare groups, see, for example, "Report of the First General Convention of the National Florence Crittenton Mission," Fourteen Years' Work Among 'Erring Girls' (Washington, D.C., 1897?), 106, CH, July 29, 1891 (14:30), 465, WWW, May, 1885, 158, and The Conqueror, October, 1895, 456.

6. CH, May 11, 1892 (15:19), 296; CH, June 15, 1892 (15:24), 368; CH, July 27, 1892 (15:30), 467; Pepper, Klopsch, 21-22; L. A. Banks, ed., T. DeWitt Talmage, His Life and Work (Philadelphia, 1902), 200.

7. CH, July 27, 1892 (15:30), 467; CH, August 3, 1892 (15:31), 481, 483; CH, August 24, 1892 (15:34), 529, 531, 534; "Closing the Relief Fund," CH, May 25, 1892 (15:21), 326; Pepper, Klopsch, 22-27; Banks, Talmage, 200-17.

8. "The Horrible Butchery of Armenians," WC, February 9, 1895 (697), 1-3; William Booth, "Armenia, a Call to Prayer," WC, October 17, 1896 (785), 9; "The Armenian Horror," WC, October 24, 1896 (786), 8; WC (L), August 29, 1896 (1049), 1, 2, 8, 9-10.

9. Pepper, Klopsch, 32-49; "Charity Balance Sheet," CH, March 4, 1896 (19:10), 188; "Corinna Shattuck's Boys," CH, October 10, 1900 (23:41), 838; "Our Armenian Orphan Work Closes," CH, July 3, 1901 (24:27), 598-99; "Dr. Klopsch's Life in Outline," CH, March 16, 1910 (33:11), 256.

10. "The Armenian Horror," loc. cit.; WC (L), October 17, 1896 (1056), 6-7, and succeeding weeks, described these efforts; WC, October 31, 1896 (787), 8; CH, October 14, 1896 (19: 42), 755; WC, November 7, 1896 (788), 1, 4, 8, 12; "Armenians Provided For," WC, November 21, 1896 (790), 8; "American Armenians," WC, December 5, 1896 (792), 15; for later aid to Turkish lands, see Pepper, Klopsch, 49-51, 151-62.

11. Editorial, AW, December 4, 1896, 517; AW, December 11, 1896, 529-31; cf. Mrs. Fuller, "The Plague and Famine," AW, April 2, 1897, 313-14; "An Unspeakable Calamity!" WC, December 19, 1896 (794), 9.

12. "The India Famine. Help! Help! Help!" WC, March 6, 1897 (805), 9; cf. WC (L), November 28, 1896 (1062), 9; WC, May 1, 1897 (813), 8; F. Booth-Tucker, "The India Famine," WC, June 5, 1897 (818), 2.

13. AW, January 8, 1897, 42-43; Editorial, AW, February 5, 1897, 132; W. Ramsey, Letter, AW, May 21, 1897, 499; for A. B. Simpson's emphasis, see "The Grounds of Missionary Obligation," AW, October 27, 1897, 416.

14. AW, April 23, 1897, 386; AW, September 22, 1897, 289-93, 301; cf. AW, March 12, 1897, 242, 259, and March 26, 1897, 307; Mrs. M. B. Fuller, "A Life Laid Down," AW, June 18, 1897, 583-84; Henry Wilson, "Our Honor Roll in India," AW, June 18, 1897, 577-79; A. B. Simpson, "The Story of the Past Year," AW, August 4, 1897, 123; Mrs. Fuller contrasted the "great privilege" the dead missionary had judged her work, with the contempt with which many in India viewed the very poor.

15. WC, May 1, 1897 (813), 8; Editorial, AW, September 22, 1897, 301.

16. Pepper, Klopsch, 56-57.

17. Pepper, Klopsch, 64; B. H. Bhatia, Famines in India; A Study in Some Aspects of the Economic History of India (1860-1945) (New York, 1963), 239, 250; see WC, December 30, 1899 (952), 16.

18. "Poor Famine Stricken India," AW, March 31, 1900, 195; AW, March 10, 1900, 152; Editorial, AW, June 13, 1903, 15; see AW, November 25, 1899, for early notice.

19. For Mrs. Fuller's communication see AW, April 14, 1900, 246, and April 21, 1900, 250; AW, May 26, 1900, 348; George P. Pardington, Twenty-five Wonderful Years, 1889-1914; A Popular Sketch of the Christian and Missionary Alliance (New York, 1914), 225-26; Mark B. Fuller, "A Plea for Immediate Reinforcements," AW, December 1, 1900, 300; for other indications of the burden on the missionaries, see AW, February 3, 1900, 65, 67, 73, 79, and March 31, 1900, 196.

20. For the Alliance, see, e.g., AW, January 20, 1900, 44; "The Famine in India," AW, February 3, 1900, 72-73; "Correspondence," AW, March 3, 1900, 142.

21. CH, May 1, 1901 (24:18), 396, 406; CH, February 12, 1902 (25:7), 138; Pepper, Klopsch, 68-73, 84-85, 88.

22. Pepper, Klopsch, 74-84, 86-88.

23. Pepper, Klopsch, 71-74, 84-85; "The British Government Thanks Our Readers," CH, February 12, 1902 (25:7), 138; "Official Recognition," CH, March 12, 1902 (25:11), 220 (the quote); for subsequent years in India, see LT, August, 1902, 18, October, 1904, 44, and November, 1904, 52-53, as well as India Alliance, November, 1911, 675-76, and March, 1912, 789-91.

24. F. Booth-Tucker, "The Indian Famine," WC, June 5, 1897 (818), 2, had reported caring for 300 orphans; WC, September 15, 1900 (989), 4; WC, November 29, 1902 (1104), 6.

25. AW, March 25, 1905, 191, claimed 1400 in four orphanages; "Old Orchard Convention," AW, August 16, 1902, 96, referred to a collection, "as usual," for the 1200 orphans; Madele Wilson and A. B. Simpson, Henry Wilson, One of God's Best (New York, 1909?), 102-03; Miss E. M. Brickensteen, "A Special Call to the Children of the Junior Missionary Alliance," AW, February 19, 1897, 182; "Extracts from President's Report," AW, May 14, 1904, 361-62; Eunice Wells, "Orphanage Work in India," LT, November, 1905, 680-87; LT, August, 1902, 14-16.

26. Pepper, Klopsch, 89-92; India Alliance, July, 1902, 8; Pardington, Wonderful Years, 113.

27. Pepper, Klopsch, 88, 91, 96-98, 102; "India's Famine Cloud Lifted," CH, October 3, 1900 (23:40), 808; "Nearly 2000 India Orphans Taken," CH, October 10, 1900 (23:41), 832; "Our Five Thousand Famine Orphans in India," CH, March 27, 1901 (24:13), 277; CH, March 29, 1905 (28:13), 293; India Alliance, July, 1902, 8, and April, 1903, 115.

28. "Famine Orphans Now China's Problems," CH, June 28, 1911 (34:26), 658; "China's President Honors Our Work," CH, March 8, 1919 (42:10), 269-72; Pepper, Klopsch, 199-201, 211-12; see Union Gospel Mission, St. Paul, Annual Report, 1913, 13, for support of orphans in China by children of the mission.

29. CH, June 12, 1901 (24:24), 533, July 10, 1901 (24:28), 615, and August 21, 1901 (24:34), 715; Pepper, Klopsch, 163-81.

30. CH, October 23, 1901 (24:43), 890; CH, March 19, 1902 (25:12), 239, 245, noted the appeal to Klopsch from U.S. Consul-General Goodnow; AW, May 10, 1902, 269-70.

31. A. E. Funk, "Famine Distress in Quang Si Province, China," AW, April 18, 1903, 221; Editorial, AW, June 13, 1903, 15; AW, June 20, 1903, 37; CH, July 15, 1903 (26:28), 594; Pepper, Klopsch, 182-85.

32. CH, February 18, 1903 (26:7), 139, March 11, 1903

(26:10), 207, and April 29, 1903 (26:17), 366; Pepper, Klopsch, 121-47.

33. "The Gift from Japan's Emperor," CH, June 5, 1907 (30:23), 505; Pepper, Klopsch, 202-04, 208-18; cf. AW, June 16, 1906, 366, and WC, September 29, 1906 (1304), 1, 13.

34. "The Call to Service," CH, February 13, 1907 (30:7), 132 (126 reprinted Root's telegram); CH, April 3, 1907 (30:14), 299; CH, July 3, 1907 (30:27), 594; "How China Welcomed the Buford," CH, July 17, 1907 (30:29), 634, 636; CH, July 24, 1907 (30:30), 652; Pepper, Klopsch, 185-201.

35. "China Again Fighting Famine," CH, January 4, 1911 (34:1), 2; "China Famine Fund," CH, January 11, 1911 (34:2), 27, 32, 35; CH, March 15, 1911 (34:11), 272, 274-75, 276; the same issues contained other relevant material, and the Herald gave much attention to this crisis each week through June, 1911.

36. "China Famine Sunday Observed Widely," CH, February 26, 1921 (44:9), 169; "Wonderful News from China," CH, June 25, 1921 (44:26), 456.

37. Pepper, Klopsch, 219-41; cf. "Earthquake in Italy," WC, January 16, 1909 (1424), 9, and January 23, 1909 (1425), 9, for the account of the Salvation Army's relief measures.

XIV. WAR AND PEACE

1. Quoted by her son, Herbert Booth, in his The Saint and the Sword (New York, 1923), 1, from her Popular Christianity, published a few years after she gave these lectures; see F. Booth-Tucker, The Life of Catherine Booth (New York, 1892), II, 462.

2. Cf. such other titles as The Officer, The Young Soldier, The Warrior, and The Staff Review.

3. WC, June 18, 1881, 3; WC, February 15, 1883 (71), 1; cf. WC, August 5, 1882 (44), 3, and April 19, 1883 (80), 1.

4. WC, May 21, 1898 (868), 1.

5. See Merle Curti, Peace or War; The American Struggle, 1636-1936 (Boston, 1959, c1936), 229, 237, 240, 249, 254-56.

6. See their attention to Independence Day, and to the birthdays of Lincoln and Washington: WC, May 30, 1891 (504), 1, 2; WC, July 4, 1891 (509), 1-4; WC, February 17, 1917 (1846), 1; G, April 11, 1896 (1), 1, July 4, 1896 (12), 1, 3 ("George Washington. The Volunteer and Defender"), July 2, 1898 (116), 1, 16-17,

and February 10, 1906 (513), 7 (the "Annual Lincoln number of the Gazette"); CH, July 20, 1910 (33:29), 654-55, and June 30, 1915 (38:26), 669, 676.

7. "The Salvation Army's Government," WC, November 13, 1884 (162), 1; "Why We Incorporated," WC, November 6, 1884 (161), 1; G, April 11, 1896 (1), 1, 2; "Peace Circles Teach Patriotism," CH, November 1, 1911 (34:44), 1105.

8. WC, May 9, 1885 (188), 1; WWW, April, 1885, 127, and May, 1885, 160, expressed Simpson's concern; cf. WC, June 21, 1902 (1081), 8, on the Boer War; "Reflections by the General," WC, February 4, 1899 (905), 9.

9. "For Peace," WC, June 10, 1899 (923), 8; for another very strong Salvationist statement, see The Officer, January, 1893, 4; Editorial, CH, July 25, 1894 (17:30), 470; cf. Editorial, CH, December 27, 1893 (16:52), 846; a recent doctoral dissertation (Michigan State University, 1973), describes Charles Spurgeon, whose sermons the Herald prominently featured during its early decades, as an "extremely outspoken" critic of war and imperialism: Albert R. Meredith, The Social and Political Views of Charles Haddon Spurgeon 1834-1892 (Ann Arbor, Mich., 1973), 79-80, 84-92.

10. A. B. Simpson, "Current Events," AW, January 3, 1896, 13 (cf. January 10, 1896, 37); "The Significance of the Spanish-American War," AW, April 27, 1898, 396; see also "Is War Right?" AW, May 4, 1898, 421; cf. varying expressions in the Gazette: March 19, 1898 (102), 8-9, April 16, 1898 (105), 20, and May 7, 1898 (108), 5, 9.

11. Editorial, AW, August 3, 1898, 108; AW, November 12, 1898, 444; see also AW, August 10, 1898, 121-24; Simpson viewed these events as providential openings for missionary work and for the Anglo-Saxon race, discussing them in sermons, editorials, articles, and finally a booklet, "Providence and Missions." See AW, December, 1898, 2, 17, and August 3, 1898, 98-100; Simpson did caution against wrong motives, as AW, May 4, 1898, 421, and December, 1898, 2; Julius Pratt, Expansionists of 1898 (Baltimore, 1936), included several references to the Christian and Missionary Alliance in his chapter, "'The Imperialism of Righteousness.'"

12. "Christianity and War," CH, October 30, 1901 (24:44), 912; AW, March 11, 1905, 148; cf. AW, March 18, 1905, 161, and September 9, 1905, 561.

13. "America's First Peace Congress," CH, April 10, 1907 (30:15), 319, 331; "The Coming Peace Conference," CH, June 5, 1907 (30:23), 506, and Editorial, 508; cf. such other articles as Charles M. Pepper, "A Peace Congress of All the Americas," CH, September 25, 1901 (24:39), 801 (Pepper, a delegate, was later

Louis Klopsch's biographer); Editorial, CH, April 29, 1903 (26:17), 364; CH, January 25, 1905 (28:4), 74-75.

14. "The Peace Congress," CH, April 10, 1907 (30:15), 326; AW, May 11, 1907, 217 (cf. October 14, 1911, 18); AW, August 28, 1915, 339; cf. AW, November 20, 1915, 113, which called the sinking of the Ancona an "eloquent commentary" on the belief that the world was growing better.

15. See Curti, Peace, 203-04, 222-23, and, for the broader context of the peace movement during the period 1900-1920, 196-261; "Carnegie's Grand Gift to Peace," CH, December 28, 1910 (33:52), 1231, 1234.

16. AW, April 15, 1911, 40.

17. CH, April 5, 1911 (34:14), 348, CH, April 19, 1911 (34:16), 400; "A Great Day for World Peace," CH, August 16, 1911 (34:33), 808.

18. "The Christian Herald Peace League," CH, June 28, 1911 (34:26), 674; "Many Peace Circles Organizing," CH, August 23, 1911 (34:34), 836; "Peace Circles Still Growing," CH, September 20, 1911 (34:38), 939; CH, November 1, 1911 (34:44), 1105; CH, November 22, 1911 (34:47), 1189.

19. "The Dawn of the World's Peace. A Great National Symposium on the Rising Tide of Arbitration and Its Future," CH, September 6, 1911 (34:36), 867-71, 884, September 13, 1911 (34:37), 903, 910, and September 20, 1911 (34:38), 934-36; Editorial, CH, September 13, 1911 (34:37); cf. William Peart, "The Abolishing of War and the Dawn of Arbitration," WC, December 16, 1911 (1576), 9; for harsh words for Italy during the Turkish-Italian fighting that same autumn see AW, November 18, 1911, 98, and CH, October 18, 1911 (34:42), 1034-35, 1036; cf. "Another War," WC, October 14, 1911 (1567), 8.

20. "Christianity and the War," CH, August 12, 1914 (37:32), 750.

21. "The 'Atrocity' Collapse," CH, September 23, 1914 (37:38), 878; "What Shall We Do?" WC, August 29, 1914 (1717), 8; WC, February 2, 1918 (1896), 9; WC, October 23, 1915 (1775), 9.

22. "Are We Keeping Up the War?" CH, January 20, 1915 (38:3), 54.

23. See CH, September 13, 1916 (39:37), 1014.

24. Editorial, CH, November 24, 1915 (38:47), 1188; "Dr. Abbott and the Bible," CH, December 8, 1915 (38:49), 1242; Editorial, CH, December 29, 1915 (38:52), 1332.

25. "Pastor Sheldon on Preparedness. An Open Letter to the President," CH, November 24, 1915 (38:47), 1181; Charles Sheldon, Letter, CH, December 29, 1915 (38:52), 1336; Charles E. Jefferson, "The Right Kind of Preparedness," CH, November 24, 1915 (38:47), 1186; cf. editorial rejection of Wilson's message on preparedness, CH, December 22, 1915 (38:51), 1300.

26. CH, January 10, 1917 (40:2) (supplemental sheet); "The President and World Peace," CH, February 7, 1917 (40:6), 138; cf. praise for Washington Gladden's, "A Thousand Million Voices for Peace," January 17, 1917 (40:3), 55 (the lead article).

27. CH, February 14, 1917 (40:7), 170 (cf. 163-64); CH, March 14, 1917 (40:11). 298.

28. "A Heart-Stirring Message," CH, April 18, 1917 (40: 16), 456; Evangeline Booth, "The Salvation Army and the War," WC, April 21, 1917 (1855), 9; cf. "Prays for President Wilson," WC, February 24, 1917 (1847), 12.

29. CH, May 23, 1917 (40:21), 590; Charles M. Sheldon, "A Sermon for War Time," CH, May 9, 1917 (40:19), 536; cf. CH, April 18, 1917 (40:16), 470.

30. "The Muzzling of the Press," CH, May 2, 1917 (40:18), 510; cf. Editorials, CH, May 16, 1917 (40:20), 562, and August 15, 1917 (40:33), 860; on taxation, see CH, April 18, 1917 (40:16), 456, and August 22, 1917 (40:34), 891; CH, September 19, 1917 (40:38), 982.

31. AW, January 5, 1918, 209; CH, May 1, 1918 (41:18), 542, also 543, 548-49; "The World's Greatest Battle," CH, April 3, 1918 (41:14), 406; Editorial, CH, May 8, 1918 (41:19), 574; cf. Editorial, AW, November 20, 1915, 113, which termed the sinking of the steamer Ancona "another shocking outrage."

32. "Glorious Peace," CH, November 20, 1918 (41:47), 1296; "What the Whole World Wants," CH, January 22, 1919 (42:4), 88.

33. "The President's Mission," CH, December 18, 1918 (41:51), 1404; CH, March 1, 1919 (42:9), 223; CH, March 22, 1919 (42:12), 323 (Williams); Charles E. Jefferson, "Religion and the League of Nations," CH, March 15, 1919 (42:11), 298, 313.

34. CH, January 22, 1919 (42:4), 88; "No Annexations; No Indemnities," CH, February 15, 1919 (42:6), 174: "Real Americanization," CH, February 15, 1919 (42:7), 174; "The President's Welcome," CH, March 8, 1919 (42:10), 262; "The Soul of the League of Nations," CH, March 15, 1919 (42:11), 292; "The President and the Plain People," CH, March 22, 1919 (42:12), 324.

35. "A Broader Patriotism," CH, July 1, 1914 (37:26), 632;

CH, September 13, 1911 (34:37), 903; cf. Sheldon's later editorial wish that the Herald would "continue to be a power ... for ... disarmament ...": February, 1931 (34:2), 28.

36. See CH, October 7, 1914 (37:40), 936.

37. CH, August 12, 1914 (37:32), 743-44, 756, August 19, 1914 (37:33), 763-64, and August 26, 1914 (37:34), 783.

38. "Multitudes Homeless and Starving," CH, September 23, 1914 (37:38), 882; cf. "How Europe's Peasants Suffered by the War," ibid., 873, "Help Us or We Perish," October 14, 1914 (37:41), 959-60, and Margaret Sangster, Jr., "The Sufferers," ibid., 970.

39. CH, September 16, 1914 (37:37), 847, 849, 854, October 7, 1914 (37:40), 930-31, October 14, 1914 (37:41), 959-60, November 4, 1914 (37:44), 1029, November 11, 1914 (37:45), 1066-67, November 18, 1914 (37:46), 1084, December 2, 1914 (37:48), 1140, and January 6, 1915 (38:1), 16.

40. CH, November 25, 1914 (37:47), 1108; "A World-Survey of the Spiritual and Benevolent Work of the Christian Herald Family Circle During 1915," CH, December 29, 1915 (38:52), 1334; see details in November 4, 1914 (37:44), 1034, November 11, 1914 (37:45), 1072, and December 9, 1914 (37:49), 1159, 1168.

41. CH, January 13, 1915 (38:2), 30; "A World-Survey," loc. cit.

42. "A World-Survey," loc. cit.; cf. Editorial, CH, November 10, 1915 (38:44), 1126; on the role of missionaries, see CH, May 1, 1918 (41:18), 555.

43. "Our Relief Work in Poland," CH, September 6, 1916 (39:36), 995; "We War Against Suffering," CH, September 13, 1916 (39:37), 1014; cf. "Our Relief Work in Austria," CH, February 9, 1916 (39:6), 170, and "Our Relief Work in Galicia and Bukovina," CH, April 12, 1916 (39:15), 447.

44. "Saving Precious Lives," CH, April 4, 1917 (40:14), 398; "Our Relief Work in Austria," loc. cit.; "The Ministries of Mercy of the Christian Herald Family," CH, May 29, 1918 (41:22), 678.

45. CH, January 6, 1915 (38:1), 16; "A World-Survey," loc. cit.; CH, May 9, 1917 (40:19), 550; "The Record of Three and a Half Years of Mercy and Relief," CH, May 29, 1918 (41:22), 679.

46. "The Worth of Sympathy," CH, February 6, 1918 (41:6), 156; "The World's Neighbor," February 7, 1917 (40:6), 142; cf. CH, January 31, 1917 (40:5), 117; CH, March 14, 1917 (40:11), 301.

47. "Multitudes Homeless and Starving," CH, September 23, 1914 (37:38), 882; CH, November 4, 1914 (37:44), 1034; Editorial, CH, April 26, 1916 (39:17), 522; Caroline V. Kerr, "The Biggest Kitchen in the World," CH, January 24, 1917 (40:4), 83-84; "Hungering to Feed the Hungry," CH, May 2, 1917 (40:18), 516.

48. "The World's Fight with Famine," CH, March 1, 1919 (42:9), 257; CH articles included "World Hunger," March 28, 1917 (40:13), 360, "This Nation's Huge Task, the Feeding of a Hungry World," December 4, 1918 (41:49), 1345, "The World's Almoners," January 29, 1919 (42:5), 114, and L. E. Theiss, "We Will Save Democracy With Food," ibid., 112-13; the Herald opened a new fund for India at about this same time in response to appeals from missionaries: January 22, 1919 (42:4), 90, February 8, 1919 (42:6), 141, and February 22, 1919 (42:8), 195-96; cf. WC, February 22, 1919 (1951), 8, for Bramwell Booth's message to President Wilson urging prompt aid to ease the "acute distress" in industrial areas of Germany.

49. See Charles M. Sheldon contribution, CH, February, 1931 (34:2), 28, for indication of very similar concern at that date.

50. "The Salvation Army's Efforts to Lessen the Horrors of War," WC, September 26, 1914 (1721), 9; "Distressing Scenes in the War Zone," WC, November 14, 1914 (1728), 1; Evangeline Booth, "Let Us Have Peace," WC, October 24, 1914 (1725), 8; "The Cost of War," WC, April 24, 1915 (1751), 1; see earlier efforts during the brief war with Spain: WC, April 2, 1898 (861), 5, May 28, 1898 (869), 4, 5, October 1, 1898 (887), 9, and October 8, 1898 (888), 6.

51. Evangeline Booth, "Pity All You Like, but for God's Sake Give," WC, October 31, 1914 (1726), 9; WC, October 17, 1914 (1724), 10; "The Salvation Army Welcomes and Entertains Belgian Refugees," WC, November 21, 1914 (1729), 11; "Salvation Army Officer Among Refugees," WC, December 5, 1914 (1731), 1; "Five Salvation Army Ambulances for the Front," WC, November 28, 1914 (1730), 6; "The Salvation Army Motor Ambulance," WC, January 23, 1915 (1738), 11; "Six More Motor Ambulances," WC, March 20, 1915 (1746), 9; Bramwell Booth, "Notes and Reflections," WC, June 19, 1915 (1759), 6.

52. "The Commander's Old Linen Campaign," WC, November 14, 1914 (1728), 8; "Wanted! Old Linen," WC, November 7, 1914 (1727), 9.

53. "The Commander's Old Linen Campaign," loc. cit.; Evangeline Booth, "I Want Your Old Linen," WC, November 14, 1914 (1728), 9; "The Old Linen Campaign," WC, November 21, 1914 (1729), 1; "Commander Addresses Distinguished Audience of Club Women," WC, November 14, 1914 (1728), 13; Evangeline Booth, "What Can I Do to Help," WC, February 13, 1915 (1741), 9.

54. WC, January 23, 1915 (1738), 9.

55. WC, November 21, 1914 (1729), 8.

56. WC, February 20, 1915 (1742), 1, 9; cf. WC, February 27, 1915 (1743), 8. The Army emphasized the relief function it accomplished in thus hiring needy and unemployed persons.

57. Though see the regular column, "Christ in the Camps," as in WC, November 11, 1916 (1832), 13.

58. WC, April 21, 1917 (1855), 9, and May 5, 1917 (1857), 12.

59. "An Important War Conference," WC, April 28, 1917 (1856), 9; "The Salvation Army and the War. The Commander's Offer and the President's Response," WC, May 12, 1917 (1858), 9; see other communications with the President, as WC, December 15, 1917 (1889), 1, 8, 9.

60. "The War Service League. Will You Join?" WC, June 30, 1917 (1865), 9; WC, August 4, 1917 (1870), 9; "Officers Farewell for France," WC, August 25, 1917 (1873), 9.

61. "Officers Farewell for France," loc. cit.

62. "Seven Huts," WC, October 27, 1917 (1882), 8; Evangeline Booth, "Wanted: One Million Dollars. Urgent War Service Appeal," WC, December 22, 1917 (1890), 21; Evangeline Booth, "That Million Dollars," WC, February 16, 1918 (1898), 8; Editorial, WC, April 13, 1918 (1906), 8; "Pershing's Men in New York," WC, May 18, 1918 (1911), 8; WC, June 29, 1918 (1917), 9; Theodore Roosevelt's son later reinforced that praise as a result of his war service in France, in WC, August 24, 1918 (1925), 4.

63. Evangeline Booth, "Wanted: Nurses, Ambulance Drivers," WC, May 12, 1917 (1858), 8; "More Cars and Drivers," WC, February 16, 1918 (1898), 7; for an earlier evaluation by Clarke, see "What Eminent Men Say About the War Work of the Salvation Army," WC, April 28, 1917 (1856), 9.

64. See reprint, Walter S. Ball, "Handing it to the Salvation Army,'" WC, August 17, 1918 (1924), 2; "Fresh From the Fighting Zone in France," WC, May 4, 1918 (1909), 4; a reprint, James Hopper, "Why the 'Boys' Like the Salvation Army," WC, June 1, 1918 (1913), 3; Margaret E. Sangster, Jr., "God's Army Under Fire," CH, March 8, 1919 (42:10), 260.

65. WC, July 13, 1918 (1918), 2, and October 19, 1918 (1933), 1, for example.

66. "Fresh from the Fighting Zone in France," loc. cit.;

Hopper, loc. cit.; WC, October 5, 1918 (1931), 4; "Pershing's Men
in New York," loc. cit.; Katherine Mayo's account of Y. M. C. A.
war service, "That Damn Y" (Boston, 1920), 386-87, while otherwise friendly to the Salvation Army, missed this point of prices in
pointing out that the Army did sell over 90 per cent of the provisions
it dispensed.

67.   Agnes L. Palmer, 1904-1922; The Time Between (New
York, 1926), 70: Evangeline Booth, "Wanted: One Million Dollars.
Urgent War Service Appeal," December 22, 1917 (1890), 21; Hopper,
loc. cit.; "'Pershing's Men' in New York," loc. cit.; "Fresh from
the Fighting Zone in France," loc. cit.; cf. Herbert Wisbey, Soldiers
Without Swords; A History of the Salvation Army in the United States
(New York, 1955), 71-72, for the respect rough miners and others
showed young women officers in California.

68.   On the need, see "Wanted!!!" WC, December 15, 1917
(1889), 7.

69.   Palmer, 1904-1922, 71; Editorial, WC, November 10,
1917 (1884), 8; "A Call to Service," WC, January 5, 1918 (1892), 8.

70.   Ball, loc. cit.; "'Pershing's Men' in New York," loc.
cit.; July 27, 1918 (1921), 13; "Fresh from the Fighting Zone in
France," loc. cit.; cf. WC, November 30, 1882 (60), 1, which included the instruction to "keep to the Army plan of putting the
poorest, roughest looking in the best seats...."

71.   "'Pershing's Men' in New York," loc. cit.; "Fresh from
the Fighting Zone in France," loc. cit.; cf. WC, July 6, 1918
(1918), 10, and July 27, 1918 (1921), 13.

72.   "'Pershing's Men' in New York," loc. cit.; WC, June
29, 1918 (1917), 9; WC, November 2, 1918 (1935), 1; "A Final Word
about the U. W. W. C.," WC, November 9, 1918 (1936), 4; WC, November 23, 1918 (1938), 11; cf. the approximately $81,000 listed in
the "Balance Sheet" for 1887 in Frank Smith, The Salvation War in
America for 1886-87 (New York, 1887), [193].

73.   "The $13,000,000 Fund," WC, April 26, 1919 (1960),
4; "The Home Service Fund," WC, April 19, 1919 (1959), 12-13.

74.   WC, June 6, 1891 (505), 12 (60,000), May 6, 1893
(605), 8 (92,000), and June 16, 1894 (663), 10 (100,000).

75.   WC, March 19, 1910 (1485), 13 (68,000); WC, February
20, 1915 (1742), 13, remonstrated about the low (60,000) circulation
after years of appealing for 100,000; WC, April 7, 1917 (1853), 14
(73,200); see higher holiday totals such as the estimate of nearly
330,000 circulation with one million readers for the Christmas War
Cry in 1911: Social News, January, 1912, 2 (cf. WC, July 16,
1904 (1189), 13).

76. WC, October 4, 1919 (1983), 14, December 13, 1919 (1993), 14, May 29, 1920 (2017), 13, July 17, 1920 (2024), 13, September 25, 1920 (2034), 8, 13, and November 27, 1920 (2043), 13.

77. Evangeline Booth, "Inaugurating a Campaign Which Will Revolutionize the Financial System of the Salvation Army," WC, March 8, 1919 (1953), 8.

XV. CRITICS OF THE SOCIAL ORDER

1. William T. Stead, Life of Mrs. Booth (New York, 1900), 195. Bramwell Booth, in his "Introduction," endorsed Stead's book for Salvationists. William T. Stead, "The Late Mrs. Booth," WC (L), October 11, 1890 (742), 8; on Henry George's influence in religious circles, see James Dombrowski, The Early Days of Christian Socialism in America (New York, 1966, c1936), 35-49.

2. Henry F. May, Protestant Churches and Industrial America (New York, 1963, c1949), 198; John F. Mecklin, The Story of American Dissent (New York, 1934), 5, directed equally strong words against the Salvation Army; cf. Howard H. Quint, The Forging of American Socialism (Indianapolis, 1964, c1953), 141, on "Bible Belt" fundamentalism.

3. "The Social Question," G, January 16, 1897 (40), 10; Editorial, WC, January 29, 1887 (278), 8; Editorial, WC, November 7, 1891 (527), 8; CH, April 29, 1889 (9:17), 264; CH, October 10, 1900 (23:41), 839; CH, February 22, 1919 (42:8), 200.

4. William Booth, In Darkest England and the Way Out (London and New York, 1890), contained numerous firsthand accounts, including the reports of his officers in the slums, e.g., 25-29, 36-38, 40; cf. Preface for his debt to his wife and to Stead (unnamed); see Robert Sandall, The History of the Salvation Army, Vol. III (London and New York, 1955), 324-25, for a letter from Stead, noting his part but assigning the major responsibility to William Booth.

5. Booth, Darkest England, 14, 35, 42.

6. Ibid., 15, 16.

7. Ibid., 36, 257.

8. Ibid., 15, 30, 31.

9. E.G., ibid., 279, 285.

10. "The Church and the Less Favored," G, September 21,

1907 (597), 8-9; "The Vagrant Rich," CH, September 3, 1902 (25: 36), 720; "Social Contrasts," CH, January 25, 1905 (28:3), 76; Stead, Mrs. Booth, 198-99; see the comments on Wall Street's "Black Thursday," brought on by the battle for control of Northern Pacific stock in 1901, in CH, May 22, 1901 (24:21), 473, and T. DeWitt Talmage, "Flight of Riches," CH, June 12, 1901 (24:24), 532. Cf. T. DeWitt Talmage, "Corners and Swindles in Stocks," CH, January 12, 1882 (5:2), 20-21, and his comments on the abuse of trust funds, CH, September 18, 1884 (7:38), 596-97.

11. CH, April 12, 1905 (28:15), 331, printed arguments, including Gladden's, for and against the Rockefeller gift; "Tainted Money," CH, April 15, 1903 (26:15), 324, opposed acceptance; "The Senate and 'Tainted Money,'" CH, June 10, 1914 (37:23), 568. With reference to the Senate's rejection of an annual gift from Rockefeller, the editor agreed in condemning his methods, but felt the Senate should accept the gift and use it for the public good; cf. the Alliance journal, LT, May, 1905, 259-60.

12. "Social Contrasts," loc. cit.

13. Booth, Darkest England, 79.

14. WC (L), November 15, 1890 (747), 2, quoting the Saturday Review; WC, December 26, 1885 (221), 8; William T. Stead, "The Late Mrs. Booth," WC (L), October 11, 1890 (742), 8; Editorial, G, June 17, 1905 (479), 8; "Jacob A. Riis, Author-Philanthropist and Originator of Settlement Work Among the New York Poor," CH, April 15, 1903 (26:15), 317, 322, 331; CH, July 19, 1905 (28:29), 609, 618-20; Jacob A. Riis, "The Battle for the Slums. What the Tenement Houses Have Accomplished in New York in 15 years," CH, September 20, 1905 (28:38), 783; Jacob A. Riis, "The Golden Rule in Poverty Row," CH, September 27, 1905 (28: 39), 795, 797; WC, September 4, 1897 (831), 6, 14.

15. CH, May 20, 1903 (26:20), 421, and Editorial, November 1, 1911 (34:44), 1092, both announced the beginning of a new serial; many sermons, as November 22, 1911 (34:47), 1180, 1198; as editor-in-chief, for example, issues of February, 1920; cf. hostility of A. B. Simpson of the Alliance to Sheldon's In His Steps: Editorial, AW, August 26, 1899, 201.

16. "Dr. Nearing and Freedom of Speech," CH, October 27, 1915 (38:43), 1076; Editorial, CH, February 23, 1916 (39:8), 222; cf. "Brandeis Attacks Price-Cutting," CH, July 30, 1913 (36: 31), 707.

17. Booth, Darkest England, 213-23, 108; Editorial, CH, March 19, 1890 (13:12), 184; "Unfit Food," CH, September 27, 1893 (16:39), 630; Editorial, CH, May 15, 1895 (18:20), 314; Editorial, CH, July 26, 1911 (34:30), 744; cf. CH, July 17, 1918 (41:29), 838-39, 852; Klopsch's biographer, Charles M. Pepper, contributed an

article on railroad rates and rebates, CH, March 1, 1905 (28:9), 202.

18. Editorial, CH, January 14, 1903 (26:2), 34; cf. protest on behalf of farmers in "High Prices and the Farmer," CH, January 18, 1911 (34:3), 69; Editorial, CH, February 2, 1910 (33:5), 96; Editorial, CH, February 9, 1910 (33:6), 124; Editorial, CH, February 16, 1910 (33:7), 148, called for legislation; the attack provoked a defense of the industry by the secretary of the American Meat Packers Assoc.: George L. McArthy, "Western Packers on the Meat War," CH, March 23, 1910 (33:12), 287-88.

19. E. G., Booth, Darkest England, 48.

20. Ibid., 46, 18, 43, 79.

21. Ibid., 214, 221, 240, 249.

22. Editorial, G, December 21, 1907 (610), 8; "Controlling the Food Supply," CH, February 16, 1910 (33:7), 148; CH, January 9, 1918 (41:2), 36, 52, which noted the wartime take-over of the railroads, made no protest.

23. Editorial, CH, April 18, 1917 (40:16), 456; Editorial, CH, June 20, 1917 (40:25), 682; Editorial, CH, July 11, 1917 (40: 27), 742.

24. "The Telephone and the Public," CH, January 7, 1914 (37:1), 10; "An Important Railroad Decision," CH, March 15, 1911 (34:11), 271; "The Child Slave's Sad Lot," CH, February 8, 1905 (28:6), 124; Editorial, CH, October 18, 1911 (34:42), 1036; "Justice to the Farmer," and "Pass the Anti-Child Labor Law," CH, August 2, 1916 (39:31), 898; "Workingmen's Rights," CH, November 26, 1913 (36:48), 1102 (cf. CH, October 3, 1900 (23:40), 802).

25. CH, November 16, 1910 (33:46), 1052 (cf. 1047, 1054); "A Labor Court at Last," CH, July 30, 1913 (36:31), 698; "Starving Oldham," WC (L), January 14, 1893 (860), 1-2; "Vagrants and Compulsory Labor Colonies," WC, March 13, 1909 (1432), 11; Editorial, WC, April 9, 1904 (1175), 8, mentioned an English vagrancy bill which embodied proposals made in a recent pamphlet by General Booth.

26. Booth, Darkest England, 108, 266; "The Workingman's Friend," G, June 24, 1899 (167), 10; CH, January 11, 1905 (28:2), 36, 28, 42; "The Church and the Less Favored," G, September 21, 1907 (597), 8-9; "The Laborers and the Lord," CH, June 25, 1913 (36:26), 602; "Can the Church Win Them Back?" CH, December 2, 1914 (37:48), 1136, 1148; Charles Howard Hopkins, The Rise of the Social Gospel in American Protestantism, 1865-1915 (New Haven, Conn., 1940), 81-87, discusses this question, as does Aaron I. Abell, The Urban Impact on American Protestantism, 1865-1900

(London, 1962, c1943), 61-67; Herbert G. Gutman, "Protestantism and the American Labor Movement: The Christian Spirit in the Gilded Age," The American Historical Review, October, 1966 (72:1), 74-101, has shown the strong religious tone which marked the labor press between 1860 and 1900.

27. See Booth, Darkest England, 16.

28. CH, April 5, 1916 (39:14), 408; for evidence of the rapprochement they desired, see, e.g., "The Laborer's Friend," G, September 2, 1899 (177), 1, "The Workman's Friend," G, September 6, 1902 (334), 1, and Samuel Brengle, "Jesus the Workingman," WC, September 2, 1916 (1822), 9.

29. Stead, Mrs. Booth, 200; for other evidence of emphasis upon the working class see "The Working Man and the Church," G, April 15, 1899 (157), 10, "Still Among the Artisan Classes," G, May 13, 1899 (161), 11, G, September 2, 1899 (177), 3, and "Can the Church Win Them Back?" loc. cit.; the following two issues continued that symposium of "leading thinkers," with the editor discussing it in CH, December 2, 1914 (37:48), 1138.

30. May, Protestant Churches, 108-09 (cf. 92-93, 100-01, 105, for the years 1877-92).

31. Booth, Darkest England, 31.

32. CH, April 29, 1886 (9:17), 264; CH, May 6, 1886 (9:18), 280.

33. Booth, Darkest England, 79.

34. G, March 29, 1902 (311), 8; "To Abolish Sweatshops," WC, September 11, 1909 (1458), 8; CH, February 23, 1916 (39:8), 222; CH, November 22, 1916 (39:47), 1276; WC, August 31, 1918 (1926), 4; "Workingmen's Rights," CH, November 25, 1913 (36:48), 1102; cf. CH, October 3, 1900 (23:40), 802.

35. "Have You Considered the Child Labor Problem?" G, May 7, 1904 (421), 1, 8; "The Child Slave's Sad Lot," CH, February 8, 1905 (28:6), 124; Editorials, G, May 7, 1904 (421), 8, and June 17, 1905 (479), 8, the latter quoting Florence Kelley at length; Kate Upsom Clark, "Child Labor and Its Victims," CH, August 9, 1911 (34:32), 782.

36. "The Coal Miner at Home," CH, August 6, 1902 (25:32), 647, 651; "Child Slavery at the Mines," CH, August 13, 1902 (25:33), 667; "New Jersey's Child Toilers," CH, September 3, 1902 (25:36), 719.

37. "The New Child Labor Laws," CH, October 14, 1903 (26:41), 860; "Pass the Anti-Child Labor Law," CH, August 2, 1916

(39:31), 898; "Tortured Childhood Set Free," CH, August 2, 1916 (39:34), 954; CH, September 6, 1916 (39:36), 988; cf. Volunteer attention, as in "Have You Considered the Child-Labor Problem," loc. cit., and "Advance Against Child Labor," G, April, 1909 (661), 8; for agitation about working conditions for women, see "Righting a National Wrong," CH, November 3, 1915 (38:44), 1113-14; CH, June 19, 1918 (41:25), 746; CH, June 26, 1918 (41:26), 774.

38. Booth, Darkest England, 262-63.

39. Ibid., 107-08, and 105-10; CH, July 13, 1892 (15:28), 437; WC (L), July 23, 1892 (835), 16; "A National Shame," WC (L), April 22, 1893 (874), 3; WC (L), September 30, 1892 (897), 15; see Robert Sandall, The History of the Salvation Army (London and New York, 1948-1955), III, 120-31; cf. WC, January 22, 1910 (1477), 7.

40. Booth, Darkest England, 87.

41. Ibid., 108, 77-78, 268-69.

42. Ibid., 268.

43. "Thanksgiving," CH, November 29, 1905 (28:48), 1004; WC, August 30, 1919 (1978), 4.

44. "Pacific Coast Laborers' Union No. 1 Approves of Our Work," WC, June 27, 1891 (508), 6; WC, September 4, 1897 (831), 6, 14.

45. Booth, Darkest England, 48, 222, Preface.

46. Ibid., 85 (cf. 241).

47. Ibid., 44, 86.

48. Ibid., e.g., 14, 31, 32, 41, 50, 217, 223, 266.

49. Ibid., 240, 111-12, 213-14.

50. Ibid., 67-75, 57-61.

51. Ibid., 213.

52. Ibid., 79-80.

53. Ibid., 43, 73, 84-89.

54. Ibid., 19-20, 44.

55. Ibid., 90-91, 108-14, 256.

56. Ibid., 210.

57. Ibid., 122.

58. Ibid., 135-36.

59. Ibid., 237-40.

60. Ibid., 194-200.

61. Ibid., 213-17

62. Ibid., 218-26.

63. Robert Bremner, From the Depths; The Discovery of Poverty in the United States (New York, 1956), 18-30, 65-66, 123-39 ("The New View of Poverty"); for the mid-twentieth century see the emphasis on attitudes in the report of the Commission on Civil Disorders, noted, for example, in Joseph Kraft, "Wanted: A New White Attitude Toward the Negro," Minneapolis Tribune, March 4, 1968, 6.

64. Booth, Darkest England, 47, 128.

65. Ibid., 129.

66. See, for example, pp. 167-76, 48-49, above.

67. See, for example, pp. 84-88, 101-02, 59, 39, 71, above.

68. Booth, Darkest England, 36, 134, 155, 219.

69. See pp. 39, 112-31, above.

BIBLIOGRAPHICAL ESSAY

The most valuable sources for this study, both for the
writings of gospel welfare leaders and for an understanding of the
movement at the lay level, were the weekly journals these organizations published between 1880 and 1920: the Salvation Army War
Cry, beginning in 1881 (most issues of which are now available on
microfilm), the Alliance Weekly (under varying names) from January,
1888, The Florence Crittenton Magazine, first issued in March,
1899, the Volunteers' Gazette, beginning in April, 1896, and the
Christian Herald, from 1878. The British War Cry, available to
me for the years 1887 to 1901 and 1911 to 1915, proved especially
helpful for the years before and after the inauguration of the Army's
"Darkest England" social program in 1890. Scattered issues of the
War Cry's predecessors, The Christian Mission Magazine and the
Salvationist, were of interest for early glimpses of the Army's
emerging social efforts. Similarly, the missionary journals A. B.
Simpson founded and edited in New York City in the early 1880s,
The Gospel in All Lands and more especially The Word, Work, and
World, illuminate his developing work before the formal organization
of his Alliances for missions in the United States and overseas.
Finally, the Christian Herald, besides presenting its own programs,
is a rich source of information about other welfare institutions, and
particularly useful for the rescue missions and rescue homes for
women with which its own interests most closely aligned it.

While no complete files are available for any of these magazines for the period before 1920, the national headquarters and
schools of these organizations have substantial holdings, as does
the Library of Congress for the Christian Herald, the Volunteers'
Gazette, and the War Cry. In addition, the headquarters of the
Christian and Missionary Alliance has holdings of the journals
Living Truths and The India Alliance, while the national headquarters
of the Salvation Army has many volumes of the special magazines
the Army published during those years, including All the World,
The Conqueror, The Field Officer, Full Salvation, Harbor Lights,
The Local Officer, The Officer, Social News, and The Young Soldier. The Public Library of Buffalo, N.Y., holds a substantial run
of Triumphs of Faith, a journal of faith healing and rescue work
published by Carrie Judd Montgomery, who had close ties to both
the Alliance and the Salvation Army. Among other periodicals not
formally aligned with these groups but often helpful were the Union

Signal, published by the Woman's Christian Temperance Union, the Watchword, published by the influential evangelical pastor, A. J. Gordon, and The Record of Christian Work, published out of D. L. Moody's Northfield, Mass., institutions, with which the Watchword later merged.

Reports of the work of individuals, institutions, and national organizations often appeared in gospel welfare magazines or as separate publications. An early example of the former category was the report of the Canal Street Mission of Buffalo, N. Y., for 1880-81, which Carrie Judd Montgomery published in her magazine Triumphs of Faith in September, 1881. The Salvation Army, while featuring a wide variety of reports in its War Cry and other publications, also printed separately many of its general and specialized reports: see Frank Smith's accounts of The Salvation War in America during his term of command in the mid-1880s, William Booth's The Salvation War, 1884 (London, 1885), War Service Report of the Salvation Army, 1917-1919, and annual prison reports under varying names. Such reports are supplemented by those from various local groups and area centers, whether for the Salvation Army (e.g., Buffalo, N. Y., Annual Report, 1898-1900, Henry Fielding, Review of the Year's Work in Chicago, 1893, and Diamonds in the Rough; Annual Report [of] Salvation Army Rescue Work in Cleveland, 1905), or for other organizations and institutions. As in the case of rescue magazines, these reports are generally available only in organizational schools and headquarters, or in special-interest collections or research-oriented libraries in the areas in which the reporting institutions were located. The New York Public Library, for example, has a file of reports from Jerry McAuley's pioneering Water Street and Cremorne missions, as well as from other rescue institutions, including the Charles Cullis group in the Boston area. Similarly, the Minnesota Historical Society Library has scattered annual reports for the St. Paul Union Gospel Mission and the Minneapolis Union Mission, as well as for the Scandinavian Rescue Mission. While similar reports exist for area institutions in Boston, Chicago, Hartford, Conn., and many other cities, I have found no significant collections of such material, except in the magazines published by gospel welfare organizations.

Leaders of rescue organizations published numerous accounts of their work. The best-known and most significant of all is William Booth's In Darkest England and the Way Out (London and New York, 1890), which analyzed England's social plight, proposed a remedy, and in the process formally launched the Army's ambitious social welfare program. In the United States as well as in England, other leaders produced reports of varying extensiveness, some of which we have already noted. Others include Maud Booth, Beneath Two Flags (New York, 1889), Ballington Booth, From Ocean to Ocean; or, The Salvation Army's March from the Atlantic to the Pacific (New York, 1891), Frederick Booth-Tucker, The Salvation Army in the United States (New York, 1899), and Evangeline Booth, Light in Darkness (New York, 1905). Several of Booth-Tucker's reports have recently been republished under the title The Salvation Army in America; Selected Reports, 1899-1903 (New York, 1972).

While almost all such accounts paid considerable attention to social work, a number of volumes focused more exclusively upon that aspect of Salvationist efforts, including The "Darkest England" Social Scheme; A Brief Review of the First Year's Work (London, 1891), Bramwell Booth, Light in Darkest England in 1895 (London, 1895), F. Booth-Tucker, The Social Relief Work of the Salvation Army in the United States (New York, 1900), Selected Papers on the Social Work of the Salvation Army (London, 1907), International Social Council Addresses, 1911 (London, 1912), and Social Problems in Solution; Papers Read at the International Social Council, London ... 1921 (London, 1923).

Other volumes by Salvationists offer a more comprehensive overview of the development of that organization's first half-century. For insight into the early decades, Frederick Booth-Tucker's two-volume Life of Catherine Booth (New York, 1892) includes many letters, reports, and other documents in its more than 1300 pages. Historical surveys and biographical sketches by Booth-Tucker and others help fill in the larger story: F. Booth-Tucker, The Consul; A Sketch of Emma Booth-Tucker (New York, 1903), William Booth; The General of the Salvation Army (New York, 1898), and his auto-biographical Muktifauj, or Forty Years with the Salvation Army in India and Ceylon (London, n.d.); George Railton, Twenty-One Years' Salvation Army Under the Generalship of William Booth (London, 1887), and The Authoritative Life of General William Booth (London, 1912); Bramwell Booth, Echoes and Memories (New York, 1925), and These Fifty Years (London, 1929); Evangeline Booth (with Grace Livingstone Hill), The War Romance of the Salvation Army (Phila-delphia, 1919); and Agnes L. Palmer, 1904-1922; The Time Be-tween (New York, 1926).

Other appraisals were penned by persons who were not mem-bers of the Salvation Army. William T. Stead, prominent reform journalist who collaborated with William Booth in the writing of In Darkest England, also published interpretive accounts of the General and of his wife: General Booth, A Biographical Sketch (London, 1891) and Life of Mrs. Booth (London, 1900). Sir Henry Rider-Haggard, novelist, social theorist, and official representative of the British government, authored two books about the Army, The Poor and the Land; Being a Report on the Salvation Army Colonies in the United States and at Hadleigh, England (London and New York, 1905), an appraisal of the most publicized facet of the Army's American social work before 1905, and Regeneration; Being an Account of the Social Work of the Salvation Army in Great Britain (London, 1910). Two other journalists who became supporters of the Army as a re-sult of their investigations were Harold Begbie, who wrote Twice-Born Men; A Clinic in Regeneration (New York, 1909), and The Life of General William Booth (2 vols., New York, 1920), and Hugh Redwood, author of God in the Slums (New York, 1931), and God in the Shadows (London, 1932). St. John Ervine's two-volume God's Soldier: General William Booth (New York, 1935) remains one of the finest interpretations of Booth and the Salvation Army.

Numerous volumes by friends and leaders give biographical and institutional accounts of the rescue mission movement, including the pioneering Water Street Mission of New York, and its founder, Jerry McAuley. Jerry McAuley; An Apostle to the Lost (New York, c1885), compiled by his friend R. M. Offord, is a collection of extracts from McAuley's talks and writings, including his Transformed; or, The History of a River Thief, dictated by McAuley a decade earlier, as well as reminiscences by those who knew him. The sequel to Offord's book, Samuel Hopkins Hadley's Down in Water Street; A Story of Sixteen Years Life and Work in Water Street Mission (New York, 1902), relates part of the subsequent history of the Water Street Mission from the standpoint of one who was also a dominant figure in the development of the larger rescue mission movement. Hadley's story was retold soon after his death by a close friend, the prominent evangelist J. Wilbur Chapman, in his S. H. Hadley of Water Street (New York, 1906). One of Hadley's converts and successors, John Wyburn, was a principal source for a book by Philip I. Roberts, The Dry Dock of a Thousand Wrecks; the McAuley Water Street Mission (New York, 1912), which continued the story McAuley and Hadley had begun in their writings. Wyburn's widow, Mrs. May Wyburn, later reviewed the larger story of the mission in the lives of its three dominant early leaders: "But Until Seventy Times Seven"; Jeremiah, Samuel, John (New York, 1936). Such was the fame of the Water Street Mission and its early superintendents that numerous contemporary reports in the secular and religious press, as well as the mission's own publications, help fill out the picture of its development.

Accounts of other city missions supplement the literature devoted to the Water Street Mission. The Christian Herald magazine, besides devoting continuing attention to its own Bowery Mission and affiliated programs, frequently featured rescue missions in New York and other American cities from its American beginnings in 1878 (April 5, 1883, 209-11; May 16, 1894, 305, 317; August 21, 1895, 537, 541; and January 15, 1896, 47, for example). One of those New York missions, operated by St. Bartholomew's Episcopal Church, and superintended for a time by Henry H. Hadley, brother and convert of S. H. Hadley, is described in E. C. Chorley, The Centennial History of St. Bartholomew's Church in the City of New York, 1835-1935 (New York, 1935). Hadley, who like his brother, ranged well beyond his immediate institution, was active in recruiting and training other rescue workers, as evidenced in one of his publications, Trained Rescue Volunteers: Report of Spring Class, 1895, of the Rescue Workers' Practical Training School of New York in Connection with St. Bartholomew's Rescue Mission (New York, 1895).

For several decades after the death of S. H. Hadley in 1906

the most important rescue mission leader was probably Mel Trotter, superintendent of the city mission of Grand Rapids, Mich., and instrumental in the founding of numerous other missions. His autobiographical These Forty Years (Grand Rapids, Mich., 1939) sheds light, therefore, on the larger movement as well as on his own career. Mel Trotter's conversion in and continuing ties with Chicago's Pacific Garden Mission accentuate the importance of that institution during the formative decades of the movement. Featured in the Christian Herald on a number of occasions (e.g., June 19, 1901 [24:25], 549), it has been the subject of several subsequent volumes, including a large anniversary publication, Commemorating the 50th Anniversary of Pacific Garden Mission (Chicago, 1927), and a history by one of the most influential of mid-twentieth century evangelicals, Carl F. H. Henry, The Pacific Garden Mission (Grand Rapids, Mich., 1942).

Many other books shed some light on various aspects of the movement. For the period preceding Jerry McAuley's Water Street Mission and the rise of modern rescue missions, see, for example, The Old Brewery, and the New Mission House at the Five Points (New York, 1954), and Lewis E. Jackson, Gospel Work in New York City; A Memorial of Fifty Years in City Missions (New York, 1878). Representative of the writings of other rescue mission workers are John G. Hallimond, The Miracle of Answered Prayer (New York, 1916), and Pat B. Withrow, A Miracle of Grace; The Life of Pat B. Withrow, Superintendent Union Mission, Charleston, W. Va. (Charlotte, N.C., 1947). Hallimond, superintendent of the Christian Herald's Bowery Mission in New York, and Withrow, who led the Charleston city mission from its beginning in 1911, were both important figures in the movement. William E. Paul, whose leadership overlapped with that of Withrow, Trotter, Emma Whittemore, and others, wrote several brief books, including Miracles of Rescue (Minneapolis, n.d.), and The Romance of Rescue (Minneapolis, c1946).

Besides the numerous articles by and about Emma Whittemore and her chain of Door of Hope rescue homes which appeared in the Alliance Weekly, the Christian Herald, the War Cry, Triumphs of Faith, and other magazines, the most useful sources for her organization are Mrs. Whittemore's books, including especially Delia (New York, 1893), a sketch of one of her early converts which also sheds light on her work to that date, and Records of Modern Miracles (Toronto, 1931), compiled by a friend after her death. The latter volume incorporates many of her other writings, including at least some of her "Door of Hope Series" of tracts. Because of the scarcity of other materials, it is invaluable for its wide-ranging coverage of Mrs. Whittemore and her homes, and even for its reflection of the sentimental and highly supernaturalistic tone she imparted to all of her work.

The Florence Crittenton Association of rescue institutions has been much more fully chronicled. Besides Charles Crittenton's autobiographical The Brother of Girls (Chicago, 1910), principal sources of information include Charlton Edholm's Traffic in Girls and Florence Crittenton Missions (Chicago, 1893), Fourteen Years' Work Among 'Erring Girls' (Washington, D.C., 1897?), separately published reports covering national and local work (e.g., Report of the National Florence Crittenton Mission and Its Affiliated Branches [1914]), Otto Wilson, Fifty Years Work With Girls, 1883-1933 (Alexandria, Va., 1933), and a number of volumes written by Kate Waller Barrett, Crittenton's successor as head of the chain of rescue homes: Some Practical Suggestions on the Conduct of a Rescue Home (Washington, D.C., 1903?), Motherhood; A Means of Regeneration (Washington, D.C., n.d.), and The Sanctity of Marriage (Washington, D.C., 1912). As in the case of the Door of Hope homes, these writings were supplemented by numerous articles in other evangelical periodicals. For the Crittenton homes, in addition, The Florence Crittenton Magazine (later Girls), is a rich source of material, including regular contributions from Charles Crittenton, Kate Waller Barrett, and other leaders.

In addition to regularly featuring a wide range of gospel welfare institutions and programs, the Christian Herald frequently included historical accounts of its own work. Among the most useful for this study were the following: "A Word About Ourselves. What 'The Christian Herald' has Accomplished in the Last Five Years" (December 5, 1894, 771); "Dr. Talmage's Philanthropies" (August 6, 1902, 652); "Dr. Klopsch's Life in Outline" (March 16, 1910, 256); "Thirty-Five Years of Christian Service, 1878-1913" (October 22, 1913, 969-72, 983); and, "The Record of Three and a Half Years of Mercy and Relief" (May 29, 1918, 555). Several volumes recount the story of Louis Klopsch and T. DeWitt Talmage, the magazine's most important leaders up to 1910: Charles M. Pepper, Life-Work of Louis Klopsch (New York, 1910), provides extensive extracts from the Herald, as well as from other documents which cover most of its welfare projects up to Klopsch's death in 1910. In contrast, the autobiographical T. DeWitt Talmage As I Knew Him (New York, 1912), compiled with concluding chapters by his wife a decade after his death, and L. A. Banks, editor, T. DeWitt Talmage, His Life and Work (Philadelphia, 1902), touch only briefly on Talmage's career with the Christian Herald. The four-volume Autobiography of Charles Haddon Spurgeon, compiled by his wife and secretary (Philadelphia, n.d.), as well as the autobiographical Charles M. Sheldon; His Life Story (New York, 1925), afford helpful sidelights because of the philanthropic interests of these two men and their close ties with the Herald. Spurgeon was also the subject of biographies by two clergymen active in the social Christianity of that era: George C. Lorimer, Charles Haddon Spurgeon (Boston, 1892), and Russell H. Conwell, Life of Charles Haddon Spurgeon, the World's Great Preacher (Philadelphia? 1892). For later developments and accounts of Herald efforts, see, for example, the "Seventy-Fifth Anniversary Issue," September, 1953, and especially Kenneth L. Wilson, "Compassion's Strong Right Arm," 46-50, 147.

For the Christian and Missionary Alliance, George Pardington, Twenty-Five Wonderful Years, 1889-1914; A Popular Sketch of
the Christian and Missionary Alliance (New York, 1914), and A. E.
Thompson, The Life of A. B. Simpson (New York, 1920), are
general accounts of the early history of the Alliance by men who
were colleagues of Simpson. Among Simpson's many books, most
of which shed more light on his religion than on historical developments, are three biographies he wrote or edited about friends, and,
in the case of Wilson and Pulis, co-workers: Henry Wilson, One of
God's Best (New York, 1909?), authored jointly with Wilson's daughter Madele, a Salvation Army officer; From the Uttermost to the
Uttermost; The Life Story of Josephus Pulis (New York, 1914); and
Michele Nardi, the Italian Evangelist (New York, 1916). Some of
Simpson's other writings, including The Gospel of Healing in its revised edition (New York, 1915), contain material of an autobiographi-
cal nature, though he wrote relatively little about his life. R. B.
Ekvall and others, After Fifty Years (Harrisburg, Pa., 1939), re-
surveyed the early decades using information drawn from Pardington
and Thompson, as well as from the official records of the Alliance.
A book published a few years later, A. W. Tozer's Wingspread;
Albert B. Simpson--A Study in Spiritual Altitude (Harrisburg, Pa.,
1943), is a highly sympathetic evaluation of the founder of the
Alliance by his most influential successor and spiritual heir.

Scores of other volumes dealt less directly with historical
developments but are invaluable for insight into the larger nature of
the evangelical rescue movement. Among these are William Booth,
Letters to Salvationists (2 vols., New York, 1902), and The Founder
Speaks Again; A Selection of Writings (London, 1960); Catherine
Booth, Papers on Practical Religion (London, 1878), and Popular
Christianity (London, 1891); Emma Booth-Tucker, Heart Messages
(London, n.d.); Maud Booth, Did the Pardon Come Too Late? (New
York, 1897), and After Prison, What? (New York, 1903); Evange-
line Booth, Love Is All (New York, 1908); A. B. Simpson, Holy
Ghost Ministries (New York, 1900), and The King's Business (New
York, 1900); and Mrs. M. B. Fuller, The Wrongs of Indian Woman-
hood (New York, 1900).

Gospel welfare groups have occasioned a number of recent
publications and academic dissertations, with the Salvation Army
and its founder, General William Booth, receiving the greatest attention. Robert Sandall, a Salvation Army officer, wrote a three-
volume History of the Salvation Army (London, 1947-1955); and
Herbert Wisbey, a history of Salvationists in the United States entitled Soldiers Without Swords (New York, 1955), a sympathetic and
careful scholarly account based on his doctoral dissertation at Colum-
bia University. Among other historical and biographical works relating to the Army published in recent decades are Harry E. Neal,
The Hallelujah Army (Philadelphia, 1961), Richard Collier, The
General Next to God; The Story of William Booth and the Salvation
Army (New York, 1965), Catherine Bramwell-Booth, Catherine Booth

(London, 1970), and Bernard Watson, Soldier Saint; George Scott Railton, William Booth's First Lieutenant (London, 1970). Herbert Wisbey has also written a History of the Volunteers of America (New York, 1954), published by the Volunteers, and, like his work on the Salvation Army, a careful and illuminating account. Susan Welty, benefitting from personal friendship with the Booths, authored a biographical account of Maud Booth and her Volunteer prison work, Look Up and Hope! (New York, 1961). Arthur Bonner's Jerry McAuley and His Mission (Neptune, N. J., 1967), sheds light on the larger development of rescue work as well as on the story of the Water Street Mission.

Among dissertations that have come to my attention are C. C. Norton, "The Salvation Army of Atlanta, Georgia (A Study in Sociology)," Emory U., 1920); Philip D. Needham, "Redemption and Social Reformation; A Theological Study of William Booth and His Movement ...," (Princeton University, 1967), and A. R. Meredith, "The Social and Political Views of Charles Haddon Spurgeon, 1834-1892," (University of Michigan, 1973).

The following studies, published during the last several decades, helped provide a clearer understanding of the era and of the relationship between religion and social welfare: One of two pioneering works, Aaron Abell, The Urban Impact on American Protestantism, 1865-1900 (London, 1962, c1943), concentrates on institutions and programs, including a chapter on the Salvation Army, while the other, Charles H. Hopkins, The Rise of the Social Gospel in American Protestantism, 1865-1915 (New Haven, Conn., 1940), places greater emphasis on social theory; Henry F. May, Protestant Churches and Industrial America (New York, 1963, c1949), relates the thought of churchmen to poverty and the labor question during the decades from the Civil War to 1900. Robert T. Handy has compiled, with a critical introductory essay, a selection of writings from three key leaders in The Social Gospel in America; Gladden, Ely, Rauschenbusch (New York, 1966).

Many other books provided valuable background for individual chapters, as well as for the larger work. Among them were Merle Curti, American Philanthropy Abroad: A History (New Brunswick, N. J., 1963), James H. Timberlake, Prohibition and the Progressive Movement, 1900-1920 (Cambridge, Mass., 1963), Roy Lubove, The Progressives and the Slums; Tenement House Reform in New York City, 1890-1917 (Pittsburgh, 1962), and The Professional Altruist; The Emergence of Social Work as a Career, 1880-1930 (Cambridge, Mass., 1965), Arthur Mann, Yankee Reformers in an Urban Age (Cambridge, Mass., 1954), Nathan I. Huggins, Protestants Against Poverty; Boston's Charities, 1870-1900 (Westport, Conn., 1971), and two volumes on social Christianity in other lands, Richard Allen, The Social Passion; Religion and Social Reform in Canada, 1914-28 (Toronto, 1971), and J. D. Bollen, Protestantism in New South Wales, 1890-1910 (Melbourne, 1972).

Representative of works not as directly related to social Christianity but important for that era were Stephen Gottschalk, The Emergence of Christian Science in American Religious Life (Berkeley, 1973), and Robert Peel, Christian Science, Its Encounter with American Culture (New York, 1958).

Several books were helpful for the decades before the Civil War and after World War I. For the former, Charles C. Cole, The Social Ideas of the Northern Evangelists, 1826-1860 (New York, 1966, c1954), and Timothy L. Smith, Revivalism and Social Reform in Mid-Nineteenth Century America (New York, 1957), concentrate, respectively, on theory and practical measures, while Anthony Armstrong, The Church of England, the Methodists and Society 1700-1850 (Totowa, N.J., 1973) is the most recent of numerous volumes dealing with the impact of the evangelical revivals on the social problems of eighteenth- and nineteenth-century England. Carroll Smith Rosenberg, Religion and the Rise of the American City; The New York City Mission Movement, 1812-1870 (Ithaca, N.Y., 1971), and John L. Dunstan, A Light to the City; 150 Years of the City Missionary Society of Boston, 1816-1966 (Boston, 1966), provide background for two of the most important centers of evangelical rescue activities.

For the years after 1918, I have used Clarke A. Chambers' general account, Seedtime of Reform; American Social Service and Social Action, 1918-1933 (Minneapolis, 1963), as well as the surveys of social Christianity by Robert M. Miller, Protestantism and Social Issues, 1919-1939 (Chapel Hill, N.C., 1958), and Paul A. Carter, The Decline and Revival of the Social Gospel: Social and Political Liberalism in American Protestant Churches, 1920-1940 (Ithaca, N.Y., 1956, c1954).

As the "Notes" for each chapter show, I am also indebted to other authors and volumes too numerous to mention here.

INDEX

84, 88; Salvation Army 3-
7, 52-3, 56, 82-3, 94, 161,
184 n19 & 20, 185 n32-35,
202 n33 & 34; Slum work
[general--visitation, etc.]
202 n33 & 34, 203 n44;
Summaries and listings
120, 159, 164, 244 n18;
Temperance 139; Volun-
teers of America 5, 48,
52, 56, 105-6; War and
peace 161
Stauffler, A. F. 130
Stead, F. H. xv
Stead, W. T. xiv, 6, 34, 88,
89-90, 115, 165, 166, 242
n2
Steele, Mrs. A. S. 123
Steele Orphanages 119, 123,
124
Stelzle, Charles 6, 28
Strachan, Margaret 84
Strong, Josiah xiv, 6, 7, 88,
145
Sully, Brigadier 61-2
Summer philanthropy 29, 34,
61-7
Summers, William 224 n30
Sunday schools 63, 73
Supernaturalism 19, 23, 35,
84, 86, 91-2
Support from non-members
52, 53, 54, 57, 58, 61,
62, 63, 67, 73-4, 75, 76,
77, 80-1, 88, 94, 95, 95-
6, 104-5, 110, 115, 135-6,
139, 142, 145, 146, 148,
150, 151, 152, 158, 161,
161-2, 162, 162-3, 163,
164, 172, 224 n31, 244
n17
Sweden 129
Swedish-Americans 129
Swedish Tabernacle (Minneapo-
lis) 129
Switzerland 114, 160
Symonds, Eliza see Shirley,
Eliza
Syracuse (N. Y.) 56

Taft, William Howard 25, 155

Talmage, Frank 28
Talmage, Thomas DeWitt
25, 26, 31, 45, 52, 101,
143-4, 154, 192 n107,
198 n150, 211 n30
Tang, Chan Yin 64
Tappan (N. Y.) 57
Temperance 1, 6, 7, 9, 11,
12, 30, 34, 73, 83, 115,
132-42, 167
Ten Talks on the Salvation
Army 97
Texas 135
Texas City (Texas) 52
Thanksgiving Day philanthropy
10, 34, 50, 59, 60, 67,
138
Thirteenth Street Presbyterian
Church (New York) 14
Thoburn, J. M. 146, 147
Tibbals, P. L. 48, 92
Tibet 15
Timberlake, James 132
The Times [London] 85
Tittle, Ernest Fremont xiii
Tobacco 133
Toledo (Ohio) 58, 74
Tolstoy, Leo 143
Tombs Prison (New York)
106, 107
Tomkins, A. S. 63-4
Topeka (Kan.) 75, 124, 125
Toronto (Ont.) 243 n16
Torrey, R. A. 12, 18, 28,
155
Toynbee Hall (London) 37
Trade unionism 172
Traffic in Girls see White
slavery
Travellers Club 50
Trotter, Mel 12, 93, 139,
140
Tulsa (Okla.) 125
Tunison, Fanny 34
Turkey 142, 256 n10, 261 n19
Tuskegee Institute 124
Twenty-Third Street Taber-
nacle (New York) 15
Tyng, Stephen 26

Unconditional, immediate